COMMAND PERFORMANCE

dBASE III®

COMMAND PERFORMANCE

dBASE III®

DOUGLAS HERGERT

The Microsoft®
Desktop Dictionary
and Cross-Reference Guide

PUBLISHED BY

Microsoft Press
A Division of Microsoft Corporation
10700 Northup Way, Box 97200, Bellevue, Washington 98009
Copyright © 1985 by Douglas Hergert

Library of Congress Cataloging in Publication Data
Hergert, Douglas.
  dBASE III: the Microsoft desktop dictionary and
  cross-reference guide.
  (Command performance)
  Includes index.
  1. dBASE III (Computer program)
I. Title. II. Series.
QA76.9.D3H48   1985   005.75′65   85-21622
ISBN 0-914845-63-2
Printed and bound in the United States of America.
     5 6 7 8 9 FGFG 8 9 0 9 8 7
Distributed to the book trade in the
United States by Harper and Row.
Distributed to the book trade in
Canada by General Publishing Company, Ltd.
Distributed to the book trade outside the
United States and Canada by Penguin Books Ltd.
Penguin Books Ltd., Harmondsworth, Middlesex, England
Penguin Books Australia Ltd., Ringwood, Victoria, Australia
Penguin Books NZ Ltd., 182–190 Wairau Road, Auckland 10, New Zealand
British Cataloging in Publication Data available

dBASE II® and dBASE III® are registered trademarks of Ashton-Tate.
IBM® is a registered trademark of International Business Machines Corporation.
WordStar® is a registered trademark of MicroPro International Corporation.
Microsoft® Word is a registered trademark of Microsoft Corporation.

ACKNOWLEDGMENTS

Dorothy Shattuck generously lent her own ideas and insightful knowledge to nearly every entry of this dictionary. Her work as the book's editor was exacting and creative, resulting throughout in improvements both technical and stylistic.

David Rygmyr and Chris Matthews also gave the book the benefit of their considerable technical expertise.

Finally, I want to express my appreciation to the entire staff at Microsoft Press for their friendly diligence and high-spirited enthusiasm.

INTRODUCTION

Command Performance: dBASE III is a complete dictionary and reference guide for users of Ashton-Tate's dBASE III database-management program. The book is designed to illuminate—through descriptions and examples—the meaning, usage, and subtleties of each element of the dBASE command set.

The entries in this book should prove useful to a wide range of dBASE users, including:

☐ Those occasional or casual users who need a conveniently organized tool to help them learn or review the most essential commands for building and using databases.

☐ Those frequent and serious users who are eager to continue expanding their knowledge of this vast and versatile database program.

☐ Those advanced users who write applications in the dBASE programming language and therefore require an in-depth understanding of the features and behavior of the language.

One of the best ways to learn about dBASE—or any application software—is to study examples of its commands in action. Appropriately, the examples in *Command Performance: dBASE III* include:

☐ Simple but "real-life" interactive dot-prompt commands.

☐ Database solutions ranging from the straightforward to the elaborate.

☐ Program segments and complete programmed applications.

The dictionary entries are arranged alphabetically, and include all the dBASE commands and functions, plus a selection of more general topics that should help answer questions about databases and the fundamentals of dBASE III. Each entry is identified with one or more "icons"—graphic symbols that should help you place the dBASE command set into categories. The key on page *ix* shows all of the icons used in this book and what they mean. Most entries are organized into the following sections:

Structure	A representation of the actual syntax of the command or function. The style of these representations has been kept simple and intuitive: dBASE reserved words appear in uppercase; information that you must supply appears in lowercase; optional syntax elements appear in italics.
Description	A paragraph or two explaining what the command or function actually does.

Usage   Additional notes about the command's behavior, along with interactive, database, and program examples.

Cautions   Situations to avoid; structures to use advisedly; pitfalls to watch out for. (Many readers will find this one of the most useful and interesting sections of the entry.)

dBASE II equivalent   The command or function that performs the same, or approximately the same, task in dBASE II. Where necessary, important differences between the two programs are noted.

Comments   Additional information—often advanced in nature—that will expand your familiarity with the command or function in question, help connect it with other dBASE commands, and improve your performance with the dBASE program.

Another significant feature of this book is the unique cross-referencing system designed specially for the *Command Performance* series. This cross-referencing will lead you directly to the pages in the book where you will find additional information about particular dBASE features. Three cross-referencing marks are used:

123★

123◆

◆

A page number followed by a star directs you to the page where you will find a complete dictionary entry covering the referenced topic. Here is an example:

...does not matter, but concatenation **65★** has the effect of...

This reference means that you will find an entire entry devoted to concatenation on page 65.

A page number followed by a diamond refers you to further important information about a particular topic that may be discussed parenthetically, or merely in passing, in an entry you are currently reading. This information is not in an entry of its own, but when you turn to the referenced page number, you will find a diamond that will help you locate the relevant definition or explanation within the entry. Here is an example of the diamond type of reference:

...attempt to use this command with a format file **365◆**, however,...

This means that you will find more detailed information about format files on page 365. Turning to page 365, you will find a mark like this:

...operations. (A format file ◆ is a user-created program that...

The diamond should help you zone in on the passage where format files are defined.

To supplement this rather elaborate cross-referencing system, the book also contains a short conceptual Index listing a selection of database, programming, and dBASE topics that you might otherwise find difficult to locate in the book itself. As you become more familiar with this book, you may want to skim through the Index occasionally, just to refresh your memory about the range of topics covered and the richness of dBASE's command set.

One large application example runs through many entries. This application is centered around a real-estate database that stores detailed information about (imaginary) houses that are for sale. An associated program provides menu-driven access to, and control over, this database. You will find an introduction to both the program and the database in the SET PROCEDURE entry, but specific information is scattered about in many different entries. For this reason, we have also provided complete listings of the database structure and the program itself in the Appendix.

As the author of *Command Performance: dBASE III*, I am enthusiastic about dBASE III as a personal-computing product, and hope that this book will contribute to your competence with—and enjoyment of—the program. I believe my own enthusiasm probably shows up most clearly in the database and program examples selected: I hope you will concentrate carefully on them and, when appropriate, incorporate the illustrated techniques into your own dBASE III applications.

THE ICONS

	database operation		environment control
	date/time operation		mathematical operation
	dictionary topic		memory operation
	disk operation		programming command
	display report operation		string operation

&

■ **Structure**
&variable_name

■ **Description**
The & symbol with the name of a character variable **459**★ results in the performance of a macro **215**★ substitution in a dBASE command or program. The term *macro substitution* means that the contents of the string variable are substituted into the syntax of the command that contains the macro.

■ **Usage**
Macros can be used in very different circumstances and for a variety of purposes. The following four examples, all taken from programs discussed elsewhere in this book, illustrate this flexibility.

Example 1: The use of a macro is important when a program receives a parameter value **245**◆ that must ultimately become part of the syntax of a command. The *Clock* program listed under the entry for the TIME() **433**★ function receives a string parameter value, which it stores in the variable *style*. The value of this variable is then used to determine the date-display format:

```
PARAMETER style
SET DATE &style
```

In this case the string value comes from an external source—the command that calls the program:

```
. DO Clock WITH "american"
```

As a result of this call, the SET DATE **337**★ command actually issued by the program reads:

```
SET DATE american
```

1

Example 2: Sometimes a program may need to "build" a list or a compound expression **207◆** that is destined to become part of a command. The difficulty here is that the length of such an expression cannot always be determined in advance. The procedure called *Reqmnts*, listed under the SET FILTER **357★** entry, is one such program: It elicits from the user a set of criteria for selecting certain records from the *Property* **384◆** database, which stores records describing houses that are for sale. These criteria are to become parts of a compound logical expression in a SET FILTER command. This logical expression may be composed of anywhere from two to seven parts, depending upon how many criteria are entered by the user.

During the input dialogue, the user's selection criteria are stored as a long string value in the variable *reqs*. By the end of the dialogue, *reqs* might contain an expression such as:

```
"(asking_pr >= 100000 .AND. asking_pr <= 125000)
.AND. bedrooms = 3 .AND. garage .AND. .NOT. sold"
```

To find all the records that match these criteria, the program issues the command:

```
SET FILTER TO &reqs
```

and the macro then allows the program to incorporate *reqs* into the command.

Example 3: Macros can contribute to program clarity and readability in some surprising ways. The *Schedule* procedure listed under the entry for the SET INDEX **372★** command contains an example. The program issues a DISPLAY **116★** command in which one of the elements to be displayed is not a field value, but rather a numeric value calculated from two fields. For clarity, the program stores the expression that performs the calculation as a string value in the variable *daystosell*, which is then used inside the DISPLAY command:

```
daystosell = "term_days - (DATE() - on_market)"
DISPLAY ALL address, &daystosell FOR .NOT. sold OFF
```

Certainly, this example presents a completely discretionary use of a macro, but it is a use that makes the passage easier to read and understand.

Example 4: In translating algorithms into executable code, programmers often resort to "tricks" to accomplish difficult tasks. Such tricks are valid, provided they get the job done without greatly compromising the clarity and readability of the program itself. Macros belong to that set of tools that encourage the trickiest of programmers to reach deep into their bags.

The programming example under the entry for PARAMETERS **245**★—the *Yesno* procedure—contains an example of a macro trick. The purpose of *Yesno* is to display a user prompt on the screen, eliciting a yes-or-no response from the keyboard. The program accepts only "Y" or "N" as appropriate input values, and stores the response in the character variable *answer*. Once *answer* contains a valid response, the program assigns a true-or-false value to the logical variable *yn*. If *answer* contains a "Y", *yn* is assigned a logical value of true; if *answer* contains an "N", *yn* becomes false. Here are the lines that assign the value:

```
answer = "." + answer + "."
yn = &answer
```

This macro substitution relies on the fact that dBASE accepts .Y. and .N. as equivalents of .T. and .F.; the sequence could also have been written as:

```
IF answer = "Y"
     yn = .T.
ELSE
     yn = .F.
ENDIF
```

The use of the macro in this case is interesting, but once again optional, and perhaps subject to the programmer's own sense of programming clarity.

■ Cautions

When employing long and complex macro substitutions, keep in mind that the maximum length of a string value in dBASE is 254 characters. (The maximum length of a command is also normally 254 characters; however, when you are using a macro in a command, the applicable length is the number of characters in the command *before* the macro substitution is made.)

Avoid using macros in DO WHILE **129**★ conditions where the value of the macro variable itself changes inside the DO loop. For example, the following passage is not reliable:

```
DO WHILE &answer
     * ... *
     answer = "." + answer + "."
     * ... *
ENDDO
```

■ **dBASE II equivalent**

&

■ **Comments**

In the interest of program clarity, you may want to avoid using macros in the condition expressions of IF **171**★, DO WHILE, and DO CASE **125**★ statements (see *Cautions*). For example, rather than including a statement like:

```
IF &answer
      *  . . .  *
```

you may want to write:

```
yn = &answer
IF yn
      *  . . .  *
```

The second form leaves no doubt about what is being evaluated.

* or NOTE

■ **Structure**

```
*  comment
NOTE comment
```

■ **Description**

The word NOTE and the symbol * are alternate ways of introducing programmer's comments **267**◆ into the text of a dBASE program. When either NOTE or * is placed at the first nonblank position in a line, dBASE ignores the line when the program is executed.

■ **Usage**

Comments ◆ should be included at the beginning of each program or procedure to identify the name and purpose of the code that follows. Comments are also often placed inside the body of the program to explain difficult passages or to call attention to important commands. Examples of commented programs appear throughout this book.

■ **Cautions**

Programmers often consider commenting a necessary but annoying task, to be put off until a programming job is complete. Unfortunately, comments postponed are seldom written. If you truly intend to write comments in a program, the time to write them is during the development of the program itself.

Comments are especially important when someone else is likely to have to maintain or modify the program later on. It is also wise to add a comment with the date and the programmer's name each time a program is modified.

■ **dBASE II equivalents**
*

NOTE

■ **Comments**
A semicolon at the end of any command line indicates that the command itself is
continued on the following line. Semicolons may also be used at the end of comment
lines as an alternate style of presenting comments. Compare the following examples:

```
* Given the principal, the interest rate, and the term
*   in years of a home loan, this program calculates the
*   monthly mortgage payment.
```

```
NOTE    Given the principal, the interest rate, and the term   ;
        in years of a home loan, this program calculates the   ;
        monthly mortgage payment.
```

Comments can also be included on the same line as the DO CASE **125★**, ELSE
146★), ENDCASE **44◆**, ENDDO **129◆**, or ENDIF **171◆** command in a conditional
structure.

? or ??

■ **Structure**
? *expression_list*
?? expression_list

■ **Description**
The ? command displays information on the screen, or sends information to the printer if the SET PRINT ON **381★** command has been issued. The list of expressions in the ?
command may include:

☐ Literal values **98◆** (strings or numbers).

☐ Variables (any type) **459★**.

☐ Operations (arithmetic **24★**, string **420★**, date **100◆**, or logical **207★**).

☐ Field values (any type **154★**, including memo fields).

In other words, the ? command can be used to display virtually any data item that can
be stored, calculated, or generated by dBASE.

If a ? command contains a list of two or more expressions, the expressions in the
list must be separated by commas. The comma generates a space character in the
resulting display, so that each expression will be separated from the next by one
space.

Within a program, the ? command issues line-feed and carriage-return characters *before* displaying the expressions in its list. The ?? command omits the line-feed
and carriage-return characters, displaying its expressions starting from the current
cursor or printer position. The following examples illustrate the difference between ?
and ?? in a command file.

Two consecutive ? commands in a program:

```
? "value1"
? "value2"
```

will display information on two different lines:

```
value1
value2
```

But a ?? command that follows a ? command

```
? "value1 "
?? "value2"
```

will place its display on the same line:

```
value1 value2
```

The ? command issued by itself, without an expression list, results in the display
of a blank line.

■ **Usage**

When a ? command includes an operation as an expression, dBASE first evaluates the operation, and then displays the result. Here are some examples—an arithmetic operation, an operation involving date arithmetic, a logical operation, and a concatenation 65★:

```
. ? 15 * 25 / 75
    5.00
.
```

```
. ? DATE() + 63
09/19/85
.
```

```
. ? 15 * 25 / 75 > 6
.F.
.
```

```
. ? "dBASE " + "III"
dBASE III
.
```

Notice that you must supply spaces explicitly in a concatenation, whereas the comma generates the space character in the following statement:

```
. ? "dBASE", "III"
dBASE III
.
```

7

Numbers in dBASE are often displayed with "leading blanks." Consider the following example, in which the variable *balance* contains the value 13572.31:

```
. ? "Balance =", balance
Balance =      13572.31
.
```

The display of these leading blank characters can be eliminated through use of the STR() **416★** function:

```
. ? "Balance =", STR(balance,8,2)
Balance = 13572.31
.
```

■ **Program example**

The program called *Price*, listed and discussed under the entry for DO...CASE **125★**, contains several examples of the use of ??. The program determines and displays ticket prices for a certain event. These prices vary according to the age of the person who is being admitted:

```
. DO Price WITH 17

==> Teenager: Admission is $4.00

.
```

Here are the passages from *Price* that produce this particular message. As you can see, the ?? command displays its message without starting a new line:

```
? " ==> "
DO CASE
      * ... *
      CASE age <= 18
            ?? "Teenager:"
            price = "4.00"
      * ... *
ENDCASE
* ... *
      ?? "Admission is $" + price
```

Further examples of ? and ?? will be found throughout this book.

■ **Caution**

Avoid using ?? from the dot prompt **62◆**, since the resulting display will overlie the query.

■ **dBASE II equivalents**

?

??

■ **Comments**

To examine the use of ? for displaying database field values, see the *Prntinfo* procedure listed under the entry for SET DEVICE **347★**. Note in particular that you can display the contents of a memo field simply by referring to the field name in a ? command. The memo value of the current record is displayed on the screen:

```
. USE Property
. GOTO 5
. ? descriptn
Stupendous ocean view.  Older row house.
Excellent condition.  Spacious rooms, modernized
kitchen.  Bedrooms upstairs.  Desirable family
home.  Good school district.  Shops and services
5 minutes.  On bus line.  Owner anxious to sell,
will carry large second for right buyer.
   .
```

See also @...SAY...GET **9★** and DISPLAY **116★**.

@...SAY...GET

■ **Structure**

@ row, col   *SAY expression   PICTURE template   GET field/variable   PICTURE template*
RANGE expression, expression   CLEAR

■ **Description**

The @...SAY...GET command gives the programmer complete control over the appearance and use of the screen, both for displaying information and for setting up input templates. The screen address represented by *row, col* is the location at which a given @...SAY...GET command will place its information. On IBM machines, the screen has 80 columns and 25 rows. The *col* component of the address may therefore be any integer from 0 through 79, and the *row* component may be any integer from 0 through 24. (dBASE itself normally uses row 0 for displaying certain messages on the screen, so in most cases you should avoid the use of this row for display of program information; see SET SCOREBOARD **379★** and RANGE **272★**.)

The SAY clause includes an expression (character **420♦**, numeric **24♦**, date **100♦**, or logical **207♦**). dBASE evaluates this expression and displays the result at the specified address. The GET clause specifies an existing variable **459★** or field and defines an input template for entering data into it. GET displays the current value of the variable or field in the input template, and allows the user to either edit the current value or enter a new value.

A single @...SAY...GET command may include either a SAY clause or a GET clause, or both. The SAY and GET clauses, in turn, may each include an optional PIC-TURE **252★** clause; the GET clause may also include an optional RANGE clause. The PICTURE clause defines the format of the information displayed by SAY or the format and requirements of the input template used by GET. The RANGE clause specifies a valid range for the input of numeric or date-type values.

If an @...SAY...GET command includes both SAY and GET clauses, the input template from GET will be displayed to the right of the information that is sent to the screen by the SAY clause. Otherwise, if there is no SAY clause, the input template appears at the specified *row, col* screen address. The GET clause does not actually initiate the input process—it only defines the input template itself. A subsequent READ **275★** command *activates* the @...GET statements.

In a program, the READ statement is the usual way to initiate the input process from a series of @...GET commands. However, dBASE also provides for the creation of a special format file **365♦** (with an .FMT extension) consisting exclusively of @...SAY...GET commands. Each format file is designed to accept input data into the fields of a specific database. When such a file has been opened (with a SET FORMAT **365★** statement), it controls the format of the entire input screen during any subsequent full-screen operations, including APPEND **19★**, CHANGE **48★**, EDIT **141★**, and INSERT **184★**.

The @...CLEAR **56★** statement clears a rectangular area of the screen, to the right of and below the corner defined by *row, col*. It is useful for eliminating unwanted information from portions of the screen before new information is displayed.

■ Usage

The following passage from the *Menu* program described under the SET PROCEDURE **383★** entry illustrates the use of the @...SAY...GET command with PICTURE and RANGE clauses.

```
choice = 7
CLEAR

@ 8, 30 SAY "Real Estate Menu"
@ 9, 30 SAY "---- ------ ----"
@ 10, 25 SAY "1. Add a new home listing."
@ 11, 25 SAY "2. Record a bid or sale."
@ 12, 25 SAY "3. Search for listing(s)."
@ 13, 25 SAY "4. Examine listing schedule."
@ 14, 25 SAY "5. Compute a mortgage."
@ 15, 25 SAY "6. Print an information sheet."
@ 16, 25 SAY "7. Quit"
@ 18, 25 SAY "Choice? <1,2,3,4,5,6,7> " ;
   GET choice PICTURE "9" RANGE 1, 7

READ
```

The first nine @...SAY commands in this passage display a menu of activities on the screen. (This menu represents all of the functions available through the real-estate program.) Then an @...SAY...GET command displays this prompt at screen address 18,25:

```
Choice? <1,2,3,4,5,6,7>
```

and to its right places a single-character input template in which the current value of the variable *choice* is displayed. (Notice that *choice* is initialized at the beginning of the passage.) Thanks to the restrictions defined by the PICTURE and RANGE clauses, this GET will accept only one digit within the range 1 through 7. The subsequent READ command actually places the cursor inside the input template, allowing the user to enter a value from the keyboard.

This book contains many more examples of @...SAY...GET; in particular, see the examples under the entries for PICTURE, RANGE, READ, and SET FORMAT for further discussion of this important command.

■ **Caution**

Unlike the input commands ACCEPT **12★**, INPUT **182★**, and WAIT **461★**, the @...GET command cannot initialize a new variable. A variable specified in the GET clause *must* already exist, or your program will terminate with a "Variable not found" error message.

■ **dBASE II equivalent**

@...SAY...GET

RANGE and CLEAR clauses are not available in dBASE II, and the SAY clause includes an optional USING , rather than PICTURE.

■ **Comment**

An @ statement that contains neither a SAY nor a GET clause simply clears information off the specified row, starting from the specified column.

ACCEPT

■ **Structure**

ACCEPT *prompt_string* TO variable_name

■ **Description**

The ACCEPT command controls an interactive dialogue between the current program and the user. ACCEPT displays an optional prompt on the screen, and waits for a character value **98♦** to be entered from the keyboard. The string value input from the keyboard need not be delimited **98♦**. Once the user has entered a value and pressed the Return key, the string is stored in the specified variable **459★**.

The ACCEPT variable does not have to be defined in advance; ACCEPT can initialize a new variable, but it will always be a character-type variable. If the user presses only the Return key in response to the ACCEPT prompt, the null value (a string consisting of no characters) will be stored in the variable.

■ **Usage**

Use ACCEPT in a program whenever you need to obtain a string of characters, specifically, from the user. ACCEPT stores even numeric and logical responses as character strings.

■ **Program example**

A program often needs to ensure the user has entered an actual value into the ACCEPT variable, and has not simply pressed the Return key. The following example:

```
*------------------------------------------------- COMPNAME.PRG
* An experiment with the ACCEPT command.
*

SET TALK OFF
SET EXACT ON

co = ""
DO WHILE co = ""
    ACCEPT "Enter your company's name: " TO co
    IF co = ""
        ?
        ? "    ---------------------------------------"
        ? "==> Please enter the name from the keyboard"
        ? "    before you press the Return key."
        ? "    ---------------------------------------"
        ?
    ENDIF
ENDDO

?
? "---------------------------------------"
? "The company's name is", co
? "---------------------------------------"

SET EXACT OFF
SET TALK ON
RETURN
```

illustrates the use of ACCEPT, and suggests one way of testing for a null string value. The ACCEPT command is performed within a DO...WHILE **129★** loop that terminates only when the ACCEPT variable, *co*, contains an actual value:

```
DO WHILE co = ""
    ACCEPT "Enter your company's name: " TO co
```

When the looping ends, the program presents an "echo" of the input value on the screen. Here is a sample run of the program:

```
. DO Compname
Enter your company's name:

------------------------------------
==> Please enter the name from the keyboard
    before you press the Return key.
------------------------------------

Enter your company's name: CompuFix, Inc.

------------------------------------
The company's name is CompuFix, Inc.
------------------------------------

.
```

Note that the user pressed only the Return key in response to the first ACCEPT prompt, and an error message from the program was the result.

■ **Caution**
A string variable may not contain a value longer than 254 characters.

■ **dBASE II equivalent**
ACCEPT

■ **Comments**
The preceding program shows one way of testing for a null string value—switch the SET EXACT **355★** status to ON and test the value of the following expression:

```
variable = ""
```

(If SET EXACT is OFF, this expression will always be true.)
    Two other techniques are possible:

▫   You can use the following form of the condition expression; if the expression is true, the variable contains a null value:

```
"" = variable
```

The SET EXACT status has no effect on the result of this expression.

□   You can use the LEN() **197**★ and TRIM() **440**★ functions, as follows:

```
LEN(TRIM(variable)) = 0
```

If this expression is true, the variable either is null or contains only space characters.

Aliases

An alias is an optional alternate name for an open database. At the time you open a database file **156**♦ with the USE **454**★ command, you can also create an alias for the database. In subsequent commands, you can refer to the file by its alias, if you wish. An alias is not stored on disk with the database, so once the file is closed again, the alias is lost.

Rules for creating aliases are the same as for creating field names: An alias can be up to 10 characters long and must begin with a letter of the alphabet; the remaining characters may be letters, digits, or an underscore.

Assigning an alias to a database is a convenience when the file name itself is difficult to remember or to use. For example, a database file that stores inventory data for the second of three company warehouses might be called *WH2INV.DBF*. When you open the file, you might want to assign a simpler alias to the database:

```
. USE Wh2inv ALIAS Inventory
```

As long as the file remains open, you can refer to the database simply as *Inventory*—a much easier name to remember than *Wh2inv*.

Aliases can be particularly useful when more than one file is open at a time, in more than one work area **454**♦. Actually, all the work areas, numbered 1 through 10, also carry *default* aliases consisting of the letters A through J. A file residing in a given work area can always be referred to by this single-letter alias. So, in fact, every open database potentially has two alias names that can be used in database commands: the alias that you assign, and the default work-area alias, a letter from A through J.

Of course, if you do not explicitly assign an alias (in the ALIAS clause of the USE **454**★ command), you simply refer to the database by its actual file name. However, this file name may *not* be used during the same dBASE session, once you have explicitly assigned an alias to the open database.

▪ Database example

The following passage illustrates the use of aliases. Two files, called *Master* and *Ju85pt3*, are opened into work areas 1 and 2, respectively. The latter (which must be indexed **176◆**) is given the alias *Monthly*:

```
. SELECT 1
. USE Master
. SELECT 2
. USE Ju85pt3 INDEX Part ALIAS Monthly
```

Let's imagine that *Master* contains year-to-date sales data for a series of items, and that *Ju85pt3*, alias *Monthly*, is a temporary file that contains last month's sales data for the same items. The following commands select the master file and establish a relation between the two files:

```
. SELECT Master
. SET RELATION TO pt_no INTO Monthly
```

Notice how the SELECT **322★** and SET RELATION **390★** commands refer to the respective databases by name (*Master*) and alias (*Monthly*).

Now, from the currently selected work area, we can access data from either database as follows:

```
. GOTO 5
.
. ? sales
69200
.
. ? Monthly -> sales
    664
.
. ? B -> pt_no
F182
.
```

Both *Monthly* and *B* are legal aliases for the database in work area 2. However, the database's actual file name, *Ju85pt3*, is *not* currently a legal name, since another alias has been assigned to the database:

```
. ? Ju85pt3 -> sales
Alias not found
           ?
? Ju85pt3 -> sales
.
```

■ **Program example**

The use of aliases in a program can contribute greatly to readability and clarity. Moreover, aliases are *essential* in the special situation where a program does not know in advance the name of a database that is to be opened.

The following short program, called *Month_up*, performs a monthly update on the master sales file called *Master*. Temporary files are created each month—by another program—to store the monthly sales figures. Each temporary file is given the name of the current month (for example, *JANUARY.DBF*, *FEBRUARY.DBF*, and so on). The task of *Month_up* is to open the current monthly file and use it to update **448**♦ the master file (this task is performed on the last day of each month):

```
*------------------------------------------------ MONTH_UP.PRG
* Performs a monthly update on the file MASTER.DBF,
*    from the monthly sales file.
*

CLEAR ALL
SET TALK OFF

mo = CMONTH(DATE())
mo = SUBSTR(mo, 1, 8)

USE Master INDEX Parts
SELECT B
USE &mo ALIAS Month
SELECT A

UPDATE ON pt_no FROM Month REPLACE sales WITH ;
   sales + Month -> sales RANDOM

SET TALK ON
RETURN
```

Month_up uses the CMONTH() **58**★ and DATE() **103**★ functions to find the name of the current monthly file, and the SUBSTR() **423**★ function to make sure that the name is not longer than eight characters. The name is assigned to the variable *mo*:

```
mo = CMONTH(DATE())
mo = SUBSTR(mo, 1, 8)
```

A subsequent USE **454**★ command opens the file, creating a macro **215**★ out of *mo*. The USE statement also assigns an alias, so that the program will have a convenient name for the file:

```
USE &mo ALIAS Month
```

Finally, the UPDATE **448**★ command uses this alias to perform the update:

```
UPDATE ON pt_no FROM Month REPLACE sales WITH ;
   sales + Month -> sales RANDOM
```

For further discussion and examples of aliases, see the entries under JOIN **189**★, SELECT, SET RELATION, and USE.

ALL

■ **Structure**

... *ALL* ...

■ **Description**

ALL is one of three optional scope **312**★ clauses available for use with some dBASE commands. A scope clause specifies the portion of the current database on which the command will operate. ALL causes the command to work on the entire database, from the first record through the last.

■ **Usage**

No matter where the record pointer **258**★ is currently positioned, a command that includes an ALL clause will begin its operation at the first record in the database, and continue to the end of the file.

■ **Database example**

The following sequence uses a database called *Staff*, which contains information concerning a group of employees. DISPLAY **116★** without a scope clause shows only the current record:

```
. USE Staff
. DISPLAY
Record#  DEPARTMENT   LASTNAME   FIRSTNAME  HIRED     YRS  EMP_ID  SALARY_MO
      1  Production   Morris     John       11/03/82  2.5    4521  1850.00
.
```

but DISPLAY ALL shows the entire database:

```
. DISPLAY ALL
Record#  DEPARTMENT   LASTNAME    FIRSTNAME  HIRED     YRS   EMP_ID  SALARY_MO
      1  Production   Morris      John       11/03/82   2.5    4521   1850.00
      2  Marketing    Southby     Anne       08/22/81   3.7    3134   2315.00
      3  Clerical     Peters      Larry      06/10/83   1.9    3412   1350.00
      4  Clerical     Broussard   Marie      05/05/81   4.0    8712   1275.00
      5  Production   James       Fred       02/22/77   8.2    6563   1675.00
      6  Marketing    Smith       June       03/29/80   5.1    6823   2475.00
      7  Clerical     Liles       Carter     09/29/77   7.6    8799   1400.00
      8  Production   Washington  Liz        11/05/74  10.5    7321   1700.00
      9  Clerical     Ludlum      Donald     03/30/77   8.1    7412   1250.00
.
```

■ **Caution**

Subsequent to the execution of a command with an ALL clause, the record pointer will be positioned *after* the last record, and the EOF() **147★** function will return a value of true. At this point, a DISPLAY command will display no record:

```
. ? RECNO()
      10
. ? EOF()
.T.
. DISPLAY
Record#  DEPARTMENT   LASTNAME   FIRSTNAME  HIRED      YRS  EMP_ID  SALARY_MO
.
```

■ **dBASE II equivalent**
ALL

■ **Comments**
A command that has a FOR **164★** condition clause but no scope clause will take on a scope of ALL. In the following example, the FOR condition is automatically applied over the entire database, regardless of the position of the pointer when the command is entered:

```
. DISPLAY FOR department = "Production"
Record#  DEPARTMENT  LASTNAME    FIRSTNAME  HIRED     YRS  EMP_ID  SALARY_MO
      1  Production  Morris      John       11/03/82  2.5    4521    1850.00
      5  Production  James       Fred       02/22/77  8.2    6563    1675.00
      8  Production  Washington  Liz        11/05/74 10.5    7321    1700.00
.
```

The following commands accept an optional ALL, NEXT **239★**, or RECORD **282★** scope clause: AVERAGE **31★**, CHANGE **48★**, COPY TO **82★**, COUNT **85★**, DELETE **106★**, DISPLAY, LABEL FORM **195★**, LIST **200★**, LOCATE **202★**, RECALL **278★**, REPLACE **291★**, REPORT FORM **295★**, SUM **426★**, and TOTAL **436★**.

APPEND

■ **Structure**
APPEND *BLANK*

■ **Description**
The APPEND command moves you into a full-screen mode designed for adding ◆ new records to the currently selected **322◆** database. Each APPEND screen is devoted to a single record **284★**. Input templates are displayed on the screen, showing the name and width of each field **154★**. APPEND allows continuous entry of records, one at a time.

In contrast, the APPEND BLANK command does not invoke full-screen mode, but rather adds one blank record at the end of the current database and returns you to the dot prompt.

■ **Usage**

Normally, APPEND displays all of the field names and templates for the current database in one or more columns on the screen. However, if you have prepared a format file **365◆** for the database, you can issue the SET FORMAT **365★** command before APPEND, to change the organization of the data-entry screen.

The following keyboard functions control the use of the APPEND mode:

Key:	*Action:*
Right-arrow, Left-arrow	Move cursor one character to the right or left.
Up-arrow, Down-arrow	Move cursor one field up or down.
PgUp, PgDn	Move to previous or next record.
Ctrl-PgDn	Edit ◆ current memo field **217★**.
Ctrl-End	Save current memo field.
Ctrl-Y	Delete contents of field template.
Ctrl-U	Mark or unmark current record for deletion (a toggle).
Ins	Activate or deactivate character-insert mode (a toggle).
Esc	Exit APPEND mode, without saving record.
Ctrl-End	Exit APPEND mode, saving current record.

(Pressing the Return key before entering any data values into a new record screen also ends the APPEND mode.)

If SET MENU **378★** is ON, a list of control keys appears at the top of the screen when you enter the APPEND mode. Even if SET MENU is OFF, you can use the F1 function key to toggle this list on or off the screen from within APPEND.

Several other SET commands affect the behavior of APPEND. SET CONFIRM **334★** and SET BELL **329★** control the action of individual field entries. SET DELIMITERS **345★**, SET INTENSITY **376★**, and SET COLOR **331★** change the appearance of the templates and the input screen. SET CARRY **330★** allows data to be carried forward (copied) from one record to the next.

If any index files **156◆** are open for the current database, they are updated after each new record is added (see INDEX **176★** and SET INDEX **372★**).

■ **Program example**

From within a program, the process of appending records can be controlled in one of two ways. The simpler way is to open up a format file, and then simply issue the APPEND command. An example appears in the *Add* procedure listed under the SET FORMAT entry:

```
SET FORMAT TO Propin
APPEND
```

This allows the user to add any number of records to the current database. When the user exits from the APPEND mode, control is passed back to the program that issued the APPEND command.

A more controlled technique is to use the APPEND BLANK command, adding a blank record to the database, and then issue a series of @...SAY...GET **9★** statements and a READ **275★** command to elicit data for the fields of the one blank record that has just been appended. These statements may all be located inside a DO...WHILE **129★** loop, for multiple-record entry. (When the user exits from this program-controlled APPEND mode, the most recently appended blank record will have to be deleted again.) The advantage of this technique is that it gives you better control over data integrity. Your program can perform any number of checks on the data just entered for the current record before allowing the user to move on to the next record.

■ **dBASE II equivalents**

APPEND

APPEND BLANK

■ **Comments**

APPEND BLANK also has an interesting interactive use. Sometimes when you are developing a new database, it is more convenient to enter data via the BROWSE **38★** command than through APPEND, since BROWSE gives you a view of a screenful of records at a time. However, the primary purpose of BROWSE is to allow editing of already existing records—you can't even get *into* the BROWSE mode if your database is empty. A way around this problem is to APPEND a series of blank records and then invoke BROWSE to enter data into them.

The following program, called *Blanks*, is a simple tool meant to facilitate data entry through BROWSE:

```
*--------------------------------------------------- BLANKS.PRG
* Appends a specified number of blank records to a database
*    and then goes into BROWSE mode.
*

PARAMETER num

SET TALK OFF
COUNT TO cur

DO WHILE num > 0
    APPEND BLANK
    num = num - 1
ENDDO
GOTO cur + 1

SET TALK ON
BROWSE
RETURN
```

To use this tool, just open any database and run the program:

```
. USE Sample
. DO Blanks WITH 10
```

The numeric parameter **245♦** value that you send to *Blanks* determines the number of blank records that will be appended to the database. The preceding example will append 10 blank records to the *Sample* database and then move into the BROWSE mode for data entry into the records. (This program works on either an empty database or one that already contains other records.)

APPEND FROM

■ **Structure**
APPEND FROM file_name *FOR condition_clause SDF/DELIMITED WITH delimiter*

■ **Description**
The APPEND FROM command copies records to the current database from a file stored on disk. The disk file may be a dBASE database, or a data file stored in one of two other formats (SDF **313★** and delimited **111★**).

■ **Usage**

You can read about the SDF and delimited file formats under their own entries in this book: If an outside program creates files in either of these two formats, the APPEND FROM command can read the data directly into a dBASE database. The example included here, however, shows how records can be appended from one dBASE database file to another.

■ **Database example**

The *Miniprop* database is a smaller version of a real-estate database called *Property* **384◆**. *Property* contains 18 fields; *Miniprop* contains only three, but the names of its fields match the names of the same three fields in *Property*:

```
. USE Miniprop
. LIST STRUCTURE
Structure for database : A:Miniprop.dbf
Number of data records :        0
Date of last update    : 07/19/85
Field  Field name  Type       Width   Dec
    1  ADDRESS     Character      28
    2  NEIGHBORHD  Character      20
    3  ASKING_PR   Numeric         9    2
** Total **                       58

.
```

Notice that the *Miniprop* database currently contains no records. The following APPEND FROM command will add selected records to *Miniprop* from *Property*:

```
. APPEND FROM Property for neighborhd = "Mission"
      3 records added
. LIST
Record#  ADDRESS                NEIGHBORHD     ASKING_PR
     1   12345 26th Avenue      Mission        149000.00
     2   50 17th Street         Mission        125000.00
     3   3555 Alta Street       Mission        179000.00

.
```

■ **dBASE II equivalent**

APPEND FROM

■ **Comment**

When dealing with the dBASE database format, APPEND FROM looks by default for a file with the .DBF **156◆** extension.

Arithmetic operators

The following arithmetic operations ♦ are available in dBASE III:

Operator:	Operation:
ˆ or **	Exponentiation
*	Multiplication
/	Division
+	Addition
−	Subtraction

When writing an arithmetic expression ♦ that includes two or more of these operations, you must carefully consider the *order of precedence*, or the order in which dBASE will evaluate a series of operations in an expression. Evaluation does not necessarily occur from the beginning of an expression to the end, from left to right; rather, some operations are normally evaluated ahead of others, as follows:

1. Exponentiation
2. Multiplication and division, left to right
3. Addition and subtraction, left to right

Here are some simple examples to illustrate the order of precedence in dBASE. In the first example, the exponentiation is performed first, then the multiplication (5 to the power of 2 is 25; 6 times 25 is 150). In the second, the multiplication is performed first, then the subtraction. And in the last, the division is performed first, then the multiplication:

```
. ? 6 * 5 ^ 2
       150.00
.
```

```
. ? 20 - 5 * 2
  10
.
```

```
. ? 18 / 3 * 5
    30.00
.
```

The result of each of these expressions would be different if the order of evaluation were changed. You will often, in fact, want to override dBASE's natural order of operations, defining a specific order that matches the requirements of the application at hand. On such occasions, you can use *parentheses* in the arithmetic expression: dBASE always evaluates operations that are inside parentheses first, and then follows its normal order of precedence.

Here are the same three examples we just considered, with parentheses to change the order in which the expressions will be evaluated:

```
. ? (6 * 5) ^ 2
        900.00
.
```

```
. ? (20 - 5) * 2
       30
.
```

```
. ? 18 / (3 * 5)
       1.20
.
```

These examples show how important the order of evaluation really is: Expressions that are otherwise identical can result in very different values when parentheses are included.

In a complex arithmetic expression, parentheses may be *nested*, to further refine the order in which the expression is to be evaluated. Nesting means placing sets of parentheses inside other sets of parentheses. To evaluate such an expression, dBASE begins with the innermost set of parentheses and works outward. Here is an example:

```
. ? (((3 + 5) * (15 - 10)) / 4) ^ 2
      100.00
.
```

In evaluating this expression, dBASE performs the addition and subtraction first, since these operations are located in the innermost set of parentheses; next comes the multiplication, then the division, and finally the exponentiation. Consider the result of the same expression if the parentheses are removed:

```
. ? 3 + 5 * 15 - 10 / 4 ^ 2
          77.38
.
```

■ **Caution**

When using parentheses, especially nested ones, you must be careful to match each opening parenthesis with a closing parenthesis; otherwise dBASE will not be able to evaluate the expression, and you will receive an error message:

```
. ? ((5 + 2) * 3
Unbalanced parenthesis
                  ?
? ((5 + 2) * 3
.
```

■ **Comment**

Parentheses actually serve two purposes in arithmetic expressions: First, they change the order in which dBASE will actually evaluate an expression; second, they make the expression easier for *people* to read. For this second reason, you may often find yourself placing parentheses in an expression even when those parentheses are not strictly necessary for the correct evaluation of the operations. This is an excellent practice, particularly when you are writing dBASE programs that other people may need to read and understand.

ASC()

■ **Structure**

ASC(character_expression)

■ **Description**

Given a string value, the ASC() function returns the ASCII **28★** numeric code of the first character in the string.

■ **Usage**

In other programming languages—BASIC, for example—the ASC() function is often used for character-by-character validation of input coming from the keyboard. In dBASE III, you can exert similar control over input, with much less programming effort, through use of the @...SAY...GET **9★** command. For this reason, ASC() is seldom used in dBASE programs.

■ **Program example**

The following short program, called *Chartest*, is an exercise to demonstrate the use of the ASC() function:

```
*-------------------------------------------------- CHARTEST.PRG
* Provides ASCII codes from the keyboard. This is an
*  endless loop, since the condition is always true.
*

SET TALK OFF

DO WHILE .T.
    WAIT "Press any key: " TO char
    ? "ASCII:", ASC(char)
    ?
ENDDO
```

The WAIT **461★** command accepts a key from the keyboard as input and stores its value in a variable—*char*, in this case. (Unlike INPUT **182★** and ACCEPT **12★**, the WAIT command does not require the user to press Return to complete the input process.) This program simply supplies the ASCII code of the given character, every time you press a key. Here is a sample:

```
. DO Chartest
Press any key: &
ASCII:    38

Press any key:
```

■ **dBASE II equivalent**

RANK()

ASCII

ASCII stands for American Standard Code for Information Interchange. On the IBM PC and other personal computers, this code is used to assign numeric codes to the computer's entire character set. The code numbers range from 0 through 255; however, only the first half of the code, 0 through 127, is actually very standard. The upper half, 128 through 255, is used for providing "extended character sets," which vary from computer to computer.

Here is an outline of the first half of the ASCII code:

ASCII value:	Character:
0–31	"Control" characters
32	Space character
33–47	Punctuation characters
48–57	Digits, 0 through 9
58–64	Punctuation and special symbols
65–90	Uppercase letters, A through Z
91–96	Punctuation and special symbols
97–122	Lowercase letters, a through z
123–126	Special symbols
127	DEL, a control character

On the IBM PC, the latter half of the code is devoted to foreign-language alphabets, special technical and mathematical symbols, and graphics characters **52♦**. The graphics characters are particularly interesting because you can use them to create the illusion of high-resolution graphics on a monitor that actually only allows the display of characters.

Two dBASE functions, CHR() **50★** and ASC() **26★**, give you access to the ASCII code in a program. The entry under CHR() contains a program that illustrates several of the IBM PC graphics characters in use.

ASSIST

■ **Structure**

ASSIST

■ **Description**

The ASSIST command invokes a menu-driven help program that performs many of the most common database commands. The operations that ASSIST will perform include:

☐ Setting the control parameters **73★**.

☐ Creating new databases.

- Appending and editing records.
- Searching for and displaying data.
- Sorting **406★** the database.
- Moving the pointer **258★**.
- Creating labels and reports.
- Working with disk files.

■ **Usage**

Using ASSIST, the newcomer to dBASE III can quickly begin performing database operations without having to learn the command language itself. ASSIST is designed to be reasonably self-explanatory, as shown in this screen:

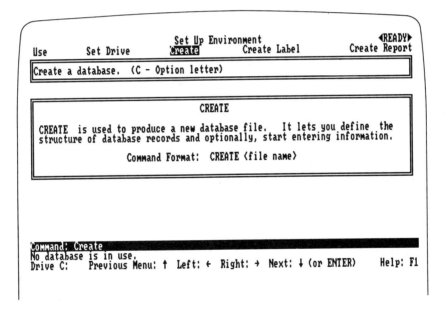

```
                         Set Up Environment                        ◀READY▶
Use          Set Drive    Create        Create Label      Create Report
┌────────────────────────────────────────────────────────────────────┐
│Create a database.  (C - Option letter)                              │
└────────────────────────────────────────────────────────────────────┘

     ┌──────────────────────────────────────────────────────────┐
     │                         CREATE                           │
     │  CREATE  is used to produce a new database file.  It lets you define  the │
     │  structure of database records and optionally, start entering information. │
     │                                                          │
     │         Command Format:  CREATE <file name>              │
     └──────────────────────────────────────────────────────────┘




Command: Create
No database is in use.
Drive C:     Previous Menu: ↑  Left: ←  Right: →  Next: ↓ (or ENTER)     Help: F1
```

■ **dBASE II equivalent**

None

■ **Comment**

After the initial learning period, most users abandon the ASSIST mode, since the command language is quicker, more efficient, and more versatile.

AT()

- **Structure**

  AT(character_expression_1, character_expression_2)

- **Description**

  Given two strings of characters, the AT() function returns a numeric value representing the position of the first string in the second string. If the first string is not found in the second string, AT() returns a value of 0.

- **Usage**

  A string that is contained within another string is referred to as a *substring*. AT() finds the position of a substring:

```
. ? AT("test", "a test of AT")
        3
.
```

This result indicates that the substring "test" begins at the third character position of the second string.

- **Program example**

  The AT() function can sometimes be useful in programming situations to check the validity of strings that are input from the keyboard. The following routine, called *Yesno*, is a very simple example. The routine makes sure that the user has entered a yes-or-no answer in response to an input prompt:

```
*-------------------------------------------------- YESNO.PRG
* This routine insists on a yes-or-no answer
* in response to an input prompt.
*

SET TALK OFF

done = .F.
DO WHILE .NOT. done
    ACCEPT "Ready to quit this program? " TO ans
    ans = UPPER(SUBSTR(ans, 1, 1))
    IF AT(ans, "YN") <> 0
        done = .T.
    ENDIF
ENDDO

IF ans = "Y"
  ? "Quitting program ..."
ELSE
  ? "Continuing program ..."
ENDIF
```

The ACCEPT **12★** command in this program places a question on the screen and stores the keyboard response in the variable *ans*. In order for the program to respond appropriately to the input, *ans* must represent a yes-or-no answer. If it does not, the user must be prompted to enter a new answer.

The following line reduces *ans* to an uppercase version of its first character:

```
ans = UPPER(SUBSTR(ans, 1, 1))
```

Then an IF **171★** statement tests to see whether the user has indeed answered the question appropriately:

```
IF AT(ans, "YN") <> 0
    done = .T.
ENDIF
```

The key to this kind of input checking is that AT() returns a value of 0 if the first string is not present in the second string. Thus, if the second string consists of all the possible appropriate answers (simply "YN" in this example), a nonzero result from AT() means that the input string, *ans*, contains a good answer.

■ **dBASE II equivalent**

@()

■ **Comment**

The SUBSTR() **423★** function actually extracts a substring value from a specified position in a string.

AVERAGE

■ **Structure**

AVERAGE   *scope_clause   expression_list   TO variable_list   condition_clause*

■ **Description**

The AVERAGE command computes and displays numeric averages from specified fields of a database. You can use the expression-list clause to specify which numeric field or fields you wish to average. The expression list may also include arithmetic expressions **24◆** involving numeric fields. The TO clause, which is optional, allows you to store the results of AVERAGE in variables **459★** that you name in the variable list. Values in the expression list are assigned in consecutive order to the variables in the variable list.

The optional scope **312★** indicator may include any one of the three scope clauses available in dBASE III: ALL **17★**, NEXT **239★**, or RECORD **282★**. The default scope is ALL, so if the scope clause is missing, AVERAGE works on the entire database. The condition expression, which is also optional, allows you to use a FOR **164★** or WHILE **463★** clause to select records conditionally for the average.

■ Usage

The results of the AVERAGE command are normally displayed on the screen immediately after you issue the command itself (be sure to SET TALK ON **398★**). To save the results of AVERAGE, you *must* include a TO clause in the command and name the variables in which you want to save the average values.

■ Database example

The following database, called *Staff*, contains information about the employees of a small company. The database has three numeric fields: *yrs*, the number of years each employee has worked for the firm; *emp_id*, the employee's personnel number; and *salary_mo*, the employee's monthly salary. Here is a complete listing of *Staff*:

```
. USE Staff
. LIST
Record#  DEPARTMENT   LASTNAME    FIRSTNAME   HIRED      YRS  EMP_ID  SALARY_MO
      1  Production   Morris      John        11/03/82   2.5    4521   1850.00
      2  Marketing    Southby     Anne        08/22/81   3.7    3134   2315.00
      3  Clerical     Peters      Larry       06/10/83   1.9    3412   1350.00
      4  Clerical     Broussard   Marie       05/05/81   4.0    8712   1275.00
      5  Production   James       Fred        02/22/77   8.2    6563   1675.00
      6  Marketing    Smith       June        03/29/80   5.1    6823   2475.00
      7  Clerical     Liles       Carter      09/29/77   7.6    8799   1400.00
      8  Production   Washington  Liz         11/05/74  10.5    7321   1700.00
      9  Clerical     Ludlum      Donald      03/30/77   8.1    7412   1250.00
.
```

The first two AVERAGE commands in the following example find the average years of service and the average monthly salary of the company's employees. The third command finds both of these averages at once.

```
. AVERAGE yrs
        9 records averaged
yrs
5.7

.
```

```
. AVERAGE salary_mo
        9 records averaged
salary_mo
  1698.89

.
```

```
. AVERAGE yrs, salary_mo
        9 records averaged
yrs salary_mo
5.7   1698.89

.
```

Here is an example of an arithmetic expression used with AVERAGE. This command finds the average *yearly* salary of all the employees:

```
. AVERAGE salary_mo * 12
        9 records averaged
salary_mo * 12
      20386.67

.
```

And here is one that uses a FOR clause to select records conditionally for the average calculation. The result is the average salary of all the clerical workers:

```
. AVERAGE salary_mo FOR department = "Clerical"
      4 records averaged
salary_mo
  1318.75

.
```

(Notice that capitalization counts when matching a string.)

- **Program example**

The entry for the SUM **426★** command contains a program that produces departmental reports from the *Staff* database. The program, called *Summary*, contains the following example of the AVERAGE command, using the TO clause to assign averages to variables:

```
AVERAGE yrs, salary_mo FOR department = deptname TO avgyrs, avgsal
```

This command computes the average years of service and the average monthly salary for a given department in the company, and assigns those values to the variables *avgyrs* and *avgsal*, which are used later in the program to produce a report for the specified department.

- **Caution**

Without any parameters at all, the AVERAGE command averages all numeric fields in a database, even those for which the average calculation serves no useful purpose. For example, consider the following command, performed on the *Staff* database:

```
. AVERAGE
        9 records averaged
YRS EMP_ID SALARY_MO
5.7   6300   1698.89
.
```

The average of all the employee numbers is meaningless, but the AVERAGE command supplies it anyway.

- **dBASE II equivalent**

AVERAGE

- **Comment**

Other statistical commands include TOTAL **436★**, SUM, and COUNT **85★**.

BOF()

■ **Structure**
BOF()

■ **Description**
BOF() is the beginning-of-file function. It returns a logical value **99◆** of true if an attempt has been made to push the record pointer **258★** above the first record in the file. Otherwise, it returns a value of false.

■ **Usage**
If the record pointer is positioned at the first record of a database, the *SKIP –1* **401◆** command sets BOF() to true. Consider the following illustration:

```
. USE Property
. GOTO TOP
.
. ? RECNO()
        1
.
. ? BOF()
.F.
.
. SKIP -1
Record no.      1
. ? RECNO()
        1
.
. ? BOF()
.T.
.
```

The RECNO() **279★** function supplies the current record number. Notice that the result of RECNO() is 1 even when BOF() is true.

■ **Program example**
A common use of BOF() in a program is to set up a DO WHILE **129★** loop that processes a database backwards—from the last record to the first. Here is an outline of the algorithm that controls such a loop:

1. Assuming that the database is not empty, move the record pointer to the bottom of the file (*GOTO BOTTOM* **169◆**).

2. Process the current record.

3. Move the record pointer up one record (*SKIP –1*).

4. Test for the beginning-of-file condition. If BOF() is true, stop processing. If BOF() is false, repeat from step #2.

This algorithm translates into the following code:

```
GOTO BOTTOM
DO WHILE .NOT. BOF()
    *  ... *
    * Process the current record.
    *  ... *
    SKIP -1
ENDDO
```

The program called *Rank* contains an example of such a loop. *Rank* deals with a simple database called *Students*, which contains fields for the names, test scores, and ranks of a group of students:

```
. USE Students
. LIST
Record#  NAME       SCORE RANK
       1 Arthur       76   0
       2 Jane         82   0
       3 Nancy        95   0
       4 Michael      62   0
       5 Donald       97   0
       6 Johnny       75   0
  .
```

The *Rank* program has two jobs: to fill in the *rank* field with appropriate numeric values, and then to produce a report listing the rank and score of each student.

```
*------------------------------------------------------- RANK.PRG
* Fills in the field Rank, and produces messages describing
*    each student in the database called Student.
*    (Illustrates BOF() and EOF().)
*

SET TALK OFF
SET SAFETY OFF

USE Students
INDEX ON score TO Score

r = 1
GOTO BOTTOM
DO WHILE .NOT. BOF()
    REPLACE rank WITH r
    r = r + 1
    SKIP -1
ENDDO
```

(continued)

36

```
INDEX ON name TO Name

GOTO TOP
DO WHILE .NOT. EOF()
    ? TRIM(name), "is #" + STR(rank, 1), "with a score of", ;
      STR(score, 3) + "."
    SKIP
ENDDO

SET SAFETY ON
SET TALK ON
RETURN
```

At the beginning of this program, the *Students* database is indexed on the field *score*. Since the INDEX **176★** command sorts only in ascending order, the scores in *Students* will be arranged from worst to best. For this reason, a backward journey through the database is required for the program to assign ranks starting from 1. This is the job of the first DO WHILE loop in the program. The variable *r* is used in a RE-PLACE **291★** command to assign the appropriate rank to each record. It is initialized with a value of 1, and then incremented by 1 after each ranking:

```
r = 1
GOTO BOTTOM
DO WHILE .NOT. BOF()
    REPLACE rank WITH r
    r = r + 1
    SKIP -1
ENDDO
```

The second DO WHILE loop in the program takes care of displaying a message about each student. (See the entry under EOF() **147★** for a discussion of this passage.) Here is the output from the program:

```
. DO Rank
Arthur is #4 with a score of  76.
Donald is #1 with a score of  97.
Jane is #3 with a score of  82.
Johnny is #5 with a score of  75.
Michael is #6 with a score of  62.
Nancy is #2 with a score of  95.
.
```

After the program is done, the *Students* database has all the values filled in for the *rank* field:

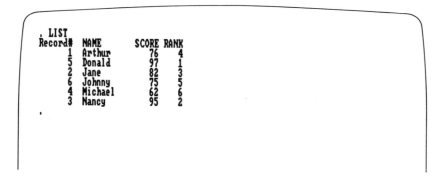

```
. LIST
Record#  NAME       SCORE RANK
      1  Arthur       76    4
      5  Donald       97    1
      2  Jane         82    3
      6  Johnny       75    5
      4  Michael      62    6
      3  Nancy        95    2
.
```

■ **Caution**

Database commands that normally work on the current record will perform on record #1 even if BOF() is true. (Contrast this with the behavior of such commands when EOF() is true.) If BOF() is true, the SKIP command will move the record pointer to record #2 and switch BOF() to false (assuming a second record exists).

■ **dBASE II equivalent**

None

■ **Comments**

BOF() is always true for an empty database—that is, a database that contains no records (see ZAP **469★**).

If two or more databases are open concurrently, the value of BOF() depends upon which database is currently selected **322◆**.

BROWSE

■ **Structure**

BROWSE   *FIELDS field_list   LOCK numeric_expression   FREEZE field   NOFOLLOW*

■ **Description**

BROWSE is a full-screen editing command. The BROWSE mode displays a screenful of records from the currently selected **322◆** database, and allows you to edit the data stored in the records. Each record is displayed on a line of its own; the columns of information represent the fields of the database. Except when the FREEZE option is used, BROWSE highlights *all* fields of the current record. You can use the cursor keys to move the highlight up and down the screen, or to move the cursor to a new field column.

The four optional clauses of the BROWSE command allow you to:

☐ Select which database fields will be included in the BROWSE screen (FIELDS).

☐ Hold the display of certain fields fixed at the left side of the screen, even when you "pan" to the right (LOCK).

☐ Specify a single field as the target for editing (FREEZE).

☐ Control the way BROWSE behaves when you are working with an indexed **176**◆ database (NOFOLLOW).

■ **Usage**

The following examples of the BROWSE command work with the real-estate database called *Property*. You can read about this database under the entry for SET PROCEDURE **383**★. *Property* contains 18 fields of information describing the characteristics of a home that is for sale. Each record applies to one home.

The first BROWSE command selects four fields from the database and uses the FREEZE option to specify one of them, *asking_pr*, as the target field for on-screen editing:

```
. BROWSE FIELDS owner_l, address, neighborhd, asking_pr ;
  FREEZE asking_pr
```

In this case, the BROWSE highlight will appear only over the *asking_pr* field.

The next example selects five fields, and locks the first two on the screen. Since there is no FREEZE clause in this command, all of the selected fields will be available for editing:

```
. BROWSE FIELDS owner_l, address, city, neighborhd, ;
  asking_pr LOCK 2
```

The rationale of the LOCK clause is as follows: When there are too many fields to be displayed all at once on the screen, you have to "pan" the screen window to the right (using Ctrl-Right-arrow) in order to see the fields that are not currently displayed. Normally, the side-effect of panning is that the initial fields on the left disappear from the screen, to make room for the new ones. LOCK lets you specify a number of fields that will remain fixed on the screen, even when panning occurs.

As a final example, the following command selects all of the fields (since the FIELDS clause is missing), and assumes that the *Property* database is currently indexed on one or more of its fields:

```
. BROWSE NOFOLLOW
```

Let's say the database is indexed on *asking_pr*. If, during the BROWSE operation, you change the *asking_pr* value in one of the records, a reindexing will occur automatically. This means that the record you have edited will be moved immediately to its new indexed position in the database. The NOFOLLOW clause specifies that the BROWSE highlight will remain at its current position in the database when the reindexing occurs. *Without* the NOFOLLOW parameter, the highlight will always follow the edited record to its new position.

If your database is small, you may think that the NOFOLLOW issue is insignificant, but if you are using BROWSE to work with a database that contains hundreds of indexed records, the position and movement of the highlight becomes a matter of great importance.

You can use the following keyboard functions to control the activity on the BROWSE screen:

Key:	*Action:*
Right-arrow, Left-arrow	Move cursor one character right or left.
End, Home	Move cursor one field right or left.
Up-arrow, Down-arrow	Move highlight one record up or down.
PgUp, PgDn	Move screen window one page up or down.
Ctrl-Right-arrow, Ctrl-Left-arrow	Pan right or left.
Ctrl-Y	Delete to right of cursor, within a field.
Ctrl-U	Mark or unmark record for deletion (a toggle). * DEL* appears on screen for marked record.
Ins	Activate or deactivate character-insert mode (a toggle).
Esc	Exit full-screen mode, without saving new edits in current record (other edits will be saved).
Ctrl-End	Exit full-screen mode, saving all edits.

The F1 function key toggles the display of a list of control keys from within the BROWSE mode. If the SET MENU **378★** status is ON, the list appears on the screen automatically when you begin BROWSE, and pressing F1 toggles the list off. Additionally, pressing Ctrl-Home brings up this menu of BROWSE options:

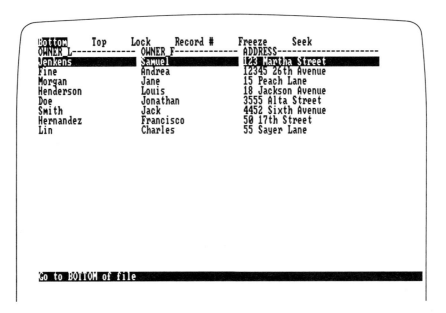

The Bottom, Top, and Record # options move the BROWSE highlight in quick jumps—to the bottom of the file, the top of the file, or a record number that you specify, respectively. The Lock and Freeze options allow you to change the values you specified for the LOCK and FREEZE clauses in the original BROWSE command. The Seek option appears in the menu only if the database is indexed. It allows a search for a specific value in the key field. To select one of the options from the menu, move the highlight (using the Right- or Left-arrow key), then press the Return key.

Finally, if you attempt to move the BROWSE record highlight to the position below the last record of the database, you will be asked if you would like to append a record. If you answer yes, blank records for you to fill in with data will continue to appear on the screen until you ask to exit the BROWSE mode.

■ **Cautions**

You may not edit memo fields **217★** in the BROWSE mode. Use the EDIT **141★** command instead.

If you specify too large a number of fields in the LOCK clause, you risk locking the entire screen in place. In locking fields at the left side of the screen, you must make sure that you are leaving enough room at the right side for panning to occur.

You must bring the first of the fields you wish to lock to the left edge of the screen *before* selecting the Lock option. If you wish to lock more than one field, the fields must be adjacent to one another in the database. Also, note that you cannot pan to the left of a locked field.

If you inadvertently lock the screen, you do not have to exit from the BROWSE mode to correct the situation. Simply bring up the options menu (Ctrl-Home) and change the Lock option.

■ **dBASE II equivalent**

BROWSE

However, the dBASE II version does not offer the LOCK, FREEZE, and NOFOLLOW options, nor does it offer a menu.

■ **Comment**

Two other commands, CHANGE **48★** and EDIT, are available for full-screen editing of the current database. Both of these commands present only one record on the screen at a time.

CANCEL

- **Structure**

  CANCEL

- **Description**

  The CANCEL command stops the execution of a program and returns control to the dBASE dot-prompt **62♦** level. CANCEL ends performance from any program level—even from a program or procedure **266♦** that has been called from another program or procedure.

- **Usage**

  In the overall structure of a program, CANCEL plays a dubious role: Its use can be compared with the use of LOOP **211★** and EXIT **150★** commands in DO...WHILE **129★** structures. All three of these commands represent abnormal interruptions to the normal flow of program control, and should therefore be used advisedly, if at all.

  A programmer might consider using CANCEL to drop completely out of program execution in the event of some unexpected error condition. In such a condition, it may not seem worthwhile to back out of the program in logical steps, moving from called to calling program, up to the "main program" level (see SET PROCEDURE **383★**). Terminating program performance from the level at which the error occurs may seem like a more sensible approach.

  For example, imagine a procedure that opens a database file that is instrumental to the remainder of program performance. If the file cannot be found on disk, there is no use continuing. To allow for such a situation, you might write a sequence of commands such as the following:

  ```
  IF .NOT. FILE("SALES.DBF")
      CANCEL
  ENDIF
  ```

  The FILE() **158★** function in the IF **171★** structure tests for the existence of the database file. If the file does not exist, the entire program is canceled.

- **dBASE II equivalent**

  CANCEL

- **Comment**

  The RETURN **301★** command is the usual and preferable way of passing control back to a calling program.

CASE

■ **Structure**
DO CASE
    CASE condition
        * ... *
   * ... *
ENDCASE

■ **Description**
A DO CASE **125★** structure consists of a sequence of CASE clauses, each representing one possible course of action that might be chosen during the performance of a program. Each CASE clause expresses a condition **286◆** that must evaluate as true in order for the case to be chosen. Performance of a DO CASE statement results in the choice of only *one* CASE clause.

    Optionally, a DO CASE structure may also include a final course of action, expressed in an OTHERWISE **242★** clause: If none of the CASE clauses is chosen during a given performance of the DO CASE statement, the OTHERWISE clause is performed. If there is no OTHERWISE clause and no CASE clause is chosen, the program simply moves on to the next command after the DO CASE structure.

CDOW()

■ **Structure**
CDOW(date-type value)

■ **Description**
Given a dBASE date-type value **99◆**, CDOW() (character day-of-week) returns a string of characters representing the name of the day of the week upon which the date falls.

■ **Usage**

The argument of CDOW() may be a date-type field or variable value, or it may be the result of the DATE() **103★** or CTOD() **92★** function:

```
. ? DATE()
07/23/85

. ? CDOW(DATE())
Tuesday

. ? CDOW(CTOD("3/14/85"))
Thursday

.
```

■ **Program example**

The following database, called *Payables*, contains a list of unpaid business bills with recent or upcoming due dates. The database has two date fields: *inv_date*, the date of the invoice; and *due*, the date the bill is due. Here is a complete listing of *Payables*:

```
. USE Payables
. LIST
Record#  COMPANY            DESCRPTION      AMOUNT INV_DATE TERMS DUE
      1  Corner Stationary  supplies        109.82 03/31/85    30 04/30/85
      2  TechCo Computer Co. floppy disks     85.22 04/21/85    45 06/05/85
      3  CompuFix, Inc.     PC Repairs       256.80 04/11/85    30 05/11/85
      4  SoftSave Corp.     software         745.32 03/29/85    15 04/13/85
      5  ConsultiComp, Inc. training         150.00 05/01/85    45 06/15/85
      6  The Tech Book Store computer books   38.92 04/21/85    30 05/21/85

.
```

The program called *Duedates* produces a four-line message describing each of the bills in the *Payables* database. The program illustrates the use of CDOW(), along with several other date functions:

```
*----------------------------------------------------- DUEDATES.PRG
* Print due date for each bill in Payables file.
*

SET TALK OFF
SET SAFETY OFF

? "Payables"
? "--------"
? "Today is ", date(), "."
?

USE Payables
INDEX ON Due to Due_ind
GOTO TOP

*----- Loop through database and display unpaid bills.
DO WHILE .NOT. EOF()
   ? "Amount due: $", amount
   ? "To:         ", company
   ? "By:         ", CDOW(due) + ",", CMONTH(due), DAY(due)
   dd = due - DATE()
   IF dd >= 0
      ? "==> Due in:", dd, "days."
   ELSE
      ? "==> Overdue!"
   ENDIF
   ?
   SKIP
ENDDO

SET TALK ON
SET SAFETY ON
RETURN
```

Duedates uses a DO WHILE 129★ loop to process each record in the database. Inside the loop, a series of ? 5★ statements displays information about the current record. In particular, notice the use of the CDOW() function in the statement:

```
? "By:         ", CDOW(due) + ",", CMONTH(due), DAY(due)
```

This print line uses both CDOW() and CMONTH() 58★ to convert the date-type value from the field *due* into a character date. The result is used with the DAY() 105★ function to produce a message in the following format:

```
By:         Saturday, April  13
```

Here is the printed output from the program, working from the *Payables* database:

```
Payables
--------
Today is  04/25/85.

Amount due: $  745.32
To:            SoftSave Corp.
By:            Saturday, April   13
==> Overdue!

Amount due: $  109.82
To:            Corner Stationary
By:            Tuesday, April   30
==> Due in:          5 days.

Amount due: $  256.80
To:            CompuFix, Inc.
By:            Saturday, May  11
==> Due in:         16 days.

Amount due: $   38.92
To:            The Tech Book Store
By:            Tuesday, May  21
==> Due in:         26 days.

Amount due: $   85.22
To:            TechCo Computer Co.
By:            Wednesday, June    5
==> Due in:         41 days.

Amount due: $  150.00
To:            ConsultiComp, Inc.
By:            Saturday, June  15
==> Due in:         51 days.
```

■ **Caution**

CDOW() works only on a date-type argument. An attempt to send a string of characters to CDOW() will result in an error message:

```
. ? CDOW("2/27/51")
Invalid function argument
                     ?
? CDOW("2/27/51")
.
```

- **dBASE II equivalent**

  None

- **Comment**

  To produce three-character abbreviations of the days of the week, use CDOW() along with the SUBSTR() **423★** function, like this:

```
. ? SUBSTR(CDOW(DATE()), 1, 3) + "."
Tue.
.
```

The DOW() **135★** function results in a *numeric* value (from 1 through 7) representing the day of the week for a given date parameter.

CHANGE

- **Structure**

  CHANGE   *scope_clause*   FIELDS *field_list*   *condition_clause*

- **Description**

  CHANGE is a full-screen command designed for editing selected records **284★** and fields **154★**, including memo fields **217★**, in the current database. It places one record on the screen at a time. The FIELDS clause, which is optional, selects certain fields to be included in the CHANGE screen. Without a FIELDS clause, CHANGE displays all fields.

  Normally, the CHANGE command begins with the first record in the database and then allows you to move forward to edit each subsequent record. However, a scope **312★** clause (NEXT **239★** or RECORD **282★**) or a condition clause (FOR **164★** or WHILE **463★**) may be included, to select only certain records for editing.

- **Usage**

  Here is an example of a CHANGE command that results in record screens containing only two fields from the *Property* **384◆** database: *address* and *asking_pr*. Only those records in which the current *asking_pr* value is greater than 175000 will be selected for editing.

```
. USE Property
: CHANGE FIELDS address, asking_pr ;
   FOR asking_pr > 175000



Record No.        1
ADDRESS       123 Martha Street
ASKING_PR     225000.00
```

You can use the following keyboard functions to control the CHANGE mode:

Key:	Action:
Right-arrow, Left-arrow	Move cursor one character to right or left.
Up-arrow, Down-arrow	Move cursor one field up or down.
PgUp, PgDn	Move to previous or next record, among selected records.
Ctrl-PgDn	Edit ◆ current memo field **217**★.
Ctrl-End	Save current memo field.
Ctrl-Y	Delete contents of field.
Ctrl-U	Mark or unmark record for deletion (a toggle).
Ins	Activate or deactivate character-insert mode (a toggle).
Esc	Exit full-screen mode, without saving new edits in current record.
Ctrl-End	Exit full-screen mode, saving all edits (not functional in version 1.00).

Pressing the F1 function key while in CHANGE mode displays a help box summarizing CHANGE keyboard functions. (If the SET MENU **387**★ status is ON, the menu automatically appears on the screen at the beginning of the CHANGE mode and pressing F1 toggles the display off.)

■ **Caution**

If a format file **365**◆ is open for the current database, the organization of the CHANGE screen will be controlled by that file (see SET FORMAT **365**★). The format file will override any FIELDS clause in the CHANGE command—in other words, *all* fields contained in the format file will appear on the CHANGE screen.

■ **dBASE II equivalent**

CHANGE

■ **Comments**

In addition to SET FORMAT and SET MENU, the following SET commands **73◆** affect the behavior or appearance of the CHANGE mode: SET BELL **329★**, SET CONFIRM **334★**, SET COLOR **331★**, SET DELIMITERS **345★**, and SET INTENSITY **376★**.

The EDIT **141★** command is similar in effect to CHANGE, but begins the editing with the current record, or with a record you specify by number. EDIT normally displays all fields from the database, including memo fields.

CHR()

■ **Structure**

CHR(ascii_number)

■ **Description**

Given a numeric argument representing an ASCII **28★** code number from 0 through 255, the CHR() function returns the ASCII character-equivalent of the number.

■ **Usage**

CHR() gives you access to the complete character set of your computer, even characters that are not on the keyboard. Of particular interest on the IBM personal computers is the upper range (127 through 255) of the ASCII code, which includes foreign-language characters and "graphics" characters suitable for creating business graphs and other special effects. A simple way to explore the ASCII code is to simply issue a series of ? commands like this:

```
. ? CHR(33)
!
. ? CHR(88)
X
. ? CHR(57)
9
.
```

■ **Program examples**

Here are two examples of the variety of uses for CHR() in dBASE programs.

Example 1: The following program, called *Ascii*, will help you examine large blocks of the ASCII code at once. The program allows up to 128 characters per screen, in 8 columns of 16 lines each:

```
*-------------------------------------------------- ASCII.PRG
* Displays the ASCII code, starting at the value passed to the
*    parameter Start.
*

PARAMETER start

SET CONFIRM OFF
SET BELL OFF
SET TALK OFF

symbol = " "
ascii = start
curcol = 0
CLEAR

*----- Loop, beginning with number input by user (START)
*--------- and continuing for 128 entries.

DO WHILE ascii < 256 .AND. ascii - start < 128
   currow = 2

   DO WHILE currow < 18
      @ currow, curcol SAY STR(ascii, 3) + " " + CHR(ascii)
      currow = currow + 1
      ascii = ascii + 1
      IF ascii > 255
         EXIT
      ENDIF
   ENDDO

   curcol = curcol + 10
ENDDO
@ 24, 24 SAY "The IBM PC Extended ASCII Code " GET symbol
READ

CLEAR
RETURN
```

(To avoid having seven to nine leading blanks in each entry, you must include a length argument in the STR() **416★** function.)

To run the *Ascii* program successfully, you must supply as a parameter **245◆** the code number where you wish the resulting display to begin—for example:

```
. DO Ascii WITH 127
```

This command will result in a screenful of ASCII code values starting from 127, and including the entire set of ASCII "graphics" characters ◆:

```
127 ⌂   143 Å   159 ƒ   175 »   191 ┐   207 ±   223 ▀   239 ∩
128 Ç   144 É   160 á   176 ░   192 └   208 ╨   224 α   240 ≡
129 ü   145 æ   161 í   177 ▒   193 ┴   209 ╤   225 β   241 ±
130 é   146 Æ   162 ó   178 ▓   194 ┬   210 ╥   226 Γ   242 ≥
131 â   147 ô   163 ú   179 │   195 ├   211 ╙   227 π   243 ≤
132 ä   148 ö   164 ñ   180 ┤   196 ─   212 ╘   228 Σ   244 ⌠
133 à   149 ò   165 Ñ   181 ╡   197 ┼   213 ╒   229 σ   245 ⌡
134 å   150 û   166 ª   182 ╢   198 ╞   214 ╓   230 μ   246 ÷
135 ç   151 ù   167 º   183 ╖   199 ╟   215 ╫   231 τ   247 ≈
136 ê   152 ÿ   168 ¿   184 ╕   200 ╚   216 ╪   232 Φ   248 °
137 ë   153 Ö   169 ⌐   185 ╣   201 ╔   217 ┘   233 Θ   249 ·
138 è   154 Ü   170 ¬   186 ║   202 ╩   218 ┌   234 Ω   250 ·
139 ï   155 ¢   171 ½   187 ╗   203 ╦   219 █   235 δ   251 √
140 î   156 £   172 ¼   188 ╝   204 ╠   220 ▄   236 ∞   252 ⁿ
141 ì   157 ¥   173 ¡   189 ╜   205 ═   221 ▌   237 φ   253 ²
142 Ä   158 ₧   174 «   190 ╛   206 ╬   222 ▐   238 ε   254 ■
```

```
The IBM PC Extended ASCII Code ■
```

Example 2: Among the ASCII "graphics" characters are six characters that allow you to draw double-line squares and rectangles on the screen. Such "boxes" can be useful for enclosing menus or other screen messages that you want the user to notice. Here are the six ASCII characters that can be used:

ASCII code:	Character:	Symbol
201	upper left corner	╔
187	upper right corner	╗
188	lower right corner	╝
200	lower left corner	╚
205	horizontal line	═
186	vertical line	║

The following program, called *Box*, uses the CHR() function to access these six characters. The program draws a box of specified size at a specified screen location:

```
*------------------------------------------------------ BOX.PRG
* Draws a box on the screen, given the parameters row1, col1
*    (upper left corner of box) and row2, col2 (lower right
*    corner of box).
*

PARAMETER row1, col1, row2, col2

SET TALK OFF

*----- Select the ASCII graphics characters.
nw = CHR(201)
ne = CHR(187)
se = CHR(188)
sw = CHR(200)
hori = CHR(205)
vert = CHR(186)

*----- Draw corners of box.
@ row1, col1 SAY nw
@ row1, col2 SAY ne
@ row2, col1 SAY sw
@ row2, col2 SAY se

*----- Draw vertical lines.
counter = row1 + 1
DO WHILE counter < row2
    @ counter, col1 SAY vert
    @ counter, col2 SAY vert
    counter = counter + 1
ENDDO

counter = col1 + 1

*----- Draw horizontal lines until corner.
DO WHILE counter < col2
    @ row1, counter SAY hori
    @ row2, counter SAY hori
    counter = counter + 1
ENDDO

RETURN
```

A call to this program requires four numeric parameters: the first two for the co-ordinates of the upper left corner of the desired box, and the second two for the lower right corner. Here is an example of a call to the program:

```
. DO Box WITH 10, 35, 15, 45
```

The result is a box drawn on the screen, connecting the following locations:

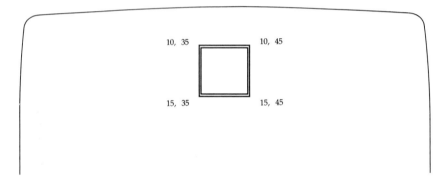

Notice the assignment statements **414◆** at the beginning of the program, accessing the six appropriate ASCII "graphics" characters and assigning them to variables:

```
nw = CHR(201)
ne = CHR(187)
se = CHR(188)
sw = CHR(200)
hori = CHR(205)
vert = CHR(186)
```

(See the entry under TIME() **433★** for an example of the *Box* program in use.)

■ **Caution**

Sending a numeric value greater than 255 to CHR() will result in an error message along with the ASCII character returned by the function:

```
. ? CHR(260)
***Execution error on CHR() : out of range
♦
  .
```

■ **dBASE II equivalent**

CHR()

■ **Comment**

Most printers accept special sequences of ASCII characters as "control" codes to switch into available printing styles. The CHR() function may be used to issue such control codes to a printer from within dBASE.

CLEAR

■ **Structure**
CLEAR
CLEAR ALL
CLEAR GETS
CLEAR MEMORY

■ **Description**
The CLEAR command performs four distinctly different tasks, depending upon its modifier:

- ☐ CLEAR alone, without a modifier, erases ♦ the current display and places the cursor at the upper left corner of the screen.

- ☐ CLEAR ALL closes all database and related files 156♦, and erases all variables 459★ from memory, giving you a new starting point in a given session with dBASE. It does not affect program or alternate 157♦ files (see CLOSE 57★).

- ☐ CLEAR GETS permanently deactivates any current @...GET 9★ commands, so that a READ 275★ command will no longer include them as part of an input screen. (CLEAR alone has the same effect on @...GET commands; the difference is that CLEAR erases the screen as well.)

- ☐ CLEAR MEMORY erases any current variables from memory (see RELEASE 288★).

■ **Caution**
Before issuing CLEAR ALL or CLEAR MEMORY, make sure you are really through with the variables currently in memory. If you are unsure, use the SAVE 309★ command first, to save them on disk.

■ **dBASE II equivalents**
ERASE clears the screen.
(Caution: ERASE is a *disk* command in dBASE III.)
CLEAR resets dBASE II by closing files.
CLEAR GETS deactivates @...GETs.

■ **Comment**
The @...CLEAR 9♦ command is also available, for erasing a portion of the screen beginning at the specified row and column.

CLOSE

■ **Structure**

CLOSE ALTERNATE
CLOSE DATABASES
CLOSE FORMAT
CLOSE INDEX
CLOSE PROCEDURE

■ **Description**

The CLOSE command closes a specified type 156♦ of file:

☐   CLOSE ALTERNATE closes the current alternate file, ending the recording process that was begun by a SET ALTERNATE 326★ command.

☐   CLOSE DATABASES closes all currently open databases and their indexes and format files.

☐   CLOSE FORMAT closes a format file in the current work area 322♦ (see SET FORMAT 365★).

☐   CLOSE INDEX closes all index files in the current work area (see SET INDEX 372★).

☐   CLOSE PROCEDURE closes the currently open procedure file, so that a new one can be opened. (Only one procedure file may be open at a time—see SET PROCEDURE 383★).

■ **Caution**

CLOSE used without a file type will return an error message:

```
. CLOSE
Unrecognized phrase/keyword in command
      ?
CLOSE
.
```

■ **dBASE II equivalent**

None
USE closes open dBASE II databases and their indexes; QUIT closes all open files and exits dBASE.

■ **Comments**

The USE 454★ command without a file name also closes the currently open database and its index. QUIT 271★ closes *all* open files and exits dBASE, returning control to DOS 133★.

CMONTH()

■ **Structure**

CMONTH(date-type value)

■ **Description**

Given a dBASE date-type value **99♦**, CMONTH() returns a string of characters repre-senting the full name of the month in which the date falls (CMONTH stands for "char-acter month"):

January	May	September
February	June	October
March	July	November
April	August	December

■ **Usage**

The argument of CMONTH() may be a date-type field or variable value; or it may be the result of the DATE() **103★** or CTOD() **92★** function:

```
. ? DATE()
07/18/85

. ? CMONTH(DATE())
July

. ? CMONTH(CTOD("3/14/85"))
March

.
```

■ **Program example**

The CDOW() 44★ entry contains database and programming examples that illustrate the use of CMONTH(). The program *Duedates* contains the following print instruction:

```
? "By:       ", CDOW(due) + ",", CMONTH(due), DAY(due)
```

In this line, the current value of the date field, *due*, is sent to the functions CDOW(), CMONTH(), and DAY() 105★, to produce messages in the following format:

```
By:        Saturday, April   13
```

■ **Caution**

CMONTH() works only on a date-type argument. An attempt to send a string of characters to CMONTH() will result in an error message:

```
. ? CMONTH("2/27/51")
Invalid function argument
              ?
? CMONTH("2/27/51")
.
```

■ **dBASE II equivalent**

None

■ **Comments**

To produce three-character abbreviations of the month names, use CMONTH() along with the SUBSTR() 423★ function, like this:

```
. ? SUBSTR(CMONTH(DATE()), 1, 3) + "."
Jul.
.
```

The MONTH() 236★ function results in a *numeric* value (from 1 through 12) representing the month of a given date argument.

COL()

■ **Structure**

COL()

■ **Description**

The COL() function (COL stands for "column") supplies the current column position of the screen cursor. The function returns a numeric value from 0 through 79, representing one of the 80 screen columns.

■ **Usage**

COL() and its companion, ROW() **304★**, are designed for use in programs that need to control the position and appearance of data displayed on the screen. The two functions are typically used in conjunction with the @...SAY...GET **9★** command to place an item of information at the current cursor position, or at some *relative address* ◆ a specified number of columns and/or rows away from the current position.

■ **Program example**

The PICTURE **252★** entry contains a demonstration program called *Picture* that illustrates the use of COL() and ROW(). The program uses the ? **5★** command to issue a series of messages to the screen; following each ?, the COL() and ROW() functions supply the current cursor position for a subsequent @...SAY command. Here is a sample passage from that program:

```
? "symbols: $##,###.##            ==>  "
@ ROW(), COL() SAY pos PICTURE "$##,###.##"
```

Given that the variable *pos* has a value of 31832.42, these lines result in the following output on the screen:

```
symbols: $##,###.##        ==) $31,832.42
```

(Note that the ? command issues a carriage return and line feed *before* it displays its message, not after.)

For relative addressing, you add to or subtract from the current address, using the COL() function:

```
? "Amount due:"
@ ROW(), COL() + 10 SAY due PICTURE "$##,###.##"
```

In this passage, the @...SAY command displays a numeric value, *due*, at an address that is 10 columns to the right of the ? message:

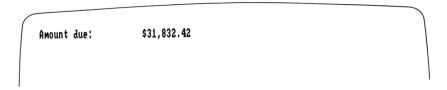

```
Amount due:        $31,832.42
```

■ **Caution**

When using COL() for relative addressing, take care not to devise a column address that is less than 0 or greater than 79. For example, consider the following passage:

```
? "Amount due:"
@ ROW(), COL() + 70 SAY due PICTURE "$##,###.##"
```

Since the expression *COL() + 70* in this case will result in a column address that is greater than 79, the program will terminate with the following error message:

```
SAY/GET position is off the screen
```

■ **dBASE II equivalent**

None

■ **Comment**

For further discussion of screen-control operations in dBASE programs, see the @...SAY...GET, CLEAR **56★**, and ? entries.

The PCOL() **250★** function is available to supply the current column position from the printer.

Command structure

In dBASE, commands may be issued directly at the "dot prompt", ♦ for immediate performance, or they may be stored as part of a program file **264♦**. In either case, every dBASE command begins with one of the command words described in this book. (The two exceptions to this rule are the alternate syntaxes of an *assignment statement* **414♦**, in which the command begins with the name of a variable, and the GOTO **169★** statement, in which the number of the target record may be entered alone.)

Included in the syntax of many dBASE commands are required or optional *clauses* that may express:

☐ The information, or source of the information, that the command is to work with.

☐ The destination of data that the command generates.

☐ The scope **312★** of a database—that is, the record or records **284★** that the command will operate on.

☐ A condition **312♦** for selecting the records that the command will operate on.

☐ The mode of operation **73♦** that the command will result in.

In many cases, the order in which these clauses appear in the command is not fixed: For example, a condition clause may appear either before or after a scope clause.

Alphabetic case is of no importance in a dBASE command; you may enter commands in all uppercase, all lowercase, or a combination of the two. (Case within a data string may be of importance in searching databases, however.) Furthermore, all dBASE vocabulary words—including command words and clauses—may be abbreviated to their first four characters. For example, instead of entering the full statement:

```
. MODIFY COMMAND
```

you may enter:

```
. modi comm
```

You may abbreviate direct (dot prompt) commands and program commands alike; however, in a program you should always consider whether abbreviation detracts from readability. Information that you supply yourself (such as variable names or field names) may not, of course, be abbreviated.

The maximum command length that dBASE can handle is 254 characters. When you write long commands that take up more than one line on the screen, you may enter them in one of two ways:

☐ Simply type the entire command, without pressing the Return key until the end. At the end of each screen line, dBASE will automatically wrap around to the following line, without adding a carriage-return character.

☐ Enter the command in one-line sections, inserting a semicolon (;) and a carriage return (the Return key) at the end of each line. The semicolon tells dBASE that the current command is continued on the following line:

```
@ 10,10 SAY "Enter your menu choice: " ;
    GET choice PICTURE "9" ;
    RANGE 1,10
```

■ Cautions

Notice that dBASE accepts extra spaces (and tabs) within a command; however, keep in mind the 254-character limit. And if you do use a semicolon to continue a command onto the next line, be sure to include at least one space character between the semicolon and a command word that falls at the end of the line.

Compiler

Within the dBASE III environment, the dBASE programming language is *interpreted*: A programmer writes *source code*—that is, the contents of a dBASE program file 57♦—and the dBASE interpreter translates the code into the low-level language that the computer can actually act upon.

An interpreter translates a given line of code each time the line is performed. Thus, if a line of code is performed several times during execution of a program (for example, inside a DO...WHILE 129★ loop), the interpreter must retranslate the line for each performance.

A *compiler* also translates source code into low-level code, but the ultimate output of a compiler is a permanent program file of executable code. Once this file exists, the program can be executed directly from DOS **133★**, without reference to the source code—translation of the source code no longer occurs during the performance of the program.

The chief advantage of a compiled program is speed of execution. A secondary advantage, for programmers, is that the source code does not need to be distributed to the ultimate user of the program.

A possible *disadvantage* of compiling is the loss of immediacy offered by the dBASE interpreter. Writing and debugging **267◆** a program in dBASE involves two basic steps:

1. Working with the source code in the dBASE word processor.

2. Running the program via a DO **122★** command.

With an interpreted program, if the program contains errors, you simply go back to the word processor and correct them—a simpler and more direct process than the steps involved in compiling, debugging, and recompiling. Maintaining the program is also less complicated, for the same reasons.

One dBASE III compiler currently on the market is called Clipper (produced by Nantucket, Inc., Culver City, CA). The Clipper package includes both a compiler and a linker, for producing DOS-executable programs (.EXE files). (A compiled dBASE program does not even require the presence of dBASE itself—the program is performed directly from DOS.)

There are a number of differences between the syntax and command set that Clipper works with and the actual language as defined in the dBASE III environment. Some of these differences are Clipper enhancements—features that may make dBASE a more powerful language for some applications. Other differences are minor syntactical issues that you must learn about to use the compiler successfully. The result of these differences is that you may be unable to compile a program that works fine in dBASE itself: Modifications of the source code are often necessary before the code can be compiled under Clipper.

In summary, a dBASE III compiler can be a considerable advantage when:

☐ Speed of performance under the dBASE interpreter is unsatisfactory for a given application.

☐ Source code must be withheld from the end user.

However, compiled programs are often more difficult to debug and maintain.

Concatenation

Concatenation ("linking together") is the combining of two strings **98♦** to form a third string. The dBASE III program has two string operators **420★**, – and +. Both produce a string whose length is equal to the combined lengths of the original strings; however, they differ in the way they handle any intervening trailing blanks. Consider these examples:

```
. d = "data    "
data

. b = "base    "
base

. ? d + b
data    base

. ? d - b
database

.
```

See the entry under *String Operators* for more information about these operations.

- **Caution**

  The elements combined in a concatenation operation *must* be string values. For occasions when you need to produce a string that combines other types of values, dBASE provides functions that convert numeric **98♦** and date-type values **99♦** into strings: STR() **416★** and DTOC() **139★**, respectively. Here are some examples of concatenation using these conversion functions. The first acts on a database with fields called *name* and *yrs*, and the second uses the DATE() **103★** function to obtain the system date:

```
. ? name + " is " + STR(yrs, 1) + " years old."
John is 6 years old.

.
```

```
. ? "Today is " + DTOC(DATE()) + "."
Today is 07/18/85.

.
```

CONFIG.DB

By creating a *CONFIG.DB* file, you can customize the default conditions under which dBASE operates on your computer (in contrast to *CONFIG.SYS* **71★**, which sets up your operating system to accommodate dBASE). *CONFIG.DB* is a user-created ASCII text file **157♦** containing only a sequence of configuration instructions. Each time you start dBASE on your computer, the program searches for this file on the *program* disk. If the file is found, dBASE takes on the new default parameters specified in it; if it is not found, dBASE opens with its normal default parameters **73♦**.

Over 40 different configuration instructions may be included in *CONFIG.DB*. You may use a subset of instructions from among these, or you may enter all of them. They may appear in any order in the file, in either upper- or lowercase letters, but each instruction should be entered on a line of its own.

The majority of the instructions deal with precisely the same control parameters **73★** as the dBASE SET commands. These parameters determine dBASE's behavior under, and reaction to, certain conditions and events. The configuration file requires its own syntax for establishing the default opening values of these parameters, but during a session with dBASE, you can change the status of any of them by issuing the appropriate SET command. Many of the settings have only two states: ON or OFF. In these cases, the syntax of the SET command is:

```
SET command ON
SET command OFF
```

where *command* is the name of the specific SET parameter. Other control parameters may take on a wider range of settings, in which case the syntax of the command is:

```
SET command TO value
```

In contrast, the syntax for establishing a new default setting for any of these parameters in *CONFIG.DB* is simply:

```
command = value
```

The *value* part of this instruction may be simply ON or OFF, or it may be some other value appropriate to the specific parameter, but in no case should it be enclosed in quotation marks. (Specific examples of syntax appear later in this entry.)

Here is a list of the SET control parameters that may be included in the CONFIG.DB file:

ALTERNATE 326★	EXACT 355★
BELL 329★	FUNCTION 368★
CARRY 330★	HEADING 369★
COLOR 331★	HELP 371★
CONFIRM 334★	INTENSITY 376★
CONSOLE 335★	MARGIN 378★
DEBUG 339★	MENU 378★
DECIMALS 340★	PATH 380★
DEFAULT 343★	PRINT 381★
DELETED 344★	SAFETY 396★
DELIMITERS 345★	SCOREBOARD 397★
DEVICE 347★	STEP 397★
ECHO 351★	TALK 398★
ESCAPE 353★	UNIQUE 399★

For example, the default settings of the F2 through F10 function keys may be established in *CONFIG.DB* or in dBASE itself. In dBASE, the SET FUNCTION command changes these settings, but in the CONFIG.DB file, the syntax is:

```
Fn = command_list
```

where *n* is a function-key number from 2 through 10.

Several other instructions can also be included in the *CONFIG.DB* file. They set parameters that cannot be controlled in any other way, and are therefore probably the most important instructions that can go into the file. These instructions deal with five general areas:

☐ The use of RAM (random-access memory) in dBASE.

☐ Optional outside text editors 466◆ used by dBASE.

☐ The number of @...GET 9★ commands that can remain pending before a READ 275★ command must be performed.

☐ The format of the dBASE prompt 62◆.

☐ The automatic performance of an opening command at the beginning of each dBASE session.

The instructions are MAXMEM, MVARSIZ, BUCKET, TEDIT, WP, GETS, PROMPT, and COMMAND, respectively. They appear in the same syntax as the other configuration instructions:

```
command = value
```

MAXMEM, MVARSIZ, and BUCKET all deal with memory use. MAXMEM specifies the amount of your system's RAM within which dBASE will operate. The value assigned to MAXMEM should be between 256 and 720 (representing K, or kilobytes), but should not exceed the actual amount of memory installed in your computer. MAXMEM's default value is 256, the minimum amount of memory required by dBASE.

If you increase the value of MAXMEM, keep in mind that the result is a decrease in the amount of memory reserved for the performance of other programs during a dBASE session. (Other programs include those performed by the RUN **306★** command and the outside word processors specified by the WP and TEDIT commands.)

MVARSIZ specifies the maximum amount of RAM available for storing variables **459★** in dBASE. Normally, dBASE allocates 6,000 bytes of memory for variables, but you can increase or decrease this amount using MVARSIZ. Note that MVARSIZ does not change the default value for the maximum *number* of defined variables; that value always remains 256.

BUCKET specifies the maximum amount of memory reserved for the performance of PICTURE **252★** and RANGE **272★** clauses in @...GET commands. The default value is 2, which stands for 2K.

TEDIT and WP control the use of outside word processors in dBASE. Normally, the built-in dBASE word processor is invoked whenever you issue MODIFY COMMAND **219★**, or whenever you create or edit a memo field **217★**. TEDIT identifies the file name of an outside word processor that will henceforth be used for MODIFY COMMAND, and WP establishes the new word processor for memo fields. Your actual ability to use an outside word processor during a session with dBASE depends upon both the amount of RAM in your system and the MAXMEM setting.

The PROMPT command allows you to define a new dBASE prompt, replacing the familiar, but hard-to-see, dot prompt. For example:

```
PROMPT = What next?
```

will result in a new screen prompt of:

```
What next?
```

Finally, the COMMAND instruction specifies an opening command that will automatically be performed at the beginning of each session with dBASE, except when you supply a program parameter in the dBASE command itself. For example, if you enter dBASE with the command:

```
A>dBASE Menu
```

dBASE will run the program *MENU.PRG* as the opening command.

A *CONFIG.DB* file may be created with any word processor or text editor, as long as the result is an ASCII text file. You can even use the built-in dBASE MODIFY COMMAND word processor. The completed file must be stored on the dBASE program disk that contains the file *DBASE.EXE* (in dBASE Version 1.1, this is System Disk #2). Once you have created the file and stored it on the correct disk, your new default parameters will take effect the next time you start dBASE on your computer. (If you create *CONFIG.DB* with MODI COMM and want to use the new defaults during the same session, you must QUIT **271★** dBASE and restart.)

Here is a sample *CONFIG.DB* file, containing a selection of both SET and .DB instructions:

```
BELL = OFF
CONFIRM = ON
DEFAULT = B
HELP = OFF
MARGIN = 10
MENUS = ON
PATH = A:\
F10 = DO Menu;
COMMAND = ? DATE(), TIME()
MVARSIZ = 12
TEDIT = Word
```

The first eight of these instructions simply establish new SET parameter values. Notice in particular that the default drive is established as B, and the alternate search path **250★** as A:\. Also, function key F10 is assigned a value that will issue the command *DO Menu*. The final three instructions accomplish tasks that are in the exclusive realm of *CONFIG.DB*. The COMMAND instruction in this case arranges to display the system date and time **102♦** on the screen when dBASE first begins. The MVARSIZ command allocates 12K for variables, and finally, the TEDIT command establishes a new word processor for MODIFY COMMAND.

There are several ways you can confirm that your new default parameters have indeed been established. First of all, dBASE will issue an error message if it finds an instruction in the *CONFIG.DB* file that it cannot perform. (This will not affect any of the other valid instructions.) Second, you can issue the DISPLAY STATUS **119★** command to make sure that the SET parameters have indeed been assigned the values that you have entered. The DISPLAY MEMORY **118★** command will show you the maximum memory space available for variables, established by the MVARSIZ command. And you can just issue a MODIFY COMMAND statement to see if the TEDIT assignment is working properly.

The SET ALTERNATE **326★** entry outlines an approach for writing a program to generate a CONFIG.DB file.

CONFIG.SYS

CONFIG.SYS is the DOS **133★** system configuration file (in contrast to *CONFIG.DB* **66★**, which configures only the dBASE environment). When you first turn on your computer and boot DOS, the system searches for the *CONFIG.SYS* file; if the file exists, DOS opens it and follows the configuration instructions it contains.

Two of the DOS configuration instructions, BUFFERS and FILES, are particularly important to dBASE III. The BUFFERS command sets aside memory buffers for temporary storage of information that is coming from, or on its way to, a disk. The FILES command specifies the maximum number of files **156◆** that may be open at one time. In order to run dBASE III successfully on your computer, the recommended settings for these two commands are:

```
BUFFERS = 15
FILES = 20
```

Your DOS boot disk may already have a *CONFIG.SYS* file on it; if so, you should make sure these two commands are included. If you do not yet have a *CONFIG.SYS* file, you may create one using a text editor (*Edlin*, for example) or a word processor. With a word processor, make sure you create an ASCII text file **156◆** by using the "nondocument" or "unformatted" mode. You may also create the *CONFIG.SYS* file directly, using the COPY command from DOS. To do this, enter the following commands from the DOS A> prompt:

```
A>COPY CON: CONFIG.SYS
BUFFERS = 15
FILES = 20
^Z
```

(To enter the ^Z, hold down the Ctrl key and simultaneously press the Z; then press Return.) The *CONFIG.SYS* file will be stored on the disk in drive A.

Before starting dBASE, you will have to reboot your system to make DOS read the instructions in *CONFIG.SYS*: Hold down Ctrl and Alt, and press Del to perform a system restart.

CONTINUE

■ **Structure**

CONTINUE

■ **Description**

CONTINUE searches forward in the current database for the next record **284★** that meets the condition expressed in a previously issued LOCATE **202★** command. Each time a CONTINUE command finds a match, the pointer **258★** is moved forward to that record. Additional CONTINUE commands may then be entered, if you wish to proceed forward through the database. When a CONTINUE command finally encounters the end of the file, the LOCATE...CONTINUE sequence is over.

■ **Usage**

CONTINUE begins its search at the *current* record position, and you can repeat the command until EOF() **147★** becomes true.

The following example illustrates both LOCATE and CONTINUE. A search is made in the *Address* **223◆** database for records whose *city* field values begin with "San":

```
. USE Address
. LOCATE FOR city = "San"
Record =        1
.
. DISPLAY OFF
LASTNAME    FIRSTNAME STREET                    CITY            STATE ZIP
Winston     Mary      57 Idaho Avenue           San Francisco   CA    94113
.
. CONTINUE
Record =        3
.
. DISPLAY OFF
LASTNAME    FIRSTNAME STREET                    CITY            STATE ZIP
Appleby     Carl      921 La Brea Drive         Santa Barbara   CA    92112
.
. CONTINUE
Record =        5
.
. DISPLAY OFF
LASTNAME    FIRSTNAME STREET                    CITY            STATE ZIP
Martin      Harris    12997 Washington Blvd.    San Diego       CA    92122
.
. CONTINUE
End of locate scope
.
```

Notice that the DISPLAY 116★ command is required if you wish to examine the record that has been located—CONTINUE does not display a record; it merely moves the record pointer.

■ **dBASE II equivalent**
CONTINUE

■ **Comment**
The LOCATE...CONTINUE sequence can be used on an unindexed file.

Control parameters

The term *control parameters* refers to those aspects of dBASE's behavior that the user can control. About three dozen commands are available that allow you to change the settings of these control parameters as often as necessary during a session with dBASE. Each of the commands begins with the word SET. Using these SET commands ♦, you can exert control over:

☐ The hardware environment.

☐ Disk drives.

☐ Programming activities.

☐ Full-screen operations.

☐ Database operations.

☐ A few other miscellaneous activities.

The SET 325★ command used alone provides you with a menu-driven guide to changing the control parameters. This menu can be used as an alternative to typing individual SET commands for each parameter.

Many of the control parameters have simple ON or OFF settings, but others specify certain conditions, hardware devices, or file names. Each parameter has a default value—the setting that will be active unless you specify otherwise. (Outside of a dBASE session, you can change these default settings by creating a *CONFIG.DB* 66★ file on your dBASE boot disk.) Here is a brief summary of the various SET commands:

Hardware controls:

☐ SET COLOR 331★ establishes the color and intensity of the screen display.

☐ SET CONSOLE 335★ turns screen output display on or off.

☐ SET DEVICE 347★ chooses the screen or the printer for output from @...SAY 9★ statements.

☐ SET FUNCTION 368★ resets the function keys 167★.

☐ SET PRINT 381★ turns the printer on or off.

☐ SET MARGIN 378★ sets the printer's left margin.

☐ SET BELL 329★ inhibits or reactivates the system bell.

Disk-drive controls:

☐ SET DEFAULT **343**★ chooses a default disk drive.

☐ SET PATH **380**★ provides a list of alternate disk directories to search in file operations.

☐ SET ALTERNATE **326**★ creates a disk file for storing a record of a session with dBASE.

☐ SET SAFETY **396**★ provides a warning message whenever a current disk file is about to be overwritten.

Programming activities:

☐ SET PROCEDURE **383**★ opens a procedure file **383**♦, making its library of procedures available to the current program **264**♦.

☐ SET DEBUG **339**★, SET ECHO **351**★, and SET STEP **397**★ provide program debugging **267**♦ tools.

☐ SET ESCAPE **353**★ activates or deactivates the Escape key as a way to stop program performance.

☐ SET TALK **398**★ inhibits or restores the display of the dBASE messages produced in response to many commands.

Full-screen operations:

☐ SET FORMAT **365**★ opens a format file **157**♦, to control the entire structure of full-screen entry or edit screens.

☐ SET MENU **378**★ activates or inhibits the display of a keyboard menu during full-screen operations.

☐ SET CARRY **330**★, SET CONFIRM **334**★, SET DELIMITERS **345**★, and SET INTENSITY **376**★ control the display and behavior of input fields.

Database controls:

☐ SET FILTER **357**★ allows a database to be *filtered*, temporarily hiding records that do not match a specified condition.

☐ SET INDEX **372**★ opens one or more index files **156**♦, to control the order in which the records of a database are displayed.

☐ SET RELATION **390**★ correlates the movements of the record pointers **258**★ in two simultaneously open databases **322**♦.

☐ SET DELETED **344**★ inhibits or restores the display of records that have been marked for deletion **106**♦.

☐ SET HEADING **369**★ inhibits or restores the display of field names in a listing of a database.

☐ SET UNIQUE **399**★ controls the display of duplicate records in an indexed database.

Miscellaneous controls:

☐ SET DATE **337**★ controls the input and display format of date-type values **99**♦.

☐ SET DECIMALS **340**★ and SET FIXED **363**★ control the display of numeric values **98**♦.

☐ SET EXACT **355**★ determines whether string values **98**♦ of unequal lengths can be considered equal.

☐ SET HELP **371**★ inhibits or restores dBASE's offers of help after a syntax error.

☐ SET SCOREBOARD **397**★ determines whether or not dBASE will use the upper right corner of the screen for special messages in full-screen operations.

COPY FILE

■ **Structure**
COPY FILE source_file_name TO destination_file_name

■ **Description**
The COPY FILE command makes a complete copy of a file that is currently stored on disk. The file you wish to copy may be of any type 156♦, but may not be open. dBASE provides no default extension names 155♦ for either the source file or the destination file, so you should supply them in the command.

■ **Usage**
The COPY FILE command is an easy way to make a backup of a disk file. For example, let's say you want to copy a program file named *Menu*, residing on the disk in drive B, to the disk in drive A. Here is the command you would issue:

```
. COPY FILE B:MENU.PRG TO A:MENUBAK.PRG
```

This command has no effect on the original source file; it simply makes a copy of the file on another disk.

■ **dBASE II equivalent**
None

■ **Comment**
The dBASE COPY FILE command does not allow wildcard characters 114♦ for copying more than one file at a time. However, if your computer has sufficient memory, you can use the dBASE RUN 306★ command to perform a DOS 133★ COPY ♦ command, which does allow wildcards:

```
. RUN COPY B:*.PRG A:
```

The command in this example copies all .PRG files from disk B to disk A. (Notice that the syntax of the DOS command does not include the word TO.)

COPY STRUCTURE

■ **Structure**

COPY STRUCTURE TO file_name   *FIELDS field_list*

■ **Description**

The COPY STRUCTURE command creates a new database file on disk, copying all or part of the field structure **100◆** of the currently selected **322◆** database. No records are copied, so the resulting disk file will be empty.

■ **Usage**

COPY STRUCTURE is used to create a new database with a structure similar or identical to that of the current database (for a transaction or update file, for instance).

■ **Database example**

The following example uses the real-estate database described in the entry for the SET PROCEDURE **383★** command. This database, called *Property*, contains 18 fields of information. Imagine that you wish to create a new database containing only a half dozen of these fields and none of the same records. Here is the sequence of commands you would use:

```
. USE Property

. COPY STRUCTURE TO Newprop FIELDS owner_l, owner_f, address, ;
  neighborhd, asking_pr, on_market

. USE Newprop
. LIST STRUCTURE
Structure for database : B:Newprop.dbf
Number of data records :      0
Date of last update    : 06/15/85
Field  Field name  Type       Width   Dec
    1  OWNER_L     Character     20
    2  OWNER_F     Character     20
    3  ADDRESS     Character     28
    4  NEIGHBORHD  Character     20
    5  ASKING_PR   Numeric        9     2
    6  ON_MARKET   Date           8
** Total **                     106

.
```

Notice that the new database, *Newprop*, contains no records. To enter data in your new file, open the database and use the APPEND **19★** or APPEND FROM **22★** command to add records.

- **Caution**

  The "Date of last update" shown in the structure display is the disk date of the *original* database, not the date on which the copy was made.

- **dBASE II equivalent**

  COPY STRUCTURE

- **Comment**

  If you wish to make a complete or partial copy of a database *with* its records, use the COPY TO **82★** command.

COPY STRUCTURE EXTENDED

- **Structure**

  COPY TO file_name STRUCTURE EXTENDED

- **Description**

  The COPY STRUCTURE EXTENDED command creates a special *structure file* from the currently selected **322◆** database. The new file is stored on disk under the specified file name, with a default extension **155◆** of .DBF.

  The purpose of a structure file is to store information about the structure **100◆** of the original database. Most important, a structure file makes this information directly accessible to a dBASE program.

  A structure file, as created by the COPY STRUCTURE EXTENDED command, always has exactly four fields, corresponding to the four items of information that define each field of a database:

Structure field:	Contents:
field_name	Field name **154◆**
field_type	Data type **98★**
field_len	Field width **154◆**, in characters
field_dec	Decimal places, if numeric field **98◆**

After creating a structure file that contains these four fields, the COPY STRUCTURE EXTENDED command appends one record of information describing each of the fields in the currently selected database. Thus, the *records* of the structure file store the *field* definitions of the original database.

The CREATE FROM **90★** command can subsequently use the field definitions stored in this structure file to create a new database.

■ **Usage**

From the dBASE dot prompt **62◆**, you can always find out the structure of an open database by simply issuing the DISPLAY STRUCTURE **121★** command, and the CREATE **88★** and MODIFY STRUCTURE **234★** commands move you into full-screen modes that allow you to create and modify the database interactively. But in the sense of lending explicit access to the structure of a database, none of these commands is available to a *program*: They are designed exclusively for use from the dot-prompt level. The purpose of the COPY STRUCTURE EXTENDED and CREATE FROM commands, then, is to allow the following activities to take place within the control of a program:

□   Accessing specific information about the structure of a database.

□   Defining the structure of a new database.

□   Modifying the structure of an existing database.

The structure file is the medium through which all these activities are possible.

■ **Program example**

The program described here illustrates the process of creating a structure file and then using it to modify the structure of the database it describes.

The database in the example, called *Office*, contains a list of items that were purchased to furnish and equip a small office. The original version of the database has only two fields, *item* and *price*:

```
. USE Office
. LIST
Record#  ITEM       PRICE
      1  Table      45.98
      2  Chair      15.29
      3  Lamp       22.95
      4  Bookcase   89.99
      5  Telephone  15.29
      6  Typewriter 99.95
.
```

The *AddTax* program modifies the structure of the *Office* database by adding one new field, called *tax*, destined to record the sales tax that was paid on the purchase price of each item.

Accomplishing this modification in the dBASE interactive mode would, of course, be quite simple: You would issue the MODIFY STRUCTURE command, add the new field, and then, back at the dot prompt, issue a REPLACE ALL **291*** command to calculate the value of the new field for each record. The *Addtax* program, however, requires a more complex sequence of steps to complete the task:

```
*------------------------------------------------- ADDTAX.PRG
* Demonstrates the use of COPY STRUCTURE EXTENDED
*    and CREATE FROM.
*
* The goal is to add a new field, called Tax,
*    to the Office database.
*

SET TALK OFF
SET SAFETY OFF
CLEAR

USE Office

COPY TO Newstruc STRUCTURE EXTENDED

USE Newstruc
APPEND BLANK
REPLACE field_name WITH "TAX"
REPLACE field_type WITH "N"
REPLACE field_len WITH 5
REPLACE field_dec WITH 2
USE

CREATE Newoff FROM Newstruc
APPEND FROM Office
REPLACE ALL tax WITH price * .065

USE
ERASE OFFICE.DBF
RENAME NEWOFF.DBF TO OFFICE.DBF
USE Office

? "--> Here is the modified version of OFFICE.DBF:"
?
LIST

SET TALK ON
SET SAFETY ON
RETURN
```

The program begins by issuing a USE **123★** statement to open the *Office* database. From there, it takes the following steps:

1. It creates the structure file called *Newstruc*, which ultimately will contain the new structure definition of the *Office* database:

```
COPY TO Newstruc STRUCTURE EXTENDED
```

2. It opens *Newstruc*, appends a blank record at the end of the file, and, with four REPLACE commands, enters the definition of the new *tax* field as the last record of the *Newstruc* database.

3. It closes *Newstruc* and issues a CREATE FROM command that creates a new database called *Newoff*:

```
CREATE Newoff FROM Newstruc
```

4. It appends all the current data values from the *Office* database to *Newoff,* and fills the new *tax* field with calculated values:

```
APPEND FROM Office
REPLACE ALL tax WITH price * .065
```

5. It erases the old version of the *Office* database, renames **291♦** the new version, and then lists the new *OFFICE.DBF*:

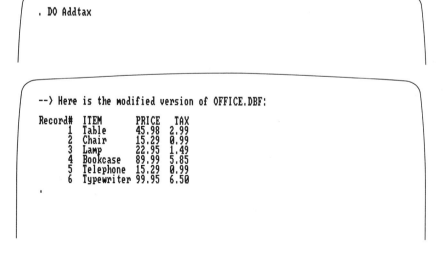

```
. DO Addtax
```

```
--> Here is the modified version of OFFICE.DBF:

Record#  ITEM       PRICE  TAX
      1  Table      45.98  2.99
      2  Chair      15.29  0.99
      3  Lamp       22.95  1.49
      4  Bookcase   89.99  5.85
      5  Telephone  15.29  0.99
      6  Typewriter 99.95  6.50
    .
```

After program execution is completed, the structure file called *Newstruc* remains stored on disk:

```
. USE Newstruc
. LIST
Record#  FIELD_NAME FIELD_TYPE FIELD_LEN FIELD_DEC
       1 ITEM       C                 10         0
       2 PRICE      N                  5         2
       3 TAX        N                  5         2
.
```

The final record, representing the *tax* field, is the one that was appended by *AddTax*.

■ **dBASE II equivalent**

COPY STRUCTURE EXTENDED

■ **Comment**

Complex and detailed though all these steps may seem, they represent an important feature of dBASE programming: the ability to control the creation and modification of databases without relying on full-screen interaction from the user.

COPY TO

■ **Structure**

COPY TO file_name *scope_clause* FIELDS *field_list condition_clause* SDF/ *DELIMITED WITH BLANK/delimiter*

■ **Description**

The COPY TO command makes a disk copy of the currently selected **322◆** database. This copy may include all or a selected subset of the original database's records and fields **154★**. Selected fields may be specified in the optional FIELDS clause (the default is all fields). The scope **312★** and condition clauses, also optional, may be used to select specific records to copy.

If the copied database is destined for use in an environment other than dBASE, you must use an SDF **313★** or DELIMITED **111◆** clause to select a specific data-file format. If neither of these clauses is included, the copy will be a normal dBASE database file, with a default extension **155◆** of .DBF (both SDF and delimited files have default extensions of .TXT).

■ **Usage**

One important use of the COPY TO command is to produce a temporary backup copy of the current database. You may want to perform this simple operation before issuing any command that may result in major changes to the contents of the current database:

```
. COPY TO Temp
```

This command produces the backup file called *TEMP.DBF*, a complete copy of the current database.

Another common use of the COPY TO command is to create an abbreviated version of the current database. The following example uses the *Property* database discussed under the SET PROCEDURE 383★ heading. This database contains 18 fields:

```
. USE Property
. LIST STRUCTURE
Structure for database : B:Property.dbf
Number of data records :        8
Date of last update    : 06/15/85
Field  Field name Type       Width    Dec
    1  OWNER_L    Character     20
    2  OWNER_F    Character     20
    3  ADDRESS    Character     28
    4  CITY       Character     20
    5  NEIGHBORHD Character     20
    6  HOME_AGE   Numeric        3
    7  BEDROOMS   Numeric        1
    8  BATHROOMS  Numeric        3      1
    9  GARAGE     Logical        1
   10  SQ_FOOTAGE Numeric        4
   11  ASKING_PR  Numeric        9      2
   12  CUR_BID    Numeric        9      2
   13  SOLD       Logical        1
   14  SALE_DATE  Date           8
   15  SALE_PRICE Numeric        9      2
   16  ON_MARKET  Date           8
   17  TERM_DAYS  Numeric        3
   18  DESCRIPTN  Memo          10
** Total **                    178

.
```

Suppose you want to create a smaller working database that contains just three of these fields, and only a selection of the records. This sequence of commands illustrates the procedure:

```
. COPY TO Miniprop FIELDS address, neighborhd, asking_pr ;
  FOR neighborhd = "Mission" .OR. neighborhd = "Sunset"
      5 records copied
.
. USE Miniprop
. LIST
Record#  ADDRESS                     NEIGHBORHD       ASKING_PR
      1  12345 26th Avenue           Mission          149000.00
      2  50 17th Street              Mission          125000.00
      3  15 Peach Lane               Sunset           275000.00
      4  4452 Sixth Avenue           Sunset           245000.00
      5  3555 Alta Street            Mission          179000.00
.
```

■ **Caution**

If you attempt to copy to an existing file name, you will receive an error message asking you to confirm your intentions:

```
. USE Property
. COPY TO Assets
Assets.dbf already exists, overwrite it? (Y/N)
```

■ **dBASE II equivalent**

COPY TO

■ **Comment**

It is not necessary to copy the database structure 100★ before using the COPY TO command. That task is handled automatically, as part of the COPY TO process.

COUNT

■ **Structure**

COUNT *scope_clause TO variable_name condition_clause*

■ **Description**

This command counts the number of database records that match a specified condition, or that are included in a specified scope 312★. The optional TO clause allows you to store the result of COUNT in a variable.

The scope indicator, which is optional, may include any one of the three scope clauses available in dBASE III: ALL **17★**, NEXT **239★**, or RECORD **282★**. The default scope is ALL, so if you omit the scope clause, COUNT works on the entire database. The condition clause, also optional, allows you to use FOR **164★** or WHILE **463★** to conditionally select records for the count.

■ **Usage**

The results of the COUNT command are normally displayed on the screen immediately after you issue the command itself. To save the result, you must include a TO clause in the command.

■ **Database example**

The database called *Staff* contains information about the employees of a small company. In addition to each employee's first and last names, the database includes department, date hired, years with firm, employee identification number, and monthly salary:

```
. USE Staff
. LIST
Record#  DEPARTMENT   LASTNAME    FIRSTNAME  HIRED      YRS  EMP_ID  SALARY_MO
      1  Production   Morris      John       11/03/82   2.5   4521    1850.00
      2  Marketing    Southby     Anne       08/22/81   3.7   3134    2315.00
      3  Clerical     Peters      Larry      06/10/83   1.9   3412    1350.00
      4  Clerical     Broussard   Marie      05/05/81   4.0   8712    1275.00
      5  Production   James       Fred       02/22/77   8.2   6563    1675.00
      6  Marketing    Smith       June       03/29/80   5.1   6823    2475.00
      7  Clerical     Liles       Carter     09/29/77   7.6   8799    1400.00
      8  Production   Washington  Liz        11/05/74  10.5   7321    1700.00
      9  Clerical     Ludlum      Donald     03/30/77   8.1   7412    1250.00
.
```

The following examples of COUNT produce information about this database. The first example finds the number of employees in the Production Department. The next shows how many employees have worked for the firm for over 5 years. Then there is a tally of the number of employees who earn less than $2,000 per month. And finally, the COUNT command without any parameters **245**◆ simply tells how many records there are in the database:

```
. COUNT FOR department = "Production"
      3 records
  .
```

```
. COUNT FOR yrs > 5
      5 records
  .
```

```
. COUNT FOR salary_mo < 2000
      7 records
  .
```

```
. COUNT
      9 records
  .
```

■ **Program example**

The entry for the SUM **426**★ command lists and discusses a program called *Summary*, which produces departmental summary reports from the *Staff* database. The program contains the following example of the COUNT command, using the TO option to assign the result to a variable:

```
COUNT FOR department = deptname TO emps
```

This command computes the number of employees in a specified department and assigns the number to the variable *emps*. Subsequently, *emps* is used by the program to produce the statistical summary for the department.

■ **dBASE II equivalent**

COUNT

■ **Comment**

Other database statistical commands include TOTAL **436**★, AVERAGE **31**★, and SUM.

CREATE

- **Structure**
CREATE file_name

- **Description**
The CREATE command invokes a full-screen mode designed for specifying the structure **100♦** of a new database. You can define from 1 to 128 fields **154★** for the database, each definition requiring three pieces of information: name, type **98♦**, and width. Numeric fields also require a fourth item: the number of decimal places.

   When you complete the structure definition and exit from the CREATE mode, dBASE gives you the option of beginning data entry immediately, or simply storing the empty database on disk (a default extension **155♦** of .DBF is added to the disk file name). If you choose to begin entering data, the new database is opened and dBASE moves you automatically into the full-screen mode for the APPEND **19★** command.

- **Usage**
Normally, you enter the name you are giving to the new database at the time you issue the CREATE command:

```
. CREATE Property
```

However, you may also issue the command alone, in which case dBASE prompts you to enter a name for the database:

```
. CREATE
Enter the name of the new file:
```

The CREATE screen immediately presents you with the input templates for the first field definition: *field name, type, width,* and *dec* (for decimal places). You may enter a single character to specify the data type of the current field:

Character:	Data type:
C	Character
D	Date
L	Logical
M	Memo
N	Numeric

or you may simply press the Spacebar one or more times and watch for the appropriate data type to appear automatically on the screen. After you complete one definition, a new line appears on the screen for the next field.

The CREATE screen allows you to move back to a previously defined field to make changes, if necessary. The following keyboard functions control the use of the CRE-ATE mode:

Key:	Action:
Right-arrow, Left-arrow	Move cursor one character to right or left.
Up-arrow, Down-arrow	Move cursor one field definition up or down.
Ctrl-Y	Delete item in field definition.
Ctrl-U	Delete field definition.
Ins	Activate or deactivate character-insert mode (a toggle).
Ctrl-N	Insert template line for new field definition.
Esc	Exit CREATE mode, without saving definition.
Ctrl-End	Exit CREATE mode, saving definition.

If SET MENU 378★ is ON, a list of control keys appears at the top of the screen when you enter the CREATE mode. Even if SET MENU is OFF, you can use the F1 function key to toggle this menu on or off from within CREATE.

■ **dBASE II equivalent**
CREATE

■ **Comments**
Date, logical, and memo fields have fixed widths of 8, 1, and 10, respectively. These widths are automatically entered into the field definition when you choose one of these data types. However, you may set character and numeric widths to suit your specific needs, within certain limits 154♦. (When determining the width of a numeric field that includes decimal places, remember to add one character for the decimal point.)

CREATE FROM

■ **Structure**

CREATE file_name FROM structure_file_name

■ **Description**

The CREATE FROM command creates a new database file from the field definitions **100♦** contained in a structure file. (A structure file is a special kind of database, usually created via the COPY STRUCTURE EXTENDED **78★** command, whose records describe the structure of some original database.)

CREATE FROM defines the new database, gives it the specified file name, and leaves it open in the currently selected work area **322♦**. The file initially contains no records.

■ **Usage**

CREATE FROM and its companion command COPY STRUCTURE EXTENDED allow a program to gain direct access to, and active control over, the structure of a database, through the medium of the structure file.

The COPY STRUCTURE EXTENDED entry contains a complete programming example that illustrates the use of both of these commands. Briefly, the program creates a structure file called *Newstruc* and then uses the CREATE FROM command to read this file and define a new database. In this case, the resulting database, *Newoff*, has three fields, each defined by a single record in *Newstruc*:

```
. USE Newstruc
. LIST
Record#  FIELD_NAME FIELD_TYPE FIELD_LEN FIELD_DEC
     1   ITEM        C               10         0
     2   PRICE       N                5         2
     3   TAX         N                5         2
     .
```

```
. CREATE Newoff FROM Newstruc
```

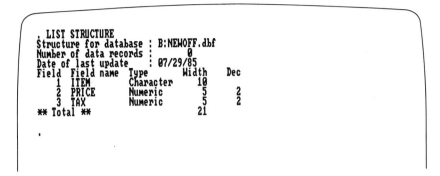

```
. LIST STRUCTURE
Structure for database : B:NEWOFF.dbf
Number of data records :        0
Date of last update    : 07/29/85
Field  Field name  Type      Width    Dec
   1   ITEM        Character    10
   2   PRICE       Numeric       5      2
   3   TAX         Numeric       5      2
** Total **                     21
.
```

Notice that it was not necessary to USE the *Newoff* file before displaying its structure, since CREATE FROM opens the file automatically.

- **dBASE II equivalent**
  CREATE FROM

- **Comment**
  A structure file always has four fields, designed to store the four elements that define the structure of a database field: name, type, width, and decimal places. Each *record* in the structure file contains the complete definition of one database *field*.

CREATE LABEL

- **Structure**
  CREATE LABEL file_name

- **Description**
  The CREATE LABEL command invokes the dBASE label-form generator. It is identical to the MODIFY LABEL **221★** command, and is discussed in detail under that entry.

CREATE REPORT

- **Structure**
  CREATE REPORT file_name

- **Description**
  The CREATE REPORT command invokes the dBASE report-form generator. It is identical to the MODIFY REPORT **226★** command, and is discussed in detail under that entry.

CTOD()

■ **Structure**

CTOD(character_date)

■ **Description**

Given a properly formatted string **98**♦ of characters representing a date, CTOD() returns the equivalent date-type value **99**♦ (CTOD stands for "character to date"). The default format for the *character_date* argument of the CTOD() function is mo/da/yr.

The argument may be any string expression that evaluates to the correct format. Most commonly, it will be a literal (constant) string, within quotes:

```
CTOD("07/18/85")
```

If you change the date-display format with the SET DATE **337**★ command, the argument of CTOD() must subsequently conform to the new format. Here are the formats available:

Format:	*Name:*
mo/da/yr	American (default)
da/mo/yr	British
da.mo.yr	French or German
da-mo-yr	Italian
yr.mo.da	ANSI

■ **Usage**

CTOD() allows you to create a date-type value, in order to perform date arithmetic **100**★ or make comparisons with other date-type values. For example, the following expression calculates and displays the number of days between today's date and the date 2/27/86:

```
. ? CTOD("2/27/86") - DATE()
       224
.
```

Without the CTOD() function, an attempt to operate on or compare a string expression and a date-type value will result in an error message, as in these two examples:

```
. ? "2/27/86" - DATE()
Data type mismatch
                    ?
? "2/27/86" - DATE()
.
```

```
. ? 2/27/86 - DATE()
Data type mismatch
                   ?
? 2/27/86 - DATE()
.
```

■ **Database example**

The following database, called *Assets*, contains a list of depreciable assets, along with their original values and the date each item was purchased:

```
. USE Assets
. LIST
Record#  ITEM                      VALUE PURCHASED  AGE
     1   typewriter              1240.00 05/30/79   0.0
     2   personal computer       2495.00 03/15/83   0.0
     3   printer, daisy-wheel     1250.00 03/15/83   0.0
     4   printer, dot-matrix       650.00 05/15/84   0.0
     5   copier                  1835.00 12/20/84   0.0
     6   office desk               850.00 02/27/80   0.0
.
```

Notice that the *purchased* field is a date-type field and that the numeric field *age* has not yet been filled in with values. The owner of these assets operates a business under a fiscal year that ends on September 30, and would like to know how old each asset will be at the end of the current fiscal year (September 30, 1985). The following REPLACE **291**★ command will calculate and store this age for each of the assets in the database:

```
. REPLACE ALL age WITH (CTOD("09/30/85") - purchased) / 365
      6 records replaced
.
```

The CTOD() function finds the date-type equivalent of the string value "09/30/85". Given this date-type value, the following expression finds the number of days between the purchase date and September 30, 1985:

```
CTOD("09/30/85") - purchased
```

And finally, this expression finds the number of years between the purchase date and September 30, 1985:

```
(CTOD("09/30/85") - purchased) / 365
```

Here is the resulting database:

```
. LIST
Record#  ITEM                    VALUE PURCHASED  AGE
      1  typewriter            1240.00 05/30/79   6.3
      2  personal computer     2495.00 03/15/83   2.5
      3  printer, daisy-wheel  1250.00 03/15/83   2.5
      4  printer, dot-matrix    650.00 05/15/84   1.4
      5  copier                1835.00 12/20/84   0.8
      6  office desk            850.00 02/27/80   5.6
.
```

■ **Caution**

After changing the date-display format with SET DATE, be careful to use the new format in CTOD(). If you mix formats, dBASE will not supply an error message, but the function will produce unexpected results. Consider the following example, which changes the date-display format to the French style (da.mo.yr), as displayed by the DATE() 103★ function, then sends a date string in the American format ("mo/da/yr") to the CTOD() function:

```
. SET DATE french
.
. ? DATE()
18.07.85
.
. ? CTOD("09/30/85")
13.06.87
.
```

■ **dBASE II equivalent**

None

■ **Comments**

CTOD() also allows you to create date-type values representing years prior to 1900 ◆. By default, if the year portion of a character date contains only two digits, the CTOD() function results in a date in the twentieth century, as in the first of the next two examples. But you may include a four-digit year in a character date, so that the date may represent a year in some other century, as shown in the second example:

```
. ? YEAR(CTOD("02/27/51"))
1951
.
```

```
. ? YEAR(CTOD("02/27/1751"))
1751
.
```

Using dates that fall before the twentieth century within a dBASE III database is problematic, since the APPEND 19★ command presents a date-input template that leaves room for only two digits in the year portion of the date. This means that any dates you enter into a database via APPEND will, by default, be taken as twentieth-century dates. To safely create non-twentieth-century date-type values in a database, you should use the CTOD() function. Here is an example of how this is done.

The following database, called *States*, is designed to store state names and the date on which each state entered the union. A final field, *state_yrs*, is for the number of years since statehood:

```
. USE States
. LIST
Record#  NAME          MO DA YR    ENTRY_DATE STATE_YRS
      1  California     09 09 1850    /  /         0.0
      2  Florida        03 03 1845    /  /         0.0
      3  Maine          03 15 1820    /  /         0.0
      4  Missouri       08 10 1821    /  /         0.0
      5  New York       07 26 1788    /  /         0.0
      6  Wyoming        07 10 1890    /  /         0.0
.
```

Examining the structure of this database, you can see that the fields *mo*, *da*, and *yr* are all character-type fields, and that *yr* has a length of 4 characters, whereas *mo* and *da* each have lengths of 2 characters:

```
. LIST STRUCTURE
Structure for database : B:STATES.dbf
Number of data records :       6
Date of last update    : 07/22/85
Field  Field name  Type        Width   Dec
    1  NAME        Character      12
    2  MO          Character       2
    3  DA          Character       2
    4  YR          Character       4
    5  ENTRY_DATE  Date            8
    6  STATE_YRS   Numeric         5     1
** Total **                      34
.
```

These three fields have been used to store the components of a character date representing the date upon which each state entered the union. From these components, we would like to create a date-type value to be stored in the *entry_date* field. The following REPLACE command uses CTOD() to create the *entry_date* values:

```
. REPLACE ALL entry_date WITH CTOD(mo + "/" + da + "/" + yr)
       6 records replaced
   .
```

In the resulting database, the year component of each *entry_date* value is displayed with only two digits, even though none of the dates falls in the twentieth century:

```
. LIST
Record#  NAME          MO DA YR   ENTRY_DATE STATE_YRS
      1  California     09 09 1850 09/09/50          0.0
      2  Florida        03 03 1845 03/03/45          0.0
      3  Maine          03 15 1820 03/15/20          0.0
      4  Missouri       08 10 1821 08/10/21          0.0
      5  New York       07 26 1788 07/26/88          0.0
      6  Wyoming        07 10 1890 07/10/90          0.0
   .
```

However, we can demonstrate that the *entry_date* values are correct by using them to calculate the age, in years, of each state. The following REPLACE command performs this task, subtracting *entry_date* from today's date (DATE()), and dividing the difference by 365:

```
. REPLACE ALL state_yrs WITH (DATE() - entry_date) / 365
       6 records replaced
. LIST
Record#  NAME          MO DA YR   ENTRY_DATE STATE_YRS
      1  California     09 09 1850 09/09/50        134.9
      2  Florida        03 03 1845 03/03/45        140.5
      3  Maine          03 15 1820 03/15/20        165.5
      4  Missouri       08 10 1821 08/10/21        164.0
      5  New York       07 26 1788 07/26/88        197.1
      6  Wyoming        07 10 1890 07/10/90         95.1
   .
```

Data types

Database fields **154★** and program variables **459★** are both characterized by the type of data they are defined to store. When you create a new database, the data type is one of the structural elements **100◆** you must define for each field the database will contain. In contrast, the data type of a variable is determined when the variable is first created: That is, the type of value that is initially assigned to the variable defines the type of the variable itself.

Five data types ◆ are available for dBASE database fields:

☐ Character.

☐ Numeric.

☐ Date.

☐ Logical.

☐ Memo.

In some contexts, dBASE refers to these types ◆ by their initials: N, C, D, L, and M, respectively. A database field may be defined to store any *one* of these types of values.

In a programming sense, only four of these types can be considered true data types: character, numeric, date, and logical. Memo-type values are available only as database fields, not for storage in variables.

Here are brief descriptions of dBASE's five data types:

Character: ◆ Character values consist of strings of characters from the ASCII **28★** character set. The maximum length of any such string, whether stored in a field or in a variable, is 254 characters. Literal (constant) strings used in dBASE commands ◆ must be enclosed in single quotes (' '), double quotes (" "), or square brackets ([ ]). (Double quotes are used throughout this book.) Three string operators **420★** are available for character values: + and –, both used for concatenation **65★**, and $, used to test for the presence of one string inside another.

Numeric: ◆ Numeric values can be either positive or negative *real numbers* with a defined number of digits after the decimal point, or positive or negative *integers*, with no digits after the decimal point. dBASE III stores numbers with up to 15 digits of precision (the legal *range* is 10^{+308} down to the fractional value 10^{-307}). The largest legal field width for a numeric value is 19 bytes. Arithmetic operations **24◆** available for numeric values include exponentiation (^ or **), multiplication (*), division (/), addition (+), and subtraction (–).

Date: ♦ Date-type values are stored internally as *scalar*, or *Julian*, date values—that is, as numbers representing the days since January 1 in the year 1 AD. Date-type values are displayed on the screen in one of several available formats, specified by the SET DATE 337★ command. Date-type fields are displayed in a width of eight spaces; date-type variables have a length of 8 bytes. The operations of *date arithmetic* 100★ include subtracting one date from another, to obtain a number representing the number of days between the two dates, and adding a number to or subtracting a number from a date, to obtain a date that is the specified number of days forward or backward in time from the first date. Date-type values are entered into a database in the current date format (from SET DATE). A date value may be assigned to a variable via the DATE() 103★ or CTOD() 92★ function.

Logical: ♦ A logical value is either true or false. Logical values in a database have a width of one space and may be entered as T, t, Y, or y (for *true* or *yes*) or F, f, N, or n (for *false* or *no*). Likewise, any of the following forms may be used to assign a true or false value to a logical variable: .T., .t., .Y., .y., .F., .f., .N., or .n.; however, dBASE III always *displays* these values as either .T. or .F.. The following relational operators 286★ are available for building conditional expressions that result in logical values: $=$, $<>$, $<$, $>$, $<=$, $>=$. Three logical operators 207★ are also available: .NOT., .AND., and .OR..

Memo: ♦ A memo field value consists of a document up to 4,096 characters long, stored on disk. In the database itself, a memo field has a width of 10 characters. The purpose of a memo field is to enable you to attach a word-processed document to each record of a database. Such fields may be created via dBASE's built-in word processor 466★. For any database that includes a memo field, dBASE creates a special disk file with the extension name 155♦ .DBT for storing the memo values of the database. (*Caution:* If the .DBT file is lost, the associated .DBF file is rendered unusable.) Memo values may be entered from full-screen edit mode 20♦, 143♦ by positioning the highlight over the memo field and pressing Ctrl-PgDn to access the dBASE word processor. To return to full-screen edit mode, press Ctrl-End or Ctrl-W. A memo value may *not* be assigned to a variable, nor can you SORT 402★, INDEX 176★, or search on a memo field. Certain other cautions also apply to the use of databases that have memo fields; see JOIN 189★.

Database structure

The complete definitions of all the fields **154★** contained in a database comprise its structure ◆. You define this structure when you first create the file, using the CREATE **88★** command. (The structure can be modified to some extent later with the MODIFY STRUCTURE **234★** command.) The definition of each field includes a name, a data type and a width (in characters). The number of decimal places is a fourth, and optional, characteristic to be defined for numeric fields.

There are several things to keep in mind when designing a database:

☐ Field widths should be kept as narrow as possible, to conserve disk space, but it is important to allow for the maximum likely entry. For instance, numeric fields must be wide enough to include the decimal point and any digits following it, and must allow for increased size resulting from arithmetic operations.

☐ When you are planning the structure of your database, it is important to consider all of the files involved in your system at the same time. If your database will need to interact with other databases, such as transaction files, it will need to have at least one field in common with each related database.

☐ If a particular type of information will be needed frequently, it may be advisable to set it up in a single, consistently formatted field that can be indexed (memo fields **217★** for instance, cannot be indexed, sorted, or searched).

☐ If the end user(s) will not be experienced with dBASE, it is especially important that field names be descriptive and indexes be in place.

Date arithmetic

Two kinds of date arithmetic ◆ are available in dBASE III, both involving the use of date-type values **99◆**:

☐ Given a date value, you can add or subtract an integer that represents a number of days. The result is a new date value. For example, the first of the following three commands displays today's date, supplied by the DATE() **103★** function.

The second adds 90 days to today's date, and displays the new date. The third subtracts 180 days from today's date and displays the result:

```
. ? DATE()
07/24/85

.
```

```
. ? DATE() + 90
10/22/85

.
```

```
. ? DATE() - 180
01/25/85

.
```

□   Given two dates, you can subtract one from the other, yielding the number of days between the two dates. The number will be positive if the first date is more recent than the second date. This next expression yields the number of days that have elapsed since 12/31/84, showing that today is the 205th day of the current year:

```
. ? DATE() - CTOD("12/31/84")
         205

.
```

Database examples of date arithmetic can be found in many of the entries in this book. In particular, see the entry under CTOD() **92★**.

Date and time functions

Nine date functions are available in dBASE III for creating and working with date-type values **99♦**. One way to categorize these functions is by the types of values that they *return*: date-type, numeric, or strings of characters.

Two of the functions yield date-type values. DATE() **103★** supplies today's date from the system's clock/calendar **♦**, and CTOD() **92★** returns a date-type value, given a properly formatted string of characters representing the date. (CTOD() is thus your way of introducing a specific date-type value into a dBASE command or program.)

Three of the functions return string values from date-type arguments. CDOW() **44★** and CMONTH() **58★** both supply specific information about the date: the name of the day of the week ("Sunday", "Monday", "Tuesday", and so on) and the name of the month ("January", "February", and so on), respectively. DTOC() **139★** returns a string conversion of its date-type argument. In this sense, DTOC() is the opposite of CTOD().

Four of the date functions supply numbers, all representing components of the date-type arguments they receive. DAY() **105★** returns a number from 1 through 31, representing the day of the month, and DOW() **135★** supplies a number from 1 through 7, representing the day of the week. Likewise, MONTH() **236★** yields a number from 1 through 12, representing the month. And finally, YEAR() **468★** supplies the four-digit value for the year in which the date falls. Since the display format **337♦** of dBASE dates gives only a two-digit year (85, for instance), the YEAR() function is the most direct way of finding out if the date is before the year 1900. Such non-twentieth-century dates **95♦** are difficult to deal with in dBASE.

The single dBASE time function, TIME() **433★**, returns the time from the system's clock/calendar. dBASE permits arithmetic operations **100♦** on all of the date functions, but not on TIME().

DATE()

■ **Structure**

DATE()

■ **Description**

The DATE() function reads the computer's system date and then supplies a date-type value **99♦** representing it. The display will be in the default format mo/da/yr, or in some other form specified by the SET DATE **337★** command.

■ **Usage**

The purpose of DATE() is to make today's date available to you in the context of dBASE III. For example:

```
. ? "Today is", DATE()
Today is 07/18/85

.
```

■ **Database example**

The following database, called *Assets*, contains a list of depreciable assets, along with their original values and the date each item was purchased:

```
. USE Assets
. LIST
Record#  ITEM                     VALUE PURCHASED  AGE
      1  typewriter             1240.00 05/30/79   0.0
      2  personal computer      2495.00 03/15/83   0.0
      3  printer, daisy-wheel    1250.00 03/15/83   0.0
      4  printer, dot-matrix      650.00 05/15/84   0.0
      5  copier                 1835.00 12/20/84   0.0
      6  office desk              850.00 02/27/80   0.0

.
```

Notice that the field named *purchased* is a date-type field, and that the numeric-type field *age* has not yet been filled in with values.

The following REPLACE **291★** command will calculate the age of each item, up to today's date:

```
. REPLACE ALL age WITH (DATE() - purchased) / 365
       6 records replaced
  .
```

In this command, the expression *DATE() – purchased* finds the difference, in days, between today's date and the date each item was purchased. Dividing the result of this expression by 365 yields the age, in years, of each asset. In the resulting database, the *age* field is now filled in with values:

```
. LIST
Record#  ITEM                     VALUE PURCHASED  AGE
      1  typewriter             1240.00 05/30/79   6.2
      2  personal computer      2495.00 03/15/83   2.4
      3  printer, daisy-wheel   1250.00 03/15/83   2.4
      4  printer, dot-matrix     650.00 05/15/84   1.2
      5  copier                 1835.00 12/20/84   0.6
      6  office desk             850.00 02/27/80   5.4
  .
```

See the CTOD() **92★** entry for another look at this database.

■ **Caution**

In order for DATE() to supply today's date, you must be sure to supply DOS with the correct date when you first turn on your computer.

■ **dBASE II equivalent**

DATE()

However, the dBASE II DATE() function returns a character-type **98◆** value, whereas the dBASE III DATE() returns a date-type value. dBASE II does not have date-type values and does not permit date arithmetic **100★**.

DAY()

■ **Structure**

DAY(date-type value)

■ **Description**

Given a dBASE date-type value **99♦**, DAY() supplies the numeric day of the month on which the date falls.

■ **Usage**

The argument of DAY() may be a date-type field or variable value, or it may be the result of the DATE() **103★** or CTOD() **92★** function:

```
. ? DATE()
07/18/85
.
```

```
. ? DAY(DATE())
18
.
```

```
. var = CTOD("5/17/85")
05/17/85
. ? DAY(var)
17
.
```

```
. ? DAY(CTOD("4/19/85"))
19
.
```

■ **Program example**

The CDOW() entry contains database and program examples that illustrate the use of DAY(). The program *Duedates* contains the following print instruction:

```
? "By:      ", CDOW(due) + ",", CMONTH(due), DAY(due)
```

The DAY() function supplies the numeric day of the month in the resulting message:

```
By:      Saturday, April  13
```

■ **Caution**

DAY() works only on a date-type argument. An attempt to send a string of characters to DAY() will result in an error message:

```
. ? DAY("2/27/51")
Invalid function argument
                    ?
? DAY("2/27/51")
.
```

■ **dBASE II equivalent**

None

DELETE

■ **Structure**

DELETE *scope_clause condition_clause*

■ **Description**

The DELETE command marks ◆ one or more records in the current database for deletion. DELETE does not physically remove the records from the database—that is the job of the PACK **243★** command.

■ **Usage**

DELETE issued alone, without a scope **312★** or condition clause, marks only the current record for deletion. DELETE does not reposition the record pointer **258★**. A scope clause (ALL **17★**, NEXT **239★**, or RECORD **282★**) or a condition clause (FOR **164★** or WHILE **463★**) may be included if you wish to mark more than one record at a time for deletion.

■ **Database example**

The following example of the DELETE command uses a database called *Bills*. This database contains records of household bills that are due within the next month:

```
. USE Bills
. LIST
Record#  DUE_TO        AMOUNT DATE_DUE PAID
      1  Bernal Bank   142.75 06/15/85 .F.
      2  Maxwell's     567.81 06/22/85 .F.
      3  Credit Union   89.00 06/01/85 .T.
      4  Ameri Mortgage 986.23 06/30/85 .F.
      5  Bernal Electric 61.15 06/18/85 .F.
      6  OC Telephone  110.52 06/05/85 .T.

.
```

Two of the bills in the list have been paid, so they contain a logical value 99♦ of .T. in the *paid* field. Once paid, a bill's record can be transferred to another database, and then permanently deleted from *Bills*. The following command marks the paid bills for deletion:

```
. DELETE FOR paid
      2 records deleted

.
```

Here is the resulting database:

```
. LIST
Record#  DUE_TO         AMOUNT DATE_DUE PAID
      1  Bernal Bank    142.75 06/15/85 .F.
      2  Maxwell's      567.81 06/22/85 .F.
      3 *Credit Union    89.00 06/01/85 .T.
      4  Ameri Mortgage 986.23 06/30/85 .F.
      5  Bernal Electric 61.15 06/18/85 .F.
      6 *OC Telephone   110.52 06/05/85 .T.

.
```

As you can see, dBASE uses the asterisk character in a display of the database to indicate records marked for deletion. The final step in deleting the records is to issue the PACK command.

■ **dBASE II equivalent**
DELETE

■ **Comments**
The RECALL **278★** command removes the deletion markers from one or more records. The SET DELETED ON **344★** command makes other database commands ignore records marked for deletion, and the DELETED() **108★** function returns a value of true if the current record is marked for deletion.

In full-screen mode (EDIT **141★**, BROWSE **38★**, or CHANGE **48★**), Ctrl-U can be used to mark (or unmark) records for deletion.

A different command altogether, DELETE FILE, is identical in effect to the disk command ERASE **149★**.

DELETED()

■ **Structure**
DELETED()

■ **Description**
The DELETED() function returns a logical value **99◆** of true if the current record has been marked for deletion. Otherwise, DELETED() returns a value of false.

■ **Usage**
The following example uses a database called *Bills*, discussed in the DELETE **106★** entry. *Bills* contains records of household bills that are due in the current month. These two commands open the database, and mark for deletion any records of bills that have already been paid:

```
. USE Bills
. DELETE FOR paid
      2 records deleted
.
```

Then the LIST **200★** command uses DELETED() in a FOR **164★** clause to display only the records that are marked for deletion:

```
. LIST FOR DELETED()
Record#  DUE_TO              AMOUNT DATE_DUE PAID
       3 *Credit Union        89.00 06/01/85 .T.
       6 *OC Telephone       110.52 06/05/85 .T.

    .
```

■ **Program example**

DELETED() can also be used for similar conditional operations in programs. For example, the following program, called *Billrecs*, copies the records of all paid bills to a new database named *Paid*:

```
*-----------------------------------------------------BILLRECS.PRG
* Uses the Bills database. Stores records of paid bills
*   in new database.
*

SET TALK OFF
SET DELETED OFF

USE Bills
DELETE FOR paid

COPY TO Paid FOR DELETED()

PACK

SET TALK ON
RETURN
```

Notice that SET DELETED **344★** must be OFF in order for the marked records to be read by the COPY **82★** command.

Here is the complete *Bills* database before the *Billrecs* program has been performed:

```
. USE Bills
. LIST
Record#  DUE_TO              AMOUNT DATE_DUE PAID
       1 Bernal Bank        142.75 06/15/85 .F.
       2 Maxwell's          567.81 06/22/85 .F.
       3 Credit Union        89.00 06/01/85 .T.
       4 Ameri Mortgage     986.23 06/30/85 .F.
       5 Bernal Electric     61.15 06/18/85 .F.
       6 OC Telephone       110.52 06/05/85 .T.

    .
```

After program performance, *Bills* contains only records of unpaid bills, and *Paid* contains the other records:

```
. DO Billrecs
. LIST
Record# DUE_TO          AMOUNT DATE_DUE PAID
      1 Bernal Bank     142.75 06/15/85 .F.
      2 Maxwell's       567.81 06/22/85 .F.
      3 Ameri Mortgage  986.23 06/30/85 .F.
      4 Bernal Electric  61.15 06/18/85 .F.
```

```
. USE Paid
. LIST
Record# DUE_TO          AMOUNT DATE_DUE PAID
      1 *Credit Union    89.00 06/01/85 .T.
      2 *OC Telephone   110.52 06/05/85 .T.
```

Notice that the records copied to the *Paid* database are still marked for deletion. The following command removes the marks:

```
. RECALL ALL
      2 records recalled
```

■ **dBASE II equivalent**
*

■ **Comments**
The PACK **243★** command permanently deletes records that have been marked by the DELETE command. SET DELETED makes other commands ignore records marked for deletion.

110

Delimited files

Through the COPY 82★ command, dBASE III can provide two ASCII text-file formats that may allow you to transport a dBASE database to another programming environment ◆. These two formats are called SDF 313★ (for "system data format") and Delimited.

The following characteristics define the structure of a delimited file:

☐ Each record is on a line of its own, ending with carriage-return and line-feed characters.

☐ Inside a record, each field is separated from the next by a comma.

☐ Character fields are enclosed in quotation marks (the default delimiter), and trailing blanks are not included in string values.

The structure of a delimited file is designed for a *sequential-access* reading scheme. Sequential access means that the file will always be read from the first record through the last, in order, as opposed to random access, where any one specific record can be read directly.

■ Database example

The following example uses the database *Assets*, which describes a company's depreciable assets. *Assets* contains four fields of information: the name of the item (a character field), its original value (a numeric field, the date it was purchased (a date-type field), and its age in years (another numeric field).

```
. USE Assets
. LIST
Record#  ITEM                     VALUE PURCHASED  AGE
      1  typewriter             1240.00 05/30/79   6.3
      2  personal computer      2495.00 03/15/83   2.5
      3  printer, daisy-wheel   1250.00 03/15/83   2.5
      4  printer, dot-matrix     650.00 05/15/84   1.4
      5  copier                 1835.00 12/20/84   0.8
      6  office desk             850.00 02/27/80   5.6
.
```

The COPY 123★ command with a DELIMITED clause creates a copy of this database in the delimited ASCII text format:

```
. COPY TO Assets DELIMITED
      6 records copied
.
```

By default, dBASE gives the new file the extension name .TXT **155◆**, so the name of the new file will be *ASSETS.TXT*. If you use the TYPE **445★** command to examine this text file, this is what you will see:

```
. TYPE Assets.txt
"typewriter",1240.00,19790530,6.3
"personal computer",2495.00,19830315,2.5
"printer, daisy-wheel",1250.00,19830315,2.5
"printer, dot-matrix",650.00,19840515,1.4
"copier",1835.00,19841220,0.8
"office desk",850.00,19800227,5.6

.
```

Notice how dBASE converts a date-type value for a delimited file: The date is represented as an eight-digit number, where the first four digits are the year, the next two are the month, and the final two are the day.

■ **Program example**

The BASIC programming language includes facilities for reading either random-access or sequential files, depending upon the structure of the file itself. The following BASIC program shows how the delimited file *Assets* can be read as a sequential file. The program reads each record in turn, from the beginning to the end of the database, and displays the records on the screen:

```
100 REM ** Read ASSETS.TXT, a delimited file from dBASE III,
110 REM ** as a sequential file.
120 REM
130 n = 1
140 OPEN "B:ASSETS.TXT" FOR INPUT AS #1
150 WHILE NOT EOF(1)
160     INPUT#1, item$, cost, dt$, age
170     PRINT "Asset #"; n; ": "; item$
180     PRINT "   Original cost:    ";
190     PRINT USING "$$#,####.##"; cost
200     PRINT "   Date of purchase: ";
210     PRINT MID$(dt$,5,2);"/";MID$(dt$,7,2);"/";MID$(dt$,1,4)
220     PRINT "   Age:              "; age; " years"
230     n = n + 1
240     PRINT : PRINT
250 WEND
260 CLOSE #1
270 END
```

The INPUT# command in line 160 controls the actual reading, relying on the quotation marks and commas in the file to distinguish one field from the next. Here is the output produced by the program:

```
Asset # 1 : typewriter
     Original cost:      $1,240.00
     Date of purchase: 05/30/1979
     Age:                6.3  years


Asset # 2 : personal computer
     Original cost:      $2,495.00
     Date of purchase: 03/15/1983
     Age:                2.5  years


Asset # 3 : printer, daisy-wheel
     Original cost:      $1,250.00
     Date of purchase: 03/15/1983
     Age:                2.5  years


Asset # 4 : printer, dot-matrix
     Original cost:        $650.00
     Date of purchase: 05/15/1984
     Age:                1.4  years


Asset # 5 : copier
     Original cost:      $1,835.00
     Date of purchase: 12/20/1984
     Age:                 .8  years


Asset # 6 : office desk
     Original cost:        $850.00
     Date of purchase: 02/27/1980
     Age:                5.6  years
```

Compare this program with the random-access program shown under the SDF entry.

■ **Comment**
See also APPEND FROM 22★.

DIR

■ **Structure**

DIR   *drive_name: path_name\   skeleton*

■ **Description**

DIR, like its DOS 133★ counterpart♦, displays information about files stored on disk. Without any parameters, the dBASE version of DIR displays the names, sizes, and last access dates of all the database files (.DBF) on the current default disk. In addition, three optional parameters allow DIR to display:

□   Information about a disk in a nondefault drive (*drive_name:*).

□   Information about the contents of a subdirectory 250♦ (*path_name*).

□   Information about file types other than databases (*skeleton*).

■ **Usage**

The *skeleton* parameter of DIR allows the use of two "wildcard" ♦ characters, * and ?. The asterisk wildcard stands for any number of characters in a file name, whereas the question-mark wildcard stands for only a single character. For example, the name *.PRG* stands for *any* file name that has an extension of .PRG, but the name *SALES??.DBF* stands only for database file names that contain five to seven characters and start with *SALES*.

Here are some examples of DIR in various formats:

```
. DIR
Database files    # records    last update    size
BKSALES.DBF            10       06/06/85        757
MAY.DBF                10       06/03/85        229
AUTHORS.DBF             7       06/06/85        587
ABOOK.DBF              10       06/03/85        611
STUDENTS.DBF            6       07/23/85        227
ADDRESS.DBF             6       06/15/85        887
STATES.DBF              6       07/22/85        431
CHILDREN.DBF            6       05/02/85        655

    4384 bytes in     8 files.
  328704 bytes remaining on drive.
    .
```

```
. DIR *.PRG
BOOKINFO.PRG        MONTH_UP.PRG        MENU.PRG

   2540 bytes in     3 files.
 328704 bytes remaining on drive.
 .
```

```
. DIR *.*
BKSALES.DBF         MAY.DBF             AUTHORS.DBF         BOOKINFO.PRG
MONTH_UP.PRG        BOOKNUM.NDX         ABOOK.DBF           CHARBASE.TXT
ASSETS.TXT          PART.NDX            AUTHOR.NDX          ADDLABEL.LBL
STUDENTS.DBF        ADDRESS.DBF         ADDRESS.NDX         AUTHORS.DBT
STATES.DBF          CHILDREN.DBF        MENU.PRG            ASCII.DOC

  24393 bytes in    20 files.
 328704 bytes remaining on drive.
 .
```

```
. DIR B:Tools\Property.*
PROPERTY.PRG        PROPERTY.DBF        PROPERTY.DBT

  10001 bytes in     3 files.
 316416 bytes remaining on drive.
 .
```

■ **Comment**

Notice that dates and sizes are provided only for database files, in response to DIR
issued without wildcards. However, all forms of DIR provide the total size, in bytes, of
all files displayed, and the total number of bytes remaining on the disk.

DISPLAY

■ **Structure**

DISPLAY *scope_clause* *expression_list* *condition_clause* OFF *TO PRINT*

■ **Description**

The DISPLAY command displays one or more records from the currently selected database **322♦**. The records appear on the screen, but can also be sent to the printer if a TO PRINT clause is included in the DISPLAY command.

By default, the DISPLAY command selects only the current record for display. A scope **312★** clause (ALL **17★**, NEXT **239★**, or RECORD **282★**) and/or a condition clause (FOR **164★** or WHILE **463★**) may be included in the DISPLAY command to select multiple records. To select specific information from each record, you may also include an optional list of fields or expressions. The OFF clause suppresses the display of the record number.

If DISPLAY results in more than one screenful of information, dBASE will pause and display the following message at the end of each screen, so that you can examine the data before proceeding:

```
Press any key to continue ...
```

■ **Usage**

The following examples display records from a real-estate database called *Property* **384♦**. The first example demonstrates DISPLAY's default behavior—to select only the current record:

```
. USE Property
. GOTO 5
. DISPLAY owner_1, address, asking_pr OFF
owner_1              address                 asking_pr
Henderson           18 Jackson Avenue       375000.00
.
```

An expression list in a DISPLAY command may include simple field names, or more complex expressions such as concatenations **65★**, arithmetic operations **24★**, or date arithmetic **100★**. This next example displays two fields and a calculated value.

The heading above each column shows the complete expression that generated the column value:

```
. DISPLAY address, sale_price, .06 * sale_price FOR sold
Record#  address                        sale_price   .06 * sale_price
      1  123 Martha Street               195000.00        11700.0000

  .
```

Use of a FOR clause in a DISPLAY command is a common way to select for display only those records that meet an expressed criterion. So the following command lists all records that contain a value greater than 175000 in the *asking_pr* field:

```
. DISPLAY address, asking_pr FOR asking_pr > 175000
Record#  address                      asking_pr
      1  123 Martha Street            225000.00
      4  15 Peach Lane                275000.00
      5  18 Jackson Avenue            375000.00
      6  4452 Sixth Avenue            245000.00
      7  55 Sayer Lane                255000.00
      8  3555 Alta Street             179000.00

  .
```

■ **Cautions**

Make sure your printer is ready to operate before you issue a DISPLAY TO PRINT command. If it is not, you may be dropped back into the operating system unexpectedly.

When records are longer than dBASE can display in one screen width, the DISPLAY output will wrap to the next line. This can make for very difficult reading, so you might want to consider using the *expression_list* option to limit the display to selected fields.

■ **dBASE II equivalent**

DISPLAY

■ **Comments**

To eliminate the display of column headings in the DISPLAY command, change the SET HEADING 369★ status to OFF. However, keep in mind that the headings can be very helpful, especially when the information being displayed is the result of a complex expression.

The LIST 200★ command is similar to DISPLAY. By default, the scope of LIST is ALL: In other words, LIST displays the entire database. If LIST results in more than one screenful of information, the display simply scrolls, without pause, down to the last record.

DISPLAY MEMORY

■ **Structure**

DISPLAY MEMORY *TO PRINT*

■ **Description**

The DISPLAY MEMORY command gives information about the currently defined variables **459★** stored in memory. The TO PRINT option sends the information to the printer.

■ **Usage**

DISPLAY MEMORY allows you to check the names and contents of all variables active during a dBASE session. If the display takes up more than one screen, DISPLAY MEMORY will pause at the end of each screen until you ask to continue.

Here is an example of the information supplied by DISPLAY MEMORY:

```
. DISPLAY MEMORY
N            pub  N       12345 (      12345.00000000)
S            pub  C   "ABCDE"
D            pub  D   07/29/85
L            pub  L   .T.
    4 variables defined,      27 bytes used
  252 variables available,  5973 bytes available
.
```

The display includes the name of the variable, its global or local status **460♦** (PRIVATE **259★** variables will be listed only if the DISPLAY MEMORY command is issued within the program or procedure **383♦** where they are created), its data type **98★**, and its actual contents. The message also tells you how many variables have been defined, how much memory space they take up, and how much room remains for additional variables.

■ **Cautions**

You can use the *DIR∗.MEM* **114♦** command to find out what memory files are on a disk, but to view the contents of one of these files with the DISPLAY MEMORY command, you must open the file for the current session with the RESTORE FROM **298★** command.

Be careful of the TO PRINT clause, both here and elsewhere. If you try to print from dBASE when the printer is not ready, you risk being dropped back into the operating system.

■ **dBASE II equivalent**
DISPLAY MEMORY

■ **Comment**
The LIST MEMORY command provides the same information, but without screen pauses.

DISPLAY STATUS

■ **Structure**
DISPLAY STATUS *TO PRINT*

■ **Description**
The DISPLAY STATUS command gives you information about your current session with dBASE. Specifically, it indicates which database files **156♦** are currently open, gives default paths and drives **343♦**, lists current settings of all the control parameters **73★**, and tells the current settings of the 10 function keys **167★**. The TO PRINT option sends all this information to the printer.

■ **Usage**
DISPLAY STATUS is especially helpful in identifying the sources of problems when something goes awry during a dBASE session: no visible response to a command, perhaps, because the SET TALK **398★** parameter is OFF, or F3 displaying a directory, instead of listing your database, because the key has been redefined.

Like all DISPLAY commands, DISPLAY STATUS provides its information in conveniently formatted screens of information, pausing at the end of each screen until you ask to continue:

```
. DISPLAY STATUS

Select area - 1, Database in use: B:MASTER.dbf   Alias - MASTER
     Index file: B:PART.ndx  key - pt_no
     Related to: MONTH

Currently selected database:
Select area - 2, Database in use: B:JUNE.dbf   Alias - MONTH
     Index file: B:MONTH.ndx  key - PT_NO

Press any key to continue...
```

```
Press any key to continue...

File search path:
Default disk drive: B:
ALTERNATE   - OFF  DEBUG       - OFF  ESCAPE     - ON   MENU      - OFF
BELL        - ON   DELETED     - ON   EXACT      - OFF  PRINT     - OFF
CARRY       - OFF  DELIMITERS  - OFF  HEADING    - ON   SAFETY    - ON
CONFIRM     - OFF  DEVICE      - SCRN HELP       - OFF  STEP      - OFF
CONSOLE     - ON   ECHO        - OFF  INTENSITY  - ON   TALK      - ON
UNIQUE      - OFF

Margin =     0

Function key  F1  - help;
Function key  F2  - modi comm
Function key  F3  - list;
Function key  F4  - dir c:\dbase *.*;
Function key  F5  - display structure;
Function key  F6  - display status;
Function key  F7  - do
Function key  F8  - display;
Function key  F9  - append;
Function key  F10 - edit;

.
```

■ **Caution**

Use the TO PRINT clause carefully. If your printer is not connected or is not ready to print, you risk being dropped unexpectedly out of dBASE.

■ **dBASE II equivalent**

DISPLAY STATUS

■ **Comment**

The LIST STATUS command produces the same message as DISPLAY STATUS, but without the screen pause.

DISPLAY STRUCTURE

■ **Structure**

DISPLAY STRUCTURE *TO PRINT*

■ **Description**

DISPLAY STRUCTURE displays the file structure **100♦** of the currently selected **322♦** database. The TO PRINT option sends the information to the printer.

■ **Usage**

DISPLAY STRUCTURE allows you to check on the field names, types, and sizes in the currently selected database, and also gives you quick-reference information on the size of your file and when it was last updated:

```
. USE Bksales
. DISPLAY STRUCTURE
Structure for database : B:Bksales.dbf
Number of data records :      10
Date of last update    : 06/06/85
Field  Field name  Type        Width    Dec
    1  BOOK_NUM    Character       6
    2  AUTHOR_NUM  Character       6
    3  TITLE       Character      20
    4  UNIT_SALES  Numeric         6
    5  PUB_DATE    Date            8
    6  MONTH_AVG   Numeric         6
** Total **                      53

.
```

Notice that the display supplies the name, type, and width of every field in the database. For numeric fields, the number of decimal places is also included. If the display takes up more than one screen, DISPLAY STRUCTURE pauses at the end of each screen until you ask to continue.

■ **Caution**

The usual cautions about printing from dBASE apply to the TO PRINT clause. These are discussed in detail in the SET PRINT **381★** entry.

■ **dBASE II equivalent**

DISPLAY STRUCTURE

■ **Comments**

Misspelled field names can be the source of irritating problems with database commands. DISPLAY STRUCTURE allows you to quickly verify that the field is indeed *Name* (for instance), not *Names*.

The LIST STRUCTURE command provides the same information, but without the screen pause.

DO

■ **Structure**

DO program_name   *WITH parameter_list*

■ **Description**

The DO command executes a program that is stored in a dBASE command file **264♦**. DO may be issued either from within a program or as a direct command from the dBASE dot prompt **62♦**.

   The program the DO command "calls" may be an individual program file on disk or part of a currently open procedure file **383♦**. If the program is in an individual disk file, DO searches the current default disk **343♦** for the specified file name with a .PRG extension **155♦** (unless you explicitly specify a nondefault disk or extension). If the program is part of a procedure file, DO must call the program by the name defined in its PROCEDURE **263★** statement.

   The WITH option is used to list values that will be sent to the called program as parameters. The number and types of values in the WITH clause must correspond to the specific parameter requirements established in the PARAMETERS **245★** statement of the program being called.

■ **Usage**

DO has two modes of operation:

☐   A DO command issued from the dot prompt "runs" a program stored on disk and then returns you once again to the dot prompt.

☐   A DO command located within a program initiates a procedure ("subroutine") and, when performance of the procedure is complete, returns control to the program that made the call.

Example 1: The following sequence from the *Sale* procedure discussed in the IF **171★** entry illustrates the use of DO as a procedure call. It also demonstrates one of the techniques a procedure can use for communicating with the program that calls it:

```
DO Get_rec
IF EOF()
    RETURN
ENDIF
```

Sale calls the *Get_rec* **319**◆ procedure to search for a record in the database *Sale* works with (*Property*). When *Get_rec* has completed its task, program control returns to *Sale*. *Sale* then needs to find out whether or not *Get_rec* has actually found a record, so it uses the EOF() **147**★ function to check the position of the record pointer **258**★. In effect, *Get_rec* communicates with *Sale* by repositioning the database pointer: If it finds a specific record, it positions the pointer at that record; otherwise, it leaves the pointer at the end of the file. Thus, *Sale* need only test the EOF() function to find out whether a record has been located.

Example 2: A dBASE program may use the WITH clause of the DO statement to pass information to a procedure it is calling. WITH sends data values to the procedure, to be stored in the PARAMETERS variables. In this example, *Sale* calls the *Yesno* procedure discussed under the PARAMETERS entry. *Yesno* performs the task of placing a prompt on the screen and eliciting a yes-or-no response. The procedure takes three parameters: two numeric values representing the screen location at which the prompt will be displayed, and a string representing the prompt itself. Here is an example of a call to *Yesno*:

```
DO Yesno WITH 13, 10, "Change the current bid?    "
```

The *Yesno* procedure contains a PARAMETERS statement that defines the local variables in which these three values will be stored:

```
PARAMETERS currow, curcol, question
```

In this case, the variables *currow* and *curcol* will receive values of 13 and 10, respectively, and the character variable *question* will receive the string value "Change the current bid?".

The sequence immediately following this call to *Yesno* illustrates another way in which a procedure can communicate with the program that calls it:

```
DO Yesno WITH 13, 10, "Change the current bid?    "
IF yn
    @ 11, 15 GET asking_pr
    READ
ENDIF
```

In a PUBLIC 269★ statement located right after the PARAMETERS declaration, *Yesno* declares *yn* as a global variable, available outside the program or procedure in which it is created. Since the variable is global, *Sale* can test its value upon regaining control of the program.

The parameter values listed in the WITH clause may be expressed as literal (constant) values, as in the preceding example, or as expressions that may include variables. Here is another call to *Yesno*, in which the first value in the WITH clause is an expression:

```
DO Yesno WITH row + 4, 19, "Try again? "
```

■ **Cautions**

If a value in the WITH clause of a DO statement is represented as a simple variable, the value stored in that variable may possibly be changed by the procedure that is being called. (See the PARAMETERS entry for details and an example.)

If a procedure file is open, DO looks for a *procedure* that has the specified name before it looks on the default disk for a *program* file with that name. For example, let's say you open a procedure file, and later you issue the command:

```
DO Tax
```

In response, dBASE will first look in your open procedure file for *PROCEDURE Tax*. If no such procedure exists, dBASE will then look on the current disk for *TAX.PRG*. If your open procedure file contains a procedure named *Tax* and your disk also contains a program named *Tax*, you must specify the disk-drive location if you wish to run the program file:

```
DO B:Tax
```

(Or, you can just close the procedure file before attempting to run the .PRG file.)

■ **dBASE II equivalent**

DO

However, dBASE II does not offer the WITH clause for passing parameters.

DO CASE...ENDCASE

■ **Structure**

DO CASE
    CASE condition
        command_list
    * ... *
    CASE condition
        command_list
    OTHERWISE
        command_list
ENDCASE

■ **Description**

DO CASE is a structured programming command that presents a set of mutually exclusive alternative courses of action for a program to choose among. Each possible course of action is preceded by a CASE **44★** statement expressing a condition **286◆**. A given action is chosen if its CASE condition evaluates as true. When a CASE statement is chosen, all of the commands located between it and the next CASE statement are executed and dBASE ignores the remainder of the DO CASE structure.

The OTHERWISE **242★** clause, which is optional, expresses one final course of action in the DO CASE statement. In the event that no previous CASE action is chosen, the action defined in the OTHERWISE clause is performed. If none of the CASE conditions evaluates to true and there is no OTHERWISE clause, the DO CASE statement results in no action at all.

The ENDCASE statement is *required*, in order to mark the end of the DO CASE structure.

■ **Usage**

The DO CASE structure is often used to control the actions of menu-driven programs such as *Menu*, listed and described under the SET PROCEDURE **383★** entry. This program displays the menu of activities for the real-estate program on the screen, and accepts the user's selection from the keyboard. The subsequent DO CASE statement then calls on one specific procedure 266♦, depending upon the value stored in the variable *choice*:

```
@ 18, 25 SAY "Choice? <1,2,3,4,5,6,7> " GET choice PICTURE "9" ;
   RANGE 1, 7
READ

DO CASE
    CASE choice = 1
        DO Add
    CASE choice = 2
        DO Sale
    CASE choice = 3
        DO Reqmnts
    CASE choice = 4
        DO Schedule
    CASE choice = 5
        DO Mortgage
    CASE choice = 6
        DO Prntinfo
    CASE choice = 7
        CLEAR
        CLOSE PROCEDURE
        SET TALK ON
        SET BELL ON
        SET CONFIRM OFF
        SET ESCAPE ON
        RETURN
ENDCASE
```

Notice how the @..SAY..GET 12★ statement uses a RANGE 272★ clause to ensure that *choice* will contain a numeric value between 1 and 7. Choices 1 through 6 result in procedure calls; choice 7 clears the screen, closes the procedure file, and ends the program.

■ Program example

This next program, called *Price*, illustrates the use of the OTHERWISE clause in a DO CASE statement. The program is designed to determine admission prices for a certain event, where the price of a ticket depends upon the age of the person who is being admitted:

```
*------------------------------------------------- PRICE.PRG
* Determines the price of admission, depending upon the
*    age of the ticket-buyer.
*

PARAMETER age

SET TALK OFF

?
? " ==> "
DO CASE     --> to determine the price according to age group.
    CASE age <= 3
        ?? "Baby:"
        price = "0.00"
    CASE age <= 12
        ?? "Child:"
        price = "1.50"
    CASE age <= 18
        ?? "Teenager:"
        price = "4.00"
    CASE age >= 65
        ?? "Senior Citizen:"
        price = "3.50"
    OTHERWISE
        ?? "Adult:"
        price = "5.00"
ENDCASE     --> for price options.

IF VAL(price) = 0
    ?? " Admission is Free!"
ELSE
    ?? " Admission is $" + price
ENDIF

?
SET TALK ON
RETURN
```

The DO CASE statement in this program processes special admission prices for four age groups: babies, children, teenagers, and senior citizens. Anyone who is not in one of these special groups pays the full adult admission price displayed by the OTHERWISE clause following the last CASE statement. Here are some samples of the program's output:

```
. DO Price WITH 17
==> Teenager: Admission is $4.00
.
```

```
. DO Price WITH 2
==> Baby: Admission is Free!
.
```

```
. DO Price WITH 68
==> Senior Citizen: Admission is $3.50
.
```

```
. DO Price WITH 11
==> Child: Admission is $1.50
.
```

```
. DO Price WITH 34
==> Adult: Admission is $5.00
.
```

■ **Caution**

Nested DO CASE statements are allowed in dBASE, and you might want to use such nested structures in a menu that leads to submenus. However, in the interest of readability and ease of debugging 267♦, consider processing submenus in procedures called from a main DO CASE statement.

■ **dBASE II equivalent**

DO CASE ... CASE ... OTHERWISE ... ENDCASE

■ **Comments**

As shown in the *Price* program, the DO CASE and ENDCASE lines may contain explanatory comments 4♦. These comments will be ignored during the performance of the DO CASE statement.

The examples in this entry show that the DO CASE structure is ideal for situations in which one course of action must be chosen from among *several* options. Compare this with the IF **171★** structure, which generally presents a choice between only *two* courses of action.

DO WHILE...ENDDO

■ **Structure**

DO WHILE condition
        command_list
ENDDO

■ **Description**

The DO WHILE structure sets up a repetition loop in a dBASE program. All of the commands located between DO WHILE and ENDDO are performed repeatedly as long as the condition 286♦ expressed in the DO WHILE statement remains true. If, after a complete iteration of the commands within the loop, the condition evaluates as false, the looping ends and the program continues at the first command after the ENDDO statement.

■ **Usage**

By using the EOF() **147★** function to check for the end of the file after each iteration, a DO WHILE loop can perform the same set of commands on each record of a database, from top to bottom:

```
DO WHILE .NOT. EOF()
```

The DO WHILE structure can also be used to ensure that the user enters valid input from the keyboard. The loop is constructed to continue its repetitions of the input commands until the input itself is valid for the application at hand, as in this short example from the *Yesno* procedure described in the PARAMETERS **245★** entry:

```
valid = .F.
answer = " "
DO WHILE .NOT. valid
    @ currow, curcol SAY question GET answer PICTURE "!"
    READ
    valid = answer $ "YN"
    * ... *
ENDDO
```

The key to this validation process is in the handling of the logical **99♦** variable *valid*. This variable is initialized to false at the beginning of the sequence, so that the DO WHILE loop, with a condition of *.NOT. valid*, will be performed at least once. Inside the loop, an @ **12★** statement reads a single uppercase character from the keyboard. If the input consists of one of two valid characters—Y or N—then *valid = answer $ "YN"* sets *valid* to true; otherwise it remains false. Thus, the @ command is performed repeatedly until it receives valid input. (The $ substring operator **421♦** tests the keyboard input in *answer* against the permissible characters listed in the string after the $ symbol.)

You may sometimes see a DO WHILE loop that begins:

```
DO WHILE .T.
```

Such a loop is atypical, because it contains no built-in conditional way of ending the looping. Instead, it must have some command inside the loop itself that will terminate the action of the DO WHILE structure. An example of this usage appears in the *Menu* program listed under the SET PROCEDURE **383★** entry:

```
DO WHILE .T.
    * ... *
    * Display the menu and accept a menu choice.
    * ... *
    DO CASE
        * ... *
        * Cases 1 through 6 result in procedure calls.
        * ... *
        CASE choice = 7
            CLEAR
            CLOSE PROCEDURE
        * ... *
            RETURN
    ENDCASE
ENDDO
```

This DO WHILE loop displays a menu on the screen, accepts a menu choice (a numeric value from 1 through 7), and then uses a CASE **44★** structure to select an appropriate activity, based upon the choice. The looping continues, accepting a new menu choice after each activity is complete, until the user enters a choice of 7 ("Quit") which selects the CASE clause that ends the program via a RETURN **301★** statement.

Some programmers may prefer to rewrite such a loop, incorporating a logical variable (*done*, in this example) that will trigger the end of the loop:

```
done = .F.
DO WHILE .NOT. done
    * ... *
    * Display the menu and accept a menu choice.
    * ... *
    DO CASE
        * ... *
        * Cases 1 through 6 result in procedure calls.
        * ... *
        CASE choice = 7
            CLEAR
            CLOSE PROCEDURE
            done = .T.
    ENDCASE
ENDDO
```

The choice between these two styles of loops depends largely upon your own personal sense of programming clarity.

■ **Caution**

There are two dBASE commands that offer abnormal escapes from the usual sequential performance of a loop: EXIT **150★** and LOOP **211★**. Unlike RETURN, which ends the performance of the *entire program* in which the loop is located, these commands simply interrupt the normal performance of the loop itself. The two commands can lead to confusion, and are best used sparingly. Except in unusual circumstances, they can easily be replaced with simpler, clearer structures.

■ **dBASE II equivalent**
DO WHILE...ENDDO

■ **Comments**
The ENDDO line may contain explanatory comments that dBASE will simply ignore during the performance of the structure, so this is a good location for a few words identifying the purpose of the DO WHILE statement of which the ENDDO is a part:

```
DO WHILE salary < 20000
    * ... *
ENDDO    --> salary evaluation
```

Like other structured commands available in dBASE, DO WHILE loops can be nested ♦—that is, one loop may be performed inside another loop. With such nested loops, it is often helpful to indicate which loop each ENDDO closes, especially if the structures are very long:

```
DO WHILE age > 16
    * ... *
    DO WHILE score > 85
        * ... *
    ENDDO score
    * ... *
ENDDO age
```

See the ASCII program listed under the CHR() **50★** entry for another example of a nested DO WHILE loop.

DOS

DOS is the name of the *disk operating system* ◆ required for running dBASE III on your computer. Several numbered versions of DOS have been issued—dBASE runs on version 2.0 or higher. In addition to providing general management of your computer's operations, DOS offers a number of file-management commands that you can use before or after a session with dBASE, to create backup files, transfer data between programs **111◆**, **313◆**, or perform other important disk operations. (Several of the DOS commands also have equivalents in dBASE itself **56◆**, **76◆**, **114◆**, **149◆**, **291◆**, **445◆**.)

Here is a selection of the most useful DOS commands:

Command:	*Action:*
DIR	Displays a directory of all the files on the current disk.
DIR*.DBF	Displays all files with .DBF extensions.
FORMAT B:	Formats the disk in drive B (no dBASE equivalent). *Caution:* The FORMAT command destroys any information previously stored on a floppy or hard disk. Do not use it on any of the dBASE program disks, or on any other disk that contains important information.
COPY B:*.* A:	Copies all the files on the disk in drive B to the disk in drive A.
COPY *.PRG A:	Copies all the .PRG files from the current disk to the disk in drive A.
COPY CON: A:NEWFILE.EXT	Copies from the console (i.e., the keyboard and the display screen) to a new disk file called *NEWFILE.EXT* (MODIFY COMMAND **219★** is the dBASE equivalent). After issuing this command, you can begin typing lines of text that you want to store in *NEWFILE.EXT*. Enter Ctrl-Z from the keyboard to end the "copy" operation.

(continued)

Command:	Action:
TYPE A:ANYFILE.EXT	Displays the contents of the disk file *ANYFILE.EXT* on the screen.
CHKDSK B:	Displays a message telling you how much storage space remains on the disk in drive B (no dBASE equivalent).
DISKCOPY B: A:	Makes an entire backup copy of the disk in drive B, onto the disk in drive A (no dBASE equivalent). *Caution:* Do not try to use this command on the copy-protected dBASE program disks. Also, see the caution under the FORMAT command.
RENAME OLD.DBF NEW.DBF	Assigns the new file name *NEW.DBF* to the file that is currently named OLD.DBF.
CLS	Clears the DOS screen.
ERASE TEST.DBF	Erases the file called *TEST.DBF* from the current disk. *Caution:* Neither DOS nor dBASE provides any way to bring the file back after it has been erased.
ERASE *.NDX	Erases all files with extensions of .NDX from the current disk.
DATE	Initiates a dialogue for resetting the system date (no dBASE equivalent).
TIME	Initiates a dialogue for resetting the system time (no dBASE equivalent).

The dBASE RUN **306**★ command allows you access to some of the DOS capabilities from within dBASE. The special memory and configuration requirements for this command are discussed in detail in the RUN entry.

DOW()

- **Structure**

DOW(date-type value)

- **Description**

Given a dBASE date-type value **99 ♦**, the DOW() function (DOW means "day of week")
returns an integer from 1 through 7, representing the day of the week on which the
date falls (Sunday through Saturday, respectively).

- **Usage**

The argument of DOW() may be a date-type field or variable value, or it may be the
result of the DATE() **103★** or CTOD() **92★** function:

```
. var = CTOD("12/25/85")
12/25/85

. ? DOW(var)
4
.
```

```
. ? DATE()
07/28/85

. ? DOW(DATE())
1
.
```

```
. ? DOW(CTOD("3/14/85"))
5
.
```

■ **Database and program example**

The following database, called *Meetings*, is a scheduling tool that might be used by a salesperson to keep track of quarterly visits to clients. The database contains four fields: the client's name (*client*), the date of the salesperson's last visit to the client (*last_visit*), and fields for scheduling the next visit and for the day of the week upon which the next visit will occur (*next_visit* and *day*, respectively).

```
. USE Meetings
. LIST
Record#  CLIENT              LAST_VISIT NEXT_VISIT DAY
      1  Jane Phillips       02/25/85    /  /
      2  Maxwell Sayers      01/15/85    /  /
      3  Dorothy Harmon      03/14/85    /  /
      4  George Conrad       02/27/85    /  /
      5  Danielle Gordon     03/29/85    /  /
      6  Charles Wheeler     04/18/85    /  /

.
```

To fill in the fields *next_visit* and *day*, the salesperson might use the following two REPLACE 291★ commands:

```
. REPLACE ALL next_visit WITH last_visit + 93
       6 records replaced

. REPLACE ALL day WITH CDOW(next_visit)
       6 records replaced

.
```

The first command calculates a date for each client's next visit, 93 days after the previous visit. The second uses the CDOW() 44★ function to determine which day of the week that will be. The following screen shows the completed database:

```
. LIST
Record#  CLIENT               LAST_VISIT NEXT_VISIT DAY
      1  Jane Phillips        02/25/85   05/29/85   Wednesday
      2  Maxwell Sayers       01/15/85   04/18/85   Thursday
      3  Dorothy Harmon       03/14/85   06/15/85   Saturday
      4  George Conrad        02/27/85   05/31/85   Friday
      5  Danielle Gordon      03/29/85   06/30/85   Sunday
      6  Charles Wheeler      04/18/85   07/20/85   Saturday
   .
```

Unfortunately, some of the dates calculated for the *next_visit* field fall on Saturday or Sunday. If the salesperson wishes to visit clients only during the business week—Monday through Friday—the database will have to be revised accordingly.

The following program, called *Weekday*, is designed to examine each record of *Meetings* and reschedule Saturday and Sunday visits to the preceding Friday or the following Monday, respectively:

```
*---------------------------------------------- WEEKDAY.PRG
* Makes sure that dates for client visits are
*    scheduled only on weekdays.
*
SET TALK OFF
USE Meetings

GOTO TOP
DO WHILE .NOT. EOF()
    next = DOW(next_visit)
    DO CASE
        CASE next = 7
            REPLACE next_visit WITH next_visit - 1
            REPLACE day WITH CDOW(next_visit)
        CASE next = 1
            REPLACE next_visit WITH next_visit + 1
            REPLACE day WITH CDOW(next_visit)
    ENDCASE
    SKIP
ENDDO

SET TALK ON
RETURN
```

The DO WHILE 129★ loop in this program steps through each record of the *Meetings* database. Within the loop, DOW() first assigns to the variable *next* the numeric value representing the day of the week for the next visit to the current client:

```
next = DOW(next_visit)
```

Then, given this value, a DO CASE 125★ statement revises the scheduled date for the next visit whenever it finds a Saturday or Sunday:

```
CASE next = 7
      * ... *
CASE next = 1
      * ... *
```

Here is how *Weekday* changes the *Meetings* database:

```
. DO Weekday
. LIST
Record#  CLIENT           LAST_VISIT NEXT_VISIT DAY
      1  Jane Phillips    02/25/85   05/29/85   Wednesday
      2  Maxwell Sayers   01/15/85   04/18/85   Thursday
      3  Dorothy Harmon   03/14/85   06/14/85   Friday
      4  George Conrad    02/27/85   05/31/85   Friday
      5  Danielle Gordon  03/29/85   07/01/85   Monday
      6  Charles Wheeler  04/18/85   07/19/85   Friday
.
```

■ **Caution**

DOW() works only on a date-type argument. An attempt to send a string of characters to DOW() will result in an error message.

```
. ? DOW("2/27/51")
Invalid function argument
                      ?
? DOW("2/27/51")
.
```

■ **dBASE II equivalent**

None

■ **Comment**

The CDOW() function supplies the character name of the day of the week, given a date-type value.

DTOC()

■ **Structure**

DTOC(date-type value)

■ **Description**

Given a dBASE date-type value **99♦**, DTOC() supplies a string **98♦** of characters identical to the format in which the date-type value would be displayed on the screen (DTOC stands for "date to character"). The default format for the string returned by the DTOC() function is mo/da/yr.

If you change the date-display format with the SET DATE **337★** command, the format of the string returned by DTOC() changes accordingly.

■ **Usage**

The argument of DTOC() may be a date-type field or variable value, or it may be the result of the DATE() **103★** or CTOD() **92★** function. DTOC() is useful for concatenation **65★**, or for those occasions when you need to use a string function **418♦** on a date string. Here is an example of concatenation, using a date-type value from a database field named *hired*:

```
. ? "Employee was hired on " + DTOC(hired) + "."
Employee was hired on 11/03/82.
.
```

In this example, an alternative ? **5★** command syntax using commas to separate the print elements might be unacceptable, because commas result in the insertion of a space between each element of the final display:

```
. ? "Employee was hired on", hired, "."
Employee was hired on 11/03/82 .
.
```

Notice the unwanted space between the date and the final period of the resulting sentence.

This next example demonstrates the use of DTOC() with the SUBSTR() **423★** function to produce a customized date-display format:

```
. ? CMONTH(DATE()) + " '" + SUBSTR(DTOC(DATE()), 7, 2)
July '85
.
```

The DTOC() function supplies the character equivalent of today's date (from DATE()) and the SUBSTR() function returns the final two characters of the date string.

■ **Caution**

If a date-type value happens to represent a date that falls before 1900, DTOC() will not return the date's correct year:

```
. STORE CTOD("07/04/1776") TO indepndnce
07/04/76

. ? YEAR(indepndnce)
1776

. ? DTOC(indepndnce)
07/04/76
.
```

The YEAR() **468★** function is dBASE's only tool for finding the complete year of a date-type value.

■ **dBASE II equivalent**

None

■ **Comments**

The CMONTH() **58★** and CDOW() **44★** functions also return string values from a date-type value.

MONTH() **236★** and YEAR() return numeric values, and can be used to isolate the components of a date-type value.

CTOD() supplies a date-type value from a correctly formatted character date.

EDIT

■ **Structure**

EDIT *RECORD numeric_expression*

■ **Description**

EDIT is a full-screen command designed for editing the information stored in the currently selected database **322◆**. EDIT places one record on the screen at a time. Each field name appears with a template displaying the current value stored in the field (if a format file **365◆** is open for the current database, the organization of the EDIT screen will be controlled by that file).

The RECORD clause allows you to edit a specific record; without a RECORD clause, the EDIT command brings up a full-screen display of the current record.

You can move forward or backward in the database while in the EDIT mode, to edit more than one record during a session.

■ **Usage**

To choose a specific record number for editing, you can use either of the following command formats:

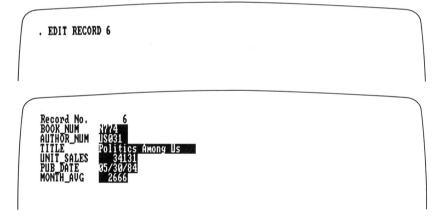

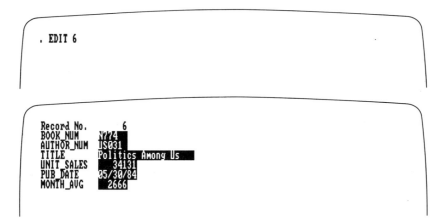

```
. EDIT 6




       Record No.       6
       BOOK_NUM    N774
       AUTHOR_NUM  US031
       TITLE       Politics Among Us
       UNIT_SALES       34131
       PUB_DATE    05/30/84
       MONTH_AVG        2666
```

The record number may also be expressed as a numeric expression or numeric variable:

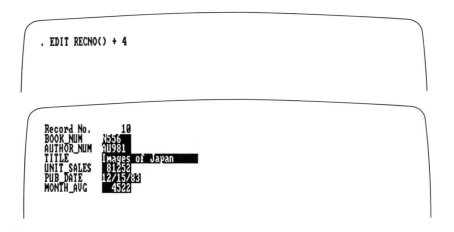

```
. EDIT RECNO() + 4




       Record No.      10
       BOOK_NUM    N556
       AUTHOR_NUM  AU981
       TITLE       Images of Japan
       UNIT_SALES       81252
       PUB_DATE    12/15/83
       MONTH_AVG        4522
```

```
. var = 5
5
.
. EDIT var
```

```
Record No.        5
BOOK_NUM     F182
AUTHOR_NUM   US528
TITLE        The Mission
UNIT_SALES       65880
PUB_DATE     09/18/84
MONTH_AVG        7240
```

Notice the use of the RECNO() **279★** function in the numeric expression that selects a record at a *relative* position in the database.

Use the following keyboard functions to control the EDIT mode:

Key:	Action:
Right-arrow, Left-arrow	Move cursor one character to right or left.
Up-arrow, Down-arrow	Move cursor one field up or down.
PgUp, PgDn	Move to previous or next record.
Ctrl-PgDn	Edit ◆ current memo field **217★**.
Ctrl-End	Save current memo field.
Ctrl-Y	Delete contents of field.
Ctrl-U	Mark or unmark record for deletion (a toggle).
Ins	Activate or deactivate character-insert mode (a toggle).
Esc	Exit full-screen mode, without saving new edits in the current record.
Ctrl-End	Exit full-screen mode, saving all edits.

Notice particularly that memo fields can be accessed and edited in the EDIT mode.

If SET MENU **378**★ is ON, a list of keyboard-control keys appears at the top of the screen when you enter the EDIT mode. Even if SET MENU is OFF, pressing the F1 function key from within EDIT toggles the list on and off.

- **dBASE II equivalent**
EDIT

- **Comments**
In addition to SET FORMAT **365**★ and SET MENU, the following SET commands affect the behavior or appearance of the EDIT mode: SET BELL **329**★, SET CONFIRM **334**★, SET COLOR **331**★, SET DELIMITERS **345**★, and SET INTENSITY **376**★.

The CHANGE **48**★ command is similar in effect to EDIT (it, too, will allow you to edit memo fields). In addition, CHANGE allows conditional selection of fields and records for the editing procedure.

EJECT

■ **Structure**
EJECT

■ **Description**
EJECT issues a form-feed command to the printer.

■ **Usage**
EJECT can be valuable both as a direct command and as a command used from within a program, whenever it is necessary to move the print position to the top of a new page. An example appears in the *Prntinfo* procedure listed and discussed under the SET DEVICE **347★** entry. This procedure issues an EJECT command before beginning to print a report from a record in the *Property* **384◆** database:

```
      *  ...  *
SET  CONSOLE  OFF
SET  PRINT  ON
SET  MARGIN  TO  12

EJECT
SET  DEVICE  TO  PRINT

?  "    XYZ  Realty"
?  "    ---  ------"
      *  ...  *
```

■ **Caution**
The use of EJECT when your printer is not on, or not available for operation, can be dangerous. Read the cautionary notes included under SET PRINT ON **381★**.

■ **dBASE II equivalent**
EJECT

■ **Comments**
This command works independently of the SET PRINT command, so SET PRINT ON is not a prerequisite for using EJECT.

The REPORT FORM **295★** command automatically issues a form-feed command before beginning a report, unless the NOEJECT clause is used.

ELSE

- **Structure**

  IF
  * ... *
  ELSE
  * ... *
  ENDIF

- **Description**

  ELSE is an optional clause that presents an alternate course of action in an IF **171**★ decision structure. An IF structure that includes an optional ELSE statement is processed as follows:

  1. If the condition is true, all of the commands located between IF and ELSE are performed; control then proceeds to the first command located after ENDIF.

  2. If the condition is false, all of the commands located between ELSE and ENDIF are performed; control of the program then continues sequentially from the first command after ENDIF.

  The *Sale* procedure **172**◆ from the *Property* **384**◆ real-estate program has several good examples of the use of ELSE clauses.

- **Comment**

  A line that begins with an ELSE statement may contain comments **4**◆. During the performance of the structure, dBASE will simply ignore anything following the word ELSE on the same line, so the ELSE statement provides a good location for a few words describing the alternate course of action:

  ```
  IF yn
      *  ...  *
  ELSE -->  "N"  entered at keyboard
      *  ...  *
  ENDIF
  ```

EOF()

- **Structure**

  EOF()

- **Description**

  EOF() is the end-of-file ◆ function. It returns a logical value **99◆** of true if the record pointer **258★** of the current database is positioned at the end of the file; otherwise it returns a value of false.

- **Usage**

  A number of database commands have the potential of setting EOF() to true. In general, commands that perform an operation on the entire database (such as LIST **200★**, DISPLAY ALL **116★**, and REPLACE ALL **291★**) set EOF() to true when the operation is complete.

  Commands that search for a specific record or records in a database will also leave EOF() set to true if the search is unsuccessful. These commands include LOCATE **202★** and CONTINUE **72★** in an unindexed database, and FIND **160★** and SEEK **317★** in an indexed database.

  Finally, if the record pointer is positioned at the last record in the database, the SKIP **400★** command will result in an end-of-file condition:

```
. USE Property
. GOTO BOTTOM

. ? EOF()
.F.

. ? RECNO()
       8

. SKIP
Record no.      9

. ? EOF()
.T.

.
```

The RECNO() **279★** function supplies the current record number. Notice that when EOF() is true, the result of RECNO() is one greater than the total number of records in the database.

■ **Program example**

A common use for EOF() in a program is to set up a DO WHILE **129★** loop that processes a database from beginning to end (several examples of such loops appear in entries throughout this book). Here is an outline of the algorithm that controls such a loop:

1. Assuming the database is not empty, move the record pointer to the top of the file (*GOTO TOP* **169♦**).

2. Process the current record.

3. Move the record pointer down one record (*SKIP*).

4. Test for the end-of-file condition (EOF()). If EOF() is true, end processing. If EOF() is false, repeat from step #2.

This translates into the following code:

```
GOTO TOP
DO WHILE .NOT. EOF()
    * ... *
    * Process the current record.
    * ... *
    SKIP
ENDDO
```

An example of this algorithm in action appears in the program called *Rank,* listed and discussed under the entry for the BOF() **35★** function. After the first part of the program has calculated the student ranks, the following passage displays a one-line message describing the information contained in each record of the database:

```
GOTO TOP
DO WHILE .NOT. EOF()
    ? TRIM(name), "is #" + STR(rank, 1), ;
      "with a score of", STR(score, 3) + "."
    SKIP
ENDDO
```

■ **Caution**

Database commands that normally work on the current record, such as DISPLAY, will perform no action at all if the end-of-file condition is true.

■ **dBASE II equivalent**

EOF()

■ **Comment**

When multiple databases are open in different work areas **454♦**, each database has its own record pointer. Movement of the pointer in one area does not *automatically* move the pointer in another area (see SET RELATION **390★**, however). The current value of EOF() applies only to the currently selected area.

ERASE

■ **Structure**

ERASE file_name

■ **Description**

Like the DOS **133**★ command ◆ of the same name, ERASE deletes a file permanently from disk. However, with the dBASE version, you can delete only one file at a time—wildcard characters **114**◆ are not available for the dBASE ERASE command. You must specify the file's entire name, *including the extension*, and if the file is not located on the disk in the default drive **343**◆, you must also indicate the disk drive and/or path **250**◆ location. Any type **156**◆ of file may be deleted.

■ **Usage**

After you issue the ERASE command, be sure to look for the message that appears on the screen to tell you whether or not the command has successfully deleted the file. (The SET TALK **398**★ parameter must be ON in order for these messages to appear.)

In the next four examples, you can see the messages for an unsuccessful attempt to delete a file without its three-character extension, a successful deletion of the same file, an unsuccessful attempt to delete a database file that is currently open, and finally, an unsuccessful attempt to delete a file that does not exist on the default disk:

```
. ERASE Test1
File does not exist

. ERASE TEST1.DBF
File has been deleted
.
```

```
. USE Test2
. ERASE TEST2.DBF
Cannot erase open file
.
```

```
. ERASE TEST3.DBF
File does not exist
.
```

■ **Caution**

Former dBASE II users may initially experience some disorientation due to changes in the ERASE and CLEAR **56★** commands. In dBASE II, ERASE merely clears the screen and CLEAR closes database files. In dBASE III, however, ERASE deletes a disk file and CLEAR erases the screen. *Use ERASE carefully in dBASE III,* to avoid deleting a file inadvertently.

■ **dBASE II equivalent**

DELETE FILE

■ **Comments**

If you are about to delete a file, but have a nagging fear that you may someday wish you hadn't, a reasonable alternative is to give the file a new name, using the RENAME **291★** command. The new name can be designed to indicate that the file is in disuse, but has been put aside for possible future reference. (You might also store the renamed file on an "archive" disk.)

The DELETE FILE command can also be used to erase dBASE III files from disk. The syntax is the same as for ERASE.

EXIT

■ **Structure**

```
DO WHILE
      *  ...  *
          EXIT
      *  ...  *
ENDDO
```

■ **Description**

The EXIT command is designed to be used inside a DO WHILE **129★** loop, to make an abnormal exit from the loop. After the EXIT command, program control passes directly to the first command after the ENDDO.

■ **Usage**

The EXIT command is best reserved for rather special circumstances. Some programmers may wish to use EXIT as a conditional escape from a loop that itself contains other structured commands—nested **132◆** DO WHILE and IF...ELSE **171★** commands, perhaps. Other programmers will prefer to avoid the use of EXIT altogether, by structuring all loops with normal logical escape paths.

■ **Caution**

In even the simplest of circumstances, the use of EXIT may make your programs less readable than you would like them to be. For example, let's say you are writing a loop that performs some processing activity on selected records of an employee database. The database is indexed on two key fields 194★: *dept* (primary) and *salary* (secondary). You want the loop to process only those employees in the Editorial Department who earn less than $1,500 per month. You might be tempted to structure your loop as follows:

```
GOTO TOP
DO WHILE dept = "Editorial"
    IF salary > 1500
        EXIT
    ENDIF

    *  ...  *
    * Process the record.
    *  ...  *
    SKIP
ENDDO
```

However, a clearer approach is to avoid the EXIT command by writing a compound condition 207◆ in the DO WHILE statement itself:

```
GOTO TOP
DO WHILE dept = "Editorial" .AND. salary < 1500
    *  ...  *
    * Process the record.
    *  ...  *
    SKIP
ENDDO
```

■ **dBASE II equivalent**

None

■ **Comment**

The LOOP 211★ command also interrupts the normal flow of repetition within a DO WHILE loop.

EXP()

- **Structure**

  EXP(numeric_expression)

- **Description**

  Given a numeric argument, x, the EXP() function supplies the value of e to the power of x. The letter e stands for the base constant of the natural logarithms and equals approximately 2.71828183.

- **Usage**

  EXP() and its converse, LOG() **205★**, are sometimes used in statistical and financial calculations.

- **Program example**

  The following program produces a short table of EXP() values in a database called *Exp*. *Exp* has two fields: x, for the argument of EXP(), and *e_to_x*, for the resulting value:

```
*------------------------------------------------- EXPTABLE.PRG
* Creates a table of natural exponentials.
*

SET TALK OFF
SET SAFETY OFF

USE Exp
ZAP

recs = 20
DO WHILE recs > 0
    APPEND BLANK
    recs = recs - 1
ENDDO

REPLACE ALL x WITH RECNO() / 10
REPLACE ALL e_to_x WITH EXP(x)

SET TALK ON
DISPLAY ALL
RETURN
```

Notice how the RECNO() **279★** function is used to create the *x* values. Here is the output from the program:

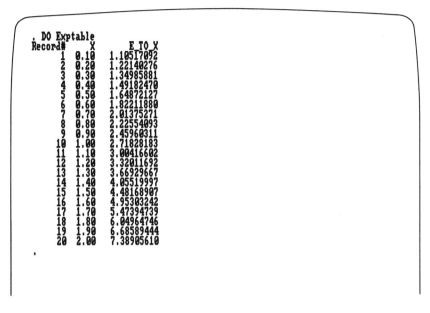

```
. DO Exptable
Record#      X         E TO X
       1   0.10    1.10517092
       2   0.20    1.22140276
       3   0.30    1.34985881
       4   0.40    1.49182470
       5   0.50    1.64872127
       6   0.60    1.82211880
       7   0.70    2.01375271
       8   0.80    2.22554093
       9   0.90    2.45960311
      10   1.00    2.71828183
      11   1.10    3.00416602
      12   1.20    3.32011692
      13   1.30    3.66929667
      14   1.40    4.05519997
      15   1.50    4.48168907
      16   1.60    4.95303242
      17   1.70    5.47394739
      18   1.80    6.04964746
      19   1.90    6.68589444
      20   2.00    7.38905610
.
```

■ **dBASE equivalent**
None

■ **Comment**
The SET DECIMALS **340★** command controls the number of decimal places that will be displayed from the EXP() function.

Fields

A field is an area in a database set up to contain one item of information, of a defined type and width, for each record **282**★ in the file. A database may contain up to 128 such fields. When a database is displayed in tabular form on the screen, the entries in each field appear in a single column.

The structural definition of a field, specified when you CREATE **88**★ the database, includes four characteristics:

☐ The field name.

☐ The type **98**◆ of information the field will contain.

☐ The width of the field, in characters.

☐ The number of places after the decimal point, for numeric fields.

A field name ◆ may be up to 10 characters long and may include letters, digits, and embedded underscore characters, but it must *begin* with a letter. It is best to avoid using dBASE reserved words for field names—the results can sometimes be unpredictable.

There are five field types ◆ available in dBASE, each with a different maximum width:

Field type:	Width:
Character	Up to 254 characters
Numeric	Up to 19 characters, with up to 15 decimal places
Date	8 characters, formatted
Logical	1 character
Memo	10 characters, formatted

The date, logical, and memo widths are assigned by dBASE and cannot be changed. The 10-character width of a memo field is just a field marker in the database itself; the real memo text is stored in an associated .DBT file **156**◆, which may be up to 4,096 characters long (however, see Word Processors **466**★).

File names

Any DOS **133★** file name, including names of files created in dBASE ◆, consists of two parts: a first name of up to eight characters, and an optional extension name ◆ of up to three characters. The first name and the extension are separated by a period (for example, *SALES.DBF*).

When you use a dBASE command to create a file, dBASE normally supplies the extension name for you. This default extension will indicate the type of file **156◆** you are creating (database, program, and so on). To create a file name with a nondefault extension, simply specify your own extension in the command itself (for instance, *OFFICE2.NY*).

The recommended rules for legal characters in file names are stricter in dBASE than in DOS:

☐ The first character should be a letter.

☐ Remaining characters may be letters, digits, or underscore characters.

☐ Embedded spaces are not allowed.

■ Cautions

DOS does not require that the first character of a file name be a letter. Furthermore, the full legal character set for DOS file names includes a number of punctuation characters in addition to the underscore character. In many contexts, you may be tempted to take advantage of these more liberal rules in naming dBASE files, but the resulting names may lead to conflicts.

It is also wise to avoid using dBASE reserved words for file names, since the results can sometimes be unpredictable.

File types

Several dBASE commands (see table) create new files on the current disk. Nine different types ♦ of files (as identified by extension name 155♦) can be created, depending upon the command that has been performed. Normally, the user need specify only the first part of the file name 155★, which can be up to eight characters long; the three-character extension indicating the file's type is supplied by dBASE, although you can override dBASE's default extension by supplying your own.

Three of the nine types of dBASE files—.PRG, .TXT, and .FMT—are ASCII 28★ text files that can be transferred directly to other programs (word-processing 466★ and spreadsheet programs, for example) via DOS 133★. The rest are specific to dBASE, and must be modified before they can be transferred.

File type:	*Origin/purpose:*
Database file (.DBF) ♦	Developed from the CREATE 88★ command and opened for a dBASE session via the USE 454★ command.
Memo file (.DBT) ♦	Created when you actually begin entering text into a memo field 217★ of a database. *Must* always remain present on the same disk as the associated .DBF file: If the .DBT file is lost, the .DBF file is rendered unusable.
Index file (.NDX) ♦	Created for a database with the INDEX 176★ command and opened via the INDEX clause of the USE command or by the SET INDEX 372★ command.
Report-form file (.FRM) ♦	Developed from the MODIFY REPORT 226★ command and opened with the REPORT FORM 295★ command to create a formatted report from a database.
Label-form file (.LBL) ♦	Developed from the MODIFY LABEL 221★ command and opened with the LABEL FORM 195★ command to create formatted labels from a database.

(continued)

File type:	Origin/purpose:
Program file (.PRG) ◆	Created in the dBASE word processor (accessed by the MODIFY COMMAND 219★ statement), or any other text editor or word processor that yields ASCII text files, and opened and executed via the DO 122★ command.
Format file (.FMT) ◆	Created in the dBASE word processor, or some other text editor such as SED 316★, and opened with the SET FORMAT TO 365★ command. Redesigns the screen format of dBASE's built-in full-screen editing and input commands. If created in the dBASE word processor, the resulting file must be renamed 291◆ with an .FMT extension (or you must specify the .PRG extension explicitly when *using* the file), since MODIFY COMMAND normally adds the .PRG extension.
Memory file (.MEM) ◆	Created by the SAVE 309★ command and read back into the computer's active memory by the RESTORE 298★ command. Saves variables and their values for use in future dBASE sessions.
Alternate file (.TXT) ◆	Created by the SET ALTERNATE 326★ command. Stores a dialogue sequence from a dBASE session in an ASCII text file that can then be transferred to a word-processing program or edited in the dBASE word processor. (The output from the REPORT FORM and LABEL FORM commands can also be directed to an ASCII text file.)
SDF and delimited files (.TXT) ◆	Created via the COPY 82★ command to store database files in ASCII text format, to facilitate data transfer from dBASE to other programs.

To use any of these files during a dBASE session, just type the file name after the appropriate command. It is not generally necessary to include the type extension (see *Format file* above, however).

FILE()

■ Structure
FILE("file_name")

■ Description
The FILE() function returns a logical value 99◆, .T. or .F., indicating whether or not the specified file exists on disk. The argument of FILE() must be a string value 98◆ indicating the complete file name, *including the extension* 155◆ (optional disk 343◆ and path 250◆ locations may also be included, as needed). The argument may take the form of a literal string value, a string variable, or a concatenation 65★.

■ Usage
The FILE() function is particularly useful in a program that needs to confirm the existence of a file before trying to open 454◆ it, since a program that tries to open a file that does not exist will terminate with an error message. For example, in the following passage, a program called *Saleprog* is called from the dot-prompt 62◆ level. It attempts to open a database file called *Junsales*, but the file does not exist. Here is what happens:

```
. DO Saleprog
File does not exist
              ?
USE Junsales
Called from - B:Saleprog.prg
Terminate command file? (Y/N) Yes
Do cancelled
    .
```

■ Program example
The FILE() function allows a program to anticipate a missing file, and to take appropriate alternate action. The following program, called *Mnthfile*, presents a simple example. Its task is to search for a monthly sales file, and display it on the screen if it exists.

A special system has been devised for naming the monthly files that this program will look for: The first three letters of each monthly file consist of the first letters of the current month itself; the remainder of the file name is *SALES.DBF*. So, for example, the file for June is called *JUNSALES.DBF*.

Notice how *Mnthfile* determines this month's file name and then searches for the designated file:

```
*---------------------------------------------- MNTHFILE.PRG
* Searches for this month's sales file, and lists
*    it if it exists.
*

SET TALK OFF

fname = SUBST(CMONTH(DATE()), 1, 3) + "SALES.DBF"

IF FILE(fname)
    USE &fname
    ? "Here is", UPPER(fname), ":"
    ?
    DISPLAY ALL
ELSE
    ? UPPER(fname), "does not exist."
ENDIF

SET TALK ON
RETURN
```

The CMONTH() **58★** and DATE() **103★** functions are used to find the name of the current month, and the SUBSTR() **423★** function then reduces the name to its first three letters:

```
fname = SUBST(CMONTH(DATE()), 1, 3) + "SALES.DBF"
```

The entire file name is assigned to the string variable *fname*. This variable is then used as the argument of the FILE() function in the expression *IF FILE(fname)*. If the program finds the file, the database is opened and displayed. Otherwise, if the file does not exist, this type of message is displayed on the screen:

```
JUNSALES.DBF does not exist.
```

- **Caution**
  If you forget to include the file name's extension in the argument of FILE(), you may be fooled into thinking that the file does not exist: FILE() requires the *entire* name.

- **dBASE II equivalent**
  FILE()

- **Comment**
  If you wish to examine all or part of the contents of a disk, use the DIR **114★** command. DIR allows wildcard characters **114◆** to designate certain groups of files, whereas FILE() does not.

FIND

■ **Structure**

FIND character_value
FIND numeric_value

■ **Description**

The FIND command searches through the key field **194★** of an *indexed* **176◆** database for a specified string or numeric value. The record pointer **258◆** will be moved to the first record in which the value is found.

If the specified value is not found in the database (and SET TALK **398★** is ON), the message *"No find"* will be displayed on the screen and the EOF() **147★** function will be set to true.

■ **Usage**

FIND always begins its search at the first record in the indexed database, and continues until the specified value is found or the end of the file is encountered.

■ **Database example**

The example presented here uses a client-billing database from a (fictitious) law firm. This database, called *Lawfirm*, is indexed by client names into an index file called *Cliname*:

```
. USE Lawfirm INDEX Cliname
. LIST
Record#  DEPARTMENT  CLIENT           AMOUNT  BILLING_DT  PAYMENT_DT
      5  Litigation  Acme Co.        4988.89  10/01/84    11/30/84
      4  Corporate   BBB Corporation 2113.20  09/15/84    11/01/84
      7  Labor Law   Doe Properties   733.28  11/01/84    01/15/85
      6  Litigation  Expo Ltd.       3889.21  10/15/84    01/20/85
      3  Labor Law   MultiGlom, Inc.  521.55  09/01/84    09/15/84
      2  Corporate   SuperTek Co.    1872.42  09/01/84    11/15/84
      1  Litigation  XYZ Enterprises 2593.88  08/15/84    12/05/84
.
```

The following FIND command searches for one of the firm's clients, using the client's full name:

```
. FIND Expo Ltd.
. DISPLAY
Record#  DEPARTMENT  CLIENT        AMOUNT BILLING_DT PAYMENT_DT
      6  Litigation  Expo Ltd.    3889.21 10/15/84   01/20/85

.
```

Notice that a successful search displays no message on the screen: To examine the record that has been found, you must issue a DISPLAY **116★** command. Also, note that the target string is not enclosed in quotation marks in the preceding command: FIND requires string delimiters **98♦** only when the target-string value contains leading blank characters.

Unless SET EXACT **355★** is ON (see *Cautions*), you do not need to supply the entire string value for FIND to be successful:

```
. FIND Super
. DISPLAY
Record#  DEPARTMENT  CLIENT          AMOUNT BILLING_DT PAYMENT_DT
      2  Corporate   SuperTek Co.   1872.42 09/01/84   11/15/84

.
```

Here is what happens when the target value is not found in the database (assuming SET TALK is ON):

```
. FIND Smith
No find
.
```

■ **Cautions**

As we've just discussed, SET EXACT is normally OFF (the default), and FIND accepts a partial string value. However, if the SET EXACT status is ON, you must supply the complete target-string value in order to perform a successful FIND:

```
. SET EXACT OFF
. FIND BBB
. DISPLAY
Record#  DEPARTMENT  CLIENT              AMOUNT BILLING_DT PAYMENT_DT
       4  Corporate   BBB Corporation 2113.20 09/15/84   11/01/84
.
```

```
. SET EXACT ON
. FIND BBB
No find
.
```

```
. FIND BBB Corporation
. DISPLAY
Record#  DEPARTMENT   CLIENT              AMOUNT BILLING_DT PAYMENT_DT
     4   Corporate    BBB Corporation    2113.20 09/15/84   11/01/84
.
```

Obviously, it is important that you know whether SET EXACT is ON or OFF when you use the FIND command: You can use either DISPLAY STATUS **119★** or SET **325★** to check on this before you begin a search.

Even with SET EXACT OFF, upper/lowercase letters are evaluated by FIND. For example, "Expo" and "expo" are never considered equivalent.

■ dBASE II equivalent
FIND

■ Comments
The SEEK **317★** and LOCATE...CONTINUE **202★ 72★** commands also search for specific values in the current database.

Within a program, the correct way to check for an unsuccessful search is to test the EOF() function.

FOR

■ **Structure**

... FOR condition_clause ...

■ **Description**

FOR is one of two optional condition clauses 312◆ available for use with some database commands (the other is WHILE 463★). A condition clause selects certain records within the default or specified scope 312★, and only those records are acted upon by the command that contains the clause. To be selected, a record must meet the condition expressed in the clause: That is, the condition expression must be true for the record in question.

The FOR clause causes the command in which it is included to begin executing at the first record in the database and continue forward sequentially through the last record, selecting and working on those records that meet the expressed condition.

■ **Usage**

A command that contains a FOR clause begins by moving the record pointer 258★ to the first record in the database. If you test the EOF() 147★ function when the action of the command is complete, it will return a value of true.

■ **Database example**

The examples in this entry use the database called *Staff*, which contains information about a group of employees:

```
. USE Staff
. LIST
Record#  DEPARTMENT  LASTNAME    FIRSTNAME  HIRED     YRS   EMP_ID  SALARY_MO
       1  Production  Morris      John       11/03/82  2.5   4521    1850.00
       2  Marketing   Southby     Anne       08/22/81  3.7   3134    2315.00
       3  Clerical    Peters      Larry      06/10/83  1.9   3412    1350.00
       4  Clerical    Broussard   Marie      05/05/81  4.0   8712    1275.00
       5  Production  James       Fred       02/22/77  8.2   6563    1675.00
       6  Marketing   Smith       June       03/29/80  5.1   6823    2475.00
       7  Clerical    Liles       Carter     09/29/77  7.6   8799    1400.00
       8  Production  Washington  Liz        11/05/74 10.5   7321    1700.00
       9  Clerical    Ludlum      Donald     03/30/77  8.1   7412    1250.00
.
```

In the first of the next three examples, the FOR clause selects all the employees in the Marketing Department. In the second, it selects all employees who were hired before January 1, 1980, and in the third it selects employees whose salaries exceed $2,000 per month:

```
. DISPLAY FOR department = "Marketing"
Record# DEPARTMENT   LASTNAME    FIRSTNAME  HIRED     YRS  EMP_ID SALARY_MO
     2  Marketing    Southby     Anne       08/22/81  3.7    3134  2315.00
     6  Marketing    Smith       June       03/29/80  5.1    6823  2475.00

.
```

```
. DISPLAY FOR hired < CTOD("01/01/80")
Record# DEPARTMENT   LASTNAME    FIRSTNAME  HIRED     YRS  EMP_ID SALARY_MO
     5  Production    James       Fred       02/22/77  8.2    6563  1675.00
     7  Clerical      Liles       Carter     09/29/77  7.6    8799  1400.00
     8  Production    Washington  Liz        11/05/74 10.5    7321  1700.00
     9  Clerical      Ludlum      Donald     03/30/77  8.1    7412  1250.00

.
```

```
. DISPLAY FOR salary_mo > 2000
Record# DEPARTMENT   LASTNAME    FIRSTNAME  HIRED     YRS  EMP_ID SALARY_MO
     2  Marketing    Southby     Anne       08/22/81  3.7    3134  2315.00
     6  Marketing    Smith       June       03/29/80  5.1    6823  2475.00

.
```

The following two examples illustrate the use of the logical operators 207★ .OR. and .AND. to create compound conditions in FOR clauses. The first command displays all employees who are in either the Marketing Department *or* the Production Department and the second uses the .AND. operator to select employees who are in the Clerical Department and have salaries less than $1,300 per month:

```
. DISPLAY FOR department = "Marketing" .OR. department = "Production"
Record#  DEPARTMENT   LASTNAME     FIRSTNAME  HIRED      YRS  EMP_ID  SALARY_MO
      1  Production   Morris       John       11/03/82   2.5   4521    1850.00
      2  Marketing    Southby      Anne       08/22/81   3.7   3134    2315.00
      5  Production   James        Fred       02/22/77   8.2   6563    1675.00
      6  Marketing    Smith        June       03/29/80   5.1   6823    2475.00
      8  Production   Washington   Liz        11/05/74  10.5   7321    1700.00
.
```

```
. DISPLAY FOR department = "Clerical" .AND. salary_mo < 1300
Record#  DEPARTMENT   LASTNAME     FIRSTNAME  HIRED      YRS  EMP_ID  SALARY_MO
      4  Clerical     Broussard    Marie      05/05/81   4.0   8712    1275.00
      9  Clerical     Ludlum       Donald     03/30/77   8.1   7412    1250.00
.
```

■ **Caution**

The FOR clause sets the default scope to ALL 17★. To examine only those records within a specific scope, you must explicitly express that scope in the command:

```
. DISPLAY NEXT 5 FOR salary_mo < 1500
```

This statement checks the next five records, starting with the current one, and displays only those that have a value less than 1500 in the *salary_mo* field.

■ **dBASE II equivalent**

FOR

■ **Comments**

The following database commands take an optional condition clause (FOR or WHILE): AVERAGE **31★**, CHANGE **48★**, COPY TO **82★**, COUNT **85★**, DELETE **106★**, DISPLAY **116★**, JOIN **189★**, LABEL FORM **195★**, LIST **200★**, LOCATE **202★**, RECALL **278★**, REPLACE **291★**, REPORT FORM **295★**, SORT **402★**, SUM **426★**, and TOTAL **436★**.

Function keys

The 10 function keys—F1 to F10—located at the left side of the IBM Personal Computer keyboard are preprogrammed in dBASE to issue selected commands at a single keystroke. The default settings of the function keys are:

Key:	Command:
F1	HELP; **170★**
F2	ASSIST; **28★**
F3	LIST; **200★**
F4	DIR; **114★**
F5	DISPLAY STRUCTURE; **121★**
F6	DISPLAY STATUS; **119★**
F7	DISPLAY MEMORY; **118★**
F8	DISPLAY; **116★**
F9	APPEND; **19★**
F10	EDIT; **141★**

The semicolon at the end of each setting means that a carriage return is also issued at the end of the command.

Except for F1 (which always remains the HELP key), you can change these default settings in any of three ways:

☐ During a dBASE session, you can use the SET FUNCTION **368★** command to make a temporary change in a function-key setting. You must issue a separate SET FUNCTION command for each key you want to reset. These changes will remain in effect until you make other changes, or until you end the current session with dBASE. The next time you start dBASE, the keys will be back to their default settings.

☐ During a dBASE session, you can use the SET **325★** command, which invokes a full-screen assist mode for changing the dBASE III control parameters **73★**. Select the Keys option, and then enter new function-key values into the templates provided on the screen.

☐ You can use the *CONFIG.DB* **66★** file to make a "permanent" change in a function-key setting. Each time you start a new session with dBASE, the computer checks for the *CONFIG.DB* file on the program disk and, if it exists, uses the information stored in it to change the default dBASE settings, including the function-key values. Thus, if you store new function-key settings in this file, the keys will take on your specified values each time you start dBASE.

Many programmers like to define DO **122★** commands for function keys, so that programs they use often can be performed with one keystroke. For example, you might assign the following value to the F10 key:

```
DO Menu;
```

Henceforth, whenever you want to run the *Menu* program, you can just press F10.

If you want to be able to enter data after a function-key command—a file name or record number, perhaps—omit the semicolon and leave a blank space:

```
EDIT RECORD
```

Then you can press the function key, supply the missing information, press Return, and the command will be executed.

The DISPLAY STATUS **119★** command displays the current settings of all the function keys, as does the SET command's Keys option.

GOTO

■ **Structure**
GOTO numeric_expression
GO*TO* TOP
GO*TO* BOTTOM

■ **Description**
The GOTO or GO command (the TO is optional) repositions the record pointer **258★** of the currently selected **322◆** database to a specified record **284★**. If the parameter of GOTO is a numeric value, the pointer is placed at the corresponding record number. If the parameter is TOP ◆, GOTO sends the record pointer to the first record in the file: record 1 if the database is not indexed **176◆**, or the first record in the index, if one is in use. GOTO BOTTOM ◆ sends the pointer to the last record in the file: either the last physical record, or the last record in the index.

■ **Usage**
A number of database commands display information from, or perform operations on, the current record in the database. For this reason, it is important to be able to move the record pointer quickly and easily. The GOTO statement is designed to provide this capability.

dBASE also allows you to simply enter the number of the record to which you would like to move the pointer, without using GOTO:

```
. 5
```

However, for the sake of clarity, it is better to use the full GOTO command when moving the pointer from within a program:

```
GOTO 5
```

■ **dBASE II equivalent**
GOTO
GOTO TOP
GOTO BOTTOM

■ **Comments**
Several other dBASE commands relate to the position of the record pointer. For instance, the SET RELATION **390★** command establishes a relation between the pointers in two open databases, and the SKIP **400★** command moves the pointer up or down the database in specified jumps. The RECNO() **279★** function supplies the number of the current record.

HELP

- **Structure**

  HELP *dBASE_command*

- **Description**

  The HELP command initiates dBASE's on-line help facility ♦. Help comes in one of two forms: menu-driven or direct. If you type HELP with no parameter, you will enter a menu-driven help mode that provides screens of both general and specific information about the dBASE program and all its commands. Alternatively, you can enter HELP along with the name of a specific command or function that you would like to read about, and dBASE will instantly supply a screenful of information about this one command.

- **Usage**

  The F1 function key is permanently programmed to issue the HELP command in dBASE. Pressing F1 is therefore a fast way to move into the menu-driven help mode.

  The help facility is particularly useful when you just want to review the syntax of one particular command. For example, the command

```
.  HELP JOIN
```

  will show you the complete syntax of the JOIN command.

- **Cautions**

  The help facility is stored in the file *HELP.DBS* on the program disk. If for some reason you remove this file from your working copy of the program, you will not be able to use the help facility.

  HELP is not the same as ASSIST **28★**. ASSIST is a menu-driven program that actually builds and performs dBASE commands for you. HELP simply offers information about the commands. Most dBASE III users ultimately outgrow ASSIST, but HELP remains important even to advanced users.

- **dBASE II equivalent**

  HELP

- **Comment**

  If you make a syntactical error when you are entering a command, dBASE will immediately *offer* help (unless you have SET HELP OFF **371★**). If you accept the offer, you will be dropped directly into the help facility.

IF...ENDIF

■ **Structure**

IF condition_expression
      command_list
ELSE
      command_list
ENDIF

■ **Description**

The IF...ELSE...ENDIF structure expresses alternate courses of action in a dBASE program. During program performance, a decision is made about the course of action, based upon the value (true or false) of the condition expression 286♦ in the IF statement.

An IF structure can be written with or without an ELSE 146★ statement, but an ENDIF is *required* in either case, to mark the end of the decision structure.

Without an ELSE statement, the IF structure works as follows:

☐ If the condition is true, all of the commands located between IF and ENDIF are performed, and the program then continues from the first command after ENDIF.

☐ If the condition is false, none of the commands located between IF and ENDIF is performed, and control passes immediately to the first command after ENDIF.

An IF decision structure that does include an ELSE statement is processed as follows:

☐ If the condition is true, all of the commands located between IF and ELSE are performed, and control then passes to the first command located after ENDIF.

☐ If the condition is false, all of the commands located between ELSE and ENDIF are performed, and the program then continues from the first command after ENDIF.

■ **Usage**

The IF condition may be any expression that evaluates to true or false, including a relation (a comparison expressed with one of the relational operators 286★), a logical-type 99♦ variable, or a function that returns a value of true or false.

171

■ **Program example**

The *Sale* procedure is part of the real-estate program described in the SET PROCE-
DURE 383★ entry. The program manages a real-estate database called *Property*, which
contains listings of houses that are for sale. *Sale* allows the realtor to revise certain
fields of a selected listing: record a change in the asking price, enter a new or different
bid, and, eventually, record the sale of the house. Here is a sample dialogue from this
procedure:

```
Address:  12345 26th Avenue
Owner:    Andrea Fine
Asking:   $149,000.00
Bid:       $136,500.00
Still available.

==========================================

Change the asking price?  N
      149000.00

Change the current bid?   N

Has the house sold?       N
```

The *Sale* procedure contains several examples of the IF structure:

```
PROCEDURE Sale
*----- Records a bid, a change in the asking price, or sale of a house.
*

CLEAR
? "          *** Record a bid or sale on a home. ***"
?
?
DO Get_rec
IF EOF()
    RETURN
ENDIF
```

(continued)

```
CLEAR
@ 2, 10 SAY "Address:  " + address
@ 3, 10 SAY "Owner:      " + TRIM(owner_f) + " " + owner_l
@ 4, 10 SAY asking_pr PICTURE "Asking:   $###,###.##"
@ 5, 10 SAY "Bid:"

IF cur_bid = 0
    @ 5, 20 SAY "None"
ELSE
    @ 5, 20 SAY cur_bid PICTURE "$###,###.##"
ENDIF

IF .NOT. sold
    @ 6, 10 SAY "Still available."
ELSE
    @ 6, 10 SAY sale_price PICTURE "Sold at:  $###,###.##"
    @ 7, 10 SAY "On:         " + DTOC(sale_date)
ENDIF

@ 8, 10 SAY "========================================="
?

IF sold
    WAIT "             Press any key to continue. "
    RETURN
ENDIF

DO Yesno WITH 10, 10, "Change the asking price? "
IF yn
    @ 11, 15 GET asking_pr
    READ
ENDIF

DO Yesno WITH 13, 10, "Change the current bid?  "
IF yn
    @ 14, 15 GET cur_bid
    READ
ENDIF

DO Yesno WITH 16, 10, "Has the house sold?      "
IF yn
    REPLACE sold WITH .T.
    @ 17, 15 SAY "Price? " GET sale_price
    READ

    DO Yesno WITH 18, 15, "Today? "
    IF yn
        REPLACE sale_date WITH DATE()
    ELSE
        @ 19, 15 SAY "When?  " GET sale_date
        READ
    ENDIF

ENDIF

RETURN
```

The IF statements in this procedure set up a rather complex web of decisions, the outcome of which depends upon both information that is entered from the keyboard during the dialogue and information that is stored in the selected database record. We'll examine three of these decisions here.

The procedure's first required action is to determine which database record it is going to work with. To do this, it calls upon another procedure called *Get_rec*, which elicits an address from the keyboard and searches in the database for that address. (*Get_rec* is listed and discussed under the entry for SEEK **317★**.) If *Get_rec* does not find the user-specified address, it leaves the record pointer **258★** positioned at the end of the file.

When control returns from *Get_rec* to *Sale*, *Sale* must find out whether or not a record has been located, so it uses the EOF() **147★** function to check the pointer position:

```
DO Get_rec
IF EOF()
     RETURN
ENDIF
```

EOF() returns a value of true if the record pointer is at the end of the file. In that case, *Sale* has no reason to continue, so it simply returns control to the main section of the real-estate program. However, if a specific record has been located, *Sale* displays its address, owner's name, asking price, current bid, and sale status on the screen.

The next IF structure determines whether or not there is a current bid, and displays an appropriate message on the screen:

```
IF cur_bid = 0
    @ 5, 20 SAY "None"
ELSE
    @ 5, 20 SAY cur_bid PICTURE "$###,###.##"
ENDIF
```

If the *cur_bid* field contains a value of zero, there is no bid pending; however, rather than place the 0 on the screen, the procedure displays the word message "None". If *cur_bid* contains a nonzero value, the value is displayed as the current bid.

```
Bid:      None
```

```
Bid:      $135,000.00
```

After displaying the current information from the record on the screen, the procedure gives the user a chance to make changes. The final IF structure in the procedure deals with a change in the sale status:

```
DO Yesno WITH 16, 10, "Has the house sold?        "
IF yn
    REPLACE sold WITH .T.
    @ 17, 15 SAY "Price? " GET sale_price
    READ

    DO Yesno WITH 18, 15, "Today? "
    IF yn
        REPLACE sale_date WITH DATE()
    ELSE
        @ 19, 15 SAY "When?   " GET sale_date
        READ
    ENDIF

ENDIF
```

If the house has sold, the logical field *sold* receives a value of .T., and the procedure elicits values for *sale_price* and *sale_date*. For *sale_date*, *Sale* is prepared to enter either today's date (DATE() **103**★) or a date entered from the keyboard.

The preceding passage illustrates a nested IF structure—that is, one structure contained within another. The first decision concerns the sale status of the house; the second determines how the sale date will be entered into the database, if the house has been sold. (Note that the *Yesno* procedure is designed to ask a yes-or-no question and return the response as a logical value in the variable *yn*. You can read about *Yesno* under the PARAMETERS **245**★ entry.)

■ **Caution**

Nesting of any programming structure must always be carefully engineered. In the case of a nested IF, the *entire* nested structure—IF, optional ELSE, and ENDIF—must be located inside the structure that contains it. Notice that the nesting example in *Sale* ends with *two* ENDIF statements: one for the inner IF and one for the outer IF. (Indentation in the program listing, although optional, is an excellent way to make such nested structures clear and readable.)

■ **dBASE II equivalent**

IF...ELSE...ENDIF

■ **Comment**

You can use the remainder of the line after an ENDIF statement for program comments **4♦**. You particularly might want to use such comment lines to reduce possible confusion in a nested structure like the one in the preceding example:

```
IF yn
     * ... *
     IF yn
          * ... *
     ELSE
          * ... *
     ENDIF  --> Date input
ENDIF  --> Sale status
```

INDEX

■ **Structure**

INDEX ON field_expression TO file_name

■ **Description**

The INDEX command sorts the currently selected **322♦** database by creating an index file, which is stored on disk under the specified file name, with an .NDX extension. Under the control of the index ♦, the records of the database appear in a sorted order.

Unlike the SORT **402★** command, INDEX does not physically rearrange the database itself. Also, INDEX sorts only in ascending order. (See the Sorting **406★** entry for a more detailed discussion of the differences between INDEX and SORT.)

INDEX can sort a database on multiple key fields **194★**. The keys may include any combination of character, numeric, and/or date-type fields, provided the appropriate type-conversion functions are included (see *Usage*). (Logical **99♦** and memo fields cannot be used in keys.)

You can open an existing index file with either the USE **454★** or the SET INDEX **372★** command.

■ Usage

The field expression in the INDEX command permits considerable versatility in the structuring of indexes. The expression may consist of a single field name, an expression joining two or more fields, and/or an expression involving a calculation. For example, by concatenating 65★ two or more fields in the key expression, you can sort a database on multiple fields.

■ Database examples

The following examples are from a database used by the Billing Department of a (fictitious) law firm. The *Lawfirm* database contains client-billing information from three departments: Litigation, Corporate, and Labor Law. The database shows the name of each client billed by a given department, the amount billed, the invoice date, and the payment date. Here is a selection from the unsorted database:

```
. USE Lawfirm
. LIST
Record#  DEPARTMENT  CLIENT            AMOUNT  BILLING_DT  PAYMENT_DT
      1  Litigation  XYZ Enterprises  2593.88  08/15/84    12/05/84
      2  Corporate   SuperTek Co.     1872.42  09/01/84    11/15/84
      3  Labor Law   MultiGlom, Inc.   521.55  09/01/84    09/15/84
      4  Corporate   BBB Corporation  2113.20  09/15/84    11/01/84
      5  Litigation  Acme Co.         4988.89  10/01/84    11/30/84
      6  Litigation  Expo Ltd.        3889.21  10/15/84    01/20/85
      7  Labor Law   Doe Properties    733.28  11/01/84    01/15/85
.
```

The firm needs to rearrange this database in several different ways, to suit various accounting requirements. First, they need an index that sorts the database by *department* (primary key), and then by *client* (secondary key) within each department:

```
. INDEX ON department + client TO Client
      7 records indexed
. LIST
Record#  DEPARTMENT  CLIENT            AMOUNT  BILLING_DT  PAYMENT_DT
      4  Corporate   BBB Corporation  2113.20  09/15/84    11/01/84
      2  Corporate   SuperTek Co.     1872.42  09/01/84    11/15/84
      7  Labor Law   Doe Properties    733.28  11/01/84    01/15/85
      3  Labor Law   MultiGlom, Inc.   521.55  09/01/84    09/15/84
      5  Litigation  Acme Co.         4988.89  10/01/84    11/30/84
      6  Litigation  Expo Ltd.        3889.21  10/15/84    01/20/85
      1  Litigation  XYZ Enterprises  2593.88  08/15/84    12/05/84
.
```

Then, they need an index that sorts the database by *department* (primary key) and *amount* (secondary key). In the preceding example, the two keys were both character fields, but when the multiple keys are of mixed types, you must deal with an additional problem: All key values must be converted to strings during the indexing process. Because *amount* is a numeric field, the STR() **416★** function must be used to convert *amount* to a string, for concatenation in the key expression for this new index:

```
. INDEX ON department + STR(amount, 7, 2) TO Amount
     7 records indexed
. LIST department, amount, client
Record#  department   amount client
       2  Corporate   1872.42 SuperTek Co.
       4  Corporate   2113.20 BBB Corporation
       3  Labor Law    521.55 MultiGlom, Inc.
       7  Labor Law    733.28 Doe Properties
       1  Litigation  2593.88 XYZ Enterprises
       6  Litigation  3889.21 Expo Ltd.
       5  Litigation  4988.89 Acme Co.

.
```

Yet another problem arises when one of the multiple keys is a date-type field: the order in which dBASE reads the resulting string. This problem is discussed in detail under *Caution*.

The INDEX command can also create an index based on a *calculated* key value. In this case, the key itself does not exist as an individual field in the database (nor is it created as a field in the index), but is only calculated during the indexing process. For example, the following command indexes the *Lawfirm* database on the number of days elapsed between billing and payment. The key value is calculated as the difference between two dates (see Date Arithmetic **100★**):

```
. INDEX ON billing_dt - payment_dt TO Paid
      7 records indexed
. LIST
Record#  DEPARTMENT  CLIENT           AMOUNT BILLING_DT PAYMENT_DT
      1  Litigation  XYZ Enterprises 2593.88 08/15/84   12/05/84
      6  Litigation  Expo Ltd.       3889.21 10/15/84   01/20/85
      2  Corporate   SuperTek Co.    1872.42 09/01/84   11/15/84
      7  Labor Law   Doe Properties   733.28 11/01/84   01/15/85
      5  Litigation  Acme Co.        4988.89 10/01/84   11/30/84
      4  Corporate   BBB Corporation 2113.20 09/15/84   11/01/84
      3  Labor Law   MultiGlom, Inc.  521.55 09/01/84   09/15/84

. LIST client, payment_dt - billing_dt
Record#  client             payment_dt - billing_dt
      1  XYZ Enterprises                       112
      6  Expo Ltd.                              97
      2  SuperTek Co.                           75
      7  Doe Properties                         75
      5  Acme Co.                               60
      4  BBB Corporation                        47
      3  MultiGlom, Inc.                        14
```

If you study this example closely, you will see that an interesting trick has occurred: The database appears to have been indexed in *descending* order, even though we know that INDEX works exclusively in *ascending* order. Here is how it was done: The calculated key in this INDEX command (*billing_dt – payment_dt*) was guaranteed to produce negative numbers, and an ascending sort on negative numbers yields an order that approaches zero. The subsequent LIST **200★** command reverses the order of the fields (*payment_dt – billing_dt*) and thus produces the positive equivalents of those same numbers.

■ **Caution**

In order to include a date-type field as one of the multiple keys of an INDEX command, the date must first be converted to a string value. The DTOC() **139★** function can be used for this purpose, as in the following example:

```
. INDEX ON department + DTOC(payment_dt) TO Payment
       7 records indexed
.
```

However, under the standard date format **337◆**, mo/da/yr, this INDEX command will fail to sort the database properly:

```
. LIST department, payment_dt
Record#  department  payment_dt
      4  Corporate   11/01/84
      2  Corporate   11/15/84
      7  Labor Law   01/15/85
      3  Labor Law   09/15/84
      6  Litigation  01/20/85
      5  Litigation  11/30/84
      1  Litigation  12/05/84
.
```

You can see that the dates of the three payments to the Litigation Department do not appear in correct chronological order. The problem is the order of elements in the standard date format: When you convert a date to a string, the indexing operation will work first on the month, then on the day, and finally on the year.

For a character date to be sorted properly, the date should be in yr/mo/da format. Fortunately, dBASE allows you to select this very format, called ANSI, through the SET DATE **337★** command:

```
. SET DATE ANSI
```

If you change the date format to ANSI before issuing the INDEX command, the indexing will work properly:

```
. INDEX ON department + DTOC(payment_dt) TO Payment
       7 records indexed
. LIST department, payment_dt
Record#  department  payment_dt
      4  Corporate   84.11.01
      2  Corporate   84.11.15
      3  Labor Law   84.09.15
      7  Labor Law   85.01.15
      5  Litigation  84.11.30
      1  Litigation  84.12.05
      6  Litigation  85.01.20
    .
```

■ **dBASE II equivalent**
INDEX

■ **Comments**
When you make a change in an indexed database—for example, adding new records, deleting records, or editing values in the key field—dBASE automatically updates the index. Furthermore, the USE and SET INDEX commands both allow you to open as many as seven indexes at a time for a given database; when changes occur, all open indexes will be updated.

If you make changes to the database at a time when an index is not open, you can update the index later with the REINDEX 284★ command.

Several dBASE commands can be used only with indexed files (see the entries for SET RELATION 390★, FIND 160★, and SEEK 317★).

INPUT

■ **Structure**

INPUT *prompt_string* TO variable_name

■ **Description**

The INPUT command controls an interactive dialogue between the current dBASE program and the user at the keyboard. INPUT displays an optional prompt on the screen, and waits for the user to enter a value from the keyboard. After the user enters the value and presses the Return key, the value is stored in the specified variable.

INPUT can accept any type **98♦** of value or legal expression from the keyboard. If an expression is entered, it is first evaluated and the *result* is then stored in the variable.

The variable specified in the INPUT statement need not be initialized in advance: INPUT can define a new variable. The type of the resulting variable will match the type of the value that was entered from the keyboard.

Character values entered in response to an INPUT prompt must be enclosed in delimiters (single quotes, double quotes, or square brackets).

■ **Usage**

Since INPUT accepts any type of value, a program will often require some way to test the type of the resulting variable before proceeding. The following program, called *Typetest*, illustrates the use of INPUT, and also suggests a way of performing a type test by using the TYPE() **445★** function:

```
*---------------------------------------------- TYPETEST.PRG
* Uses the TYPE() function to test the data type
*    of an INPUT value.
*

SET TALK OFF
?

DO WHILE .T.
    INPUT "Enter any type of expression: " TO var
    ?
    ?? "==> "
    t = TYPE("var")
    DO CASE
        CASE t = "C"
            ?? "character value: "
        CASE t = "N"
            ?? "numeric value: "
```

(continued)

```
        CASE t = "D"
            ?? "date value: "
        CASE t = "L"
            ?? "logical value: "
    ENDCASE
    ?? var
    ?
ENDDO

SET TALK ON
RETURN
```

The program accepts a value or expression from the keyboard, displays the value's type—character, numeric, date, or logical—and then displays the value itself. In order to enable the user to repeat the exercise, this activity all takes place within an endless loop (to end the program, press the Escape key). Here is a sample run:

```
. DO Typetest

Enter any type of expression: DATE()
==) date value: 07/28/85

Enter any type of expression: 19 - 14 = 4
==) logical value: .F.

Enter any type of expression: 45 ^ 5
==) numeric value:   184528125.00

Enter any type of expression: SUBSTR(CMONTH(DATE()), 1, 3)
==) character value: Jul

Enter any type of expression:
```

As you can see, INPUT accepts and evaluates any type of expression—even one that contains one or more dBASE functions or operations.

■ **Caution**
If the user merely presses the Return key in response to the INPUT statement, there will be no change in the status or value of the INPUT variable. If the variable already exists, its value will remain the same; if it does not yet exist, it will *not* be created.

■ **dBASE II equivalent**
INPUT

■ **Comments**

If an expression entered in response to an INPUT prompt is not a legal expression, dBASE will display an error message and request another input value, using the same prompt as before. For instance, in the following example, the input expression is missing its final parenthesis:

```
Enter any type of expression: SUBSTR(CMONTH(DATE()), 1, 3
Syntax error, try again:
Enter any type of expression:
```

The INPUT command and its counterpart, ACCEPT **12**★, are convenient, but rather informal, tools for accepting input from the keyboard. For greater control over both the prompt display and the input process, use the @...SAY...GET **9**★ command instead.

INSERT

■ **Structure**

INSERT *BLANK   BEFORE*

■ **Description**

The INSERT command moves you into a full-screen mode so that you can add a new record **282**★ to a database, just after the current position of the record pointer **258**★. The BEFORE clause, which is optional, permits you to insert the new record *before* the current position of the record pointer.

The INSERT BLANK command does not move you into full-screen mode, but simply inserts an empty record after (or before, if specified) the current position of the record pointer.

■ **Usage**

Normally, the INSERT command results in the addition of just one record at a time. However, if you use INSERT at the end of a database, you will be allowed to add multiple records. And in fact, if the database is indexed **176**◆, INSERT *always* appends records at the end of the file.

■ **Database example**

The following database, called *Furniture*, contains a list of items purchased to furnish and equip an office. The database is sorted **402**◆ by the *item* field.

```
. USE Furniture
. LIST
Record#  ITEM       PRICE  TAX
       1 Bookcase   89.99  5.85
       2 Chair      15.29  0.99
       3 Lamp       22.95  1.49
       4 Table      45.98  2.99
       5 Telephone  15.29  0.99
       6 Typewriter 99.95  6.50
.
```

Imagine that you want to add two items to this database: an armchair and a map. Since the database is already sorted, you would like to insert the records for these items in correct alphabetical order. Here is how you might proceed:

```
. GOTO 3
. INSERT BLANK
. GOTO 1
. INSERT BLANK BEFORE
. LIST
Record#  ITEM       PRICE  TAX
       1
       2 Bookcase   89.99  5.85
       3 Chair      15.29  0.99
       4 Lamp       22.95  1.49
       5
       6 Table      45.98  2.99
       7 Telephone  15.29  0.99
       8 Typewriter 99.95  6.50
.
```

With the two blank records inserted in the correct places, you can now enter the data, using either the BROWSE 38★ or the EDIT 141★ command. (Alternatively, you could have used the full-screen INSERT mode to create each record and filled in the data at the same time.)

■ **Caution**

When a new record is inserted within a database, dBASE automatically renumbers the existing records (see the preceding example).

■ **dBASE II equivalent**

INSERT

■ **Comment**

The APPEND 19★ and APPEND BLANK commands also allow you to add records, but only at the end of the current database.

INT()

■ **Structure**

INT(numeric_value)

■ **Description**

Given a real number, the INT() function returns the number's integral value. In other words, INT() truncates (without rounding) any digits located after the decimal point.

■ **Usage**

INT() can be used to supply an integer whenever the result of a numeric calculation includes undesired decimal digits. For example, the following commands calculate the straight-line yearly depreciation on an asset that has a 30-year useful life:

```
. value = 112000
. life = 30
. deprec = value / life
. ? deprec
     3733.33
.
```

Assuming that this dollar value does not need to include cents, the INT() function can be used to reduce the value to an integer:

```
. deprec = INT(deprec)
. ? deprec
     3733
.
```

INT() is also important in the dBASE formula for the arithmetic operation called *modulus*. This operation, often referred to simply as *mod*, results in the *remainder* from the division of two integers. Many programming languages include mod as one of their built-in arithmetic operations; dBASE does not. However, the following formula can be used as a replacement for the mod operator:

```
x mod y = x - y * INT(x / y)
```

The mod evaluation is useful whenever you need to determine whether or not one number is evenly divisible by another: That is, if *x mod y* produces a value of zero, then *x* is evenly divisible by *y*.

■ **Program example**

The following program, called *Groups*, illustrates the use of an INT() mod operation to solve a sampling problem. In this example, a personnel manager wishes to divide the company's employees into two groups, for a study of worker efficiency. He would like the groups to be randomly selected, or at least not based on any significant character-istics of the employees in the groups, so he decides to base the group assignment on the employee's birth date—specifically, the day of the month on which the employee was born. If the day is an even number, the employee will go into group A; if odd, group B.

The database the personnel manager is using is called *Employee*. Along with other information, it contains the fields *last_name*, *birthdate*, and *group*. The manager has written the *Groups* program to calculate the "random" group assignment and then place an A or a B in the *group* field of each record:

```
*---------------------------------------------------- GROUPS.PRG
* Divides employees into two study groups, A and B.
*

SET TALK OFF

USE Employee
GOTO TOP

DO WHILE .NOT. EOF()
    bday = DAY(birthdate)
    randval = bday - 2 * INT(bday / 2)
    IF randval = 0
        REPLACE group WITH "A"
    ELSE
        REPLACE group WITH "B"
    ENDIF
    SKIP
ENDDO

SET TALK ON
RETURN
```

The following commands from this program create two variables: *bday*, to hold a given employee's day of birth, and *randval*, to hold the calculated value of *bday mod 2*:

```
bday = DAY(birthdate)
randval = bday - 2 * INT(bday / 2)
```

After each evaluation, *randval* contains a value of 0 if the day is an even number, or 1 if the day is an odd number. Depending upon this value, a subsequent IF **171★** statement then makes the appropriate replacement in the *group* field.

Here are listings of the *Employee* database before and after the *Groups* program:

```
. USE Employee
. LIST last_name, birthdate, group
Record#  last_name  birthdate group
       1  Arden      05/23/47
       2  Birch      07/19/39
       3  Carr       12/18/56
       4  Dalton     02/26/51
       5  Harte      09/13/48
       6  Martin     11/24/57
   .
```

```
. DO Groups
. LIST last_name, birthdate, group
Record#  last_name  birthdate group
       1  Arden      05/23/47  B
       2  Birch      07/19/39  B
       3  Carr       12/18/56  A
       4  Dalton     02/26/51  A
       5  Harte      09/13/48  B
       6  Martin     11/24/57  A
   .
```

■ **dBASE II equivalent**

INT()

■ **Comment**

A ROUND() **302★** command is also available in dBASE, for rounding numbers up or down on a specified decimal place.

JOIN

■ Structure

JOIN WITH database TO file_name FOR condition_list   *FIELDS field_list*

■ Description

The JOIN command copies information from two databases that are currently open in separate work areas **454♦**, and saves the merged information in a new database file on disk. The two databases from which information will be copied are:

☐ The database that is currently selected **322♦** at the time the JOIN command is issued.

☐ The database referred to (by name or by alias **14★** in the WITH clause of the JOIN command.

The TO clause specifies a file name for the new database that will result. The FIELDS clause, which is optional, selects the fields **154★** that will be copied into the new file from the two open databases: In other words, FIELDS determines the ultimate file structure **100♦** of the newly created database. If the FIELDS clause is omitted, JOIN includes all fields from both databases.

With the structure thus determined, JOIN copies records **284★** of information into the new file from the two open databases. Potentially, JOIN can combine every record from the first database with every record from the second database, creating one new record for every possible combination. For example, if the first open database has 25 records and the second open database has 10 records, JOIN can create a new database that will contain up to 250 records. In most cases, however, you will want to include only a certain portion of these many combinations: The required FOR **164★** clause enables you to control the selection by expressing conditions that each record must meet in order to be included in the newly created database.

When the action of JOIN is complete, the new database will be stored on disk; however, JOIN does not open the database.

■ **Usage**

JOIN is a convenient way to merge data from two related files in a system of databases. For example, the following database, called *Bksales* ♦, belongs to the sales manager of an (imaginary) American bookstore chain. *Bksales* contains information about the chain's best-selling books. The database has the following six fields of information:

Field:	Contents:
book_num	A unique alphanumeric code for each book in the database.
author_num	A unique alphanumeric code for each author.
title	The title of the book.
unit_sales	The number of copies of the book sold to date.
pub_date	The date on which the book was published.
month_avg	The average monthly sales, in copies, since the book was published.

Here is a sample record entry from *Bksales*:

```
. DISPLAY
Record#  BOOK_NUM AUTHOR_NUM TITLE                  PUB_DATE UNIT_SALES MONTH_AVG
     1   N556     AU981      Images of Japan        12/15/83      81252      4548
.
```

The manager also keeps a sorted version of *Bksales*, called *Salesort*, in which the books are arranged in order of total copies sold, from high to low. (The SORT **402★** entry shows how *Salesort* was created.)

Since the *Bksales* and *Salesort* databases may well contain more than one book by a given author, the manager of the bookstore chain keeps author profiles in a second database called *Authors*. *Authors* and *Bksales* have one field in common: *author_num*. In addition, the *Authors* database has fields for the author's last name and first name (*last_name, first_name*), for the name of the publisher (*publisher*), and finally, a memo field **217★** that contains a short description of the author's career to date (*profile*). Here is a sample entry from the *Authors* database:

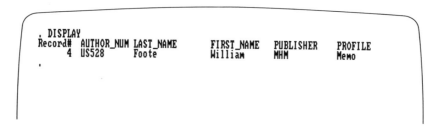

```
. DISPLAY
Record#  AUTHOR_NUM LAST_NAME    FIRST_NAME  PUBLISHER  PROFILE
     4   US528      Foote        William     MHM        Memo
.
```

From these databases, the manager can use the JOIN command to merge information about sales and authors, for selected titles, into a single database. The following passage shows how JOIN works. In this case, it creates a new file called *Top5* that contains information about only the top five best-sellers in the database. The example uses *Salesort* rather than *Bksales*, for reasons that will be clear when you examine the results:

```
. SELECT 1
. USE Salesort ALIAS Books
. SELECT 2
. USE Authors
. SELECT Books
. JOIN WITH Authors TO Top5 FOR RECNO() <= 5 .AND. ;
  author_num = B -> author_num FIELDS title, last_name, ;
  unit_sales, publisher
      5 records joined
.
```

The JOIN command is issued from work area 1, the location of the *Salesort* database. The WITH clause specifies *Authors* as the second open database, which will be merged with *Bksales* in the file *Top5*. The FOR clause contains two conditions:

```
RECNO() <= 5
author_num = B -> author_num
```

The first condition ensures that only the first five records of *Salesort* will be included in the merge operation: Since *Salesort* is arranged in order of sales, these first five records will be the top five best-sellers. The second condition matches books with authors. For each book title selected from *Salesort*, the corresponding author number will be located in *Authors* (*B -> author_num*).

Finally, the FIELDS clause of this JOIN statement specifies the four fields that will be included in the new database: the title of the book, the author's last name, the number of copies sold, and the publisher. The following commands open *Top5* in work area 3 and list the database:

```
. SELECT 3
. USE Top5
. LIST OFF
TITLE              LAST_NAME     UNIT_SALES PUBLISHER
Images of Japan    Barton           81252 MHM
The Perfect Cook   Harte            76835 Book House
Mountain Romance   Bloomfield       67646 Linton
Mystery of the East Bloomfield      66834 Linton
The Mission        Foote            65880 MHM
.
```

As you can see, the order of the records in the newly created database is the same as the order in the *first* of the two merged databases (*Salesort*, in this case).

■ **Cautions**

As you have already seen, the FIELDS clause of the JOIN command may include field names from both of the databases that are being merged. During the merge process, dBASE searches first in the currently selected database for each field listed in the FIELDS clause; if a field is not part of the structure of the current database, dBASE then searches for it in the database named in the WITH clause. Normally, you do not need to (and, in fact, should not try to) specify the alias of the file in which a field is included.

However, a special problem occurs when each of the two databases includes a field with the same name. Let's say, for example, that you are joining two databases, both of which have a field named *sales*. You want the newly formed database to include the *sales* fields from both databases. A reasonable approach seems to be to write a FIELDS clause in the JOIN command like this:

```
FIELDS sales, B -> sales
```

Unfortunately, however, dBASE III versions 1.0 and 1.10 will not accept the syntax *alias -> field_name* in the FIELDS clause. There is, in fact, no way for you to include both *sales* fields in the new database without renaming one of them. Version 1.11 corrects this problem, however, by allowing the necessary *alias -> field_name* syntax.

The JOIN command does not work gracefully with memo fields. In the *Salesort and Authors* example, we did not try to include the memo field *profile* in the new database. If we had, the field itself would have been included structurally, but none of its data would have been copied from the *Authors* database. So, if the database that you specify in the WITH clause contains a memo field, don't expect to be able to use JOIN to merge that field successfully into a new database. (See the SET RELATION 390★ entry for an alternate approach to working with multiple databases and memo fields.)

Unfortunately, there is an even more serious problem associated with JOIN and memo fields: If the currently selected database in a JOIN operation (that is, the database that is selected when the JOIN command is issued) contains a memo field, the new database that JOIN creates will be unusable—*whether or not* you include the memo field in the FIELDS clause. Consider the following example, which attempts to create a database file named *Abook*, containing a list of authors and their books:

```
. SELECT 1
. USE Authors
. SELECT 2
. USE Bksales ALIAS Books
. SELECT Authors
. JOIN WITH Books TO Abook FOR author_num = B -) author_num ;
  FIELDS last_name, first_name, title
      10 records joined

.
```

So far, it appears that the operation has been successful, as you can see from the dBASE message following the JOIN command. However, this is what happens when we try to open the new database:

```
. SELECT 3
. USE Abook
File does not exist
Memo file cannot be opened
      ?
USE Abook
Do you want some help? (Y/N) No

.
```

Even though we did not include the *profiles* field in the FIELDS clause of the command, dBASE is still, inexplicably, attempting to find a memo file for the new database. Since this file does not exist, dBASE cannot open *ABOOK.DBF* either.

In this situation, you can fool dBASE into opening *ABOOK.DBF* by creating an empty file named *ABOOK.DBT* (the SET ALTERNATE **326★** command can be used for creating this file); however, a better solution is to anticipate the problem in advance and avoid using a database that contains memo fields as the current file in a JOIN operation.

Note: These problems with the JOIN command and memo fields apply to both versions 1.0 and 1.1 of dBASE III.

■ **dBASE II equivalent**
JOIN
The memo problems do not apply, since dBASE II does not offer memo-type fields.

■ **Comment**
In many applications, the SET RELATION command is an alternative way of working with two databases at once. All in all, SET RELATION is easier to use than JOIN. As a rule of thumb, try to think of a way to use SET RELATION to solve a given database problem, before you resort to the JOIN command.

Key Field

A key field is a reference field **154★** on which certain classes of commands perform their database operations. (Logical **99◆** and memo fields cannot be keys.) Under certain conditions, dBASE permits the use of multiple-field keys: In such cases, the keys are entered in order of their importance to the operation—primary, secondary, and so forth. (Details on how to create multiple-field keys are presented under INDEX **176★** and SORT **402★**.)

The INDEX and SORT commands both require one or more keys by which to rearrange the order of the records **284★** in a database. The JOIN **189★**, SET RELATION **390★**, and UPDATE **448★** commands all perform operations on *two* open databases, so they require a key field that is common to both in order to match records. Finally, the TOTAL **436★** command, which creates a totals file from an open database, requires that the original database be indexed or sorted by a key field whose values are used to determine the totals categories.

You will find a more comprehensive discussion of key fields under the Sorting **406★** entry and also in the entries for the commands listed above.

LABEL FORM

■ **Structure**

LABEL FORM file_name   *scope_clause   condition_clause   SAMPLE   TO PRINT*
TO FILE file_name

■ **Description**

The LABEL FORM command opens a specified label-form file **156♦** and follows its directions for creating labels from the currently selected **322♦** database. (A label-form file is created via the MODIFY LABEL **221★** command and is given a default extension **155♦** of .LBL.) The resulting labels can be sent to the printer (TO PRINT) or to a specified text file **157♦** (TO FILE). If neither of these clauses is included in the command, the labels will just be displayed on the screen.

Normally, LABEL FORM creates one label for each record in the current database. However, a scope **312★** (NEXT **239★** or RECORD **282★**) or condition clause (FOR **164★** or WHILE **463★**) may be used to select a subset of records for which to print labels.

The SAMPLE clause causes one or more dummy labels to be printed before the first real label. These dummies allow you to adjust the printing position properly, so that subsequent labels will be printed where you want them.

■ **Usage**

Before using the LABEL FORM command, you must:

☐ Create a label-form file on disk, using either the MODIFY LABEL or the CREATE LABEL **91★** command.

☐ Make sure that the target database is open in the selected work area.

■ **Database example**

The following examples use the *Addlabel* file from the MODIFY LABEL entry. *Addlabel* produces mailing labels from a database called *Address,* in response to the following command:

```
. USE Address
. LABEL FORM Addlabel TO PRINT
Mary Winston                    Bob Peters
57 Idaho Avenue                 1142 Pine Street
San Francisco,                  Los Angeles,
CA 94113                        CA 90250


Carl Appleby                    Olive Wadsworth
921 La Brea Drive               84 7th Street
Santa Barbara,                  Los Angeles,
CA 92112                        CA 90047


Harris Martin                   George Wren
12997 Washington Blvd.          16 10th Avenue
San Diego,                      Oakland,
CA 92122                        CA 94710


.
```

This next example illustrates two other optional parameters of the LABEL FORM command—the condition clause and the SAMPLE clause:

```
. LABEL FORM Addlabel FOR city = "Los Angeles" SAMPLE TO PRINT
**********************************   **********************************
**********************************   **********************************
**********************************   **********************************
**********************************   **********************************
**********************************   **********************************
**********************************   **********************************

Do you want more samples?  (Y/N) No
Bob Peters
1142 Pine Street                Olive Wadsworth
Los Angeles,                    84 7th Street
CA 90250                        Los Angeles,
                                CA 90047


.
```

As you can see, the "dummy" labels resulting from the SAMPLE clause consist of strings of asterisks filling the entire width of the label. If one set of dummy labels is not sufficient for you to establish the correct alignment of the printer, you can request additional samples before the real labels are printed.

The FOR clause results in the conditional selection of a subset of the records from the *Address* database—in this case, all records that have the value *"Los Angeles"* in the *city* field.

■ **Caution**

Make sure your printer is turned on and ready to operate *before* you issue a LABEL FORM command with a TO PRINT clause. (See the cautionary notes under the SET PRINT **381**★ entry.)

■ **dBASE II equivalent**

None

■ **Comments**

If you enter the command LABEL, alone, dBASE will prompt you for the name of the form-file to use, but if you enter LABEL FORM without a file name, you will receive an error message.

A REPORT FORM **295**★ command is also available in dBASE. This command works with a report-form file **156**◆ (created via MODIFY REPORT **226**★) to print tabular reports from the current database.

LEN()

■ **Structure**

LEN(character_expression)

■ **Description**

Given a string **98**◆ of characters, the LEN() function returns the number of characters in the string.

■ **Usage**

The argument of LEN() may be any valid expression that results in a string of characters, including:

    □   A character-type field or variable.

    □   The result of a function **418**◆ that returns a string.

    □   A literal (constant) string value enclosed in quotation marks.

    □   A concatenated **65**★ string expression combining two or more strings.

```
. ? LEN("dBASE III")
      9

.
```

```
. ? LEN(TIME())
      8

.
```

```
. sl = "test"
test
. ? LEN(sl)
      4

.
```

If its argument is a database field, LEN() returns the structurally defined width 154♦ of that field, not the length of any data value that the field happens to contain.

■ **Program example**

The *Kidlist* program presented in the SPACE() 407★ entry uses the LEN() function in the process of right justifying strings of characters within display fields of specified length. This sequence is one example:

```
name = TRIM(firstname) + " " + TRIM(lastname)
? "Name:                "
?? SPACE(25 - LEN(name)) + name
```

The first line uses the TRIM() **440★** function to eliminate any trailing spaces from the string contents of the fields *firstname* and *lastname*. The trimmed and concatenated strings are assigned to the variable *name*. In the third line, the expression containing the LEN() function determines the number of spaces that must precede the first letter of each name in order to right justify it within a display field of 25 spaces.

■ **Caution**

When working with database fields and the values contained in them, be careful to note the difference between the following two kinds of statements:

```
name1 = firstname + lastname
```

```
name2 = TRIM(firstname) + " " + TRIM(lastname)
```

The length of *name1* will be equal to the entire combined widths of the fields *firstname* and *lastname*, as defined in the structure **100◆** of the database. The length of *name2* will be equal to the combined lengths of the actual *values* stored in *firstname* and *lastname*, plus the added space character between them. Thus, if *firstname* and *lastname* are both empty, *name2* will contain only the one space character.

■ **dBASE II equivalent**

LEN()

■ **Comments**

The LEN() function is unique in that its role is simply to supply a piece of information about a string. Other string functions perform such tasks as:

☐ Changing the case of the characters in a string (UPPER() **451★** and LOWER() **213★**).

☐ Supplying access to the ASCII code (ASC() **26★** and CHR() **50★**).

☐ Working with substrings (AT() **30★** and SUBSTR() **423★**).

☐ Supplying or eliminating spaces in strings (SPACE() and TRIM()).

☐ Converting between numeric and string values (STR() **416★** and VAL() **456★**).

LIST

- **Structure**

  LIST *scope_clause   expression_list   condition_clause   OFF   TO PRINT*

- **Description**

  The LIST command displays records from the currently selected **322◆** database. The records appear on the screen, but can also be sent to the printer if a TO PRINT clause is included in the LIST command.

  By default, LIST displays all records, starting from the first record in the database. (If the database is indexed **176◆**, LIST displays the records in indexed order.) A scope **312★** (NEXT **239★** or RECORD **282★**) and/or condition clause (FOR **164★** or WHILE **463★**) may be included in the LIST command to select particular records for display. To select specific information from within each record, you may also include an optional list of fields or expressions.

  The OFF clause suppresses the display of the record number.

- **Usage**

  The following examples display records from a real-estate database called *Property* **384◆**. The first example demonstrates LIST's default behavior—to display the entire database:

```
. USE Property
. LIST
```

```
    1  Jenkens            Samuel           123 Martha Street
San Francisco      Noe Valley        74        4        1.0 .F.
   1500 225000.00 195000.00 .T.  05/18/85   195000.00 04/25/85        90 Memo
    2  Fine               Andrea           12345 26th Avenue
San Francisco      Mission           70        4        2.5 .T.
   2000 149000.00 136500.00 .F.   / /        0.00 03/20/85        90 Memo
    3  Hernandez          Francisco        50 17th Street
San Francisco      Mission           60        2        1.0 .F.
   1000 125000.00     0.00 .F.   / /        0.00 01/30/85       180 Memo
    4  Morgan             Jane             15 Peach Lane
San Francisco      Sunset            60        4        2.0 .T.
   2500 275000.00     0.00 .F.   / /        0.00 12/15/84       180 Memo
    5  Henderson          Louis            18 Jackson Avenue
San Francisco      Nob Hill          55        7        5.0 .T.
   5000 375000.00     0.00 .F.   / /        0.00 02/27/85       180 Memo
    6  Smith              Jack             4452 Sixth Avenue
San Francisco      Sunset            45        4        2.5 .T.
   2500 245000.00     0.00 .F.   / /        0.00 03/01/85        90 Memo
    7  Lin                Charles          55 Sayer Lane
South San Francisco Central          25        5        3.0 .T.
   2500 255000.00     0.00 .F.   / /        0.00 05/19/85       180 Memo
    8  Doe                Jonathan         3555 Alta Street
San Francisco      Mission           75        4        2.5 .T.
   2000 179000.00     0.00 .F.   / /        0.00 03/15/85        90 Memo
  .
```

The expression list in the LIST command may include simple field names, or more complex expressions such as concatenations 65★, arithmetic operations 24★, or date arithmetic 100★. This next example shows concatentation of two character fields:

```
. LIST TRIM(owner_l) + ", " + owner_f, address OFF
TRIM(owner_l) + ", " + owner_f               address
Jenkens, Samuel                              123 Martha Street
Fine, Andrea                                 12345 26th Avenue
Hernandez, Francisco                         50 17th Street
Morgan, Jane                                 15 Peach Lane
Henderson, Louis                             18 Jackson Avenue
Smith, Jack                                  4452 Sixth Avenue
Lin, Charles                                 55 Sayer Lane
Doe, Jonathan                                3555 Alta Street

.
```

Notice that no record numbers are displayed, thanks to the OFF clause. Also note that the heading above each column displays the complete expression that generated the column.

A LIST command with a FOR clause is a common way to display records that meet an expressed criterion. The following command lists all records that contain a value greater that 175000 in the *asking_pr* field:

```
. LIST address, asking_pr FOR asking_pr > 175000
Record#  address                             asking_pr
      1  123 Martha Street                   225000.00
      4  15 Peach Lane                       275000.00
      5  18 Jackson Avenue                   375000.00
      6  4452 Sixth Avenue                   245000.00
      7  55 Sayer Lane                       255000.00
      8  3555 Alta Street                    179000.00

.
```

This final example contains a condition clause and an arithmetic expression that finds the difference between two numeric fields. The command selects those records (in this case only one) in which the logical field *sold* contains a value of .T.:

```
. LIST address, asking_pr - sale_price FOR sold
Record#  address                       asking_pr - sale_price
      1  123 Martha Street                        30000.00
.
```

■ **Cautions**

If LIST results in more than one screenful of information, the display simply scrolls down to the last record without pause.

Make sure your printer is ready to operate *before* you issue a LIST TO PRINT command or you may be dropped back to the operating system unexpectedly (see SET PRINT **381★**).

■ **dBASE II equivalent**

LIST

■ **Comments**

To eliminate the display of column headings in the LIST command, change the SET HEADING **369★** status to OFF. However, keep in mind that the headings can be very helpful when the information being listed is the result of a complex expression.

The DISPLAY **116★** command is similar to LIST. However, DISPLAY alone selects only the current record. If a DISPLAY command with a scope or condition clause results in multiple screens of information, dBASE will pause automatically between screens.

LOCATE

■ **Structure**

LOCATE   *scope_clause*   FOR condition_clause

■ **Description**

The LOCATE command searches through the currently selected **322◆** database for a record that meets the criterion expressed in the condition **312◆** clause. If a record is found, the pointer **258★** is moved to that record, the record number is displayed, and LOCATE's action is temporarily over.

Subsequently, CONTINUE **72★** commands are used to search forward from the current pointer position for additional records that match the LOCATE criterion. Like LOCATE, CONTINUE identifies only the *next* eligible record, so a series of CONTINUE commands may be required in order to locate all of the relevant records. The LOCATE...CONTINUE sequence is finally complete when a CONTINUE command fails to find a record that meets the criterion. At that point, the message "End of locate scope" is displayed on the screen and the end-of-file condition is set to true.

■ **Usage**

The current database need not be sorted **402◆** or indexed **176◆** for the LOCATE command to work successfully. When the LOCATE command contains a FOR **164★** clause alone, the default scope **312★** becomes ALL **17★**, which means that LOCATE begins searching at the first record in the database and moves forward, with each subsequent CONTINUE command, to the end of the file. However, NEXT **239★** may be included to restrict the number of records (starting with the current record) over which the LOCATE...CONTINUE sequence is to operate.

■ **Database example**

The following LOCATE...CONTINUE sequence searches through a database called *Address* **223◆** for records in which the *city* value begins with the letters "San" (SET EXACT **355★** must be OFF to search for a partial match like this). Notice that LOCATE does not *display* a record that meets the criterion—it simply moves the pointer to that record. You must issue a DISPLAY **116★** command if you wish to examine the record that has been located:

```
. SET EXACT OFF
. USE Address
. LOCATE FOR city = "San"
Record =        1

. DISPLAY OFF
LASTNAME   FIRSTNAME STREET                          CITY          STATE ZIP
Winston    Mary      57 Idaho Avenue                 San Francisco CA    94113

. CONTINUE
Record =        3

. DISPLAY OFF
LASTNAME   FIRSTNAME STREET                          CITY          STATE ZIP
Appleby    Carl      921 La Brea Drive               Santa Barbara CA    92112

. CONTINUE
Record =        5

. DISPLAY OFF
LASTNAME   FIRSTNAME STREET                          CITY          STATE ZIP
Martin     Harris    12997 Washington Blvd.          San Diego     CA    92122

.
```

After three records that meet the criterion have been located, a final CONTINUE command encounters the end of the file. At this point the EOF() **147**★ function is true:

```
. CONTINUE
End of locate scope

. ? EOF()
.T.
```

■ **Cautions**

Despite documentation to the contrary, the LOCATE command does not allow a WHILE **463**★ clause in version 1.1 of dBASE III. An attempt to use a WHILE clause results in a syntax error.

If SET TALK **398**★ is OFF, the record number won't be displayed when the pointer is moved to a new location. You can still use the DISPLAY command to show the record on the screen, however.

Upper/lowercase letters are evaluated by the LOCATE command, even with SET EXACT OFF: That is, "San" and "san" are never considered equivalent.

■ **dBASE II equivalent**

LOCATE

■ **Comment**

The FIND **160**★ and SEEK **317**★ commands also search for specific values in the current database; however, the database must be indexed.

LOG()

- **Structure**

  LOG(numeric_value)

- **Description**

  Given a positive nonzero numeric argument, x, the LOG() function supplies the natural logarithm of x: that is, the power to which e must be raised to yield x. The letter e stands for the base constant of the natural logarithms, and equals approximately 2.71828183.

- **Usage**

  The LOG() function and its converse, EXP() **152★**, are sometimes used in statistical and financial calculations.

- **Program example**

  The following program, called *Logtable*, produces a short table of LOG() values in a database called *Log*. The database has two fields: *x*, for the argument of LOG(), and *log_x*, for the resulting value:

```
*------------------------------------------------- LOGTABLE.PRG
* Creates a table of natural logarithms.
*

SET TALK OFF
SET SAFETY OFF

USE Log
ZAP

recs = 20
DO WHILE recs > 0
    APPEND BLANK
    recs = recs - 1
ENDDO

REPLACE ALL x WITH RECNO() / 2
REPLACE ALL log_x WITH LOG(x)

DISPLAY ALL
SET TALK ON
SET SAFETY ON
RETURN
```

Here is the output from *Logtable*:

```
. DO Logtable
Record#       X       LOG X
      1    0.50  -.69314718
      2    1.00  0.00000000
      3    1.50  0.40546511
      4    2.00  0.69314718
      5    2.50  0.91629073
      6    3.00  1.09861229
      7    3.50  1.25276297
      8    4.00  1.38629436
      9    4.50  1.50407740
     10    5.00  1.60943791
     11    5.50  1.70474809
     12    6.00  1.79175947
     13    6.50  1.87180218
     14    7.00  1.94591015
     15    7.50  2.01490302
     16    8.00  2.07944154
     17    8.50  2.14006616
     18    9.00  2.19722458
     19    9.50  2.25129180
     20   10.00  2.30258509
.
```

■ **Caution**

The argument of LOG() may not be negative or zero. If SET TALK **398★** is ON, an attempt to use LOG() with an invalid argument will result in an error message and string of asterisks; if TALK is OFF, the result will be only the string of asterisks:

```
. ? LOG(-2)

***Execution error on LOG() : zero or negative
*********
.
```

```
. SET TALK OFF
. ? LOG(-2)
*********
.
```

■ **dBASE II equivalent**

None

■ **Comment**

The SET DECIMALS **347★** command controls the number of decimal places displayed from the LOG() function. Values are rounded according to the standard mathematical conventions.

Logical operators

Three logical operators are available in dBASE, for use in constructing complex condition expressions:

Operator:	Action:
.NOT.	Modifies the result of a condition expression.
.AND.	Builds compound condition expressions ◆ that are true only when all parts are true.
.OR.	Builds compound condition expressions that are true when any part is true.

A condition expression is one that dBASE can evaluate to one of only two values: true or false. Such an expression most commonly consists of a relation built with one of dBASE's six relational operators **286★**: $=$, $<>$, $>$, $<$, $>=$, $<=$. However, a condition expression may also be a function that results in a logical value, a variable that contains a logical value, or simply one of the two dBASE logical constants, .T. or .F..

(Notice the format of the logical operators: Each is preceded and followed by a period, and there are no spaces between the beginning and ending periods. The values they return—.T. and .F.—have this same structure.)

The .NOT. operator reverses the value of the condition that follows it. Given a true condition, .NOT. yields a value of false; given a false condition, .NOT. yields a value of true:

```
. c1 = .T.
.T.
. c2 = .F.
.F.
. ? .NOT. c1
.F.
. ? .NOT. c2
.T.
.
```

A common use of the .NOT. operator is in a DO WHILE **129★** loop that processes the records of a database from beginning to end:

```
DO WHILE .NOT. EOF()
     * ... *
ENDDO
```

In this example, the EOF() **147★** function returns a value of false as long as the record pointer **258★** is not positioned at the end of the database. Thus, the condition expression *.NOT. EOF()* is true, and processing within the loop continues, until the pointer is pushed beyond the last record in the database. (See the programming examples under the entries for SPACE() **407★** and CDOW() **44★** for further examples of this usage.)

The .AND. operator combines two conditions. An .AND. compound condition yields a value of true only if *both* of the combined conditions are true. If either one is false, or if both are false, the .AND. compound yields a false:

```
. c1 = .T.
.T.
.
. c2 = .F.
.F.
.
. c3 = .T.
.T.
.
. c4 = .F.
.F.
.
```

```
. ? c1 .AND. c3
.T.
.
```

```
. ? c1 .AND. c2
.F.
.
. ? c2 .AND. c4
.F.
.
```

The following DISPLAY **123★** statement makes use of an .AND. compound to select only those records that match both of two conditions (see also the example under the FOR **164★** entry).

```
DISPLAY FOR department = "Clerical" .AND. salary_mo < 1300
```

The .OR. operator results in a value of true if *either* one or both of the combined conditions are true. If both conditions are false, the .OR. compound results in a false:

```
. ? c1 .OR. c3
.T.

. ? c1 .OR. c2
.T.
.
```

```
. ? c2 .OR. c4
.F.
.
```

This next DISPLAY statement makes use of an .OR. compound to select records that match either of two conditions:

```
DISPLAY FOR department = "Production" .OR. department = "Marketing"
```

(Notice that the field or variable name must be stated in each condition, even when the same value is being tested.)

When a compound condition expression contains more than one logical operator, dBASE follows a specific *order of precedence* for evaluating the parts of the expression:

1. .NOT.
2. .AND.
3. .OR.

(Arithmetic operators **24★** are also evaluated in a defined order of precedence.)

Parentheses may be used to change the default order of precedence: The expressions within parentheses are always evaluated first. When sets of parentheses are nested inside one another, evaluation begins with the innermost pair and proceeds outward.

The following illustrations again make use of the logical variables $c1$, $c2$, and $c3$. In the first expression, the .AND. compound results in a value of false; then the .OR. compound yields a true. In the second example, however, the parentheses cause the .OR. to be evaluated first, yielding a value of true. Then the resulting .AND. compound yields a false:

```
. c1 = .T.
.T.
.
. c2 = .F.
.F.
.
. c3 = .T.
.T.
.
```

```
. ? c2 .AND. c1 .OR. c3
.T.
.
```

```
. ? c2 .AND. (c1 .OR. c3)
.F.
.
```

■ **Caution**

The logical operators provide great versatility and flexibility for extracting very specific information from your dBASE data files, as well as for controlling program execution. However, it is important to think through your criteria carefully before choosing which operator to use, since certain compound expressions occasionally produce unexpected results.

LOOP

■ **Structure**
DO WHILE
        * ... *
        LOOP
        * ... *
ENDDO

■ **Description**
The LOOP command is designed to be used inside a DO WHILE **129**★ structure, to interrupt the normal flow of control within the loop.

Usually, all the commands located between DO WHILE and ENDDO are performed sequentially, and then ENDDO sends control back up to the DO WHILE statement for a new evaluation of the looping condition. However, a LOOP command located inside the loop structure causes an early return to the DO WHILE statement, skipping the commands located between LOOP and ENDDO for that iteration.

■ **Usage**
The LOOP command is best reserved for rather special circumstances. Some programmers may wish to use LOOP as a kind of conditional ENDDO within a loop that itself contains other structured commands—nested DO WHILE and IF...ELSE **171**★ commands, perhaps. Others will prefer to avoid the use of LOOP altogether, by structuring all DO WHILE loops with normal logical paths to the ENDDO statement.

■ **Caution**
In even the simplest of circumstances, the use of LOOP may result in a program that is not very clear or readable. For example, let's say you are writing a loop that performs two different processing activities on selected records in an employee database. The database is indexed on the key field **194**★ *dept*. You want the loop to perform the first processing activity for all the employees in the Editorial Department.

The secondary processing is reserved for only those Editorial employees who earn less than $1,500 per month. You might be tempted to write your loop as follows:

```
GOTO TOP
DO WHILE dept = "Editorial"
    * ... *
    * Perform main processing activity.
    * ... *
    IF salary > 1500
        SKIP
        LOOP
    ENDIF
    * ... *
    * Perform secondary processing activity,
    *    only for salaries < 1500.
    * ... *
    SKIP
ENDDO
```

However, a much clearer and more direct approach is to avoid using the LOOP statement by restructuring the IF command located within the DO WHILE loop:

```
GOTO TOP
DO WHILE dept = "Editorial"
    * ... *
    * Perform main processing activity.
    * ... *
    IF salary < 1500
        * ... *
        * Perform secondary processing activity,
        *    only for salaries < 1500.
        * ... *
    ENDIF
    SKIP
ENDDO
```

■ **dBASE II equivalent**
LOOP

■ **Comment**
The EXIT 150★ command also interrupts the normal flow within a DO WHILE loop structure. However, EXIT actually terminates the loop, moving on to the statement following ENDDO.

212

LOWER()

■ **Structure**

LOWER(character_expression)

■ **Description**

Given a string **98◆** of characters, the LOWER() function returns a new version of the same string in which the letters of the alphabet are converted to lowercase.

■ **Usage**

The argument of LOWER() may be any of the following:

☐ A character-type field or variable.

☐ The result of a function that returns a string.

☐ A literal (constant) string value enclosed in quotation marks.

☐ A concatenated **65★** expression combining two or more strings.

```
. ? LOWER("dBASE III")
dbase iii
.
```

```
. ? LOWER("Today is " + CDOW(DATE()))
today is thursday
.
```

■ **Database example**

The following database, called *Invntory*, contains five fields of information about items of inventory. The character field *item* stores a brief description of each:

```
. USE Invntory
. LIST
Record#  ID      ITEM            QTY  COST  VALUE
      1  12B123  ruler           150  0.21   31.50
      2  76C987  NOTEBOOK        225  0.45  101.25
      3  32A971  Blotter          76  1.51  114.76
      4  76F971  CALCULATOR       35  3.75  131.25
      5  23D971  Desk Clock       25  7.88  197.00
      6  32H231  desk ORGANIZER  110  2.37  260.70
.
```

Notice that the *item* values are stored in inconsistent and random case formats: Some of the descriptions are all uppercase, others are all lowercase, and still others are mixed case. This situation often occurs when records are entered into a database by several different people, or over a long period of time. The following REPLACE **291**★ command uses the LOWER() function to put all of the *item* values into a consistent lowercase format:

```
. REPLACE ALL item WITH LOWER(item)
      6 records replaced
. LIST
Record#  ID      ITEM            QTY  COST  VALUE
      1  12B123  ruler           150  0.21   31.50
      2  76C987  notebook        225  0.45  101.25
      3  32A971  blotter          76  1.51  114.76
      4  76F971  calculator       35  3.75  131.25
      5  23D971  desk clock       25  7.88  197.00
      6  32H231  desk organizer  110  2.37  260.70
      .
```

■ **Caution**

If the values stored in a character field follow an intentional pattern of combined upper- and lowercase formats (in identification codes, perhaps), that pattern can be difficult to restore after a REPLACE ALL command that converts everything to lowercase.

■ **dBASE II equivalent**

None

■ **Comment**

The UPPER() **451**★ function converts the letters of a string to uppercase.

Macros

A macro is a programming tool that allows you to substitute the contents of a string variable **459**★ into the actual command structure **62**★ of a dBASE command. The & **1**★ symbol designates a macro: Placing this symbol before the first character of a string variable's name results in a *macro substitution*.

Normally, dBASE reads a character variable as a string-type value, as in this example:

```
. language = "French"
. ? "I speak a little " + language + "."
I speak a little French.

.
```

However, when the & character precedes a string variable's name, dBASE substitutes the variable's value into the syntax of the command itself, as in the following sequence:

```
. language = "french"
. SET DATE &language
```

dBASE does not normally accept a string value in the SET DATE **337**★ command; rather, it looks for a one-word command option that specifies a standard date-display format. Macro substitution permits you to provide this option indirectly, perhaps as the result of evaluation of a condition within a program. The completed command is then performed by the program:

```
. SET DATE french
```

Another frequently used macro substitution involves the TO PRINT option available with many dBASE commands. In the following program sequence, the user is allowed to choose whether to display the current database only on the screen, or send it to the printer as well:

```
*-------------------------------------------------------PRMAC.PRG
* Demonstrates the use of a macro for the TO PRINT clause.
*

pr = ""
ACCEPT "Do you wish to print the database listing? (Y or N) " TO ans
IF UPPER(ans) = "Y"
     pr = " TO PRINT"
ENDIF

LIST &pr
RETURN
```

Note the use of the macro &pr in this passage. The variable pr is initialized as an empty string. If the user indicates that a printed listing of the current database is required, pr receives a new value:

```
IF UPPER(ans) = "Y"
     pr = " TO PRINT"
ENDIF
```

Depending upon the value of pr—either an empty string or the string " TO PRINT"— the subsequent LIST 200★ command will output the database listing to the screen only, or to both the screen and the printer:

```
LIST &pr
```

Both of the preceding examples involve simple uses of macros to complete the syntax of a command. However, macros have other, more complex uses, including:

☐ Interactively building command lists whose exact lengths may not be known in advance.

☐ Simplifying the expression of complex formulas.

☐ Designing imaginative "tricks" to simplify the task of writing programs.

You will find examples of all of these uses in the & entry, and you will find a variety of other examples in programs throughout this book.

Mathematical functions

dBASE provides a small but important group of mathematical functions for use in rounding numbers, finding integral values, and formulating advanced mathematical equations:

- The ROUND() **302★** function rounds any number to a specified decimal place.
- The INT() **186★** function reduces a real number to its integral value, eliminating any decimal portion of the number without rounding.
- The EXP() **152★** function returns the value of the natural logarithmic constant ϵ raised to a specified power.
- Its converse, the LOG() **205★** function, returns the natural (base ϵ) logarithm of a given value.
- The SQRT() **412★** function provides the square root of a positive number.

EXP(), LOG(), and SQRT() are most commonly used in financial and statistical calculations.

For examples and further information about these functions, see the individual entries and also the discussions of arithmetic operators **24★** and data types **98★**.

Memo fields

A memo field makes it possible to attach a small word-processed document to any record of a database. All that is stored in the database itself is the marker for the memo field, which occupies only 10 spaces; the actual contents of the memo are stored in a separate disk file **156◆** with the extension name .DBT.

You can create or edit a memo document via the APPEND **19★**, CHANGE **48★**, or EDIT **141★** command, by positioning the cursor in the memo field and pressing Ctrl-PgDn to access dBASE's built-in word processor **466★**. When your memo is completed, press Ctrl-End to return to the record template.

The list of possible uses for memo fields is nearly endless. In an employee database, you might keep personal notes about an individual employee's performance; in an inventory database, descriptions of each item in the inventory; in a scheduling database, notes about meetings that have taken place, or outlines for future discussions; in a research database, notes on the last series of experiments. In short, a memo field can be used for any kind of prose description that does not lend itself readily to the columnar structure of the other types of database fields.

■ **Database example**

The *Property* database described in the SET PROCEDURE **383**★ entry, and discussed in many other entries in this book, contains information about houses that are for sale. It includes a memo field called *descriptn*, which holds promotional-type descriptions of each house in the database. The following sequence shows a quick way to examine the contents of *descriptn* for an individual record:

```
. USE Property
. LIST address
Record#   address
        1  123 Martha Street
        2  12345 26th Avenue
        3  50 17th Street
        4  15 Peach Lane
        5  18 Jackson Avenue
        6  4452 Sixth Avenue
        7  55 Sayer Lane
        8  3555 Alta Street

. GOTO 8
. ? descriptn
This charming, spacious Edwardian home, located
near the Church Street shopping district, is
perfect for a growing family. Priced to sell;
owner must relocate. A two-car garage plus large
basement has great potential as an in-law
apartment. Quiet traditional neighborhood, near
schools, churches, shopping, and restaurants.
Appliances included. Assumable mortgage available
at 12.75%. Owner willing to carry a small second
mortgage if necessary.

```

(The same technique, using the **? 5**★ command, may also be used to print the contents of a memo field. See the program example in the SET DEVICE **347**★ entry for an illustration.)

■ **Cautions**

Versatile as memo fields are, there are certain restrictions on their use:

☐   A memo field cannot be used as a key **194**★ for a record search in a database.

☐   A database cannot be indexed **176**◆ or sorted **402**◆ on a memo field.

☐   Some commands, such as JOIN **189**★, may have problems handling databases that contain memos.

Also, be aware that if a database that contains a memo field becomes separated from its .DBT file, the database itself will be unusable.

MODIFY COMMAND

■ **Structure**
MODIFY COMMAND file_name

■ **Description**
MODIFY COMMAND activates the dBASE word processor, allowing you to create or edit a program file, a format file, or any other text file **157♦** that will be saved on disk.

dBASE expects you to include a file name **155★** in the MODIFY COMMAND statement. If you do not, it will prompt you for one:

```
. MODIFY COMMAND
Enter filename:
```

Once you have provided a name, dBASE looks on the current or specified disk to see if the file already exists. If it does, it is loaded into memory, so that you can begin an editing session. (After the session, the previous version of the file will be retained on disk as a backup, with a .BAK extension.) If the file does not yet exist, dBASE opens the word processor and allows you to create the file. (Unless you specify otherwise, MODIFY COMMAND always assigns a .PRG extension to files created in the word processor.)

■ **Usage**
Once you are in the MODIFY COMMAND word processor, you can use a set of keyboard control commands to move around in the program or document you are creating or editing (see Word Processing **466★**). When you are done, you can exit the session in either of two ways: Press Ctrl-End to save the work you have just completed, or press Escape to abandon it. In the latter case, dBASE will ask you to confirm that you truly do not wish to save your work.

■ **Caution**

A program or document file created in dBASE's MODIFY COMMAND word processor may be no longer than 4,096 bytes. Although dBASE is perfectly capable of *running* programs that are longer than this, you will have to create long program files in an external word processor or text editor (such as DOS's *Edlin*). Most of these external programs allow you to create files in a "nondocument" or "unformatted" mode that yields ASCII **28★** text files. (If you do use an external word processor to write programs, remember to give your files the .PRG extension.)

■ **dBASE II equivalent**

MODIFY COMMAND

■ **Comments**

To use the MODIFY COMMAND word processor to create a *CONFIG.DB* **66★** file, issue the command:

```
. MODIFY COMMAND CONFIG.DB
```

The following form of the dBASE DIR **114★** command will show you all the program files on your current disk:

```
. DIR *.PRG
```

and you can use the dBASE TYPE **444★** command to display or print their contents.

The MODIFY FILE command is an acceptable but seldom-used alternative to MODIFY COMMAND.

MODIFY LABEL

■ **Structure**
MODIFY LABEL file_name

■ **Description**
The MODIFY LABEL command invokes the dBASE label-form generator. Using this command, you can design multiline labels (address, product-identification, or personnel-file labels, for example) to be produced from the records **284★** of the currently selected **322◆** database. Once designed, the label format is stored on disk under the specified file name, with an .LBL extension **156◆**.

CREATE LABEL is an alternate form of this command. Both forms may be used either to generate a new label-form file, or to edit the specifications in an existing one.

MODIFY LABEL does not actually generate the labels: This is the job of the LABEL FORM **195★** command. LABEL FORM opens an existing .LBL file and follows its instructions to create labels from the records of the currently selected database. The resulting labels may be sent to the printer, stored in a disk file, or just displayed on the screen.

■ **Usage**
To guide you through the process of creating a label form, the MODIFY LABEL command presents you with two input screens. Each screen has information templates for you to fill in, to define the format and contents of the labels:

1. *The layout screen* asks for information about the dimensions and margins of each printed label, and the number of labels that will be printed across a sheet. (The gummed labels available for use in your computer's printer typically come in single-, double-, or triple-column strips.) This screen also allows you to enter descriptive remarks about the labels—purpose or label size, perhaps, or date last printed.

2. *The label-contents screen* supplies a template in which you specify the field **154★** contents of each line of the labels you wish to generate. Each line may consist of a single field name, a list of field names, or an expression containing one or more field names (see *Caution*).

The MODIFY LABEL command provides some special features that simplify and clarify the process of defining a label format. First, an area is reserved at the top of each screen for information that you may need while you are using MODIFY LABEL. This area displays either a table of the field structures of the currently selected database or a list of the keyboard functions you can use to control the label generator. The F1 function key toggles between these two displays.

Second, dBASE offers a menu of five standard label formats that you can choose from. If you choose one of these standard formats, you do not need to enter individual layout values for your label form. To bring up the format menu, just press Ctrl-Home:

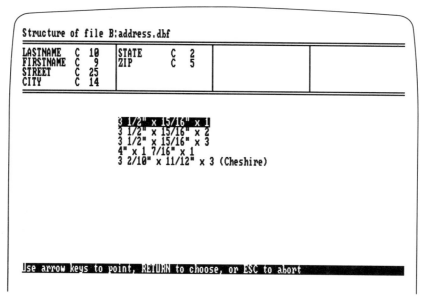

The first three of these selections represent the standard 5-line, 35-character address labels, with 1, 2, or 3 labels across. The last two represent other sizes and shapes commonly used in business offices and laboratories. To select any one of these five formats, move the highlight over the format you want and press the Return key. When you return to the layout screen, you will see that the specifications you chose have automatically been entered into the layout fields and the format description added to *Remarks*.

■ **Database example**

To illustrate the use of MODIFY LABEL, we'll use an indexed **176**♦ database called *Address* ♦, which contains only names and addresses:

```
. USE Address
. INDEX ON lastname + firstname TO Nameind
      6 records indexed
. LIST OFF
LASTNAME    FIRSTNAME STREET                          CITY           STATE ZIP
Appleby     Carl      921 La Brea Drive               Santa Barbara  CA    92112
Martin      Harris    12997 Washington Blvd.          San Diego      CA    92122
Peters      Bob       1142 Pine Street                Los Angeles    CA    90250
Wadsworth   Olive     84 7th Street                   Los Angeles    CA    90047
Winston     Mary      57 Idaho Avenue                 San Francisco  CA    94113
Wren        George    16 10th Avenue                  Oakland        CA    94710
.
```

Let's say you wish to produce mailing labels from this database, and you have purchased standard 5-line, 35-character gummed labels in strips containing two labels across. Here are the steps necessary to prepare the label format:

1. After opening the *Address* database with the *Nameind* index, issue the MODIFY LABEL command, supplying a file name for the label form:

```
. MODIFY LABEL Addlabel
```

2. When the layout screen appears, press Ctrl-Home to bring up the standard labels menu and select the format. You need enter no further information into the layout screen, so press the PgDn key to move on to the label-contents screen.

3. Enter the following information to define the contents of your label:

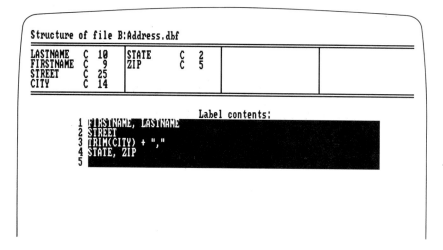

```
Structure of file B:Address.dbf
LASTNAME   C  10   STATE    C   2
FIRSTNAME  C   9   ZIP      C   5
STREET     C  25
CITY       C  14

                           Label contents:
        1 FIRSTNAME, LASTNAME
        2 STREET
        3 TRIM(CITY) + ","
        4 STATE, ZIP
        5
```

4. Press Ctrl-End to save the completed label-format file on disk.

At the end of this process, the file *ADDLABEL.LBL* will be stored on the default disk. Now, to print the labels, use the LABEL FORM command:

```
. LABEL FORM Addlabel TO PRINT
```

Here are the resulting printed labels:

```
Carl Appleby              Harris Martin
921 La Brea Drive         12997 Washington Blvd.
Santa Barbara,            San Diego,
CA 92112                  CA 92122


Bob Peters                Olive Wadsworth
1142 Pine Street          84 7th Street
Los Angeles,              Los Angeles,
CA 90250                  CA 90047


Mary Winston              George Wren
57 Idaho Avenue           16 10th Avenue
San Francisco,            Oakland,
CA 94113                  CA 94710
```

Since the *Address* database was indexed by the *lastname* and *firstname* fields, the labels are presented in alphabetical order.

■ **Caution**

The label-form generator accepts only character data for the contents list. If you wish to include dates or numeric values, you must use the appropriate conversion function **139♦, 416♦** in the contents input template:

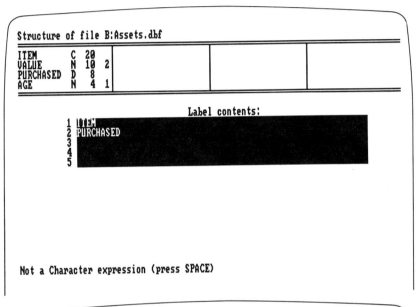

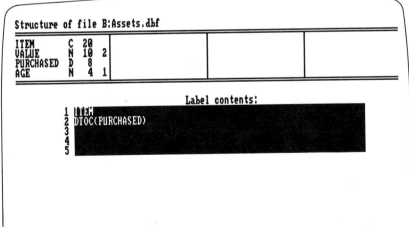

■ **dBASE II equivalent**

None

A program file is necessary for creating labels in dBASE II.

■ **Comments**

The LABEL FORM command's SAMPLE option permits you to test and align your labels before actually printing them.

A report generator is also available in dBASE III; see the MODIFY REPORT **226★** and REPORT FORM **295★** entries.

MODIFY REPORT

■ **Structure**

MODIFY REPORT file_name

■ **Description**

The MODIFY REPORT command invokes the dBASE report-form generator. Using this command, you can design a tabular, *column-oriented* report format for the currently selected **322◆** database. Once designed, the report format is stored on disk under the specified file name, with an extension of .FRM **156◆**.

CREATE REPORT is an alternate form of this command. Both forms may be used either to generate a new report-form file or to edit the specifications of an existing one.

MODIFY REPORT does not actually create a copy of the report: This is the job of the REPORT FORM **295★** command. REPORT FORM opens an existing .FRM file and follows its instructions to generate a report from the currently selected database. The resulting report may be sent to the printer, stored in a disk file, or just displayed on the screen.

■ **Usage**

To guide you through the process of creating a report form, the MODIFY REPORT command presents you with three types of input screens. Each screen has questions for you to answer and field templates for you to fill in, to define the format and contents of the resulting report:

1. *The page layout screen* asks you for a page heading (that is, a title for your report) and for information about the margins, dimensions, and desired line spacing of a printed page. You can either accept the default values (which are set up for a standard 8½-by-11 page), or you can change the settings to meet your own specific requirements.

2. *The group/subtotal screen* allows you to specify optional group divisions ◆ in your report, with group headings and group totals. These groups must correspond to the key groups of records in your sorted **402**◆ or indexed **176**◆ database. You may prepare a complete report showing all the records in each group, or a summary report containing only the the total value of numeric fields in the group. Finally, you may also organize your report into subgroups within each primary group.

3. *The field-column screen* is a repeating screen that you fill in once for each column of information you want to appear in your report. You use this screen to specify the field contents and the header for a given column. The field contents may be a single field name from your database or an expression that includes one or more field names. Fields may be of any data type; if the column is to contain numeric values, you must also specify the number of decimal places that will be displayed, and indicate whether or not you want the column to be totaled at the bottom of the report. The field header may be up to four lines long. Column width is calculated automatically to accommodate the contents and headings, but you may change this value if you prefer different spacing between columns in the final report.

Several helpful features are available to simplify and clarify the process of defining a report format. First, an area is reserved at the top of each screen for information that you may need while you are using MODIFY REPORT. This area displays either a table of the field structures of the currently selected database or a list of the keyboard functions you can use to control the report generator. The F1 function key toggles between these two displays.

Second, each field-column screen contains a visual display of all the columns you have defined so far and a running tally of the number of spaces still available on the line (negative numbers mean that the report will wrap to the next line). The display includes column headers and field-width indicators (strings of Xs for character fields and strings of # characters for numeric fields).

Finally, if you are preparing a very long and complex report format, you may have occasion to use a special menu that is available to help you jump forward or backward from one screen to another. You invoke this menu by pressing Ctrl-Home:

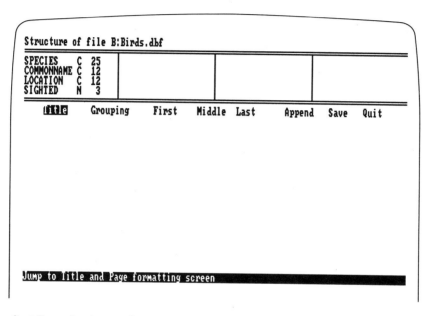

The first five selections refer to the various screens of the format generator itself; the last three supply ways to continue or end the definition process. Use the Right- and Left-arrow keys to highlight one of the options on this menu: A brief explanation of the selection will appear at the bottom of the screen. Then press the Return key to perform your selection.

■ **Database example**

To illustrate the use of MODIFY REPORT, we'll turn to a database called *Birds*. (Most of the database examples in this book are business oriented, but dBASE III can be equally valuable to people working in other pursuits, including the natural and social sciences and the humanities.)

The *Birds* database contains information gathered by two ornithologists who are studying bird populations in urban settings. They have selected several avian species for their study, and have chosen a representative group of cities to work in. In each city, they have selected typical residential, downtown, and park environments, and are counting the individual sightings of each species over a given seasonal period. Here is a sample passage from their database:

```
. USE Birds
. INDEX ON commonname TO Birdind
      9 records indexed
. LIST
Record#  SPECIES                  COMMONNAME  LOCATION     SIGHTED
      1  Falco sparverius         Kestrel     residential      2
      4  Falco sparverius         Kestrel     downtown         0
      7  Falco sparverius         Kestrel     park            12
      3  Mimus polyglottos        Mockingbird residential      5
      6  Mimus polyglottos        Mockingbird downtown        14
      9  Mimus polyglottos        Mockingbird park            16
      2  Aphelocoma coerulescens  Scrub Jay   residential     12
      5  Aphelocoma coerulescens  Scrub Jay   downtown         2
      8  Aphelocoma coerulescens  Scrub Jay   park            21

.
```

The ornithologists want to produce a report on the total number of sightings for each species in all the selected city environments. As you can see, they have indexed their database on the field *commonname*. They want the report to contain two columns of information within each group division: the location in which the birds were sighted, and the number of individual birds sighted. Here are the steps necessary to prepare the report:

1. After opening the *Birds* database with the *Birdind* index, issue the MODIFY RE-PORT command, supplying a file name for the report form:

```
. MODIFY REPORT Citybird
```

2. On the page-layout screen, enter the title *Birds Residing in City Habitats* in the space for the page heading. Then, to accept default values for the remainder of the page-layout screen, simply press the PgDn key to move to the next screen.

3. On the group/subtotal screen, first indicate the field name for the report's divisions (*commonname*). Then, because this will be a complete report rather than a summary, and no page eject is required after each group division in the report, enter N for each of these options. Finally, enter the heading *Common name*: for the group divisions.

```
Structure of file B:Birds.dbf

SPECIES      C  25
COMMONNAME   C  12
LOCATION     C  12
SIGHTED      N   3

Group/subtotal on:       commonname



Summary report only? (Y/N): N      Eject after each group/subtotal? (Y/N): N

Group/subtotal heading:  Common name:



Subgroup/sub-subtotal on:



Subgroup/subsubtotal heading:
```

Since there will be no subgroups, press PgDn to move to the next screen.

4. Now you can begin formatting the report. The first column will contain the *location* field and the header for this column will be two lines long.

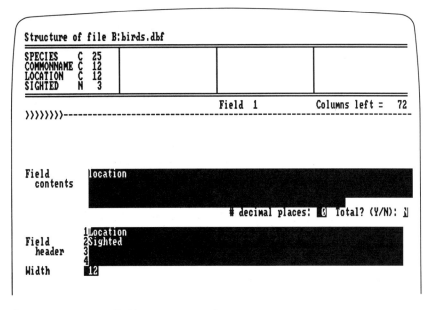

```
Structure of file B:birds.dbf
SPECIES      C  25
COMMONNAME   C  12
LOCATION     C  12
SIGHTED      N   3
                                    Field  1        Columns left =   72
>>>>>>>>------------------------------------------------------------------

Field        location
   contents

                              # decimal places: 0  Total? (Y/N): N

              1Location
Field        2Sighted
   header     3
              4
Width         12
```

Once again, press PgDn to move to the next screen.

5. The second column of the report will contain the numeric field *sighted*. The column values should be displayed as integers (no decimal places) and the column should be totaled. This column will also have a two-line header.

```
Structure of file B:birds.dbf
SPECIES      C  25
COMMONNAME   C  12
LOCATION     C  12
SIGHTED      N   3
                                    Field  2        Columns left =   59
>>>>>>>>Location    ------------------------------------------------------
        Sighted

              XXXXXXXXXXX

Field        sighted
   contents

                              # decimal places: 0  Total? (Y/N): Y

              1Individuals
Field        2Sighted
   header     3
              4
Width         11
```

6. Press Ctrl-End to save the completed report definition on disk.

At the end of this process, the file *CITYBIRDS.FRM* will be stored on the default disk. Now, to print out a copy of the report, use the REPORT FORM command:

```
. REPORT FORM Citybird PLAIN NOEJECT TO PRINT
```

Here is the resulting printed report:

```
                    Birds Residing in City Habitats

    Location       Individuals
    Sighted          Sighted


** Common name: Kestrel
  residential           2
  downtown              0
  park                 12
** Subtotal **
                       14

** Common name: Mockingbird
  residential           5
  downtown             14
  park                 16
** Subtotal **
                       35

** Common name: Scrub Jay
  residential          12
  downtown              2
  park                 21
** Subtotal **
                       35

*** Total ***
                       84
```

Notice that dBASE automatically supplies certain default formatting elements in the report, including the headings * * *Subtotal* * * and * * * *Total* * * * , the spaces between report divisions, and the asterisks before each division heading.

If you have trouble relating to ornithological studies, imagine generating this same report format for another database. For example, the groups in the report might represent a company's regional sales divisions, and the individual lines within each group might be salespeople and their quarterly earnings. Then the group totals would be the quarterly sales for each division, and the bottom line would be the total sales for all the divisions.

■ **dBASE II equivalent**
REPORT FORM

■ **Comments**
If a report you want to generate does not happen to conform to the tabular format generated by MODIFY REPORT, you can always write a program to produce exactly the format you require. Examples can be found throughout this book; in particular, see CDOW() **44★**, SET DEVICE **347★**, and SET RELATION **390★**.

The REPORT FORM command may also be used in dBASE programs, either directly or to "patch" together reports containing different formats and/or information from different databases (see the REPORT FORM entry).

A label generator is also available in dBASE III; see the MODIFY LABEL **221★** and LABEL FORM **195★** entries.

MODIFY STRUCTURE

- **Structure**

  MODIFY STRUCTURE

- **Description**

  The MODIFY STRUCTURE command puts you into a full-screen mode that enables you to change the field structure 100♦ of an existing database. Through this command, you can add new fields, make changes in the definitions of existing fields, or delete unwanted fields.

- **Usage**

  When you issue the MODIFY STRUCTURE command, dBASE assumes that you want to change the structure of the currently selected 322♦ open database. If no database is open, dBASE issues the following prompt:

  ```
  No database is in USE, enter filename:
  ```

  Unless you specify otherwise, dBASE will look for a file with a .DBF extension.

  In the MODIFY STRUCTURE mode, each field definition is displayed on a line of its own. You can use the same keyboard control commands that are available in CREATE 88★:

Key:	Action:
Right-arrow, Left-arrow	Move cursor one character to right or left.
Up-arrow, Down-arrow	Move cursor one field definition up or down.
Home, End	Move cursor one field element left or right.
Ctrl-Y	Delete item in field definition.
Ctrl-U	Delete field definition.
Ins	Activate or deactivate character-insert mode (a toggle).
Ctrl-N	Insert template line for new field definition.
Esc	Exit MODIFY STRUCTURE mode, without saving definition.
Ctrl-End	Exit MODIFY STRUCTURE mode, saving definition.

If SET MENU 378★ is ON, a list of control keys appears at the top of the screen when you enter the MODIFY STRUCTURE mode. Even if SET MENU is OFF, you can use the F1 function key to toggle this menu on or off from within MODIFY STRUCTURE.

When you exit MODIFY STRUCTURE with Ctrl-End, dBASE will copy records from the old version of the database into the modified version (see *Cautions*). Of course, no data can be copied for new or deleted fields. After the MODIFY STRUCTURE session, the previous version of the database is retained on disk as a backup file, with a .BAK extension.

■ **Cautions**

MODIFY STRUCTURE can successfully perform type conversions only between numeric and character data types. If you make other type changes, no data will be copied into the modified field.

Normally, if you change either the name of a field or the width of a field, dBASE will copy data back into the field. However, if you change *both* in the same MODIFY STRUCTURE session, dBASE will not copy data back into the field.

■ **dBASE II equivalent**

MODIFY STRUCTURE

However, the dBASE II version of the command does not automatically copy records from the old version to the new version. To modify a dBASE II database, it is necessary to COPY the old version to a backup file, define the new structure via MODIFY STRUCTURE, and then APPEND the data from the backup version. Data will not be appended to any field whose name or type has been modified.

■ **Comment**

In addition to the help provided by the SET MENU option, dBASE displays brief explanatory messages at the bottom of the screen as you work through the MODIFY STRUCTURE process:

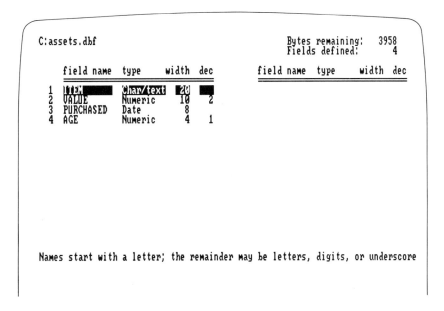

```
C:assets.dbf                               Bytes remaining:   3958
                                           Fields defined:       4

       field name   type     width  dec    field name   type      width  dec

    1  ITEM         Char/text   20          
    2  VALUE        Numeric     10    2
    3  PURCHASED    Date         8
    4  AGE          Numeric      4    1



    Names start with a letter; the remainder may be letters, digits, or underscore
```

MONTH()

■ **Structure**

MONTH(date-type value)

■ **Description**

Given a dBASE date-type **99**♦ value, MONTH() supplies a number from 1 through 12, representing the month in which the date falls.

■ **Usage**

The argument of MONTH() may be a date-type field or variable value, the value returned by the DATE() **103**★ or CTOD() **92**★ function, or the result of a date-arithmetic **100**★ expression. In these next two examples, the first command finds the month of the date value stored in the variable *birthday*, and the second finds the month for a date that is 100 days forward from the system date:

```
. ? MONTH(birthday)
5
.
```

```
. ? MONTH(DATE() + 100)
7
.
```

■ **Program example**

The following database, called *Booklist*, contains a list of book titles, their authors, and the dates on which the publisher expects to release the books:

```
. USE Booklist
. LIST
Record#  TITLE                AUTHOR    PUB_DATE
      1  Feeding Your Cat     Smith     09/18/85
      2  Understanding Cats   Jones     06/30/85
      3  Cats of the West     Jackson   12/15/85
      4  Night Cats           Carlson   04/10/86
      5  Modern Cats          Miller    06/25/86
      6  Adventures with Cats Mason     11/18/86
.
```

From this database, the publisher wishes to produce a list announcing the books by the seasons in which they will appear. The following program, called *Books*, uses the MONTH() function to determine the season for each book:

```
*------------------------------------------------------ BOOKS.PRG
* Announces the season in which each book will be available.
*

SET TALK OFF
SET SAFETY OFF

USE Booklist
INDEX ON pub_date TO Pub_ind

CLEAR
SET PRINT ON

? "Book List"
? "---- ----"
?

GOTO TOP
DO WHILE .NOT. EOF()
    ? title
    ? "By", author
    ? "Available "

    mo = MONTH(pub_date)
    DO CASE
        CASE (mo >= 3 .AND. mo <= 5)
            ?? "Spring"
        CASE (mo >= 6 .AND. mo <= 8)
            ?? "Summer"
        CASE (mo >= 9 .AND. mo <= 11)
            ?? "Fall"
        OTHERWISE
            ?? "Winter"
    ENDCASE

    ?? YEAR(pub_date)
    ?
    SKIP
ENDDO

SET PRINT OFF
SET TALK ON
SET SAFETY ON
RETURN
```

This program uses a DO WHILE 129★ loop to step through the entire *Booklist* database and produce a three-line announcement for each book. For a given book, the month in which the book will be published (*pub_date*) is assigned to the variable *mo*:

```
mo = MONTH(pub_date)
```

Then *mo* is used in a DO CASE **125★** statement within the loop to select the correct season.

Here are the announcements that the *Books* program produces:

```
Book List
---- ----

Understanding Cats
By Jones
Available Summer 1985

Feeding Your Cat
By Smith
Available Fall 1985

Cats of the West
By Jackson
Available Winter 1985

Night Cats
By Carlson
Available Spring 1986

Modern Cats
By Miller
Available Summer 1986

Adventures with Cats
By Mason
Available Fall 1986
```

■ **Caution**

MONTH() works only on a date-type argument. An attempt to send a string of characters to MONTH() will result in an error message:

```
. ? MONTH("2/27/51")
Invalid function argument
                      ?
? MONTH("2/27/51")
.
```

■ **dBASE II equivalent**

None

■ **Comments**

The CMONTH() **58★** function returns the *name* of the month represented by a date-type value. The DAY() **105★** and YEAR() **468★** functions return numeric values representing the day and the year, respectively, from a date-type value.

NEXT

■ **Structure**

... NEXT number ...

■ **Description**

NEXT is one of three optional scope **312★** clauses (ALL **17★** and RECORD **282★** are the other two) available for use with some dBASE commands. A scope clause specifies the portion of the current database that the command will operate on. The number in the NEXT clause specifies how many records **284★**, from the current record forward, will be included in the action of the command.

■ **Usage**

The NEXT clause causes a command to begin its action at the current position of the record pointer **258★** and work sequentially forward over the specified number of records. When the command is finished, the record pointer will be positioned at the last record that was *included* in the action.

■ **Database examples**

The database called *Staff* contains information about a group of employees. In the *Deptind* index, which we will use in the following examples, the *Staff* records are arranged alphabetically by department:

```
. USE Staff INDEX Deptind
. LIST
Record#  DEPARTMENT  LASTNAME    FIRSTNAME  HIRED     YRS  EMP_ID  SALARY_MO
      3  Clerical    Peters      Larry      06/10/83  1.9   3412    1350.00
      4  Clerical    Broussard   Marie      05/05/81  4.0   8712    1275.00
      7  Clerical    Liles       Carter     09/29/77  7.6   8799    1400.00
      9  Clerical    Ludlum      Donald     03/30/77  8.1   7412    1250.00
      2  Marketing   Southby     Anne       08/22/81  3.7   3134    2315.00
      6  Marketing   Smith       June       03/29/80  5.1   6823    2475.00
      1  Production  Morris      John       11/03/82  2.5   4521    1850.00
      5  Production  James       Fred       02/22/77  8.2   6563    1675.00
      8  Production  Washington  Liz        11/05/74 10.5   7321    1700.00
.
```

In the following sequence, the FIND **160★** command positions the record pointer at the first record for the Marketing Department and the subsequent DISPLAY **116★** command lists that record and the one following it. After the display is completed, the RECNO() 279★ function shows that the command left the record pointer at the last record in the specified scope:

```
. FIND Marketing
. DISPLAY NEXT 2
Record#  DEPARTMENT   LASTNAME   FIRSTNAME  HIRED      YRS  EMP_ID  SALARY_MO
      2  Marketing    Southby    Anne       08/22/81   3.7    3134   2315.00
      6  Marketing    Smith      June       03/29/80   5.1    6823   2475.00
.
```

```
. ? RECNO()
       6
.
```

(The DISPLAY command issued without a scope clause displays the current record only: In other words, the default scope of DISPLAY is *NEXT 1*.)

■ **Caution**

As we have already seen, a command with a NEXT clause normally leaves the pointer at the last record that was included in the command's action. However, if the NEXT clause specifies a greater number of records forward than are actually contained in the database, the command will attempt to search beyond the last record and the EOF() 147★ function will therefore be set to true. The following example illustrates such a situation:

```
. FIND Production
. DISPLAY NEXT 4
Record#  DEPARTMENT   LASTNAME    FIRSTNAME  HIRED      YRS   EMP_ID  SALARY_MO
      1  Production   Morris      John       11/03/82   2.5     4521   1850.00
      5  Production   James       Fred       02/22/77   8.2     6563   1675.00
      8  Production   Washington  Liz        11/05/74  10.5     7321   1700.00
.
. ? RECNO()
      10
.
. ? EOF()
.T.
.
```

RECNO() returns a value of 10 at the completion of the command (the database currently contains only nine records), and the EOF() function returns a value of .T..

■ **dBASE II equivalent**

NEXT

■ **Comments**

When a command contains both a NEXT clause and a FOR **164★** condition clause, the condition is applied only over the specified scope, beginning from the present pointer position. For example, consider the following two sequences:

```
. FIND Production
. DISPLAY NEXT 3 FOR yrs > 8
Record#  DEPARTMENT   LASTNAME    FIRSTNAME  HIRED      YRS  EMP_ID SALARY_MO
      5  Production   James       Fred       02/22/77   8.2   6563   1675.00
      8  Production   Washington  Liz        11/05/74  10.5   7321   1700.00
.
```

```
. DISPLAY FOR yrs > 8
Record#  DEPARTMENT   LASTNAME    FIRSTNAME  HIRED      YRS  EMP_ID SALARY_MO
      9  Clerical     Ludlum      Donald     03/30/77   8.1   7412   1250.00
      5  Production   James       Fred       02/22/77   8.2   6563   1675.00
      8  Production   Washington  Liz        11/05/74  10.5   7321   1700.00
.
```

The first DISPLAY command might be paraphrased as, "Find the first entry for the Production Department and then display all records among the next three that have *yrs* values greater than 8." In contrast, note that when no other scope is specified, as in the second example, a FOR clause normally changes the default scope to ALL.

The following database commands accept an optional scope clause (ALL, NEXT, or RECORD): AVERAGE **31★**, CHANGE **48★**, COPY **82★**, COUNT **85★**, DELETE **106★**, DISPLAY, LABEL FORM **195★**, LIST **200★**, LOCATE **202★**, RECALL **278★**, REPLACE **291★**, REPORT FORM **295★**, SUM **426★**, and TOTAL **436★**.

OTHERWISE

■ **Structure**

DO CASE
    CASE condition
        command_list
    * ... *
    OTHERWISE
        command_list
ENDCASE

■ **Description**

The OTHERWISE clause is an optional part of the DO CASE **125★** structure. It expresses a course of action that will be chosen if none of the previous CASE conditions evaluates as true. For instance, in this segment from *Price* **127◆**, the program evaluates several possible age groups and finally concludes that if the buyer doesn't fit any of those groups, he should pay the adult admission price:

```
DO CASE
    * ... *
    CASE age >= 65
        ?? "Senior Citizen:"
        price = "3.50"
    OTHERWISE
        ?? "Adult:"
        price = "5.00"
ENDCASE
* ... *
```

■ **Comment**

See the DO CASE entry for a detailed discussion of the OTHERWISE option in action.

PACK

■ **Structure**

PACK

■ **Description**

PACK deletes records **284★** permanently from a database. Specifically, PACK removes all records that have been marked for deletion by previous DELETE **106★** commands.

■ **Usage**

The following example of PACK involves a database called *Bills*, which contains information about household bills that fall due in the current month:

```
. USE Bills
. LIST
Record#  DUE_TO          AMOUNT DATE_DUE PAID
      1  Bernal Bank     142.75 06/15/85 .F.
      2  Maxwell's       567.81 06/22/85 .F.
      3  Credit Union     89.00 06/01/85 .T.
      4  Ameri Mortgage  986.23 06/30/85 .F.
      5  Bernal Electric  61.15 06/18/85 .F.
      6  OC Telephone    110.52 06/05/85 .T.

.
```

If you wish to delete the records of bills that have already been paid, two commands are required—DELETE and PACK:

```
. DELETE FOR paid
       2 records deleted
.
. LIST
Record#  DUE_TO           AMOUNT DATE_DUE PAID
      1  Bernal Bank      142.75 06/15/85 .F.
      2  Maxwell's        567.81 06/22/85 .F.
      3 *Credit Union      89.00 06/01/85 .T.
      4  Ameri Mortgage   986.23 06/30/85 .F.
      5  Bernal Electric   61.15 06/18/85 .F.
      6 *OC Telephone     110.52 06/05/85 .T.
.
. PACK
       4 records copied
.
```

As you can see, the DELETE command marks the appropriate records for deletion, and the PACK command then physically removes the records. Here is the resulting database:

```
. LIST
Record#  DUE_TO         AMOUNT DATE_DUE PAID
      1  Bernal Bank    142.75 06/15/85 .F.
      2  Maxwell's      567.81 06/22/85 .F.
      3  Ameri Mortgage 986.23 06/30/85 .F.
      4  Bernal Electric 61.15 06/18/85 .F.
  .
```

■ **Cautions**

PACK cannot be made to work on only part of a database. No scope 312★ or condition clauses are allowed in the PACK syntax. If you wish to delete only a selection of the records marked for deletion, you must RECALL 278★ the records you wish to save before performing PACK.

PACK does not save a backup copy of the database before deleting the records, so if you are in any doubt about the deletions, use the COPY 82★ command to save the database under another name before issuing the PACK command:

```
. COPY TO BILLS.BAK
: PACK
```

Otherwise, the deletions performed by PACK are permanent and irretrievable.

■ **dBASE II equivalent**

PACK

■ **Comments**

It is always wise to examine records that have been marked for deletion before you issue a PACK command. This DISPLAY 116★ command will list only the marked records:

```
. DISPLAY ALL FOR DELETED()
```

The ZAP 469★ command deletes all records in a database, whether they are marked for deletion or not.

PARAMETERS

■ **Structure**

PARAMETERS variable_list

■ **Description**

A PARAMETERS statement sets up local (PRIVATE 259★) variables 459★ in a program or procedure 383♦, for the purpose of receiving data values from a calling program 387♦ (which may be dBASE itself).

If used, PARAMETERS must be the first performable statement in a program (that is, the first statement other than comment lines 4♦), or the first performable statement after the PROCEDURE 263★ line in a procedure.

Actual values are assigned to the PARAMETERS variables from the WITH clause of the calling DO 122★ statement. The expressions in the WITH clause, which may be of any of dBASE's four data types 98★, are evaluated in the order listed and the results assigned sequentially to the variables in the PARAMETERS list. The number of expressions in the WITH clause *must* equal the number of variables in the PARAMETERS list.

■ **Usage**

The use of parameters ♦ "generalizes" the task performed by a procedure: That is, parameters allow the procedure to perform differently under different conditions, as defined by the specific needs of the calling program.

■ **Program example**

Yesno is a procedure that is called from several different locations in the real-estate program. (The real-estate program is discussed in detail under the SET PROCEDURE 383★ entry.) The purpose of *Yesno* is to place a prompt at some specified location on the display screen, elicit a yes-or-no response, and store the response as a logical value in the global 269♦ variable *yn*.

The calling program passes three parameter values to *Yesno*: the two numeric coordinates of the screen location where the prompt is to appear, and a string value representing the prompt itself. *Yesno* receives these three values in the variables *currow*, *curcol*, and *question*, respectively. Here is *Yesno*:

```
PROCEDURE Yesno
*----- Handles prompt and input for a yes-or-no question.
*        Returns answer in the logical variable yn.
*

PARAMETERS currow, curcol, question

PUBLIC yn
valid = .F.
answer = " "

SET BELL OFF

DO WHILE .NOT. valid
    @ currow, curcol SAY question GET answer PICTURE "!"
    READ
    valid = answer $ "YN"
    IF valid
        answer = "." + answer + "."
        yn = &answer
    ELSE
        ? CHR(7)
    ENDIF
ENDDO

RETURN
```

As required, the PARAMETERS statement is the first executable statement in the program:

```
PARAMETERS currow, curcol, question
```

Here is an example of the way a DO...WITH statement calls *Yesno*, passing the desired parameter values in the call:

```
DO Yesno WITH 10, 10, "Is the printer ready? "
```

In this case, the parameter variables *currow* and *curcol* will each receive a value of 10, and the variable *question* will receive the prompt string "Is the printer ready?".

Yesno uses the three parameter values passed by the DO statement in the following @ 9★ statement:

```
@ currow, curcol SAY question GET answer PICTURE "!"
```

This statement is located inside a DO...WHILE 129★ loop that continues displaying the prompt until the user has entered a single valid character: Y or N. This value is then converted into a logical value of .T. or .F. and stored in *yn*. (For further discussion of *Yesno*, see the & 1★ entry.)

■ **Caution**

A special condition exists when you pass a variable as a parameter to a procedure: If the procedure changes the value of the variable internally, its value is changed externally as well. Let's say, for example, that a program called *Prog* passes the variable *var* to the *Proc* procedure:

```
DO Proc WITH var
```

Proc receives the parameter value in a local variable called *p*:

```
PROCEDURE Proc
PARAMETER p
```

If, during the performance of the procedure, a new value is assigned to *p*, the value of *var* will also change, because *var* and *p* are, in effect, the same variable. When *Proc* passes control back to *Prog*, *var* contains whatever new value was assigned to *p* and the old value of *var* is lost.

The following example is a simple exercise that illustrates this phenomenon. The *Tally* program totals the prices of a series of items (the prices are input from the keyboard) and then adds sales tax. To do this, *Tally* first stores the sum of the prices in the variable *ttl* and then calls the procedure *Califtax*, passing it the current value of *ttl* as a parameter:

```
*--------------------------------------------------------- TALLY.PRG
* Illustrates the use of a variable as a parameter.
*

SET TALK OFF

ttl = 0
item = " "

?
?
DO WHILE .NOT. LEN(item) = 0
    ACCEPT "       ==>      " TO item
    ttl = ttl + VAL(item)
ENDDO
? "           ------------"
? "          ", STR(ttl, 13, 2)

DO Califtax WITH ttl

? "           ------------"
? "Total : ", STR(ttl, 13, 2)

SET TALK ON

RETURN
```

Califtax, whose task is to calculate the state sales tax and add it to the total, receives the value of *ttl* in the variable *num*:

```
*--------------------------------------------------- CALIFTAX.PRG
* Illustrates the use of a variable as a parameter.
*

PARAMETER num

tax = ROUND(num * .065, 2)
? "Tax   : ", STR(tax, 13, 2)
num = num + tax

RETURN
```

During program performance, *Califtax* changes the value of *num* by adding the value of *tax* to it. When control returns to *Tally*, the value of *ttl* has also been changed. Here is a sample run of the program:

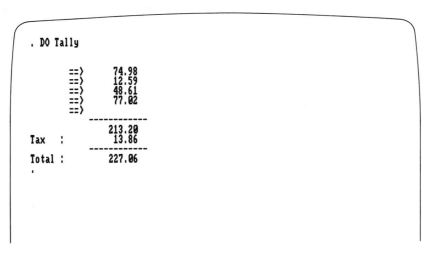

```
. DO Tally

            ==>      74.98
            ==>      12.59
            ==>      48.61
            ==>      77.02
            ==>
                  ------------
                    213.20
    Tax   :          13.86
                  ------------
    Total :         227.06
    .
```

Note that the original value of *ttl* is lost. If a record of the pre-tax total were required, *Tally* would have to be modified to save that value in another variable before passing *ttl* to *Califtax*.

■ **dBASE II equivalent**
None

■ **Comment**
Parameter-passing is a fairly sophisticated programming tool usually found only in full-blown computer languages. It is one of the advanced features that make dBASE III such a powerful microcomputer application.

Path names

The main directory of a disk is called the root directory. The root directory may contain subdirectories ♦, which simply constitute division of the storage space on a hard or floppy disk. These subdirectories, in turn, may have subdirectories of their own, and so on, like branches—in fact, we often refer to this system as a tree-structured directory. A path name indicates a file's location within this structure.

The default directory in dBASE is the root directory of the current disk. If you issue a command that is to work with a file located in some other directory (or on some other disk), you must specify the path to that directory, so that dBASE can find the file.

Like files, subdirectories have user-assigned names. The rules for creating these subdirectory names are the same as those for creating file names in DOS 133★. In a path name, the root directory of a disk is always referred to by a backslash symbol (\), and the name of each subdirectory is separated from the next by another backslash symbol. A backslash also separates the final subdirectory name from the file name.

For example, let's say the disk in drive B contains a subdirectory called *Accounts*, which in turn contains two subdirectories called *New* and *Old*. You want to open a database file called *PARTSCO.DBF*, which is stored in *Old*. You would issue the dBASE USE 454★ command as follows:

```
. USE B:\Accounts\Old\Partsco
```

Notice that the path name supplies the complete subdirectory hierarchy that leads to the desired file.

To establish alternate subdirectory paths for file searches, use the SET PATH 380★ command. If dBASE does not find a given file in the default directory, it will search the alternate paths in the order listed. (If you use the same alternate search paths regularly, you may want to include them in the *CONFIG.DB* 66★ file.)

PCOL()

- **Structure**
  PCOL()

- **Description**
  The PCOL() function returns a numeric value representing the current column position of the printer.

■ **Usage**

PCOL() and its companion, PROW() 268★, are useful whenever you are using a combination of the ? 5★ and @...SAY 9★ commands to produce a printed document from a dBASE program. After a series of ? commands, PCOL() and PROW() supply the current printer position for use in the subsequent @...SAY command. For example:

```
? "Net Income: "
@ PROW(), PCOL() SAY income PICTURE "$###,###"
```

If the variable *income* in the preceding statement contains a value of 512780, these statements will result in the following output to the printer:

```
Net Income: $512,780
```

The reason for using @...SAY rather than ?? after a ? command is to take advantage of the number-formatting features of the PICTURE 252★ clause.

■ **Caution**

Like PROW(), PCOL() can be used in addresses determined *relative* to the current printer position:

```
? "Net Income: "
@ PROW(), PCOL() + 25 SAY income PICTURE "$###,###"
```

to achieve displays like this:

```
Net Income:                       $512,780
```

However, it is best to avoid using same-row negative values in such statements (*@ PROW(), PCOL() – 15*, for example), since not all small printers can move the print head from right to left, and in any case, the danger of inadvertently overwriting other data on the same line is great.

■ **dBASE II equivalent**

None

■ **Comments**

The SET DEVICE TO PRINT 347★ command is required in order to use @...SAY for printer output.

For further discussion of printer control, see the entries under @...SAY...GET, EJECT 145★, SET DEVICE, and SET PRINT 381★.

The COL() 60★ function is available to supply the current column position from the screen.

PICTURE

■ **Structure**

@ row,col   *SAY value   PICTURE template   GET field/variable   PICTURE template*

■ **Description**

PICTURE is an optional clause in the @...SAY...GET **9**★ command. The clause offers special formatting features for displaying data with @...SAY and for reading data with @...GET. These features are implemented through a "sublanguage" of functions and template symbols that appear in quotes as part of the PICTURE clause.

The general form of the PICTURE clause is:

```
PICTURE "@f xxxxxxxxxx"
```

where @f represents one of PICTURE's 10 formatting functions and the x's represent some combination of template symbols. A PICTURE clause may contain one function (which may be a compound), a set of template symbols, or both. If both are present, a space character *must* separate the function from the template symbols.

The functions and template symbols are characterized by the type of data they work with and the command they are appropriate to (SAY, GET, or both). The largest single set of functions and symbols is for numeric display:

☐ The @C and @X functions display *CR* and *DB* after positive and negative numbers, respectively.

☐ The @(function ◆ places negative numbers in parentheses.

☐ The @B function left justifies a number within a specified field width.

☐ The @Z function displays zero as a blank.

☐ The comma (,) and period (.) template symbols are available for displaying numbers with commas and decimal points.

☐ The * and $ template symbols fill leading blanks in a right-justified number with asterisks or dollar signs, respectively.

There are two functions for displaying and reading date-type **99**◆ values:

☐ The @D function uses the American mo/da/yr date format.

☐ The @E function uses the European da/mo/yr date format.

(however, keep in mind that the SET DATE **337**★ command offers far greater versatility in working with dates).

There are four character functions and symbols:

□   @A restricts input to alphabetic characters.

□   @! converts all characters to uppercase.

□   @R, when used with an @...GET command, indicates that literal (constant) characters contained in the template will *not* be considered as part of the input value. (Without @R, any literals in the PICTURE template will be stored in the input variable along with other characters entered from the keyboard.)

□   The ! template symbol both displays and reads alphabetic characters as uppercase only, and has no effect on other characters.

In addition, there are several more template symbols available for restricting the type and nature of input values for the @...GET command:

□   9 limits input to digits and signs.

□   # limits input to digits, blanks, and signs.

□   A limits input to letters.

□   L limits input to logical values **99♦**.

□   N limits input to letters and digits.

□   X accepts any character (unrestricted input).

■ **Usage**

The PICTURE sublanguage is best learned through use and experimentation. The following program illustrates a selection of the functions and template symbols. You will find it helpful as a beginning exercise in mastering the PICTURE clause.

```
*-------------------------------------------------- PICTURE.PRG
* Demonstrates the use of the PICTURE clause in the @ command.
*

SET TALK OFF

*----- Create variables that will be used in the demonstration.
*
neg = -31832.42
pos = 31832.42
dt = CTOD("03/14/85")
logic = .T.
char = "the picture clause"

CLEAR

? "            Using the PICTURE Clause"
? "            ======================="
?
? "  *** The PICTURE Functions ***"
? "      ---------------------"
? "@C  (positive number)        ==>  "
@ ROW(), COL() SAY pos PICTURE "@c"
? "@X  (negative number)        ==>  "
@ ROW(), COL() SAY neg PICTURE "@x"
? "@(  (negative number)        ==>  "
@ ROW(), COL() SAY neg PICTURE "@("
? "@B  (positive number)        ==>  "
@ ROW(), COL() SAY pos PICTURE "@b"
? "@D  (date)                   ==>  "
@ ROW(), COL() SAY dt PICTURE "@d"
? "@E  (date)                   ==>  "
@ ROW(), COL() SAY dt PICTURE "@e"
? "@!  (character value)        ==>  "
@ ROW(), COL() SAY char PICTURE "@!"

?
? " *** The PICTURE Template Symbols ***"
? "     ----------------------------"
? "symbols: $##,###.##          ==>  "
@ ROW(), COL() SAY pos PICTURE "$##,###.##"
? "symbols: *99,999.99          ==>  "
@ ROW(), COL() SAY pos PICTURE "*99,999.99"
? "symbol:  !!!!!!!!!!!!!!!!!!!  ==>  "
@ ROW(), COL() SAY char PICTURE "!!!!!!!!!!!!!!!!!!!!"
?
? "combination: @C $##,###.##      ==>  "
@ ROW(), COL() SAY pos PICTURE "@c $##,###.##"
? "combination: @( $###,###.##     ==>  "
@ ROW(), COL() SAY neg PICTURE "@( $###,###.##"
?

RETURN
```

Here is the output from *Picture*:

```
        Using the PICTURE Clause
        ========================

   *** The PICTURE Functions ***
   -------------------------
 @C  (positive number)      ==)       31832.42 CR
 @X  (negative number)      ==)       31832.42 DB
 @(  (negative number)      ==)  (    31832.42)
 @B  (positive number)      ==)  31832.42
 @D  (date)                 ==)  03/14/85
 @E  (date)                 ==)  14/03/85
 @!  (character value)      ==)  THE PICTURE CLAUSE

   *** The PICTURE Template Symbols ***
   ------------------------------
 symbols: $##,###.##         ==)  $31,832.42
 symbols: *99,999.99         ==)  *31,832.42
 symbol:  !!!!!!!!!!!!!!!!!   ==)  THE PICTURE CLAUSE

 combination: @C $##,###.##   ==)  $31,832.42 CR
 combination: @( $###,###.##  ==)  ($31,832.42)

   .
```

You can experiment with this program by changing the values of the variables or trying different formatting functions and symbols, until you feel comfortable managing the PICTURE options.

- **Program example**

The following procedure, called *Mortgage*, is part of the real-estate program described in the SET PROCEDURE **383★** entry. Given three input values—the principal loan amount, the interest rate, and the term of the loan—*Mortgage* calculates a monthly mortgage payment. The procedure conducts an input dialogue to obtain the three values, and then presents a screen displaying all the values entered, along with the calculated result. Both the input dialogue and the final screen output require the use of PICTURE clauses. Here is the procedure:

```
PROCEDURE Mortgage
*----- Calculates a monthly mortgage payment.
*

SET CONFIRM ON
SET BELL OFF
SET TALK OFF
CLEAR

@ 6, 25 SAY "Monthly Mortgage Calculation"
@ 7, 25 SAY "------- -------- ------------"

princ = 0
rate = 0.00
term = 0

@ 9, 25 SAY "Principal amount? " GET princ PICTURE "######" ;
   RANGE 10000, 999999
@ 11, 25 SAY "Percent interest? " GET rate PICTURE "##.##" ;
   RANGE 5, 25
@ 13, 25 SAY "Term in years?    " GET term PICTURE "##" ;
   RANGE 10, 50
READ

r1 = rate / 1200
t1 = term * 12
fact = (r1 + 1) ^ (-t1)
mort = (princ * r1) / (1 - fact)

CLEAR

@ 8, 25 SAY princ PICTURE "Principal:      $###,###"
@ 9, 25 SAY rate  PICTURE "Interest:        ##.##"
@ 10, 25 SAY term  PICTURE "Years:             ##"
@ 11, 25 SAY "------------------------"
@ 12, 25 SAY mort  PICTURE "Payment:      $#,###.##"
?
?
WAIT "                      Press any key to continue."

RETURN
```

Notice that a PICTURE string may contain words and symbols that are not part of the formatting template:

```
@ 8, 25 SAY princ PICTURE "Principal:       $###,###"
```

Here is a typical interaction with the *Mortgage* procedure:

```
Monthly Mortgage Calculation
------- -------- -----------

Principal Amount?  120000

Percent Interest?  13.25

Term in Years?     30
```

```
Principal:    $120,000
Interest:       13.25
Years:            30
--------------------------
Payment:      $1,350.93

Press any key to continue.
```

You can read more about *Mortgage* in the entries for RANGE 272★ and WAIT 461★.

■ **dBASE II equivalent**
PICTURE

■ **Comment**
See @...SAY...GET and RANGE for more detailed discussions of the uses and variations of the @ command.

Pointer

When you open a database, dBASE always keeps track of the number of the current record 284★ in the database. Metaphorically, we speak of a *record pointer* that moves up and down the database, and is always positioned at (or pointing to) the currently active record.

The importance of the record pointer lies in the fact that many database commands work, by default, on only the current record. For example, DISPLAY 116★ shows the current record on the screen; REPLACE 291★ stores new field 154★ data in the current record; and EDIT 141★ puts the current record in full-screen edit mode.

When you plan to use commands like these, you will often want to find out where the record pointer is currently located, and you may want to move the pointer to a new position: RECNO() 279★ supplies the current position of the record pointer; GOTO 169★ and SKIP 400★ allow you to move the pointer to a specific record; query commands like FIND 160★ SEEK 317★, and LOCATE 202★ move the pointer to the record that contains specific information you are looking for.

Many other commands move the pointer as a side effect of their actual tasks. For example, commands that perform operations over the entire database generally move the pointer to the end of the file and leave it there, setting the EOF() 147★ function to true. In this special case, the record pointer will be located *after* the last record in the database.

When multiple databases are open simultaneously in different work areas 454♦, each has its own record pointer. These pointers are generally left independent of one another. However, the SET RELATION 390★ command allows you to establish a relationship between two databases, so that when the pointer of the first database moves, the pointer of the second also moves accordingly.

You will find many references to the record pointer throughout this book, along with examples that illustrate the uses of the pointer concept.

PRIVATE

■ **Structure**

PRIVATE variable_list
PRIVATE ALL
PRIVATE ALL LIKE skeleton
PRIVATE ALL EXCEPT skeleton

■ **Description**

The PRIVATE command declares one or more variables **459★** as local **460♦** to a given procedure **383♦**, even when the same variable names have been declared global **460♦** (PUBLIC **269★**) at another level of the program. The variables included in the PRIVATE command may therefore have the same names as global variables used elsewhere in the program, without interfering with the values of the global variables (or vice versa).

PRIVATE variables are available only to the procedure in which they are declared, and are released from memory as soon as that procedure relinquishes control.

Like the RELEASE **288★** syntax, the PRIVATE syntax allows several ways of specifying the variable names affected:

☐   A list of variable names.

☐   An ALL clause, specifying all currently defined variables.

☐   An ALL LIKE clause, using the wildcard characters **114♦** * and ? to specify variable names with common elements.

☐   An ALL EXCEPT clause, also using wildcard characters, but this time to specify variable names that are to be *excluded* from the PRIVATE list.

■ **Usage**

The use of PRIVATE is essentially a convenience, not a necessity: PRIVATE does allow local duplication of variable names without loss of global-variable values, but you can always program the same tasks using unique names for the local variables.

■ **Program example**

The following programming exercise demonstrates how dBASE organizes global and local variables, and suggests how PRIVATE variables might be put to use. The program consists of a routine called *Pubvar* and a subroutine called *Privvar*, both of which assign values to the same three variables: *a*, *b*, and *c*. However, *Pubvar* declares the variables as PUBLIC, whereas *Privvar* declares them as PRIVATE. Here are the two routines:

```
*----------------------------------------------------- PUBVAR.PRG
* Part of an experiment with the PRIVATE statement.
*    Calls Privvar.
*

PUBLIC a, b, c
SET TALK ON

? "Assigning public values:"
?
? "a = "
a = 1
?
? "b = "
b = 2
?
? "c = "
c = 3
?
? "Now calling Privvar."
DO Privvar

?
? "Back from Privvar."
DISPLAY MEMORY

RETURN


*----------------------------------------------------- PRIVVAR.PRG
* Part of an experiment with the PRIVATE statement.
*    Called from Pubvar.
*

PRIVATE a, b, c

?
? "Assigning private values:"
?
? "a = "
a = 4
?
? "b = "
b = 5
?
? "c = "
c = 6
?
DISPLAY MEMORY

?
? "Returning control to Pubvar."
?
RETURN
```

Pubvar calls *Privvar*, and both routines perform the DISPLAY MEMORY 118★ command before relinquishing control. Here is the output from a performance of the program:

```
. Do Pubvar
Assigning public values:

a =
1

b =
2

c =
3

Now calling Privvar.

Assigning private values:

a =
4

b =
5

c =
6

A          pub  (hidden) N        1 (          1.00000000)
B          pub  (hidden) N        2 (          2.00000000)
C          pub  (hidden) N        3 (          3.00000000)
A          priv N           4 (          4.00000000)     C:privvar.prg
B          priv N           5 (          5.00000000)     C:privvar.prg
C          priv N           6 (          6.00000000)     C:privvar.prg
    6 variables defined,       54 bytes used
   250 variables available,   5946 bytes available

Returning control to Pubvar.


Back from Privvar.
A          pub  N        1 (          1.00000000)
B          pub  N        2 (          2.00000000)
C          pub  N        3 (          3.00000000)
    3 variables defined,       27 bytes used
   253 variables available,   5973 bytes available

    .
```

When you study the results of the DISPLAY MEMORY commands in this output, you will notice that there are actually *six* variables defined in memory after performance of *Privvar*—three of them PRIVATE, available only to *Privvar*; the other three PUBLIC (though temporarily "hidden"), but with the same names as the PRIVATE variables. However, when *Privvar* returns control to *Pubvar*, the three PRIVATE variables are released from memory: Only the PUBLIC variables remain, no longer hidden. Furthermore, these PUBLIC variables have the same values they had when *Privvar* was first called—the lower-level procedure (*Privvar*) that declared the local variables used them without interfering with the global variables declared by the higher-level procedure (*Pubvar*).

■ Cautions

As you can deduce from the preceding output, dBASE's imposed maximum of 256 defined variables applies to *all* current variables, PUBLIC and PRIVATE alike.

PRIVATE variables can make program debugging difficult, because their values are lost as soon as the program exits the procedure in which the variables were created or declared PRIVATE. See the PUBLIC entry for some suggested solutions to this problem.

■ dBASE II equivalent

None

All variables are global in dBASE II.

■ Comment

Generally, the PUBLIC statement is more important than the PRIVATE statement in dBASE programming situations, because PUBLIC is often the only means by which a lower-level procedure can pass information back to the procedure that called it. (See the PUBLIC entry for details.)

PROCEDURE

■ **Structure**

PROCEDURE procedure_name

■ **Description**

A PROCEDURE statement marks the beginning of each program in a procedure file **383◆**. The purpose of the statement is to assign a unique name by which the procedure can be called with a DO **122★** command (*DO Minmax*, for example).

■ **Usage**

The rules for procedure names are similar to the rules for dBASE III file names **155★**:

☐ A procedure name may be up to 8 characters long.

☐ The first character must be a letter.

☐ The remaining characters may be any combination of letters, digits, and under-score characters.

☐ The name may not include embedded spaces.

Unlike file names, however, procedure names have no extensions.

For examples of the PROCEDURE statement in use, see the SET PROCEDURE **383★** entry. Additional examples occur throughout the book.

■ **Caution**

Because only one procedure file can be open at a time, it is possible to use the same name for procedures stored in different files. However, this can lead to confusion during development or maintenance of large applications, and the practice should, therefore, be avoided.

■ **dBASE II equivalent**

None

Programming

dBASE III can operate in either of two modes:

☐ Direct-command mode.

☐ Program mode.

Direct-command mode is undoubtedly the side of dBASE most new users encounter first. In this mode of operation, you issue a command at dBASE's "dot prompt" **62♦**:

If the *syntax* is correct, dBASE immediately performs the command and, normally, displays the results on the screen (see Control Parameters **73★**). Using the vocabulary of direct commands available in dBASE III, you can create and work with databases and exploit all the data-management facilities dBASE has to offer. Many dBASE users never need anything more than this direct use of the command set.

However, for those whose needs are more complex, dBASE also functions as a complete programming language. (A program ♦ is simply a sequence of commands structured to accomplish a defined task and stored together in a disk file **157♦**.)

To write or edit ♦ a dBASE program, you can access the dBASE word processor **466♦** via the MODIFY COMMAND **219★** statement, or you can use an external word processor to create an ASCII text file. To "run" the program—that is, to instruct dBASE to open the program file and begin a sequential performance of the commands the file contains—you issue a DO **122★** command that includes the program's disk-file name. The program then temporarily takes control of the computer's activity and performs its defined task. When program performance is complete, you are returned to the dBASE dot prompt.

All but a few of the dBASE direct commands are designed for practical use within a program, as well as from the dot prompt. This, of course, is what distinguishes dBASE from other personal-computer programming languages such as BASIC or Pascal. These other programming languages also have the *potential* for creating and managing databases, but dBASE's uniquely rich collection of *built-in* resources can save the programmer considerable time and effort in database programming tasks.

In addition to the vocabulary of direct commands involved primarily in working with databases, dBASE includes a set of commands designed specifically to define the logic and structure of a program. Together, these commands provide the essential features of a traditional programming language, making dBASE far more than just a command-driven database manager.

■ Loops

A loop is a program structure that sets off a group of commands for repetitive performance. The DO WHILE...ENDDO **129★** command defines a loop in a dBASE program: The commands located between the DO WHILE statement and the ENDDO statement are performed repeatedly, as long as the WHILE condition remains true; looping ends when the condition becomes false. One common example of such repetitive action in a dBASE program is a loop that performs one set of commands on each record of a database. Looping stops when the program comes to the end of the database (the end-of-file **147◆** condition becomes true).

■ Decision structures

A decision structure defines alternative courses of action in a program. The choice of which course to take depends upon the value—true or false—of a condition expression **286◆**. The IF...ELSE...ENDIF **171★** statement creates a two-choice decision structure in a dBASE program: The commands located between IF and ELSE are performed whenever the IF condition is true; otherwise, the commands located between ELSE and ENDIF are performed. The DO CASE...ENDCASE **125★** structure presents *several* possible courses of action, the choice depending upon which of the mutually exclusive CASE **44★** conditions is true. Only one course of action (or none) will be chosen during a given performance of the statement.

■ Input and Output

Programs often require the ability to communicate with the user during program performance—to display certain messages to the user, perhaps, or to obtain information or responses at various points. The program may, in fact, be designed to choose one of several different courses of action on the basis of choices indicated from the keyboard during program execution. These activities in a program—receiving information from the keyboard and sending messages and information to the display screen or printer—are referred to as *input* and *output*. dBASE provides several input and output commands:

☐ The print commands ? and ?? 5★ are simple ways to send lines of text to the screen or printer.

☐ The @...SAY 9★ command presents formatted data at a specific location on the screen.

☐ The INPUT 182★, ACCEPT 12★, @...GET 9★, READ 275★, and WAIT 461★ commands accept information from the keyboard in a variety of ways. (An important aspect of the @...GET command is that it allows a program to take control over the format of a database input or editing screen.)

■ Variables

Programs typically need storage space for specific data items that are required (or acquired) during program performance. In a dBASE program, the major data structure usually consists of the open database (or databases) the program is working with. However, other intermediate data items may also come into play, and the program sets aside memory space for such items through the creation of variables 459★. In the program itself, a variable is simply a name that represents a certain data item; however, in the computer's memory, the variable name is associated with a memory address at which the actual data item is stored. The data item (value) that a variable "contains" may change during the course of program performance, but the variable's type 98◆ (numeric, character, date, or logical) normally will not.

Ordinarily, dBASE uses the STORE 414★ command or its alternative syntax, the equal sign (=), to assign a value to a variable. However, a program can also store an input value in a variable via an INPUT, ACCEPT, @...GET, or WAIT command. To gain access to the data item, the program simply refers to the name of the variable in which the value is stored.

(A useful technique for writing "self-documenting" programs is to assign variable names that are descriptive of the data the variables hold—*tax* to hold a computed sales-tax value, for example, or *choice* to hold an option selected from a menu.)

■ Subroutines

A large programming task is best organized into small, easily managed pieces called *subroutines* or *procedures* ◆. Once a subroutine is written, it may be called upon to perform its specific task again and again, whenever it is needed. Professional programmers recognize the importance of a hierarchical "top-down" structure, where routines at the top control the major action by calling upon specific task-oriented routines located farther down in the structure. The dBASE language encourages this modularized, top-down approach to programming in several ways:

☐ A programmer can create a "library" of procedures, stored together in a single disk file. When that file is opened (via the SET PROCEDURE 383★ command), all of the procedures are available to the controlling program.

☐ DO commands can be used *within* a program to "call" procedures in the same manner they are used to open program files for performance.

☐ When a program calls a procedure, it may also "send" the procedure specific data items called *parameters*. These values are listed in a WITH clause in the DO command. (With this construct, the called procedure must contain a PARAMETERS 245★ statement to establish the variables in which the data values will be stored when received.)

☐ Variables can be defined as PUBLIC 269★ (available to any procedure) or PRIVATE 259 ★ (available only in the procedure that establishes them).

When a subroutine has completed its task, it normally returns control to the procedure that called it (which, of course, may be the main program).

■ Comments

Programs should contain internal documentation, or comments ✦, explaining their overall purpose and how specific sections of the program work. These comments are not performable parts of the program, but simply aids to the person reading or maintaining the program. In the dBASE language, comment lines must begin with an asterisk (* 4★) or with the word NOTE.

Although comments are important for clarity and documentation, they do consume disk space, so they should be kept brief. See the * entry for a more detailed discussion of program commenting.

■ Debugging

Very few programs perform perfectly the first time you use them. The process of locating and correcting the sources of program error is called debugging ✦. dBASE provides the SET TALK 398★, SET STEP 397★, SET ECHO 351★, and SET DEBUG 339★ commands to help with this critical stage of program development.

All of the programming commands mentioned in this entry are described in detail, with examples, under their own headings, and are also used in programming examples throughout the book.

PROW()

- **Structure**

  PROW()

- **Description**

  The PROW() function returns a numeric value representing the current row position of the printer.

- **Usage**

  PROW() and its companion, PCOL() **250★**, are useful whenever you are using a combination of the ? **5★** and @...SAY **9★** commands to produce a printed document from within a dBASE program. After a series of ? commands, PROW() and PCOL() are called to supply the current printer position, for use in the subsequent @...SAY command.

- **Program example**

  The *Printinfo* program listed in the SET DEVICE **347★** entry produces a printed home description from a selected record in a real-estate database called *Property*. The beginning of the description is produced by a series of ? commands. Then, an @...SAY command is used to produce a formatted display of the home's price. This command uses PROW() to find the current printer-row location:

  ```
  @ PROW() + 1, 15 SAY asking_pr PICTURE "$###,###.##"
  ```

  Notice that the command prints its data at a *relative address* **60♦**, one row down from the previous printer row position.

- **Cautions**

  The SET DEVICE TO PRINT command is required in order to use @...SAY for printer output.

  A relative row address for the printer must not exceed 254.

  Do not attempt to move backwards up the paper with a relative address such as *PROW() – 2*. The resulting problems can range from annoying to catastrophic, depending upon your printer.

- **dBASE II equivalent**

  None

- **Comments**

  Other commands used for printer control include EJECT **145★** and SET PRINT **381★**.

  The ROW() **304★** function is available to supply the current row position of the screen cursor.

PUBLIC

■ **Structure**

PUBLIC variable_list

■ **Description**

The PUBLIC statement declares one or more variables **459★** as global ◆. Global variables are available to every procedure **383◆** of the program in which they were declared. Furthermore, they are retained in memory after program performance is complete. Variables that are not explicitly declared as PUBLIC are released from memory as soon as the procedure that created them relinquishes control.

■ **Usage**

A PUBLIC declaration enables one procedure in a program to make information stored in a variable available to other procedures in the same program. The following example from the real-estate program described in the SET PROCEDURE **383★** entry illustrates this point.

■ **Program example**

The real-estate program maintains a database called *Property*, which contains listings of homes that are for sale. One of the important functions of the program is to locate all homes that match the specific requirements of a potential home-buyer. The *Reqmnts* procedure described under SET FILTER **357★** is in charge of this task. *Reqmnts* uses a special-purpose input procedure called *Minmax* to obtain two values from the user at the keyboard and store them in the variables *min* and *max*, respectively. These values represent the potential home-buyer's minimum and maximum requirements for a given characteristic of a home (sale price or square footage, for example). To make these values available to *Reqmnts* (the procedure that calls *Minmax*), a PUBLIC statement in *Minmax* declares the variables as global:

```
PROCEDURE Minmax
*----- Accepts min and max requirements for the REQMNTS procedure.
*

PARAMETER loc

PUBLIC min, max
min = "      "
max = "      "

DO WHILE LEN(TRIM(min)) = 0 .OR. LEN(TRIM(max)) = 0
    @ 16, 16 SAY "from: " GET min PICTURE "999999"
    @ 17, 16 SAY "to:   " GET max PICTURE "999999"
    READ
ENDDO

@ loc, 40 SAY min + " TO " + max
RETURN
```

Notice that the PUBLIC statement is located near the beginning of the procedure, *before* the variables are assigned their initial values (see *Caution*).

■ **Caution**

If a variable is to be declared PUBLIC, it should not be assigned an initial value before the PUBLIC statement is executed. For example, the *Reqmnts* program should not initialize *min* and *max* before calling upon *Minmax* to do its work. A syntax error will result if a PUBLIC statement is performed on a variable that has been initialized.

■ **dBASE II equivalent**

None

■ **Comments**

Declaring variables as PUBLIC can often prove to be an excellent tool for debugging **267◆** programs. Since global variables remain in memory after program performance is complete, you can use direct ? commands to investigate the contents of the variables the program creates and works with. These values will often reveal the problem in a program that is not working properly.

Variables that are initialized at the dot-prompt **62◆** level are *always PUBLIC*. Hence, another way to track a variable used in a program is to assign the variable an initial value *before* running the program. Then, after the program has been executed, you can use a ? statement to examine the new value of the variable.

QUIT

- **Structure**

  QUIT

- **Description**

  QUIT performs a graceful exit from dBASE, closing all open database, program, and alternate files **157♦**, and returning you to DOS **133★**.

- **Usage**

  You can safely issue a QUIT command even if you have made unsaved changes in the currently open database: QUIT will save the database in its new version before leaving dBASE.

  You can also safely use QUIT at the end of a dBASE command file **264♦**, if you wish to exit dBASE and return to the operating system upon completion of the program.

- **Caution**

  The consequences of exiting dBASE in any other way than through the QUIT command can be serious. See the cautionary notes under the SET PRINT **381★** entry for a detailed discussion.

- **dBASE II equivalent**

  QUIT

- **Comment**

  The RETURN **301★** command transfers program control back to a calling program or procedure *within* dBASE.

RANGE

■ **Structure**

@...GET... *RANGE expression, expression*

■ **Description**

RANGE is an optional clause of the @...GET **9★** command that allows the programmer to specify a valid range for numeric **98◆** or date **99◆** input values. When the subsequent READ **275★** command is performed, dBASE will accept only values that are within the specified range. In response to an invalid value, dBASE will display an error message at the upper right corner of the screen and prompt for another input value.

■ **Usage**

The RANGE clause offers a simple technique for restricting input to values that fall within a realistic range for a specific application. This kind of input validation is one way of avoiding nonsensical computed output.

■ **Program examples**

Here are two typical examples of the use of RANGE in interactive applications.

Example 1: The *Mortgage* procedure **256◆** from the real-estate program **384◆** requires three input values: the principal, the mortgage rate, and the term (in years) of a mortgage. From these values the program calculates the monthly mortgage payment. The three input values are stored in the variables *princ*, *rate*, and *term*, respectively:

```
@ 9, 25 SAY "Principal amount? " GET princ PICTURE "######" ;
  RANGE 10000, 999999
@ 11, 25 SAY "Percent interest? " GET rate PICTURE "##.##" ;
  RANGE 5, 25
@ 13, 25 SAY "Term in years?    " GET term PICTURE "##" ;
  RANGE 10, 50
```

In each of these @...SAY...GET statements, the RANGE clause specifies the range of numeric values it is reasonable for the application to accept. The range will be enforced by dBASE, rather than by the logic of the program itself. For example, if you were to enter a value of 4 for the interest rate, dBASE would display the following message at the upper right corner of the screen:

RANGE is 5 to 25 (hit SPACE)

To recover from this error, you would press the Spacebar and then enter a new and appropriate value for the interest rate.

Example 2: This next program, called *Birthday,* illustrates the use of the RANGE clause for validating date input. The program accepts birth dates of adults who are in the age range 18 through 65:

```
*-------------------------------------------------- BIRTHDAY.PRG
* Accepts birth dates of people who are between
*   18 and 65 years old.
*

CLEAR
SET CONFIRM ON
SET BELL OFF
SET TALK OFF

bday = DATE()
d1 = DATE() - (65 * 366)
d2 = DATE() - (18 * 365)

ok = .F.
DO WHILE .NOT. ok
    @ 10,10 SAY "Enter your birth date: " GET bday ;
      RANGE d1, d2
    READ
    IF bday <> DATE()
        answer = " "
        @ 12, 10 SAY "Is this your birth date:"
        @ 13, 10 SAY CMONTH(bday) + " " + STR(DAY(bday), 2) + ;
        ", " + STR(YEAR(bday), 4)
        @ 15, 10 SAY "Y or N? " GET answer PICTURE "!"
        READ

        IF answer = "Y"
            ok = .T.
        ENDIF

    ENDIF
    CLEAR
ENDDO

SET TALK ON
SET BELL ON
RETURN
```

Birthday assigns calculated date values to the variables *d1* and *d2*. These values will become the chronological limits for the valid input range:

```
d1 = DATE() - (65 * 366)
d2 = DATE() - (18 * 365)
```

(Notice that each of these statements subtracts a calculated number of days from today's date: *d1* receives a date that is approximately 65 years ago, and *d2* receives a date that is approximately 18 years ago.)

With the date limits established, the following @...SAY...GET command elicits a birth date, and restricts the range accordingly:

```
@ 10, 10 SAY "Enter your birth date: " GET bday ;
   RANGE d1, d2
```

If, in response to this command, you enter a date that is outside the correct range, dBASE will display a message similar to the following:

```
                              RANGE is 09/03/20 to 10/09/67 (hit SPACE)




     Enter your birth date:  06/18/14
```

(Of course the exact range of dates depends upon the value of the system date when the program is performed.)

■ **Cautions**

The RANGE clause checks only data entered from the keyboard. If the user fails to enter a value and simply presses Return to accept the current value, the RANGE clause will not validate the input response. For example, in the *Birthday* program, the input variable *bday* is initialized to today's date:

```
bday = DATE()
```

This results in an initial input prompt that looks like this:

```
     Enter your birth date:  10/22/85
```

If today's date were entered as a value from the keyboard, the value would not be accepted as an input date, thanks to the RANGE clause. However, if the user simply presses the Return key to accept the initial value located in the input template, the value will be accepted unchecked. For this reason, the program requires the following logical check, in addition to the checking performed by the RANGE clause:

```
READ
IF bday <> DATE()
     * ... *
```

The SET SCOREBOARD OFF **397★** command disables the message area at the upper right corner of the screen. If you use the RANGE clause, you should make sure that SET SCOREBOARD is ON (the default setting).

■ **dBASE II equivalent**
None

■ **Comments**
If you wish, you may supply only a single boundary for RANGE (upper or lower), but you must still include the comma in the appropriate position so that dBASE will know which boundary you are supplying.

The @...GET command also has a PICTURE **252★** clause that can be used to define the input *format* of numeric, date, and character input.

READ

■ **Structure**
READ *SAVE*

■ **Description**
The READ command works along with one or more @...GET **9★** commands to initiate a full-screen editing session from within a dBASE program. A full-screen session can be designed for inputting or editing the values of variables **459★**, database fields **154★**, or both. The programming steps required for setting up full-screen editing include:

1. Defining a series of @...GET (or @...SAY...GET) commands, to place prompts and input templates at specified locations on the screen.

2. Issuing a single READ command, to activate all of the corresponding @...GET commands. READ places the cursor at the beginning of the first input template, ready for the user to begin editing or entering data from the keyboard.

In full-screen mode, the user is free to move the cursor backward or forward among the input templates displayed on the screen. No single input value is "final" until the user exits from full-screen mode (by moving the cursor to the last input template and pressing Return, or by pressing Escape from any template on the screen).

A given READ command activates all the @...GET commands that have been issued since exit from the previous full-screen session, or since the last CLEAR 56★ or CLEAR GETS command was issued.

When the user exits from the current full-screen session, an implicit CLEAR GETS command is generated. This means that all the current @...GET commands are permanently deactivated. However, if READ SAVE is used to initiate a full-screen session, this CLEAR GETS is not generated and a subsequent READ command will reactivate the same full-screen session. (For further discussion, see CLEAR GETS and the *Comment* section of this entry.)

■ **Usage**

The following example is from the procedure called *Mortgage*, listed in its entirety under the PICTURE **252★** entry. The passage demonstrates how to set up a full-screen input session in a program:

```
princ = 0
rate = 0.00
term = 0

@ 9, 25 SAY "Principal amount? " GET princ PICTURE "######" ;
  RANGE 10000, 999999
@ 11, 25 SAY "Percent interest? " GET rate PICTURE "##.##" ;
  RANGE 5, 25
@ 13, 25 SAY "Term in years?   " GET term PICTURE "##" ;
  RANGE 10, 50
READ
```

In this case, the purpose of the full-screen session is to receive values for three variables: *princ*, *rate*, and *term*. Each of the three variables is initialized to zero at the beginning of the passage. Then, three @...SAY...GET commands display prompts and formatted input templates on the screen. Finally, the READ command initiates the full-screen input session, allowing the user to enter or edit values for the three variables.

■ **Caution**

The @...GET command has no effect as an input statement on its own: A READ statement *must* be issued to begin the full-screen input session. (A maximum of 128 @...GET commands can be activated by a given READ command.)

■ **dBASE II equivalent**
READ

■ **Comment**
You can use the SAVE clause of the READ command for certain kinds of input validation. The idea is to enable a program to repeat the performance of a given full-screen session until the user has entered data values that satisfy the requirements of the program. The following illustration, called *Get_exp*, will help you experiment with the use of READ SAVE:

```
*--------------------------------------------------GET_EXP.PRG
* An experiment with GET, READ SAVE, and CLEAR GETS.
*

CLEAR

SET TALK OFF

num = 0.00
char = "        "

DO WHILE num = 0 .OR. LEN(TRIM(char)) = 0
    @ 10,10 SAY "number:  " GET num PICTURE "###.##"
    @ 12,10 SAY "string:  " GET char
    READ SAVE
ENDDO

CLEAR GETS
SET TALK ON

RETURN
```

This program sets up a full-screen session for the purpose of receiving input values into the numeric variable *num* and the string variable *char*. At the beginning of the program, *num* is initialized to zero and *char* is initialized to a string of spaces. The program requires that new values be entered into both variables before the input session can be ended. In other words, the user must enter a non-zero value for *num* and a non-blank value for *char*, or the looping continues.

The technique for repeating the input session is to place the READ SAVE command inside a DO WHILE **129★** loop. The condition **207♦** of the loop expresses the data-entry requirements of the program. Each performance of the READ SAVE command retains the @...GET commands for a possible subsequent performance. Only when the looping ends—when the data-entry requirements have been satisfied—does the program issue a CLEAR GETS command to deactivate the @...GET statements.

RECALL

■ **Structure**

RECALL   *scope_clause   condition_clause*

■ **Description**

The RECALL command undoes the work of the DELETE **106★** command. That is, RE-CALL removes the deletion marker from one or more records **284★** in the current database.

■ **Usage**

RECALL alone, with no scope **312★** or condition clause, removes the deletion marker from only the current record. (RECALL has no effect on a record that is not marked for deletion.) A scope (ALL **17★**, NEXT **239★**, or RECORD **282★**) or condition clause (FOR **164★** or WHILE **463★**) may be added to the RECALL command to extend its effect over more than one record.

■ **Database example**

The following example uses a database called *Bills*, which contains records of house-hold bills that fall due in the current month. Two of the records in the database have been marked for deletion, since those bills have been paid:

```
. USE Bills
. LIST
Record#  DUE_TO          AMOUNT DATE_DUE PAID
      1  Bernal Bank     142.75 06/15/85 .F.
      2  Maxwell's       567.81 06/22/85 .F.
      3 *Credit Union     89.00 06/01/85 .T.
      4  Ameri Mortgage  986.23 06/30/85 .F.
      5  Bernal Electric  61.15 06/18/85 .F.
      6 *OC Telephone    110.52 06/05/85 .T.
.
```

As you can see, the display of a record that is marked for deletion contains an asterisk character at the left side of the first field. The following RECALL command removes all these deletion markers from the database:

```
. RECALL ALL
       2 records recalled
.
. LIST
Record#  DUE_TO        AMOUNT DATE_DUE PAID
       1  Bernal Bank   142.75 06/15/85 .F.
       2  Maxwell's     567.81 06/22/85 .F.
       3  Credit Union   89.00 06/01/85 .T.
       4  Ameri Mortgage 986.23 06/30/85 .F.
       5  Bernal Electric 61.15 06/18/85 .F.
       6  OC Telephone  110.52 06/05/85 .T.
.
```

Now, with no records marked for deletion, a PACK **243★** command will have no effect on the database.

■ **Caution**

Once records have been physically removed from a database with the PACK command, the RECALL command can no longer bring them back.

■ **dBASE II equivalent**

RECALL

■ **Comments**

DELETE marks a record for deletion and PACK physically removes these marked records. The DELETED() **108★** function returns a logical value **99◆** indicating whether or not the current record is marked for deletion, and SET DELETED ON **344★** causes other dBASE commands to ignore marked records.

RECNO()

■ **Structure**

RECNO()

■ **Description**

The RECNO() function returns a number representing the position of the record pointer **258★** in the currently selected **322◆** database. In other words, RECNO() supplies the number of the current record **284★**.

■ **Usage**

RECNO() can be entered from the dot prompt, to determine your position in a database, but it is most useful in programming situations. The following three examples are all taken from programs described elsewhere in this book.

Example 1: An exercise under the JOIN **189★** entry performs a merge operation between two bookstore databases called *Bksales* and *Authors*. The goal is to find the top five best-selling books listed in *Bksales* and match them with their authors and publishers, listed in *Authors*. The JOIN example works with a sorted version of *Bksales* called *Salesort*, in which the books are arranged in order of copies sold, from high to low. To merge the correct records, the FOR **164★** clause of the JOIN statement uses the RECNO() function to select the first five records in *Salesort*:

```
. JOIN WITH Authors TO Top5 FOR RECNO() <= 5 .AND. ;
author_num = B -> author_num FIELDS title, last_name ;
unit_sales, publisher
```

Example 2: The *Bookinfo* program listed under the SET RELATION **390★** entry uses the same two databases to create individual reports about the books and their sales. One line in this report tells how a selected book ranks in sales, compared with all the other books in the list:

```
This book is # 3 on our list.
```

The program line that produces this message uses the RECNO() function:

```
? "This book is #" + STR(RECNO(), 2) + " on our list."
```

The numeric value returned by RECNO() is converted into a string **98♦** value (using the STR() **416★** function) in order to control the width of the output field.

By the way, one form of the SET RELATION command uses record numbers to establish a relation between two open databases:

```
. SET RELATION TO RECNO() INTO Sales
```

Example 3: A final example, from the *Exptable* program listed under the EXP() **152★** entry, illustrates how the RECNO() function may be used in a REPLACE **291★** statement to fill in an entire field of data. This particular exercise fills in the field named *x*, for all 20 records of the database, with an evenly incremented series of numbers from 0.10 to 2.00:

```
REPLACE ALL x WITH RECNO() / 10
```

■ **Caution**

When the end-of-file condition is true—that is, when the EOF() **147★** function returns a .T. for the currently selected database—the value of RECNO() may seem misleading. In this special case, RECNO() returns a value that is 1 greater than the record number of the last record in the database. For example, if a database has 25 records, and some event has set EOF() to true, RECNO() will behave as follows:

```
. ? RECNO()
       26
.
```

There would be no sense in trying to access data from a nonexistent record, so a program should always consult the EOF() function before performing an action that depends upon the value returned by RECNO().

■ **dBASE II equivalent**

#

■ **Comment**

Several database commands move the record pointer, as either a primary (GOTO **169★**, SKIP **400★**) or a secondary effect (LIST **200★**, DISPLAY ALL **116◆**).

RECORD

■ **Structure**

... RECORD number ...

■ **Description**

RECORD is one of three optional scope 312★ clauses (the other two are ALL 17★ and NEXT 239★) available for use with some dBASE commands to specify the portion of the current database on which the command will operate. The RECORD clause specifies a single record 284★, by its record number, as the scope of the command's operation.

■ **Usage**

A command that contains a RECORD clause first repositions the pointer 258★ to the specified record number and then performs its operation on that record. The pointer remains at this position after the command's performance is complete.

■ **Database example**

The following sequences use the database called *Staff*, which contains information about a group of employees. The DISPLAY 116★ command is an example of a database command that takes an optional scope clause. By default—without a scope clause—DISPLAY operates on the current record, whatever it may be:

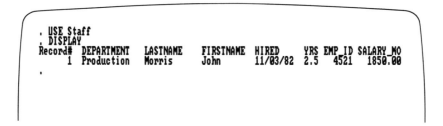

```
. USE Staff
. DISPLAY
Record#  DEPARTMENT  LASTNAME  FIRSTNAME  HIRED     YRS  EMP_ID  SALARY_MO
      1  Production  Morris    John       11/03/82  2.5  4521    1850.00
.
```

but with a record number, DISPLAY lists only the record specified.

```
. DISPLAY RECORD 5
Record#  DEPARTMENT    LASTNAME    FIRSTNAME  HIRED     YRS EMP_ID SALARY_MO
      5  Production    James       Fred       02/22/77  8.2    6563  1675.00
.
```

```
. DISPLAY RECORD 2
Record#  DEPARTMENT    LASTNAME    FIRSTNAME  HIRED     YRS EMP_ID SALARY_MO
      2  Marketing     Southby     Anne       08/22/81  3.7    3I34  2315.00
.
```

```
. DISPLAY RECORD 8
Record#  DEPARTMENT    LASTNAME    FIRSTNAME  HIRED     YRS EMP_ID SALARY_MO
      8  Production    Washington  Liz        11/05/74 10.5    7321  1700.00
.
```

Notice that a RECORD clause can send the record pointer either up or down the database from its current position.

- **dBASE II equivalent**

  RECORD

- **Comments**

  The NEXT clause defines the scope of a command as a specified number of records, beginning with the current one. The ALL clause defines the scope as the entire database. The condition 312◆ clauses FOR 164★ and WHILE 463★ are also available for selecting specific records in a database; in the absence of a specified scope, FOR uses a default scope of ALL.

  The following database commands accept an optional scope clause (ALL, NEXT, or RECORD): AVERAGE 31★, CHANGE 48★, COPY 82★, COUNT 85★, DELETE 106★, DISPLAY, LABEL FORM 195★, LIST 200★, LOCATE 202★, RECALL 278★, REPLACE 291★, REPORT FORM 295★, SUM 426★, and TOTAL 436★.

Records

A record is the complete description of one entity (person, place, item, event, transaction, or the like) in a database. When dBASE displays the database in tabular form, a record corresponds to a row of information.

A record may contain up to 128 fields 154★. The maximum width of a record—the sum of the widths of all of its fields—is 4000 characters. (This does not count the textual information contained in memo fields 217★. Such text is stored in a .DBT file, not a .DBF file 156♦.)

The practical limit on the number of records that can be stored in a database is set by the amount of disk space that is available on your particular system.

Each record in a database is automatically given a record number ♦. These numbers are assigned sequentially, starting with 1, in the order in which records are appended 19♦ to the database. (However, if the database is indexed 176♦, the records might not be *displayed* in record-number order.) If new records are added within the database via the INSERT 184★ command, dBASE automatically renumbers the rest of the records in the file.

The *record pointer* 258♦ is a number, stored internally by dBASE, that keeps track of the current position in the database file. This information can be important in programs, or with those dBASE commands that operate, by default, on only the current record (DISPLAY 116★ and EDIT 141★, for example). The RECNO() 279★ function returns the number of the record at which the pointer is currently located.

REINDEX

■ **Structure**
REINDEX

■ **Description**
REINDEX updates an index file 156♦ so that it matches the current version of its associated database.

■ **Usage**
When you revise an indexed database, all open indexes are automatically updated to reflect the changes. However, if an index happens to be closed when database records are added, deleted, or edited, it will not be updated and therefore will no longer be a valid tool for sorting 406★ the database.

But sometimes it is not practical to keep all the indexes of a given database open during revisions. The REINDEX command solves this problem: You can update the out-of-date indexes later, by simply opening both the database and the target indexes, and then issuing the REINDEX command. REINDEX will update all the open indexes.

■ **Database example**

In the following example, the client-billing database of a (fictitious) law firm has recently been increased in size by one record. Here is the latest version of the *Lawfirm* database:

```
. USE Lawfirm
. LIST
Record#  DEPARTMENT  CLIENT                 AMOUNT BILLING_DT PAYMENT_DT
      1  Litigation  XYZ Enterprises 2593.88 08/15/84   12/05/84
      2  Corporate   SuperTek Co.    1872.42 09/01/84   11/15/84
      3  Labor Law   MultiGlom, Inc.  521.55 09/01/84   09/15/84
      4  Corporate   BBB Corporation 2113.20 09/15/84   11/01/84
      5  Litigation  Acme Co.        4988.89 10/01/84   11/30/84
      6  Litigation  Expo Ltd.       3889.21 10/15/84   01/20/85
      7  Labor Law   Doe Properties   733.28 11/01/84   01/15/85
.
```

Lawfirm was originally indexed on the key field **194★** *client*. The index file, called *Cliname,* is still stored on disk, but it was not open at the time of the most recent APPEND **19★** operation. As a result, *Cliname* has information about only six of the seven records in the database:

```
. SET INDEX TO Cliname
. LIST
Record#  DEPARTMENT  CLIENT                 AMOUNT BILLING_DT PAYMENT_DT
      5  Litigation  Acme Co.        4988.89 10/01/84   11/30/84
      4  Corporate   BBB Corporation 2113.20 09/15/84   11/01/84
      6  Litigation  Expo Ltd.       3889.21 10/15/84   01/20/85
      3  Labor Law   MultiGlom, Inc.  521.55 09/01/84   09/15/84
      2  Corporate   SuperTek Co.    1872.42 09/01/84   11/15/84
      1  Litigation  XYZ Enterprises 2593.88 08/15/84   12/05/84
.
```

To update this index, just issue the REINDEX command:

```
. REINDEX
Rebuilding index - B:CLINAME.ndx
     7 records indexed
.
```

If you now list the database under control of the updated *Cliname* index, all of the records appear:

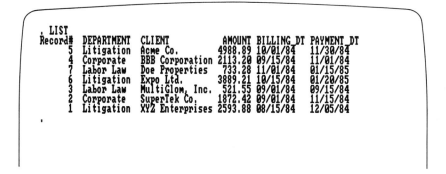

```
. LIST
Record#  DEPARTMENT  CLIENT            AMOUNT  BILLING_DT  PAYMENT_DT
      5  Litigation  Acme Co.         4988.89  10/01/84    11/30/84
      4  Corporate   BBB Corporation  2113.20  09/15/84    11/01/84
      7  Labor Law   Doe Properties    733.28  11/01/84    01/15/85
      6  Litigation  Expo Ltd.        3889.21  10/15/84    01/20/85
      3  Labor Law   MultiGlom, Inc.   521.55  09/01/84    09/15/84
      2  Corporate   SuperTek Co.     1872.42  09/01/84    11/15/84
      1  Litigation  XYZ Enterprises  2593.88  08/15/84    12/05/84
.
```

■ **Caution**

Interestingly, no error message is generated through the use of an outdated index. You have to recognize for yourself that the index needs to be rebuilt.

■ **dBASE II equivalent**

REINDEX

■ **Comments**

USE **254**★ and SET INDEX **372**★ can both open multiple indexes for a given active database. With either command, the first index listed is the one that takes control of the database; the rest are open only for potential updating.

Relational operators

The relational operators are "verbs" that specify the nature of a comparison in a condition expression ♦. The six relational operators available in dBASE are:

Operator:	Meaning:
=	Is equal to
<> or #	Is not equal to
>	Is greater than
<	Is less than
>=	Is greater than or equal to
<=	Is less than or equal to

A condition expression (also referred to as a logical expression) is a statement that dBASE can evaluate to one of two values: true or false. The specific action of many dBASE statements depends upon the presence of such an expression. For example:

☐ The DO WHILE 129★ statement creates a loop in a dBASE program. The loop repetitively performs a group of statements as long as the condition expressed in the DO WHILE statement remains true.

☐ The IF...ELSE 171★ statement chooses between two courses of action in a program, depending upon the evaluation of a condition expression.

☐ The DO CASE 125★ command chooses among several courses of action, depending upon evaluation of its mutually exclusive CASE 44★ conditions.

☐ The FOR 164★ and WHILE 463★ clauses, which are optional parts of many database commands, specify conditions by which certain records of a database are selected for action.

Here are some examples of these kinds of statements. Each contains a condition expression using one of the relational operators:

```
DO WHILE n <= 10
     *  ...  *
     *  Perform action of loop.
     *  ...  *
ENDDO


IF ans = "Y"
     *  ...  *
     *  Perform action 1.
     *  ...  *
ELSE
     *  ...  *
     *  Perform action 2.
     *  ...  *
ENDIF


DISPLAY FOR duedate < CTOD("05/08/85")
```

The first example shows a DO WHILE loop whose condition specifies that the repetition shall continue as long as the variable *n* contains a value less than or equal to 10. The second shows an IF statement whose action depends upon the value of the string variable *ans*: If the variable contains the value "Y", action 1 will be taken; otherwise, action 2 will be taken. And finally, the third example shows a DISPLAY 116★ command with a FOR clause that selects for display only those records whose *duedate* field contains a date earlier than 05/08/85. The condition is evaluated for each record in the database.

　　Compound condition expressions can also be constructed, using the logical .AND. and .OR. operators 207★. You will find many examples of such expressions throughout this book.

RELEASE

■ Structure

RELEASE variable_list
RELEASE ALL
RELEASE ALL LIKE skeleton
RELEASE ALL EXCEPT skeleton

■ Description

The RELEASE command erases one or more of the currently defined variables **459★** from active memory.

The RELEASE syntax allows several ways of specifying which variables are to be released:

☐ A list of variable names.

☐ An ALL clause, to erase all current variables.

☐ An ALL LIKE clause, using the wildcard characters **114◆** * and ? to erase certain groups of variables.

☐ An ALL EXCEPT clause, also using wildcard characters, but this time to *exclude* certain groups of variables from erasure.

A RELEASE ALL command within a program erases only private (local) variables **460◆**—that is, only those variables actually created in the procedure **266◆** containing the RELEASE statement (see *Comments* at the end of this entry).

■ Usage

The purpose of RELEASE is to free memory and variable space when certain variables are no longer needed. The following exercise shows how RELEASE works.

At the beginning of the exercise, the DISPLAY MEMORY **118★** command shows 10 variables stored in memory:

```
. DISPLAY MEMORY
A1        pub   N        1  (        1.00000000)
A2        pub   N        2  (        2.00000000)
A3        pub   N        3  (        3.00000000)
A4        pub   N        4  (        4.00000000)
A5        pub   N        5  (        5.00000000)
B1        pub   N        2  (        2.00000000)
B2        pub   N        4  (        4.00000000)
B3        pub   N        6  (        6.00000000)
B4        pub   N        8  (        8.00000000)
B5        pub   N       10  (       10.00000000)
    10 variables defined,      90 bytes used
   246 variables available,  5910 bytes available
.
```

A series of RELEASE commands gradually erases them all. The first RELEASE specifies an explicit list of variables to be erased. The next erases all variables whose names begin with the letter A. The third removes all remaining variables except B3, and finally, a RELEASE ALL command deletes all remaining currently defined variables (in this case, only one):

```
. RELEASE a3, b1, b4
. DISPLAY MEMORY
A1          pub  N      1 (              1.00000000)
A2          pub  N      2 (              2.00000000)
A4          pub  N      4 (              4.00000000)
A5          pub  N      5 (              5.00000000)
B2          pub  N      4 (              4.00000000)
B3          pub  N      6 (              6.00000000)
B5          pub  N     10 (             10.00000000)
     7 variables defined,     63 bytes used
   249 variables available,  5937 bytes available

.
```

```
. RELEASE ALL LIKE a?
. DISPLAY MEMORY
B2          pub  N      4 (              4.00000000)
B3          pub  N      6 (              6.00000000)
B5          pub  N     10 (             10.00000000)
     3 variables defined,     27 bytes used
   253 variables available,  5973 bytes available

.
```

```
. RELEASE ALL EXCEPT b3
. DISPLAY MEMORY
B3          pub  N      6 (              6.00000000)
     1 variables defined,      9 bytes used
   255 variables available,  5991 bytes available

.
```

```
.  RELEASE ALL
.  DISPLAY MEMORY
     0 variables defined,      0 bytes used
   256 variables available,  6000 bytes available
.
```

■ **Caution**

Once a variable is released from memory, its value cannot be retrieved.

■ **dBASE II equivalent**

RELEASE

■ **Comments**

The CLEAR MEMORY 56★ command also erases current variables from memory. Within a program, there is an important distinction between CLEAR MEMORY and RELEASE ALL: As we have already discussed, RELEASE ALL erases only private variables defined in the procedure that currently has control of the program; CLEAR MEMORY, on the other hand, releases *all* variables, public (global) 460◆ and private alike. (At the dot-prompt 62◆ level, the two commands behave identically.)

You can use the SAVE 309★ command to store variables and their values on disk before they are released from current memory. They can then be read back into memory later with the RESTORE 298★ command.

RENAME

■ **Structure**
RENAME old_name TO new_name

■ **Description**
The RENAME command gives a new name ◆ to an existing disk file.

■ **Usage**
RENAME may be used on any type of file, but it works on only one file at a time and does not allow wildcard characters 114◆. An extension name 155◆ must always be included in the RENAME command, even for .DBF files:

```
. RENAME PROPERTY.DBF TO REAL_EST.DBF
```

■ **Caution**
RENAME will not work on a file that is currently open.

REPLACE

■ **Structure**
REPLACE *scope_clause* field_name WITH expression ,*field_name WITH expression* ,... *condition_clause*

■ **Description**
The REPLACE command stores new field data in one or more records of the currently selected 322◆ database. The new data items replace whatever was previously stored in the specified field.

■ **Usage**
Without a scope 312★ or condition clause, REPLACE works, by default, on only the current record, storing the value of the expression in the WITH clause in the specified field.

For global, block, or conditional replacements, you may include a scope (ALL 17★, NEXT 239★, or RECORD 282★) or condition clause (FOR 164★ or WHILE 463★) in the RE-PLACE command.

■ **Database example**

The database called *Bksales* 190◆ contains sales data about a list of best-selling books. Here, we are interested in just four of the database's fields—*title*, *pub_date*, *unit_sales*, and *month_avg*:

```
. USE Bksales
. LIST title, pub_date, unit_sales, month_avg OFF
title               pub_date unit_sales  month_avg
The Orchid          02/19/84     59643           0
Mountain Romance    09/18/84     67646           0
Nights of London    01/18/85     39806           0
Paris: Art at Home  03/18/84     51193           0
The Mission         09/18/84     65880           0
Politics Among Us   05/30/84     34131           0
The Perfect Cook    02/19/84     76835           0
Traveler in Europe  09/30/84     40749           0
Mystery of the East 02/15/84     66834           0
Images of Japan     12/15/83     81252           0
.
```

The unit-sales figure represents the number of copies of a given book that have been sold since its publication date. Now, we would like to place the average number of copies sold per month into the *month_avg* field, which is currently empty. Here is the formula for calculating this value:

```
unit sales / ((days since publication) / 30)
```

This translates into the dBASE formula:

```
unit_sales / ((DATE() - pub_date) / 30)
```

292

And here is the REPLACE command that uses this formula in a global replacement of the *month_avg* field:

```
. REPLACE ALL month_avg WITH ;
  unit_sales / ((DATE() - pub_date) / 30)
```

```
. LIST title, pub_date, unit_sales, month_avg OFF
  title                 pub_date unit_sales  month_avg
  The Orchid            02/19/84    59643        3689
  Mountain Romance      09/18/84    67646        7434
  Nights of London      01/18/85    39806        7908
  Paris: Art at Home    03/18/84    51193        3361
  The Mission           09/18/84    65880        7240
  Politics Among Us     05/30/84    34131        2666
  The Perfect Cook      02/19/84    76835        4753
  Traveler in Europe    09/30/84    40749        4684
  Mystery of the East   02/15/84    66834        4100
  Images of Japan       12/15/83    81252        4424
.
```

■ **Program example**

Impressive though this kind of global replacement might seem, it is certainly not the only use for the REPLACE command. In some situations, REPLACE acts more like an assignment statement 414♦, storing one new value in a specific field, much as the STORE 414★ statement assigns a value to a variable 459★.

An example appears in the *Sale* procedure listed and discussed under the IF **171**★ entry. *Sale's* task is to find and display a requested record from a real-estate database and allow the user to enter information about a sale into the record. The following

passage contains two REPLACE commands—one for changing the values of the logical **99♦** field *sold,* and one for changing the values of the date **99♦** field *sale_date*:

```
DO Yesno WITH 16, 10, "Has the house sold?       "
IF yn
    REPLACE sold WITH .T.
    @ 17, 15 SAY "Price? " GET sale_price
    READ

    DO Yesno WITH 18, 15, "Today? "
    IF yn
        REPLACE sale_date WITH DATE()
    ELSE
        @ 19, 15 SAY "When?  " GET sale_date
        READ
    ENDIF

ENDIF
```

(Actually, this passage uses two techniques for storing a new data value in a field of
the current record: first, the REPLACE command; second, the @...GET **9★** and READ
275★ commands.)

■ **Caution**

It is best to avoid making multiple replacements in the key field **194★** of an indexed
176♦ database, since each replacement potentially can move the record to a new position, leading to unpredictable results.

■ **dBASE II equivalent**

REPLACE

■ **Comment**

A REPLACE command that operates globally on the entire database leaves the record
pointer **258★** at the end of the file and sets EOF() **147★** to true. A REPLACE that works on
only one record does not move the record pointer.

REPORT FORM

■ **Structure**

REPORT FORM file_name   *scope_clause   condition_clause   PLAIN   HEADING string*
NOEJECT   TO PRINT   TO FILE file_name

■ **Description**

The REPORT FORM command opens a specified report-form file 156♦, and follows its directions for creating a report from the currently selected 322♦ database. (Report-form files are created via the MODIFY REPORT 226★ command and are given a default extension 155♦ of .FMT.) The resulting report can be sent to the printer (TO PRINT) or to a specified text file 157♦ (TO FILE). If neither of these clauses is included in the command, the report will be displayed only on the screen.

Normally, REPORT FORM creates a report from all the records 284★ of the current database. However, a scope 312★ (NEXT 239★ or RECORD 282★) or condition clause (FOR 164★ or WHILE 463★) may be used to select a subset of records to be included in the report.

REPORT FORM automatically includes a page number and the system date at the top of each page of the report. The HEADING clause allows you to specify an additional string of characters that will be included on the same line as the page number. The PLAIN clause suppresses *all* of these page elements.

If the report is sent to the printer, the REPORT FORM command normally performs a form feed before printing the first page of the report. The NOEJECT clause suppresses this first form feed.

■ **Usage**

Before using the REPORT FORM command, you must:

☐   Create a report-form file on disk, using either CREATE REPORT 91★ or MODIFY REPORT.

☐   Index 176♦ or sort 402♦ the database appropriately, if the report includes group divisions 227♦.

☐   Make sure that the target database is open in the selected work area.

■ **Database examples**

The following example uses the *Citybird* report-form file from the MODIFY REPORT entry:

```
. REPORT FORM Citybird PLAIN NOEJECT TO PRINT
```

This command searches for and opens the format file called *CITYBIRD.FRM*, and then, without an initial form feed, prints the report without page numbers:

```
              Birds Residing in City Habitats

     Location      Individuals
     Sighted          Sighted


** Common name: Kestrel
   residential          2
   downtown             0
   park                12
** Subtotal **
                       14

** Common name: Mockingbird
   residential          5
   downtown            14
   park                16
** Subtotal **
                       35

** Common name: Scrub Jay
   residential         12
   downtown             2
   park                21
** Subtotal **
                       35
*** Total ***
                       84
```

Here is another example, showing how to send a report to a text file rather than to the printer. The example deals with a database of regional sales records:

```
. REPORT FORM Salesrpt FOR division = "Atlantic" TO FILE Sales
```

This command creates the *SALES.TXT* file, and stores the report in the new file. Subsequently, you can use *SALES.TXT* to incorporate the report into a word-processed document. The command also uses a FOR clause to select only certain records for the report—in this case, those that have a value of "Atlantic" in the *division* field.

■ **Caution**
Make sure your printer is on and ready before you issue a REPORT FORM command with a TO PRINT clause. (See cautionary notes under the SET PRINT 381★ entry.)

■ **dBASE II equivalent**
REPORT FORM
In dBASE II, the same command can be used both to create a report-form file and to print the resulting report.

■ **Comments**
If you enter the command REPORT, alone, dBASE will prompt you for the name of the form file to use, but if you enter REPORT FORM without a file name, you will receive an error message.

The NOEJECT option is useful in programs that build custom reports whose parts differ in format or draw upon different databases. NOEJECT allows you to "patch" report forms together, without a page break.

A LABEL FORM 195★ command is also available in dBASE III. This command works with a label-form file (created via MODIFY LABEL 221★) to print a series of labels from the currently open database.

RESTORE

- **Structure**

RESTORE FROM file_name   *ADDITIVE*

- **Description**

The RESTORE command opens a specified memory file **309✦** and retrieves the variable names and values stored in it. (The SAVE **309★** command creates memory files.)

    With the ADDITIVE clause, RESTORE adds the newly retrieved variables to the group of variables currently stored in memory. Without ADDITIVE, the current variables are cleared from memory before the saved ones are retrieved.

- **Usage**

In the SAVE entry, you can read about one important use of memory files: providing general information about a company or organization to all the different programs that might require it. The use we are going to discuss here, however, is quite different. In general terms, this example illustrates a situation in which each new performance of a given program requires access to a data value that was generated during the previous performance of the program. To provide this access, the final value in memory at the end of each run is stored in a memory file.

- **Program example**

Suppose you are in charge of a large database that stores a variety of transaction records. To a large extent, the database is processed automatically by a program, but one of your daily jobs is to double-check small groups of records, selected randomly from the database, to make sure that transactions are being entered and processed correctly.

    The following program, called *Randcheck*, contains a "random-number generator" that you can use to select records randomly from the file. Since the dBASE language does not include the RND() or RAND() function available in some other programming languages, *Randcheck* uses its own algorithm for generating numbers sufficiently random to satisfy the needs of the application:

```
*------------------------------------------------- RANDCHEK.PRG
* Selects records randomly from a large database file.
*

PARAMETER checks

SET TALK OFF
SET SAFETY OFF

* USE Bigfile
* COUNT TO numrecs

numrecs = 1000
```

(continued)

```
IF FILE("RANDBASE.MEM")
    RESTORE FROM Randbase ADDITIVE
ELSE
    base = VAL(SUBSTR(TIME(), 8, 1))
ENDIF

num = 1
DO WHILE checks >= num

    *----- The random-number routine:
    t = (base + 3.1415926) ** 5
    base = t - INT(t)
    rnd = base

    rec = INT(numrecs * rnd) + 1

    ? STR(num, 3) + ":", "Check record #" + STR(rec, 4)

    * GOTO rec
    * IF .NOT. checked
        * DISPLAY
        * REPLACE checked WITH .T.
        num = num + 1
    * ENDIF
ENDDO

SAVE ALL LIKE base TO Randbase

SET SAFETY ON
SET TALK ON
RETURN
```

The random-number algorithm produces each new number through a calculation that includes the value of the previously generated number. During a given performance, the program simply saves each number in memory, for use in the next calculation. But at the end of the run, the program needs a way of saving the final "random" number for the next session, so that the process can continue as though uninterrupted. The solution to this problem is to save the last generated number in a memory file called *Randbase*, where it will be found the next time the program is executed.

At the beginning of each performance, the program looks for *RANDBASE.MEM*, and retrieves its contents if it exists:

```
IF FILE("RANDBASE.MEM")
    RESTORE FROM Randbase ADDITIVE
```

The file will contain one variable, *base*, which stores the last number generated by the previous performance of the program. The ADDITIVE clause is used in the RESTORE statement to avoid loss of the other variables the program works with. At the end of the program, the following statement saves the newest value of *base* in the *Randbase* file:

```
SAVE ALL LIKE base TO Randbase
```

Notice that the portions of the program that actually deal with a specific database have been "commented out." In its present state, the program simply produces and displays random record numbers that fall between 1 and 1000. Here are two consecutive sample runs:

```
. DO Randchek WITH 10
  1: Check record # 333
  2: Check record # 305
  3: Check record # 722
  4: Check record # 117
  5: Check record #  14
  6: Check record # 708
  7: Check record # 369
  8: Check record # 543
  9: Check record # 286
 10: Check record # 424
.
```

```
. DO Randchek WITH 10
  1: Check record # 827
  2: Check record # 201
  3: Check record # 163
  4: Check record # 656
  5: Check record # 291
  6: Check record # 356
  7: Check record # 280
  8: Check record # 423
  9: Check record # 788
 10: Check record # 872
.
```

■ **dBASE II equivalent**
RESTORE

■ **Comment**
Other commands relating to memory management include CLEAR **56★**, DISPLAY MEMORY **118★**, RELEASE **288★**, and STORE **414★**.

RETURN

■ **Structure**

RETURN *TO MASTER*

■ **Description**

The RETURN command ends the performance of the current program 264♦ or procedure 383♦, and transfers control back to the level from which the program was originally called. (If the current program was called from the dBASE dot prompt 62♦, the RETURN command will return the user to the dot prompt.)

RETURN TO MASTER returns control to the "main program" of a structured program 266♦, from any procedure level.

■ **Usage**

In many cases, RETURN is the last statement in a program, and terminates the program only after all other commands have been performed. (Programs that do not have a RETURN statement also are simply terminated after the last command is performed; nevertheless, the use of a RETURN at the end of every program is good "housekeeping" practice.) Sometimes, however, a RETURN is conditional: The point at which a program relinquishes control might depend upon the current situation. For example, the following sequence returns control to the calling level if the end-of-file (EOF() 147★) condition is true:

```
IF EOF()
      RETURN
ENDIF
```

In cases like this, the program might actually contain more than one RETURN statement, only one of which will be encountered and executed during the program's performance.

■ **Cautions**

Some programmers use the RETURN TO MASTER command in unusual circumstances where it is necessary for a deep-level procedure to send control directly up to the main program. In a well-structured program, however, procedures almost always relinquish control one step at a time, each to the procedure that called it.

RETURN does not close database, index, or format files opened by the program, so you may want to include CLOSE 57★ commands, when appropriate, just before the RETURN command.

■ **dBASE II equivalent**

RETURN

■ **Comment**

The QUIT 271★ command is used within a program to terminate program performance, close all files, and exit dBASE, returning control to the operating system 133♦.

ROUND()

■ **Structure**

ROUND(numeric_expression, places)

■ **Description**

The ROUND() function returns a number that is rounded to a specified number of decimal places. ROUND() takes two arguments:

☐ The number that is to be rounded.

☐ The number of decimal places for the rounding operation.

If the second argument is a positive number, rounding will take place on the right side of the decimal point; if it is negative or zero, rounding will take place on the left side of the decimal point.

■ **Usage**

The result of ROUND() depends upon whether a positive or negative number is being rounded. The following short program, *Roundtst*, is designed to demonstrate the behavior of the ROUND() function:

```
*---------------------------------------------- ROUNDTST.PRG
* An exercise with the ROUND() function.
*

SET TALK OFF

num = 987.6543
done = .F.

? "Rounding a positive number:"
? "---------------------------"

DO WHILE .NOT. done
    places = 3
    DO WHILE places > -3
        ? "ROUND(" + STR(num, 9, 4) + ", " + STR(places, 2) + ") = "
        ?? ROUND(num, places)
        places = places - 1
    ENDDO
    ?
    IF num > 0
        ? "Rounding a negative number:"
        ? "---------------------------"
        num = -1 * num
    ELSE
        done = .T.
    ENDIF
ENDDO

SET TALK ON
RETURN
```

Here is the output generated by the program (notice the use of concatenation 65★ and the STR() 416★ function to format the display):

```
. DO Roundtst
Rounding a positive number:
---------------------------
ROUND( 987.6543,  3) =       987.6540
ROUND( 987.6543,  2) =       987.6500
ROUND( 987.6543,  1) =       987.7000
ROUND( 987.6543,  0) =       988.0000
ROUND( 987.6543, -1) =       990.0000
ROUND( 987.6543, -2) =      1000.0000

Rounding a negative number:
---------------------------
ROUND(-987.6543,  3) =      -987.6530
ROUND(-987.6543,  2) =      -987.6400
ROUND(-987.6543,  1) =      -987.6000
ROUND(-987.6543,  0) =      -987.0000
ROUND(-987.6543, -1) =      -980.0000
ROUND(-987.6543, -2) =      -900.0000

.
```

As you can see, ROUND() follows very different rules for rounding positive and negative numbers.

The *RoundTst* program can easily be used for further experimentation by simply changing the value of the variable *num* at the top of the program.

■ **dBASE II equivalent**
None

■ **Comment**
The INT() 186★ function truncates a positive or negative real number (without rounding), resulting in an integer value.

ROW()

- **Structure**
  ROW()

- **Description**
  The ROW() function supplies the current row position of the screen cursor. On the IBM PC, this is a numeric value from 0 through 24, representing one of the 25 screen rows.

- **Usage**
  ROW() and its companion, COL() **60★**, are designed for use in programs that need to control the position and appearance of data displayed on the screen. The two functions are typically used in conjunction with the @...SAY...GET **9★** command, to place an item of information at the current cursor position or at some *relative address* **60◆** a specified number of columns and/or rows away from the current position.

  In the following example, the @...SAY command places a data item immediately after the message displayed by the ? **5★** command (? executes its carriage return and line feed *before* it displays its message, not after):

  ```
  ? "Balance: "
  @ ROW(), COL() SAY bal PICTURE "@( $###,###.##"
  ```

  Given a value of –12345.67 for the variable *bal*, the result of these two commands is the following display:

  ```
  Balance: ($12,345.67)
  ```

  (Notice the effect of the @(**252◆** in the PICTURE **252★** statement, for formatting the display of negative values.)

  Relative addressing means specifying an address in relation to the current address. In the following example, for instance, a number is added to the value returned by ROW(), resulting in a new row address:

  ```
  ? "Balance: "
  @ ROW() + 2, COL() SAY bal PICTURE "@( $###,###.##"
  ```

The resulting display will be:

```
Balance:
        ($12,345.67)
```

■ **Caution**

When using ROW() for relative addressing, take care not to devise a column address that is less than 0 or greater than 24. For example, consider the following passage:

```
? "Balance: "
@ ROW() + 25, COL() SAY bal PICTURE "@( $###,###.##"
```

Since the expression *ROW() + 25* results in a row address that is greater than 24, the program will terminate with the following error message:

```
SAY/GET position is off the screen
```

■ **dBASE II equivalent**

None

■ **Comments**

For further discussion of screen-control operations in dBASE programs, see the entries under @...SAY...GET, CLEAR **56★**, and ?.

The PROW() **268★** function is available to supply the current row position from the printer.

RUN

■ **Structure**

RUN command
! command

■ **Description**

RUN allows you to perform a DOS **133**★ command or execute an external program during a dBASE session. When the performance of the DOS program is complete, you are automatically returned to dBASE.

RUN can perform programs that reside on disk and have extension names **155**◆ of .COM or .EXE. In addition, it can perform the DOS "internal" commands, including COPY, DATE, DIR, ERASE, RENAME, TIME, and TYPE.

■ **Usage**

You may sometimes want to use a DOS disk command rather than its dBASE equivalent, particularly to take advantage of DOS wildcard characters **114**◆. For example, the following command copies all database files from disk B to disk A, from within dBASE:

```
. RUN COPY B:*.DBF A:*.DBF
```

The equivalent dBASE command, COPY FILE **76**★, does not allow the use of wildcards for copying more than one file at a time.

Other DOS programs may also be of value during a session with dBASE. The first command in the following example checks the status of disk B and the second switches from monochrome to color-graphics display in a system that contains both:

```
. RUN CHKDSK B:
```

The RUN command also works successfully with DOS batch files. The commands in the file are performed sequentially and then control is returned to dBASE.

You may also want to use RUN to perform other application programs without leaving dBASE. For example, you can run a text editor or a word processor **466★**:

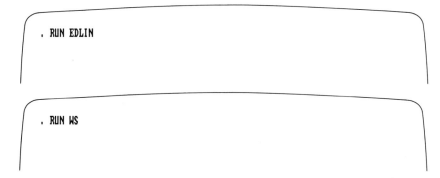

You can even perform a BASIC program:

(In this case, an exit from BASIC via the SYSTEM command will return you to dBASE.)

■ **Cautions**

For successful use of RUN, the DOS *COMMAND.COM* file must be available in an identified disk location. One simple solution is to copy this file onto the working dBASE program disk.

The dBASE MAXMEM command in the *CONFIG.DB* **66★** file determines how much RAM will be allocated for running DOS programs. By default, MAXMEM is set at 256K—the minimum amount of memory required by dBASE itself. If your system has only this minimum amount of RAM, you will not be able to use the RUN command. If you do have sufficient memory to use the RUN command, be aware that increasing the value of the MAXMEM setting allots more memory to dBASE, resulting in a *decrease* in the amount of memory allocated for running DOS programs, so you will need to plan accordingly.

■ **dBASE II equivalent**

None

■ **Comment**

If your system has sufficient memory to handle the RUN command, but dBASE can't find the *COMMAND.COM* file, you will still receive an "Insufficient memory" error message.

SAVE

■ Structure

SAVE TO file_name   *ALL LIKE skeleton*
SAVE TO file_name   *ALL EXCEPT skeleton*

■ Description

The SAVE command stores defined variables **459★** and their current values in a memory file ◆ on disk. The values stored in such a memory file can be loaded back into memory via the RESTORE **298★** command whenever they are needed. Unless you specify otherwise, SAVE creates a file with the extension name **155◆** .MEM.

By default, SAVE stores all currently defined variables in the memory file, but you can include an optional ALL LIKE or ALL EXCEPT clause to select only certain groups of variables for inclusion in, or exclusion from, the file.

■ Usage

If you are creating a system of programs and databases all centered around the activities of a single entity—a business, a research center, or some other type of organization—a memory file is an excellent place to keep general information about the entity itself. Then, any program that requires access to this information can simply open the memory file and read the data from the variables contained in the file. Furthermore, if some parts of the general information change over time, you can simply revise the contents of the memory file, rather than having to revise each program in your system.

■ Program example

The *General* program is designed to create and maintain a general-information file for a club—specifically, a computer-users group. This file, called *GENERAL.MEM*, contains eight variables that store the name and address of the club, the names of the club's officers, the day of the week when the club meets, the founding date, the number of members, and the annual dues.

General initializes the information file if it does not exist yet, or permits you to revise it if it does. Here is a sample input screen from the program:

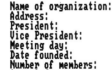

And here is the program itself:

```
*------------------------------------------------ GENERAL.PRG
* Saves general information about an organization
*    in a memory file on disk.
*

SET TALK OFF
SET SAFETY OFF

IF FILE("GENERAL.MEM")
    RESTORE FROM General
ELSE
    STORE SPACE(30) TO name, address, president, vicepres
    STORE SPACE(10) TO meetday
    STORE date() TO founded
    STORE 0 TO members
    STORE 0.00 TO dues
ENDIF

CLEAR

@ 3, 10 SAY "General Information"
@ 4, 10 SAY "-------------------"
@ 5, 10 SAY "Name of organization: " GET name
@ 6, 10 SAY "Address:              " GET address
@ 7, 10 SAY "President:            " GET president
@ 8, 10 SAY "Vice President:       " GET vicepres
@ 9, 10 SAY "Meeting day:          " GET meetday
@ 10, 10 SAY "Date founded:         " GET founded
@ 11, 10 SAY "Number of members:    " GET members PICTURE "#,###"
@ 12, 10 SAY "Annual dues:          " GET dues PICTURE "$##.##"
READ

SAVE TO General
CLEAR
SET TALK ON
SET SAFETY ON
RETURN
```

General begins by checking the current disk to see if the file *GENERAL.MEM* exists yet (the FILE() **158★** function supplies a value of true if the file does exist). If the file is on disk, the program uses a RESTORE command to load its contents into memory; otherwise, it uses a series of STORE **414★** statements to initialize the eight variables required for the general information. The subsequent @...SAY...GET **9★** commands display the current values on the screen (if the variables are newly initialized, these values may be spaces or zero). Then READ **275★** activates full-screen mode so that the user can enter or revise the eight values. As soon as the user exits from full-screen mode, the following command saves all eight variables and their current values to *GENERAL.MEM* (notice that the program toggles the SET SAFETY **396★** parameter to OFF, so that there will be no interruption when the memory file is overwritten):

```
SAVE TO General
```

From now on, any program that needs access to this information about the organization can find it in *GENERAL.MEM*.

Of course, this is a very simple example. An actual business organization would probably require a much more elaborate general-information file that included, among other things, data about accounting, personnel, branch offices, and even perhaps the names of dBASE files that are part of the company's database system.

■ **Cautions**

A program that requires access to information in a memory file must have advance knowledge of the names of the variables in the file. There is no way for the program to acquire these names from the file itself. If you forget the names of the variables in a memory file, you can examine the file's contents from the dBASE dot prompt **62♦** by retrieving the file and issuing the DISPLAY MEMORY **118★** command, as illustrated in the following passage:

```
. RESTORE FROM General
. DISPLAY MEMORY
NAME         pub   C   "dBase III Users Club      "
ADDRESS      pub   C   "123 M Street, SF, CA 94110 "
PRESIDENT    pub   C   "Dorothy Wood               "
VICEPRES     pub   C   "Samuel Mann                "
MEETDAY      pub   C   "Wednesdays"
FOUNDED      pub   D   12/01/84
MEMBERS.     pub   N          462  (        462.00000000)
DUES         pub   N        49.00  (         49.00000000)
     8 variables defined,     167 bytes used
   248 variables available,  5833 bytes available
.
```

Keep in mind, however, that unless you include the ADDITIVE option, the RESTORE command will erase all other currently defined variables when it loads the memory file. (Note that a memory file is not stored in ASCII text format, so you may not use the TYPE **444★** command to examine its contents.)

Don't try to use both ALL LIKE and ALL EXCEPT in the same SAVE command. dBASE will not display any error message, but when you examine the memory file later, you will find it empty.

■ **dBASE II equivalent**

SAVE

■ **Comments**

The ALL LIKE and ALL EXCEPT clauses use "skeletons" ♦ that allow you to select certain variable names for inclusion, in or exclusion from, the memory file. These skeletons are built with any combination of the two wildcard characters, * and ? (see the DIR **114★** entry for a description of these characters). The use of either ALL clause in the SAVE command presupposes that you have carefully planned the names of your variables in advance: If you wish to include only a certain group of variables in a memory file, the names of all those variables must have some common element that can be exploited in a skeleton clause.

ALL LIKE can also be used for specifying one single variable name for inclusion in the memory file. This special case is illustrated in the *Randchek* program from the RESTORE entry. *Randchek* stores one variable—*base*—in a memory file called *Randbase*:

```
SAVE ALL LIKE base TO Randbase
```

The skeleton is unique, so only *base* will be included in the file and RESTOREd to memory the next time the program is performed.

To rename a variable, you must assign its value to a new variable and then use the RELEASE **288★** command to erase the former version.

Scope

The term *scope* refers to the portion of a database over which a given dBASE command is to work. dBASE offers three optional scope clauses for use in many database commands:

Scope:	Effect:
ALL **17★**	Command will work on the entire current database, from the first record **284★** to the last.
NEXT **239★**	Command will affect the specified number of records forward, beginning with the current record.
RECORD **282★**	Command will affect a single record, identified by its record number.

Each dBASE database command has a default scope—that is, the scope that will apply if no specific scope clause is included in the command itself. For example, the DISPLAY **116★** command works, by default, on only the current record. In contrast, the LIST **200★** command, whose default scope is ALL, displays the entire database.

Two other optional clauses may also affect the specific records that a command will operate on. These are the condition clauses ♦, FOR **164★** and WHILE **463★**. Both of these cause the command to select only those records that match a criterion expressed in a condition expression **286♦**: The FOR clause selects all records within the defined scope that match the criterion; the WHILE clause selects records sequentially, starting with the current record, until a record is found that does not match the criterion.

A database command may include both a scope clause and a condition clause. In the absence of an explicitly expressed scope, a FOR condition clause changes the default scope to ALL.

For examples and more detailed discussions of all of these modifiers, see their specific entries.

SDF files

Through the COPY **82★** command, dBASE III can provide two ASCII file formats that may allow you to transport a dBASE database to another program environment ♦. These formats are called SDF (for "system data format") and delimited **111★**.

The following elements define the structure of an SDF file:

☐ All records are of equal length, in characters, and each record is followed by a carriage return and a line-feed character.

☐ The structure of each record is identical, in that the field widths **154♦** of the original database are maintained even when the data do not entirely fill each field.

☐ Each record is stored as a line of text. Space characters are used to "pad" the contents of each field, if necessary, to maintain the correct field widths. (No other delimiting characters, such as commas or quotation marks, are introduced into the records to separate one field from the next, so the only way a program can read individual field values is by counting the defined number of characters in each field width.)

Because each record follows a consistent structure, an SDF file is ideally suited for *random access*: That is, any record in the database can be accessed directly (as opposed to a sequential-access scheme, where the entire database must be read in sequence from beginning to end).

■ Database and program example

The following example uses the database called *Assets*, which contains four fields describing a small firm's depreciable assets: the name of the item (*item*), its original value (*value*), the date it was purchased (*purchased*), and its age in years (*age*). The *item* is a string value, *value* and *age* are numeric values, and *purchased* is a date-type value. Here is a listing of the database:

```
. USE Assets
. LIST
Record#  ITEM                    VALUE PURCHASED  AGE
       1 typewriter            1240.00 05/30/79   6.3
       2 personal computer     2495.00 03/15/83   2.5
       3 printer, daisy-wheel  1250.00 03/15/83   2.5
       4 printer, dot-matrix    650.00 05/15/84   1.4
       5 copier                1835.00 12/20/84   0.8
       6 office desk            850.00 02/27/80   5.6
.
```

The COPY command with an SDF clause creates a copy of this database in the SDF format:

```
. COPY TO Assets SDF
     6 records copied

    .
```

By default, dBASE gives the new file the extension name 155♦ .TXT; hence, the file's entire name will be *ASSETS.TXT*. We can examine the file via the TYPE 444★ command:

```
. TYPE ASSETS.TXT
typewriter             1240.0019790530 6.3
personal computer      2495.0019830315 2.5
printer, daisy-wheel   1250.0019830315 2.5
printer, dot-matrix     650.0019840515 1.4
copier                 1835.0019841220 0.8
office desk             850.0019800227 5.6

    .
```

The field widths in this SDF file are: *item*, 23; *value*, 7; *purchased*, 8; *age*, 4. In addition, each record ends with a carriage return and a line feed. Thus, the total record length is 44 characters. (Notice how dBASE converts date-type values for an SDF file: In an eight-character field, the first four characters are the year, the second two represent the month, and the final two the day.)

The BASIC programming language includes facilities for reading either random-access or sequential files, depending upon the structure of the file itself. The following BASIC program shows how the *Assets* SDF file can be read as a random-access file:

```
100 REM ** Read ASSETS.TXT, an SDF file created from
110 REM ** dBASE III, as a random-access file.
120 REM
130 OPEN "B:ASSETS.TXT" AS 1 LEN = 44
140 FIELD#1, 23 AS item$, 7 AS cost$, 8 AS dt$, 4 AS age$, 2 AS rtn$
150 PRINT
160 INPUT "Which asset do you want to see? (0 = stop) ", n
170 IF n = 0 THEN CLOSE: STOP
180 GET#1, n
190 PRINT
```

(continued)

```
200 PRINT "Asset #"; n; ": "; item$
210 PRINT "Original cost:      ";
220 cost = VAL(cost$)
230 PRINT USING "$$#,###.##"; cost
240 PRINT "Date of purchase:  ";
250 PRINT MID$(dt$, 5, 2); "/"; MID$(dt$, 7, 2); "/"; MID$(dt$, 1, 4)
260 PRINT "Age:               "; age$; " years"
270 PRINT : PRINT
280 GOTO 150
```

To enable the program to read the SDF file, the OPEN and FIELD statements in lines 130 and 140 define the file's structure: Its record length is 44 characters (line 130) and each record contains five fields, of lengths 23, 7, 8, 4, and 2, respectively (line 140). (The carriage return and line-feed characters are read into a subsequently unused field named *rtn$*.)

The following sample output from the program demonstrates the advantage of a random-access file:

```
Which asset do you want to see? (0 = stop) 3

Asset # 3 : printer, daisy-wheel
Original cost:     $1,250.00
Date of purchase: 03/15/1983
Age:               2.5 years


Which asset do you want to see? (0 = stop) 5

Asset # 5 : copier
Original cost:     $1,835.00
Date of purchase: 12/20/1984
Age:               0.8 years


Which asset do you want to see? (0 = stop) 1

Asset # 1 : typewriter
Original Cost:     $1,240.00
Date of purchase: 05/30/1979
Age:               6.3 years
```

Compare this with the sequential-access program example shown in the Delimited Files **111★** entry.

See the APPEND FROM **22★** entry for further discussion of the uses of SDF and delimited data files.

SED and dFORMAT

The SED and dFORMAT programs are special form editors for developing dBASE input screens. (SED comes with dBASE III, version 1.1; dFORMAT came with version 1.0.) These programs can be used to simplify the process of producing a screen-format file **157♦** for use with the SET FORMAT **365★** command.

Either SED or dFORMAT can be accessed during a dBASE session by using the RUN **306★** command:

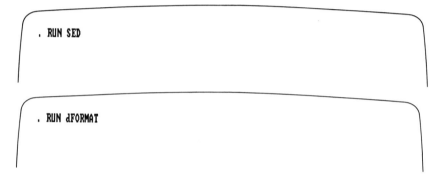

```
. RUN SED
```

```
. RUN dFORMAT
```

Each of the programs contains extensive "on-line" documentation explaining how to create an input screen and how to use the program itself. Essentially, the programs allow you to enter information directly onto a screen, visually planning the exact positioning and format of the input fields. Then, the programs translate your screen template into a dBASE program file containing a series of @...SAY...GET **9★** commands. You can develop a set of sequential input screens in one file by including selected dBASE command words in square brackets ([ ]) at appropriate positions on the template screen.

Alternatively, of course, you can write your own program files, using the built-in dBASE word processor **466★**.

■ **Caution**

Both SED and dFORMAT produce files with a .PRG extension name. For ease of use with the SET FORMAT command, it is best to rename **291♦** them, using the .FMT extension instead.

SEEK

■ **Structure**

SEEK expression

■ **Description**

The SEEK command searches for a specified field **154★** value in an indexed **176◆** database. If the value is found, the pointer **258★** is positioned at the corresponding record **284★** in the database. If the value is not found, the end-of-file condition **147◆** becomes true.

The expression in the SEEK command indicates the field value for which the command will search. This expression may be a literal (constant) string or numeric value (a string **98◆** must be enclosed in quotes) or the name of a variable **459★** (character, numeric, or date), in which case SEEK looks for the *value* contained in the variable.

■ **Usage**

SEEK is perhaps most useful when the target field value is stored in a variable. In this case the syntax of the command becomes:

```
SEEK variable_name
```

■ **Database example**

The next few examples use a database called *Booklist*, which contains a publisher's schedule for the appearance of new books:

```
. USE Booklist
. LIST
Record#  TITLE                AUTHOR    PUB_DATE
      1  Feeding Your Cat     Smith     09/18/85
      2  Understanding Cats   Jones     06/30/85
      3  Cats of the West     Jackson   12/15/85
      4  Night Cats           Carlson   04/10/86
      5  Modern Cats          Miller    06/25/86
      6  Adventures with Cats Mason     11/18/86
.
```

The following sequence of commands indexes the database by book title and then creates four string variables, each containing the title of a book:

```
. INDEX ON title TO Titleind
       6 records indexed
.
. t1 = "Cats of the West"
Cats of the West
.
. t2 = "Adventures with Cats"
Adventures with Cats
.
. t3 = "Modern Cats"
Modern Cats
.
. t4 = "Cats I Have Known"
Cats I Have Known
.
```

The three examples that follow show how the SEEK command repositions the record pointer at a target record, and how the DISPLAY 116★ command is subsequently used to display the record on the screen or printer (like FIND 160★ and LOCATE 202★, SEEK itself does not list the record it has found). Notice that SEEK always begins its search at the beginning of the indexed database, no matter where the record pointer is positioned when the command is issued:

```
. SEEK t1
. DISPLAY
Record#  TITLE                   AUTHOR    PUB_DATE
      3  Cats of the West        Jackson   12/15/85
.
. SEEK t2
. DISPLAY
Record#  TITLE                   AUTHOR    PUB_DATE
      6  Adventures with Cats    Mason     11/18/86
.
. SEEK t3
. DISPLAY
Record#  TITLE                   AUTHOR    PUB_DATE
      5  Modern Cats             Miller    06/25/86
.
```

If SEEK does not find the target value, the end-of-file condition becomes true, and dBASE issues a "No find" message:

```
. SEEK t4
No find
   .
```

(In a program, the "No find" message can be suppressed via the SET TALK OFF **398★** command.)

■ **Program example**

The following procedure, called *Get_rec*, is part of the real-estate program described in detail under the SET PROCEDURE **383★** entry. (Briefly, the program's overall purpose is to provide management functions for a database called *Property*, which contains listings of houses that are for sale.) *Get_rec*'s task is to locate a specific record in the *Property* database. It begins by conducting an input dialogue that obtains an address from the user at the keyboard, and then searches for that address in the database. Here is *Get_rec*:

```
PROCEDURE Get_rec
*----- Finds a record in the Property database,
*         given an address.
*

SET TALK OFF
SET BELL OFF
SET CONFIRM ON
SET EXACT OFF

SET INDEX TO Address

done = .F.
r = ROW()

DO WHILE .NOT. done
    street = SPACE(28)
    @ r + 1, 10 SAY "What is the street address?" GET street
    READ
    street = TRIM(street)
```

(continued)

```
      SEEK street
      IF EOF()
          @ r + 3, 15 SAY "*** Record not found. ***"
          DO Yesno WITH r + 4, 19, "Try again? "
          IF yn
              @ r + 1, 10
              @ r + 3, 15
              @ r + 4, 15
          ELSE
              done = .T.
          ENDIF
      ELSE
          done = .T.
      ENDIF

   ENDDO

   RETURN
```

The index file *ADDRESS.NDX* already exists at the time *Get_rec* is called. The key field **194★** on which this index orders the database is a character field called *address*. *Get_rec* first opens the index file:

SET INDEX TO Address

Then, in the input dialogue that follows, *Get_rec* places a prompt on the screen:

```
What is the street address?
```

and stores the value input in the character variable *street*. The next step is to look for the field variable stored in *street*:

SEEK street

If the record is found, *Get_rec*'s job is complete and control returns to the procedure that called it, leaving the record pointer positioned at the target record so that the calling program will be able to access the required information. If the record is not found, the user is given a chance to enter a new address:

```
IF EOF()
    @ r + 3, 15 SAY "*** Record not found. ***"
    DO Yesno WITH r + 4, 19, "Try again? "
```

Notice that the EOF() **147★** function returns a value of .T. if SEEK does not find a record that contains the target field value. In *Get_rec*, all of this activity occurs inside a loop that continues processing until either a record is found or the user gives up trying. The original calling program will be able to determine whether or not a record has been located by checking the value of EOF().

(To examine the procedures that use *Get_rec*, see the programming examples included in the IF **171★** and SET DEVICE **347★** entries. For further discussion of *Get_rec* itself, see @...SAY...GET **9★** and ROW() **304★**.)

■ **Cautions**

SEEK works only on an indexed database, not on a sorted **402♦**, one. The index provides not only an ordered database, but also the key field for the search that SEEK conducts.

When you use SEEK to search for a string value, be careful to note the status of the SET EXACT **355★** command. When this control parameter **73★** is ON, an exact match (both length and content) will be required for the search to be successful. When SET EXACT is OFF, however, the string expression in the SEEK command may be shorter than the actual target field value. For example, if the variable *street* contains only the value "50 Westin" and SET EXACT is OFF, then the command *SEEK street* will successfully locate the *address* field value "50 Westin Avenue". This is why the *Get_rec* procedure sets EXACT OFF and also trims **440♦** any spaces from the end of the *street* string before attempting a search:

```
street = TRIM(street)
SEEK street
```

As a result, the user is not required to enter the entire street address in order to locate a target record.

■ **dBASE II equivalent**

None

However, the FIND command used with a macro **215★** duplicates the function of SEEK.

■ **Comment**

FIND is another dBASE command that searches for a field value in an indexed database; however, its syntax has different features and requirements.

SELECT

■ **Structure**

SELECT work_area
SELECT alias

■ **Description**

The SELECT command chooses among the 10 available dBASE III work areas **454◆**. Each of these work areas may contain an open database, but only one of the areas may be "current" ◆ at any given time. In general, any database command issued during a dBASE session applies to the currently selected work area.

■ **Usage**

The SELECT syntax allows you to refer to the 10 work areas in several different ways:

☐ The work areas are numbered from 1 through 10, and you can always select a work area by referring to one of these numbers.

☐ You can use the default alias **14★** (a single letter from A through J) of the database that is open in a given work area.

☐ You can use an optional alias assigned at the time you opened the database with the USE **454★** command. If you do not assign an alias, the SELECT syntax accepts the actual name of the database.

■ **Database example**

In the following example, databases are opened in work areas 1 and 2. The first database, called *Bksales*, contains data about the sales of best-selling books. The second, called *Authors*, stores information about the authors of the books:

```
. SELECT 1
. USE Bksales ALIAS Books
. SELECT 2
. USE Authors INDEX Author
```

Since *Bksales* was opened with an alias, *Books*, this alias can now be used in the SELECT command:

```
. SELECT Books
```

With these two databases open in different work areas, you can find related records 284★ in the two files and display information from both records: For example, given a title in work area 1, find its author and publisher in work area 2. The database in each work area has its own independent record pointer 258★, however, the SET RELATION 390★ command allows you to establish a relationship between two open databases, so that when the pointer is moved in the first database, a corresponding move occurs in the second:

```
. SET RELATION TO author_num INTO Authors
. GOTO 2
.
. ? title
Mountain Romance
.
. ? unit_sales
   67646
.
. ? Authors -> last_name
Bloomfield
.
. ? Authors -> publisher
Linton
.
```

Even though the currently selected database is in work area 1, we can still access information from work area 2 simply by referring to the name or alias of the database in that work area. As you can deduce from the examples above, the general forms of such a reference are:

```
alias -> field_name
database_name -> field_name
```

In the case of the *Authors* database, no optional alias was explicitly assigned, so *Authors* remains the working name of the file.

■ **Cautions**

The *alias −> field_name* notation fails when the field involved is a memo field **217★**. In this case, to display the information that the field contains, you must select the actual work area in which the field is stored. For example, the *Authors* database contains a memo field called *profile*. From within another work area, you cannot access this field with the reference:

```
Authors -> profile
```

Instead you must take the following steps:

```
. SELECT Authors
. ? profile
Janice Bloomfield has written over one-hundred
romance novels during her twenty-year career as a
storyteller.
.
```

(See the entries under SET RELATION and JOIN **189★** for more discussion of the problems with memo fields.)

In principle, each work area may contain not only an open database, but also any of the database's related files, including a memo file **156◆** (.DBT), one or more index files **156◆** (.NDX), and a format file **157◆** (.FMT). However, a maximum of 15 files may be open at once, and this limit includes all types of files, in all work areas. Furthermore, any one file—a format file, for example—may be open in only one work area at a time.

■ **dBASE II equivalent**

SELECT

However, dBASE II has only two work areas, called PRIMARY and SECONDARY.

■ **Comment**

When you first begin a session with dBASE, work area 1 is automatically selected. The CLEAR ALL **56★** command also selects work area 1 after closing all files.

SET

■ **Structure**

SET

■ **Description**

SET invokes a full-screen menu-driven assist mode that allows you to view and select options for many of the dBASE III control parameters **73★**. This assist mode is an alternative to issuing a separate SET command for each control setting.

■ **Caution**

Several control parameters, including SET DATE **337★** and SET SCOREBOARD **397★**, are not included in the SET menu. These must be entered from the dot prompt **62♦** or included in your *CONFIG.DB* **66★** file (see *Comments*).

■ **dBASE II equivalent**

None

■ **Comments**

There are three other ways to set control parameters:

□ Include appropriate instructions in a *CONFIG.DB* file, stored on the dBASE III program disk. (There are some control parameters that can be set *only* via *CONFIG.DB*.)

□ Write a program file that includes all your favorite SET commands and run this program at the beginning of each dBASE session to invoke the settings.

□ Include settings specific to a particular program within that program, and reset them before exiting the program.

SET can also be used to perform a quick check on the present status of the control parameters, as can the DISPLAY STATUS **119★** command.

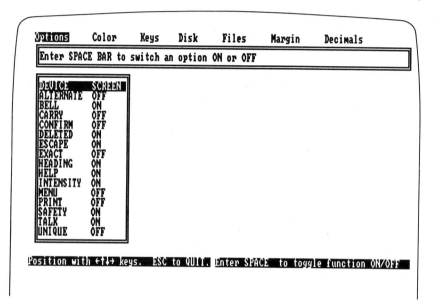

SET ALTERNATE

■ **Structure**

SET ALTERNATE TO file_name
SET ALTERNATE ON
SET ALTERNATE OFF

■ **Description**

SET ALTERNATE TO creates and opens an ASCII text file **157♦** on disk, to capture screen activity during a dBASE session. After SET ALTERNATE ON is issued, all normal screen activity (with the exception of information displayed in any of the full-screen modes) is sent concurrently to this text file. SET ALTERNATE OFF temporarily stops the flow of data to the disk file, but leaves the file open. CLOSE ALTERNATE **57♦** closes the file.

Unless you specify otherwise, SET ALTERNATE creates a file with a .TXT extension name **155**◆.

■ **Usage**

You might decide to use the SET ALTERNATE command for any of three purposes:

☐ To record—for future study—a sequence of direct commands and the screen displays that the commands generate.

☐ To save on disk the screen output from a program.

☐ To create a functional text file that serves some specific purpose.

We'll discuss each of these activities in turn.

Capturing direct commands: The following exercise illustrates how SET ALTERNATE captures a series of direct commands in a text file:

```
. SET ALTERNATE TO Test
. SET ALTERNATE ON
. * This first comment will appear in the file.
. SET ALTERNATE OFF
. * This second comment will not appear.
. SET ALTERNATE ON
. * This third comment will be included.
. CLOSE ALTERNATE
```

Since the resulting file, called *TEST.TXT*, is an ASCII text file, you can use the TYPE **444**★ command to display it on the screen:

```
. TYPE TEST.TXT

. * This first comment will appear in the file.

. SET ALTERNATE OFF

. * This third comment will be included.

. CLOSE ALTERNATE

.
```

Capturing screen output: To record the screen output generated by a specific program, issue SET ALTERNATE TO and SET ALTERNATE ON commands before you run the program. For example, the following sequence records the output from a program called *Prog*:

```
. SET ALTERNATE TO Prog_out
. SET ALTERNATE ON
. DO Prog
* ... *
. CLOSE ALTERNATE
```

After the program is run, its output will be stored in a text file called *PROG_OUT.TXT*.

Creating special files: Finally, some programmers may want to consider using SET ALTERNATE for creating specific kinds of text files from within a program. For example, SET ALTERNATE makes it possible to write a program that generates a *CONFIG.DB* 66★ file. The program will obtain a user's preferences for specific control parameters 73★, and then store those parameters in a text file in the format required by *CONFIG.DB*. This next command creates the file:

```
SET ALTERNATE TO A:CONFIG.DB
```

Then, command sequences like the following obtain settings from the user and send appropriate instructions to the *Config* file:

```
INPUT "Enter the new default printer margin: " TO marg
SET ALTERNATE ON
? "MARGIN =", marg
SET ALTERNATE OFF
```

■ **Cautions**

The SET SAFETY 396★ command does not apply to SET ALTERNATE: If a file created by a SET ALTERNATE TO command already exists, it will be overwritten *without warning*.

Because of its inability to record any full-screen activity generated by @...SAY 12★ commands, SET ALTERNATE has only limited value as a debugging 267◆ tool for use in conjunction with SET ECHO ON 351★.

■ **dBASE II equivalent**

SET ALTERNATE

■ **Comment**

Text files produced by SET ALTERNATE can be incorporated into word-processed documents. For example:

□ In WordStar, use the Ctrl-KR command to read an alternate file into your current document.

□ In Microsoft Word, create a second window (with the Window Split Horizontal command), use the Transfer Load command to read the text file into the new window, and then use the Copy command to transfer a copy of the text from window 2 to your original document in window 1.

SET BELL

■ **Structure**

SET BELL ON
SET BELL OFF

■ **Description**

The SET BELL command determines whether or not dBASE will sound the system bell in either of two circumstances involving full-screen data input:

□ When the input value fills the width of an individual field **154★** template.

□ When the user enters an input value that isn't of the expected data type **98★**.

SET BELL ON (the default) means that the bell will operate in these situations; OFF means that it will not.

■ **Usage**

The choice between these two modes of operation is a matter of personal preference. Some people are annoyed by having to listen to the system bell sound frequently during data-input sessions. On the other hand, touch typists may appreciate the audio warning, especially when the SET CONFIRM **334★** option is OFF.

■ **dBASE II equivalent**

SET BELL

■ **Comment**

ASCII **28★** character 7 controls the ringing of the system bell. The following command can be used to ring the bell from within a program:

```
? CHR(7)
```

This command works no matter which SET BELL setting is in effect. For an example, see the *Yesno* procedure listed under the PARAMETERS **245★** entry.

SET CARRY

- **Structure**

  SET CARRY ON

  SET CARRY OFF

- **Description**

  Normally, the input screens presented by the APPEND **19★** and INSERT **184★** commands contain empty templates for each new input field **154★**. The SET CARRY ON command arranges to carry field data forward from the previous record **284★** and display it in the current input template. SET CARRY OFF is the default status.

- **Usage**

  When a database contains many records that have one or more field values in common, the SET CARRY ON command may help streamline the data-input process. In the following example, you can imagine the *date_due* and *paid* fields—and perhaps occasionally even the *due_to* field—containing identical data from one record to the next:

  The user may change any fields that require new data, and simply press Return to accept those whose carried-forward values are correct.

■ **Caution**

Even with data carried forward, at least one character must be typed into the record template in order to append a new record.

■ **dBASE II equivalent**

SET CARRY

■ **Comment**

An alternative approach for entering an identical data item into many records of a database is to use the REPLACE **291★** command. In this case, you may simply leave the relevant fields blank during the input process.

SET COLOR

■ **Structure**

SET COLOR TO   fore1/back1 , *fore2/back2* , *border*

■ **Description**

The SET COLOR command allows you to control the display colors on a color monitor, or special display effects on a monochrome monitor.

SET COLOR takes three parameters—two of them optional—that control the display characteristics for normal text (*fore1/back1*), full-screen enhanced text (*fore2/back2*), and the screen border (*border*), respectively. Normal text is usually displayed as white against a black background. Enhanced text—that is, special full-screen displays such as input templates and help-screen highlights—normally appears as black text against a white background (see SET INTENSITY **376★**). The default color for the screen border is black.

The parameters for normal text and enhanced text are pairs of color codes, with a slash character separating the foreground code from the background code. The border parameter is a single color code. The color codes consist of either single numbers from 0 through 7 or a corresponding set of characters:

Number code:	Color:	Letter code:
0	Black	Space
1	Blue	B
2	Green	G
3	Cyan	BG
4	Red	R
5	Magenta	BR
6	Brown	GR
7	White	W

In addition, you may select "high-intensity" colors by including a plus sign (+) after any of the eight basic color codes. In most cases, this simply produces a brighter version of the same color; however, high-intensity brown (6 +) produces yellow.

■ Usage

Here is an example of the SET COLOR command, using all three parameters:

```
. SET COLOR TO 6+/4, 7/1, 3
```

This command selects yellow text against a red background for the normal display mode; white against blue for the enhanced display mode; and cyan for the border.

This next command produces high-intensity light text against a dark background, and can be used on either a color or a monochrome monitor:

```
. SET COLOR TO 7+/0
```

SET COLOR TO without any parameters sets the display to dark letters on a light background (0/7).

If you decide to work with dBASE in color, you will want to choose foreground and background colors that improve the readability of your screen. From the normal-intensity colors alone, there are 56 possible foreground/background combinations. The following program, called *Colortst*, lets you quickly examine each of these combinations, so that you can select the ones you like best:

```
*------------------------------------------------ COLORTST.PRG
* Steps through all possible screen color combinations.
*

SET TALK OFF

fore = 0
DO WHILE fore < 8
    back = 0
    DO WHILE back < 8
        IF fore <> back
            stfore = STR(fore, 1)
            stback = STR(back, 1)
            SET COLOR TO &stfore/&stback
            CLEAR
```

(continued)

```
        TEXT

                With the SET COLOR command,
                you can choose any color combination
                that improves readability on
                your color display screen.

            ENDTEXT
            WAIT
        ENDIF
        back = back + 1
    ENDDO
    fore = fore + 1
ENDDO

SET COLOR TO 7/0
CLEAR
SET TALK ON
RETURN
```

Within a nested DO WHILE loop, *Colortst* displays a short paragraph of text in each of the different color combinations and gives you a chance to examine the screen. Notice the use of macros 215★ in the program's SET COLOR command:

```
SET COLOR TO &stfore/&stback
```

The SET COLOR syntax does not allow the use of simple variables 459★ for the foreground/background parameters.

■ **Caution**
Be careful not to set the foreground and background to the same color. If you do, text display will disappear from the screen altogether.

■ **dBASE II equivalent**
SET COLOR
This option became available in version 2.4 of dBASE II. It is not available in earlier versions.

■ **Comment**
Along with the normal- and high-intensity colors, two other display effects can be produced with the SET COLOR command:

Effect:	Code:
Blinking text	*
Underlining	U

(Underlining is possible only on a monochrome monitor.)

The following short program, called *Scrntest*, illustrates the appearance of blinking and underlined text on a monochrome monitor:

```
*-------------------------------------------------- SCRNTEST.PRG
* Creates blinking and underlining effects
*    on a monochrome screen.
*

CLEAR
SET COLOR TO U
@ 10, 10 SAY "This sentence will be underlined. "

SET COLOR TO 7*
@ 12, 10 SAY "This sentence will be blinking on and off."

SET COLOR TO 7/0
?
?
WAIT

CLEAR
RETURN
```

SET CONFIRM

- **Structure**
  SET CONFIRM ON
  SET CONFIRM OFF

- **Description:**
  The SET CONFIRM command determines whether or not dBASE will require the use of the Return key for entering data into individual input templates in a full-screen mode. The default status is OFF: Under this setting, the cursor will automatically move to the next input field 154* as soon as the width of the current field is filled. When SET CONFIRM is ON, the person who is entering data will have to confirm each entry item by pressing the Return key.

- **Usage**
  The status of the SET CONFIRM option is largely a matter of personal preference. The disadvantage of the OFF status is that it creates an inconsistent data-entry requirement: When a data item does not completely fill an input field, the Return key is required; when the item does fill a field, a Return not only is not required, but in fact will advance the cursor two fields because of the automatic Return issued when a field is filled. For these reasons, most dBASE users seem to prefer the SET CONFIRM ON setting.

■ **Caution**

When both SET CONFIRM and SET BELL 329★ are OFF, data too long for an input field may inadvertently be run over into the subsequent field, if both fields are of the same data type 98★. A touch typist who does not check the screen after each record entry may not become aware of the error until much later, when data are accessed from the record.

```
. SET BELL OFF
. SET CONFIRM OFF
. USE Address
. APPEND
```

```
Record No.        7
LASTNAME     Blenheim-Y
FIRSTNAME    ork
STREET
CITY
STATE
ZIP
```

■ **dBASE II equivalent**

SET CONFIRM

■ **Comment**

The SET BELL command determines whether or not dBASE will sound the system bell when the width of an input field is filled or the user attempts to enter data of the wrong type.

SET CONSOLE

■ **Structure**

SET CONSOLE ON
SET CONSOLE OFF

■ **Description**

The SET CONSOLE command controls program output to the display screen. The default state is ON: In this normal condition, direct keyboard input and the results of all data-display commands in a program appear on the screen. When the CONSOLE setting is OFF, output to the display screen is inhibited, although dBASE continues to *read* both file and keyboard input. The OFF state does not inhibit the display of dBASE messages (see SET TALK **398★**).

■ Usage

The SET PRINT ON **381★** command normally sends display output to both the printer and the screen. In some programming situations, however, you may wish to send information only to the printer, maintaining an unchanging display on the screen. Such a situation requires the use of both SET CONSOLE OFF and SET PRINT ON.

The *Prntinfo* procedure listed and discussed under the SET DEVICE **347★** entry contains an example of the SET CONSOLE command. The procedure prepares a printed report from a selected record of the *Property* real-estate database **384♦**. During the printing of the report, the screen identifies the record that is being printed, but does not display the report itself. To achieve this effect, *Prntinfo* issues the following commands before beginning the report:

```
SET CONSOLE OFF
SET PRINT ON
```

When the report is complete, the reverse settings are established, so that the display screen will once again be the output device, and the printer will be turned off:

```
SET CONSOLE ON
SET PRINT OFF
```

■ Caution

A procedure that turns the console off should always take care to turn it back on again before returning control to the calling program or procedure, so that other routines within the same program can display their output on the screen. (The SET CONSOLE status is automatically restored to ON when a program or procedure returns control to dBASE.)

■ dBASE II equivalent

SET CONSOLE

■ Comment

The SET DEVICE command directs the output from @...SAY **9★** statements to the screen or the printer.

SET DATE

■ **Structure**

SET DATE date_display_type

■ **Description**

The SET DATE command establishes the display format for subsequent date-type 99♦ values used in the current dBASE session. Five different display formats ♦ are available, as shown in the following table:

Format:	Display type:
mo/da/yr	American
da/mo/yr	British
da.mo.yr	French or German
da-mo-yr	Italian
yr.mo.da	ANSI

■ **Usage**

Normally, the default format is American (mo/da/yr). To change this format, you simply issue a SET DATE command indicating the new format in which you wish to see dates displayed. To return to the default format, issue the command:

```
. SET DATE american
```

Here is an example of the SET DATE command in action:

```
. SET DATE french
. ? DATE()
27.08.85
. SET DATE american
. ? DATE()
08/27/85
.
```

■ **Database example**

The database called *Payables*, discussed in the CDOW() **44★** entry, shows invoice dates and due dates for a series of monthly bills. In the next few examples, you will see the database listed several times, each time after a different SET DATE command has been issued. Notice the changes in the date displays from one listing to the next:

```
. USE Payables
. LIST
Record#  COMPANY              DESCRPTION       AMOUNT INV_DATE TERMS DUE
      1  Corner Stationary    supplies         109.82 03/31/85    30 04/30/85
      2  TechCo Computer Co.  floppy disks      85.22 04/21/85    45 06/05/85
      3  CompuFix, Inc.       PC repairs       256.80 04/11/85    30 05/11/85
      4  SoftSave Corp.       software         745.32 03/29/85    15 04/13/85
      5  ConsultiComp, Inc.   training         150.00 05/01/85    45 06/15/85
      6  The Tech Book Store  computer books    38.92 04/21/85    30 05/21/85
.
. SET DATE british
. LIST
Record#  COMPANY              DESCRPTION       AMOUNT INV_DATE TERMS DUE
      1  Corner Stationary    supplies         109.82 31/03/85    30 30/04/85
      2  TechCo Computer Co.  floppy disks      85.22 21/04/85    45 05/06/85
      3  CompuFix, Inc.       PC repairs       256.80 11/04/85    30 11/05/85
      4  SoftSave Corp.       software         745.32 29/03/85    15 13/04/85
      5  ConsultiComp, Inc.   training         150.00 01/05/85    45 15/06/85
      6  The Tech Book Store  computer books    38.92 21/04/85    30 21/05/85
.
```

```
. SET DATE french
. LIST
Record#  COMPANY              DESCRPTION       AMOUNT INV_DATE TERMS DUE
      1  Corner Stationary    supplies         109.82 31.03.85    30 30.04.85
      2  TechCo Computer Co.  floppy disks      85.22 21.04.85    45 05.06.85
      3  CompuFix, Inc.       PC repairs       256.80 11.04.85    30 11.05.85
      4  SoftSave Corp.       software         745.32 29.03.85    15 13.04.85
      5  ConsultiComp, Inc.   training         150.00 01.05.85    45 15.06.85
      6  The Tech Book Store  computer books    38.92 21.04.85    30 21.05.85
.
. SET DATE ansi
. LIST
Record#  COMPANY              DESCRPTION       AMOUNT INV_DATE TERMS DUE
      1  Corner Stationary    supplies         109.82 85.03.31    30 85.04.30
      2  TechCo Computer Co.  floppy disks      85.22 85.04.21    45 85.06.05
      3  CompuFix, Inc.       PC repairs       256.80 85.04.11    30 85.05.11
      4  SoftSave Corp.       software         745.32 85.03.29    15 85.04.13
      5  ConsultiComp, Inc.   training         150.00 85.05.01    45 85.06.15
      6  The Tech Book Store  computer books    38.92 85.04.21    30 85.05.21
.
```

■ **Cautions**

SET DATE affects only dBASE date-type values—not dates that are represented as strings **98♦** of characters. Date-type values include fields and variables that are defined as dates, and the results of the DATE() **103★** and CTOD() **92★** functions.

SET DATE is not included in the on-line (HELP **170★**) documentation in early releases of dBASE III.

■ **dBASE II equivalent**

None

The SET DATE TO command is used to change the system date in dBASE II, and accepts only a mo/da/yr date string.

■ **Comments**

SET DATE determines the format for date input and verification. For example, if you set a new date format and then APPEND **19★** a record to a database that contains a date field, the input template for the date field will appear in the new format you have chosen.

SET DATE also determines the correct format for the argument of the CTOD() function and the result of the DTOC() **139★** function.

To change the system date from within dBASE, use the RUN **306★** command to perform the DOS **133★** *DATE* routine.

If you wish to change the default date format, include the new setting in your *CONFIG.DB* **66★** file.

SET DEBUG

■ **Structure**

SET DEBUG ON
SET DEBUG OFF

■ **Description**

The SET DEBUG command is a program-debugging **267♦** tool that works in conjunction with the SET ECHO **351★** command. When SET ECHO is ON, each program command is displayed at the time that dBASE actually performs it. Normally, this display appears on the screen, along with the actual screen output that the program itself produces. SET DEBUG ON sends the display of the commands to the printer instead, so that the program's screen output will not be mixed up with the command displays generated by SET ECHO. The default status of SET DEBUG is OFF.

■ **Caution**

SET DEBUG has no effect at all unless SET ECHO is ON.

■ **dBASE II equivalent**

SET DEBUG

■ **Comment**

You can also use the SET ALTERNATE **326★** command to record the results of SET ECHO, as in the following sequence:

```
. SET ALTERNATE TO Prog_out
. SET ECHO ON
. SET ALTERNATE ON
. DO Prog
      * ... *
. CLOSE ALTERNATE
. SET ECHO OFF
```

As a result of these commands, the file *PROG_OUT.TXT* will receive most of the screen output from *Prog* (see SET ALTERNATE for the exceptions), including all of the command displays generated by SET ECHO.

SET DECIMALS

■ **Structure**

SET DECIMALS TO numeric_expression

■ **Description**

The SET DECIMALS command establishes a default number of decimal places to be displayed in the results of the SQRT() **412★**, EXP() **152★**, and LOG() **205★** functions, and in the results of arithmetic division. dBASE's default setting for these operations is two decimal places.

■ **Usage**

Normally, the number of digits displayed after the decimal point in the result of a numeric expression depends upon either the default (two decimal places) or the number of decimal places in the arguments or operands of the expression. However, with the four operations listed above, you can use the SET DECIMALS command to control the decimal places more specifically. (Where necessary, the displayed values will be rounded according to the usual arithmetic conventions.)

The following examples illustrate the effects of SET DECIMALS. The first two show how dBASE displays numeric values on the basis of the number of decimal places in the operands. The third shows the result of a division displayed with the default decimal setting. The remaining examples show how the SET DECIMALS command can be used to change the numeric displays for division, SQRT(), EXP(), and LOG():

```
. x = 5
5
. ? x + 2
         7
. ? x + 2.0
           7.0
. ? x / 3
          1.67

.
```

```
. SET DECIMALS TO 6
.
. ? x / 3
         1.666667

. ? SQRT(x)
2.236068

. ? EXP(x)
148.413159

. ? LOG(x)
  1.609438

.
```

```
. SET DECIMALS TO 4
.
. ? x / 3
         1.6667

. ? SQRT(x)
  2.2361

. ? EXP(x)
148.4132

. ? LOG(x)
  1.6094

.
```

■ **Caution**

Unless SET FIXED **363**★ is ON, dBASE will disregard a SET DECIMALS value that is *less than* the number of decimal places in the arguments or operands:

```
. z = 7.326
7.326
: SET DECIMALS TO 1
:
: ? SQRT(z)
      2.707
:
: SET FIXED ON
:
: ? SQRT(z)
      2.7
:
```

■ **dBASE II equivalent**

None

■ **Comments**

SET DECIMALS affects only the *display* of numeric values. Results of arithmetic operations or variable assignments **414**✦ are stored in memory to maximum dBASE precision:

```
. x = 5
. y = 7
:
: numvar = x / y
:
. LIST MEMORY
X           pub   N        5 (        5.00000000)
Y           pub   N        7 (        7.00000000)
NUMVAR      pub   N        0.71 (     0.71428571)
    3 variables defined,      27 bytes used
  253 variables available,  5973 bytes available
.
```

If the numeric result of a function or calculation is stored in a database, the SET DECIMALS command has no effect on the number of decimal places. Rather, the field definition **100**✦ itself is the controlling factor.

SET DEFAULT

- **Structure**
  SET DEFAULT TO drive

- **Description**
  The SET DEFAULT command allows you to designate a default disk drive ◆ where dBASE will look whenever you issue a command that results in reading from or writing to disk.

- **Usage**
  When you first begin a dBASE session, the default drive is the one from which the dBASE program itself was loaded. For example, if you have a system with two floppy disks, you will load dBASE from drive A; therefore, A is the default drive. However, you will probably want to save database files on drive B, so after starting dBASE, you can issue the following command to designate B as the drive containing the data disk (notice that the colon that is normally part of the drive name is optional here):

> . SET DEFAULT TO B

Once you have issued this command, dBASE will save files to and read files from drive B unless you explicitly specify otherwise in a database command.

- **Caution**
  If you cannot locate a file that you are certain is on your data disk, use the DISPLAY STATUS **119**★ command to verify that your default drive is set properly (see *Comment*).

- **dBASE II equivalent**
  SET DEFAULT

- **Comment**
  Since the default drive is a parameter that you will almost always want set to a drive different from the one holding the dBASE program disk, you may want to include this specification in your *CONFIG.DB* **66**★ file, so that you won't have to issue the SET DEFAULT command every time you work in dBASE.

SET DELETED

■ **Structure**

SET DELETED ON
SET DELETED OFF

■ **Description**

SET DELETED affects the way dBASE treats records **284★** that are marked for deletion **106◆**. When the SET DELETED status is ON, most dBASE commands behave as though such records have actually been removed: That is, they ignore marked records. The default status of SET DELETED is OFF.

■ **Usage**

The following example illustrates the use of SET DELETED. A database called *Bills* contains records of household bills that are coming due. Records of bills that have already been paid are marked for deletion:

```
. USE Bills
. LIST
Record#  DUE_TO         AMOUNT DATE_DUE PAID
      1  Bernal Bank    142.75 06/15/85 .F.
      2  Maxwell's      567.81 06/22/85 .F.
      3 *Credit Union    89.00 06/01/85 .T.
      4  Ameri Mortgage 986.23 06/30/85 .F.
      5  Bernal Electric 61.15 06/18/85 .F.
      6 *OC Telephone   110.52 06/05/85 .T.
.
```

When the SET DELETED ON command is issued, the marked records are ignored by most other dBASE commands:

```
. SET DELETED ON
. LIST
Record#  DUE_TO         AMOUNT DATE_DUE PAID
      1  Bernal Bank    142.75 06/15/85 .F.
      2  Maxwell's      567.81 06/22/85 .F.
      4  Ameri Mortgage 986.23 06/30/85 .F.
      5  Bernal Electric 61.15 06/18/85 .F.
.
```

■ **Caution**

The RECALL ALL **278**◆ command is disabled when SET DELETED is ON. However, RECALL RECORD can still be used to recall a specific record by number **284**◆ (see *Comments*).

■ **dBASE II equivalent**

SET DELETED

■ **Comments**

SET DELETED does not affect indexing **176**◆ or sorting **402**◆.

Commands that operate only on the current record and commands that refer to a specific record by number (via a RECORD **282**★ clause) will disregard the SET DE-LETED status and operate as usual.

The DELETE **106**★ command marks records for deletion; the PACK **243**★ command deletes them permanently. The DELETED() **108**★ function returns a value of true if the current record has been marked for deletion.

SET DELIMITERS

■ **Structure**

SET DELIMITERS TO character(s)/DEFAULT
SET DELIMITERS ON
SET DELIMITERS OFF

■ **Description**

The SET DELIMITERS command allows you to change the display format of input templates in dBASE full-screen modes.

■ **Usage**

Normally, input templates for database fields and variables are simply displayed in reverse-video mode: black text on a light background. You can modify this display so that the width of the input template is defined visually by a beginning and ending delimiting character ◆. If you include only one character in the SET DELIMITERS TO command, the beginning and ending delimiters will be the same.

The steps for changing the delimiter status are:

1. Issue a SET DELIMITERS TO command, to indicate the character or characters that will become the delimiters.

2. Issue the SET DELIMITERS ON command, to initiate the use of the defined delimiters.

Here is an example:

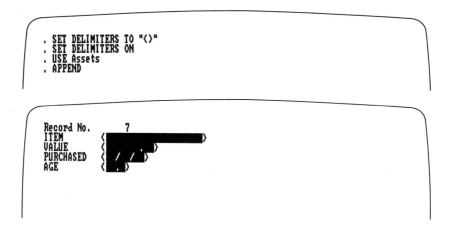

The two DELIMITERS commands establish the characters < and > as the beginning and ending delimiters for all full-screen input templates.

If you issue SET DELIMITERS ON without first specifying the delimiting characters, dBASE will use the default delimiter, which is the colon. If you have changed the delimiters, SET DELIMITER TO DEFAULT will re-establish the colon as the delimiting character.

- **dBASE II equivalent**

None

SET COLON controls the display of the colon dBASE II delimiter.

- **Comments**

As you can see from the preceding example, the SET DELIMITERS command does not affect the reverse video in the display of input templates: After SET DELIMITERS ON was issued, the selected delimiters simply appeared on either side of the reverse-video template. To eliminate the reverse-video display, leaving only the delimiting characters, you must also SET INTENSITY OFF **376★**.

```
. SET INTENSITY OFF
: APPEND
```

```
Record No.        8
ITEM         <                    >
VALUE        <      , >
PURCHASED    <  / / >
AGE          <  . >
```

If you wish to use the new delimiters in all future dBASE sessions, just include them and the SET DELIMITERS ON command in your *CONFIG.DB* **66★** file, so that they will automatically be reset each time you load dBASE.

SET DEVICE

■ **Structure**
SET DEVICE TO device_name

■ **Description**
The SET DEVICE command controls the destination of output from the @...SAY ...PICTURE **9★** command. One of two device names may be used in the SET DEVICE command: SCREEN or PRINT. By default, @...SAY displays its output on the screen; the SET DEVICE TO PRINT command enables you to send the formatted output of @...SAY commands to the printer instead.

■ **Usage**

The PICTURE 252★ clause of the @...SAY command includes a versatile "sublanguage" of formatting symbols, offering the programmer an important set of tools for controlling the way data are displayed on the screen. Thanks to the SET DEVICE command, this versatility is also available for formatting data sent to the printer.

■ **Database and program example**

The *Property* database and its companion, the real-estate program, are designed to store and manage listings of homes that are for sale. (Both the program and the database are described in detail under the SET PROCEDURE 383★ entry.) One of the procedures in the real-estate program—*Prntinfo*—has the task of printing out a promotional "spec sheet" that agents can distribute to potential buyers of a given home. *Prntinfo* uses SET DEVICE to print this spec sheet:

```
PROCEDURE Prntinfo
*----- Prints out a specification sheet for distribution
*         to potential buyers of a given home.
*

CLEAR
? "         *** Print a specification sheet for a home. ***"
?
?
DO Get_rec
IF EOF()
    RETURN
ENDIF

ok = .F.
DO WHILE .NOT. ok
    DO Yesno WITH 10, 10, "Is the printer ready? "
    ok = yn
ENDDO

SET CONSOLE OFF
SET PRINT ON
SET MARGIN TO 12
EJECT
SET DEVICE TO PRINT

? "     XYZ Realty"
? "     --- ------"
?
? "   Home Listing"
?
?
? "                 " + address
? "                 " + city
?
? "                 (" + TRIM(neighborhd) + " District.)"
?
```

(continued)

```
@ PROW() + 1, 15 SAY asking_pr PICTURE "$###,###.##"
?
?
? "                Features of home:"
? "                --------- -- -----"
? "                    > ", sq_footage, "sq. feet"
? "                    > ", bedrooms, "bedrooms"
? "                    > ", bathrooms, "bathrooms"
IF garage
    ? "                    >  garage"
ENDIF
?
?
? "=========================================================="
?
? descriptn
?

SET CONSOLE ON
SET DEVICE TO SCREEN
SET MARGIN TO 0
SET PRINT OFF
RETURN
```

The procedure begins by calling *Get_rec*, another of the procedures in the real-estate program. *Get_rec* obtains an address from the user, identifying which home listing is to be printed as a spec sheet (you can read more about *Get_rec* under the SEEK 317★ entry). Once a record in the *Property* database has been selected and the printer is ready to go, *Prntinfo* begins sending field information to the printer.

A number of different SET commands are issued before the printing begins, among them:

```
SET DEVICE TO PRINT
```

Subsequently, when *Prntinfo* issues an @...SAY command to display the asking price of the home:

```
@ PROW() + 1, 15 SAY asking_pr PICTURE "$###,###.##"
```

the output is sent to the printer in a dollars-and-cents format.

```
XYZ Realty
--- ------

Home Listing

          18 Jackson Avenue
          San Francisco

          (Nob Hill District.)

          $375,000.00


          Features of home:
          --------- -- -----
            >   5000 sq. feet
            >   7 bedrooms
            >   5.0 bathrooms
            >   garage


========================================================

Stupendous ocean view.  Older row house.
Excellent condition.  Spacious rooms, modernized
kitchen.  Bedrooms upstairs.  Desirable family
home.  Good school district.  Shops and services
5 minutes.  On bus line.  Owner anxious to sell,
will carry large second for right buyer.
```

When the printing of the spec sheet is complete, *Prntinfo* reinstates the display screen as the device for @...SAY output, to ensure that subsequent @...SAY commands will display their output on the screen rather than the printer:

```
SET DEVICE TO SCREEN
```

(For further discussion of the *Prntinfo* procedure, see the EJECT **145★**, Memo Fields **217★**, PROW() **268★**, SET CONSOLE **335★**, SET PRINT **381★**, and SET MARGIN **378★** entries.)

■ **Cautions**

You must use the word PRINT, not PRINTER, as a device name in the SET DEVICE command.

   If you want the output of an @...SAY command to be sent to both the screen and the printer, you will have to issue the @...SAY command twice—once after each SET DEVICE command.

   When the printer is the output device, an @...SAY command that attempts to move upward from the current output position will result in a form feed—almost always an undesirable effect. To ensure that each @...SAY command will move *down* the page from the current position, use the PROW() function to determine the current printing row (see PROW() and the preceding example).

■ **dBASE II equivalent**

None

■ **Comment**

The @...GET command has no effect when the printer is the output device.

SET ECHO

■ **Structure**

SET ECHO ON
SET ECHO OFF

■ **Description**

SET ECHO is a tool for use in debugging 267◆ dBASE programs—that is, for locating the error or errors in a program that isn't working the way you want it to. After you issue the SET ECHO ON command, any subsequent program run will result in a display of each individual command line on the screen as the command itself is performed. The default SET ECHO status is OFF.

■ **Usage**

When SET ECHO is ON, the normal screen output of the program will still appear on the screen along with the display of the command lines. You can also turn the SET TALK 398★ status to ON to obtain even more information from dBASE during a program run.

■ **Program example**

The following short program is an exercise designed to demonstrate the effects of the SET ECHO ON command:

```
*------------------------------------------------- ECHOTEST.PRG
* Experiment with the SET ECHO ON command.
*

SET TALK ON
SET ECHO ON

i = 1
DO WHILE i < 3
    ? "Outer loop: iteration #" + STR(i, 1)
    j = 1

    DO WHILE j < 3
        ? "    Inner loop: iteration #" + STR(j, 1)
        j = j + 1
    ENDDO

    i = i + 1
ENDDO

SET ECHO OFF
RETURN
```

Notice that the *Echotest* program contains a nested DO WHILE **129★** loop. Performance of the program produces the following display, which shows each loop iteration and also the successive values of the loop "counters," *i* and *j*:

```
. DO Echotest

i = 1
1
DO WHILE i < 3
    ? "Outer loop: iteration #" + STR(i, 1)
Outer loop: iteration #1
    j = 1
1
    DO WHILE j < 3
        ? "    Inner loop: iteration #" + STR(j, 1)
    Inner loop: iteration #1
        j = j + 1
        2
    ENDDO
        ? "    Inner loop: iteration #" + STR(j, 1)
    Inner loop: iteration #2
        j = j + 1
        3
    ENDDO
    i = i + 1
    2
ENDDO
    ? "Outer loop: iteration #" + STR(i, 1)
Outer loop: iteration #2
    j = 1
1
    DO WHILE j < 3
        ? "    Inner loop: iteration #" + STR(j, 1)
    Inner loop: iteration #1
        j = j + 1
        2
    ENDDO
        ? "    Inner loop: iteration #" + STR(j, 1)
    Inner loop: iteration #2
        j = j + 1
        3
    ENDDO
    i = i + 1
    3
ENDDO

SET ECHO OFF

.
```

As you can see from this example, SET ECHO is a powerful debugging tool when you are looking for an error in nested loops, where the logical mechanism that terminates the looping is a common source of program errors.

Normally, you probably would not include the SET ECHO command inside the program itself, but rather issue the command from the dBASE dot prompt:

```
. SET ECHO ON
. DO Newprog
*  ...  *
. SET ECHO OFF
```

- **dBASE II equivalent**
  SET ECHO

- **Comments**
  When SET ECHO is ON, you can use the SET DEBUG **339★** command to send the display of each command to the printer rather than to the screen.
  Another debugging tool, SET STEP **397★**, causes the program to pause after performance of each program line.

SET ESCAPE

- **Structure**
  SET ESCAPE ON
  SET ESCAPE OFF

- **Description**
  The SET ESCAPE command specifies whether or not a dBASE program or command can be interrupted from the keyboard via the Escape key. The default setting is ON, meaning that Escape can terminate the current activity. For example, if you press Escape during a program, dBASE will halt the program and display a prompt that gives you a choice between exiting the program or resuming:

```
. DO Ascii
*** INTERRUPTED ***
Called from - B:Ascii.prg
Terminate command file? (Y/N)
```

If you press Escape during performance of a dot-prompt 62♦ command, (and SET TALK 398★ is ON) you will receive an INTERRUPTED message, as in the following example:

```
. USE Assets
. LIST
Record# ITEM                   VALUE PURCHASED  AGE
      1 typewriter            1240.00 05/30/79  6.3
*** INTERRUPTED ***
.
```

If the SET ESCAPE option is OFF, the Escape key will not, in general, have any effect on program or command performance. Note, however, that Escape does continue to terminate full-screen mode.

■ **Usage**

During program development, the SET ESCAPE ON command can be helpful in debugging 267♦. For example, if you see that some unexpected event is taking place in the performance of your program, you can press the Escape key to stop the action and dBASE will show you exactly where you were in the program's structure when the interruption occurred:

```
Called from - B:PROPERTY.PRG
Called from - B:MENU.PRG
Terminate command file? (Y/N) Yes
Do cancelled
```

However, when a program is in use, the prevention of accidental or even intentional interruptions can be a great asset, so the SET ESCAPE OFF command should be inserted into the debugged program.

■ **dBASE II equivalent**

SET ESCAPE

■ **Comment**

You can include the SET ESCAPE OFF command when you write your program, but "comment it out" (disable it) with an asterisk (* 4★). When debugging is complete, just delete the * to activate the command.

SET EXACT

■ **Structure**

SET EXACT OFF

SET EXACT ON

■ **Description**

SET EXACT determines how dBASE evaluates a comparison between two character strings **98♦** of unequal length. The default setting is OFF: Under this setting, a string *s1* and a second string, *s2*, will be considered equal as long as all of the characters in *s2* are identical with the characters in the corresponding positions of *s1*. Thus, *s1* = *s2* can be true even when *s2* contains fewer characters than *s1*.

If SET EXACT is ON, two strings must be identical in both length and content to be considered equal.

■ **Usage**

The SET EXACT status has great significance to database commands that search for specific records **284★**. Consider the following example using the *Students* database, which contains the first names, scores, and class ranks of a group of students. The teacher would like to find all the students whose names begin with the letter J. With SET EXACT in its OFF setting, the following search is possible:

```
. SET EXACT OFF
. LIST FOR name = "J"
Record#  NAME        SCORE RANK
      2  Jane           82    3
      6  Johnny         75    5
.
```

In performing this LIST **200★** command, dBASE matches the string "J" with all names that *begin* with "J"; hence, the LIST yields two names. When SET EXACT is ON, however, no match is found, because there is no student whose full name is "J".

```
. SET EXACT ON
. LIST FOR name = "J"
Record#  NAME        SCORE RANK
.
```

■ **Program example**

Another illustration of SET EXACT OFF can be found in the *Get_rec* procedure listed and described in the SEEK **317★** entry. This procedure searches for records in a real-estate database called *Property* **384♦**. To locate a given record, *Get_rec* prompts the user for an address from the keyboard, and then uses the SEEK command to search for the address (the database is indexed **176♦** by the *address* field). Consider the following passage from the program:

```
SET EXACT OFF
*  ...  *
    street = SPACE(28)
    @ r + 1, 10 SAY "What is the street address?" GET street
    READ

    street = TRIM(street)
    SEEK street
```

An important element of the program's design is that the user need enter only the *first part* of a given address to perform a successful search. For example, let's say the user is searching the database for the address "18 Jackson Street, Apt B" but can remember only the number and street name, "18 Jackson". If this shorter string is entered into the variable *street* when SET EXACT is OFF, the SEEK command will successfully locate the record.

■ **Caution**

Trailing blanks at the end of an incomplete key string will spoil the effect of SET EXACT OFF. For example, if the partial-address string above contains spaces, as follows:

```
"18 Jackson               "
```

the string will *not* match the target address, even with SET EXACT OFF. This is why the *Get_rec* procedure uses the TRIM **440★** function to eliminate any trailing blanks from the contents of *street* before performing the SEEK command:

```
    street = TRIM(street)
    SEEK street
```

■ **dBASE II equivalent**

SET EXACT

■ **Comments**

SET EXACT also affects the FIND **160★** and LOCATE **202★** commands, and commands with condition clauses **312♦** (FOR **164★** and WHILE **463★**).

For more about string values, see the entries for Data Types **98★**, the various string functions **418★**, and String Operators **420★**.

SET FILTER

■ **Structure**

SET FILTER TO condition_expression

■ **Description**

The SET FILTER command temporarily "hides" database records **284★** that do not meet the condition **286♦** expressed in the command. Subsequently, many database commands that would normally operate on the entire database will work only on those records that have not been hidden by the filter. To disable the filter, bringing back all the previously hidden records, issue the command:

```
. SET FILTER TO
```

■ **Usage**

SET FILTER is useful whenever you wish to perform a series of commands on a subset of all the records in a database: Rather than including the same FOR **164★** clause in each command, you can issue one general SET FILTER command before entering the database commands.

■ **Database example**

The following short example filters a database called *Assets*:

```
. USE Assets
. LIST
Record#  ITEM                    VALUE PURCHASED  AGE
      1  typewriter            1240.00 05/30/79   6.3
      2  personal computer     2495.00 03/15/83   2.5
      3  printer, daisy-wheel  1250.00 03/15/83   2.5
      4  printer, dot-matrix    650.00 05/15/84   1.4
      5  copier                1835.00 12/20/84   0.8
      6  office desk            850.00 02/27/80   5.6
    .
```

```
. SET FILTER TO value > 1000
. COUNT
        4 records
.
. LIST
Record#  ITEM                    VALUE PURCHASED  AGE
      1  typewriter            1240.00 05/30/79   6.3
      2  personal computer     2495.00 03/15/83   2.5
      3  printer, daisy-wheel  1250.00 03/15/83   2.5
      5  copier                1835.00 12/20/84   0.8
.
. COPY TO Temp
        4 records copied
    .
```

Normally, the database commands COUNT 85★, LIST **200**★, and COPY **82**★ would all work on the entire database. In this case, however, they perform their respective tasks on only the four records that remain after the filter is activated.

■ **Program example**

The *Reqmnts* procedure is part of the real-estate program described in detail under the SET PROCEDURE 383★ entry. *Reqmnts* (the name stands for "requirements") works with a database called *Property*, which contains descriptions of homes that are for sale. The procedure finds all the homes in the database that match the requirements of a given potential buyer. On the following page is a listing of *Reqmnts*.

```
PROCEDURE Reqmnts
*----- Filters the Property database, searching for homes that
*        match the requirements of a given client.
*

CLEAR
?
? "   ** Search for homes that match these requirements: **"
?
? "          1. price range...............>"
? "          2. square footage range......>"
? "          3. age range.................>"
?
? "          4. number of bedrooms........>"
? "          5. number of bathrooms.......>"
? "          6. garage required...........>"
done = .F.
reqs = ""
validate = ""
choice = 1

DO WHILE .NOT. done
    @ 12, 12 CLEAR
    @ 12, 12 SAY "Which requirement? <1,2,3,4,5,6> ";
      GET choice PICTURE "9" RANGE 1, 6
    READ
    stchoice = str(choice)

    IF stchoice $ validate
        ? CHR(7)
        @ 14, 14 SAY "You have already specified"
        @ 15, 14 SAY "a value for this requirement."
    ELSE
        IF LEN(validate) <> 0
            reqs = reqs + " .AND. "
        ENDIF

        DO CASE
            CASE choice = 1
                @ 14, 14 SAY "price range:"
                DO Minmax WITH 4
                reqs = reqs + " (asking_pr >= " + min;
                    + " .AND. asking_pr <= " + max + ")"
            CASE choice = 2
                @ 14, 14 SAY "footage range:"
                DO Minmax WITH 5
                reqs = reqs + " (sq_footage >= " + min;
                    + " .AND. sq_footage <= " + max + ")"
```

(continued)

359

```
                CASE choice = 3
                    @ 14, 14 SAY "age range:"
                    DO Minmax WITH 6
                    reqs = reqs + "(home_age >= " + min;
                        + " .AND. home_age <= " + max + ")"
                CASE choice = 4
                    bdrms = "  "
                    DO WHILE LEN(TRIM(bdrms)) = 0
                        @ 14, 14 SAY "number of bedrooms: " GET bdrms ;
                            PICTURE "99"
                        READ
                    ENDDO
                    @ 8, 40 SAY bdrms PICTURE "99"
                    reqs = reqs + "bedrooms = " + bdrms
                CASE choice = 5
                    bthrms = "   "
                    DO WHILE LEN(TRIM(bthrms)) = 0
                        @ 14, 14 SAY "number of bathrooms: " GET bthrms ;
                            PICTURE "9.9"
                        READ
                    ENDDO
                    @ 9, 40 SAY bthrms PICTURE "9.9"
                    reqs = reqs + "bathrooms = " + bthrms
                CASE choice = 6
                    @ 10, 40 SAY "Yes"
                    reqs = reqs + "garage"
            ENDCASE

        validate = validate + stchoice
    ENDIF

        IF LEN(validate) < 60
            DO Yesno WITH 19, 16, "Another requirement? "
            done = .NOT. yn
        ELSE
            done = .T.
        ENDIF

ENDDO

reqs = reqs + " .AND. .NOT. sold"
SET FILTER TO &reqs
COUNT TO n
CLEAR

IF n = 0
    ?
    ? "** No homes available matching those requirements. **"
ELSE
    SET HEADING ON
    DISPLAY ALL address, asking_pr, sq_footage, home_age, ;
        bedrooms, bathrooms OFF
ENDIF
?

WAIT

SET FILTER TO
RETURN
```

The bulk of the procedure is designed to create an input dialogue eliciting a set of selection criteria from the user:

```
** Search for homes that match these requirements: **
     1. price range...............>  100000 to 200000
     2. square footage range......>
     3. age range.................>

     4. number of bedrooms........>
     5. number of bathrooms.......>
     6. garage required...........>

        Which requirement? <1,2,3,4,5,6>  ▯

           price range:

           from:  100000
           to:    200000

        Another requirement?  ▯
```

The program stores all of the criteria in the string variable *reqs*. Each time a new criterion is expressed, the program concatenates 65♦ an additional condition expression (in string form) onto the end of *reqs*, like this:

```
reqs = reqs + " (sq_footage >= " + min ;
    + " .AND. sq_footage <= " + max + ")"
```

When the user has expressed all of the requirements for selecting homes from the database, the procedure uses *reqs* as a macro 215★ to filter the database appropriately:

```
SET FILTER TO &reqs
```

(See the & 1★ entry for an explanation of the macro substitution in this statement.)

The COUNT command then tells the procedure how many records remain in the filtered database and, assuming there is at least one, the DISPLAY 116★ command lists selected fields 154★ from the records that match the requirements:

```
address                  asking_pr sq_footage home_age bedrooms  bathrooms
12345 26th Avenue        149000.00      2000       70         4        2.5
50 17th Street           125000.00      1000       60         2        1.0

Press any key to continue...
```

Before returning control to the calling program, *Reqmnts* uses SET FILTER TO to disable the filter, returning the database to its original unfiltered state.

■ **Caution**

It is not safe to assume that all database commands will work only on the unhidden records in a filtered database. INDEX 176★ and ZAP 469★, for example, both ignore the filter and continue working on the entire database. Consider the following example, again using the *Assets* database:

```
. USE Assets
. SET FILTER TO value > 1000
:
. COUNT
        4 records
:
. INDEX ON item TO Itemind
        6 records indexed
:
. ZAP
Zap B:Assets.dbf? (Y/N) Yes
:
. SET FILTER TO
. COUNT
        No records
:
```

As you can see, after ZAP, the entire database is gone—not just the records remaining after the filter.

■ **dBASE II equivalent**

None

■ **Comments**

The SET FILTER command always works on the entire database, even if another filter is currently in effect. In other words, a second SET FILTER command does not impose a filter on the previously filtered database, but rather establishes a new filter over the entire database. To establish a filter with multiple criteria, you must write a compound condition expression like that shown in the *Reqmnts* example.

Different filter conditions may be applied to databases open in different work areas **454♦**, without interfering with one another.

SET FIXED

■ **Structure**

SET FIXED ON
SET FIXED OFF

■ **Description**

SET FIXED determines the extent to which the SET DECIMALS **340★** command controls numeric displays. SET FIXED is normally OFF: In this mode, SET DECIMALS affects only the displays from the EXP() **152★**, LOG() **205★**, and SQRT() **412★** functions, and the results of arithmetic division **24♦**.

When SET FIXED is ON, the number of decimal places specified in SET DECIMALS is applied to all numeric expressions.

■ **Usage**

Compare the following numeric displays, with SET FIXED first ON, then OFF:

```
. SET DECIMALS TO 5
. SET FIXED ON
.
. ? 2 / 3
0.66667
.
. ? SQRT(3)
   1.73205
.
. ? 2 * 3
  6.00000
.
. ? 2 + 3
 5.00000
.
. ? 2 - 3
-1.00000
.
```

```
. SET FIXED OFF
.
. ? 2 / 3
0.66667
.
. ? SQRT(3)
   1.73205
.
. ? 2 * 3
   6
.
. ? 2 + 3
  5
.
. ? 2 - 3
-1
.
```

■ **dBASE II equivalent**
None

■ **Comments**
The number of decimal places displayed for numeric values resulting from mathematical operations is normally determined by the number of decimal places in the arguments or operands involved. SET DECIMALS alone, without SET FIXED, will establish a maximum display, but will not affect this minimum. (See the SET DECIMALS entry for examples.)

Values affected by the SET DECIMALS and SET FIXED commands are rounded according to the usual arithmetic conventions.

SET FORMAT

■ **Structure**
SET FORMAT TO file_name

■ **Description**
The SET FORMAT command opens a format file, placing it in control of the screen design used in subsequent full-screen operations. (A format file ◆ is a user-created program 157◆ that maps out directions for a customized data-entry screen. Each file is generally designed for use with a specific database.) As long as the format file is in control, all full-screen data-entry commands (including APPEND 19★, CHANGE 48★, EDIT 141★, and INSERT 184★) conform to the specified input-screen format. When a format file is not in control, dBASE follows its standard default data-entry screen format, where the field input templates are simply arranged in a column.

■ **Usage**
The first step in establishing a customized data-entry screen is to plan and create a format file containing the @...SAY...GET 9★ commands that define the screen locations, prompts, and input templates of the customized screen. Like other program files, a format file can be created in the built-in dBASE word processor accessed via the MODIFY COMMAND 219★ statement, or in an external word processor 466★ or text editor.

SET FORMAT expects a format file to have an .FMT extension name 155◆ (see *Comments*). For example, the following command will cause dBASE to search on the current disk for a file called *PROPIN.FMT*:

```
. SET FORMAT TO Propin
```

If the file has any other extension, it must be specified in the SET FORMAT command.

■ **Database and program example**
The real-estate program described under the SET PROCEDURE 383★ entry works with a database called *Property*, which contains descriptions of homes that are for sale and listed with a particular realtor. The real-estate program consists of a top-level 266◆ controlling program plus several procedures. One of the procedures, *Add*, shown on the following page, allows the realtor to add new home listings to the *Property* database.

```
PROCEDURE Add
*----- Appends a new record to the Property database.
*

SET FORMAT TO Propin
APPEND

CLOSE FORMAT
RETURN
```

This short procedure begins by opening a format file called *PROPIN.FMT* (the name stands for "property input") and then uses the APPEND command to allow the user to enter new records into the *Property* database. When the user exits from the APPEND mode, control returns to *Add*, which closes the format file with the CLOSE FORMAT 57◆ command and returns control to the main program.

Here is a listing of the *Propin* format file ◆:

```
*-------------------------------------------------- PROPIN.FMT
* Data-entry format for the Property database.
*

@ 1, 1 SAY "Record #" + str(recno(), 2)
@ 1, COL() SAY " ---------------------------------------------------------"

@ 3, 1 SAY "The Home:"
@ 4, 1 SAY "--- -----"
@ 5, 1 SAY "Owner:"
@ 6, 1 SAY "  Last name: " GET owner_l
@ 7, 1 SAY "  First name:" GET owner_f
@ 9, 1 SAY "Street address:"
@ 10, 1 SAY "        " GET address
@ 12, 1 SAY "City:          " GET city
@ 13, 1 SAY "Neighborhood:" GET neighborhd
@ 14, 1 SAY "Age of home: " GET home_age range 1, 150
@ 16, 1 SAY "No. of bathrooms: " GET bathrooms
@ 17, 1 SAY "No. of bedrooms:  " GET bedrooms
@ 18, 1 SAY "Garage? (Y or N): " GET garage
@ 20, 1 SAY "Square footage:   " GET sq_footage

@ 3, 41 SAY "The Negotiations:"
@ 4, 41 SAY "--- -------------"
@ 5, 41 SAY "Asking price:  " GET asking_pr
@ 7, 41 SAY "Current bid:   " GET cur_bid
@ 8, 41 SAY "Sold? (Y or N) " GET sold
@ 9, 41 SAY "Date of sale:  " GET sale_date
@ 10, 41 SAY "Sale price:    " GET sale_price

@ 13, 41 SAY "The Contract:"
@ 14, 41 SAY "--- ---------"
@ 15, 41 SAY "Date on market: " GET on_market
@ 16, 41 SAY "Term of contract:  " GET term_days
@ 18, 41 SAY "Description:"
@ 19, 41 SAY "  Press Ctrl-PgDn to "
@ 20, 41 SAY "  write spec sheet:  " GET descriptn
```

The input screen created under the control of this file looks like this:

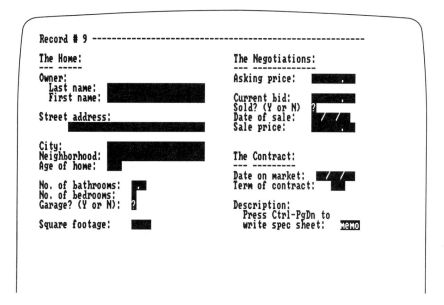

- **Caution**

  In addition to APPEND, CHANGE, EDIT, and INSERT, the READ **275★** command will also activate the full-screen mode according to the specifications of an open format file. However, in the case of READ, this is often undesirable.

  READ is most commonly used in association with @...GET statements located inside a program file, rather than in a format file. If a program uses @...GET and READ to obtain an input value for a variable or for a single database field, an open format file would interfere with this specific input sequence. That is why the *Add* procedure closes the *Propin* format file before returning control to the main program. Other parts of the real-estate program make use of @...GET and READ for individual data entry, and these sequences would not function as planned if *Propin* were left open throughout the entire program.

- **dBASE II equivalent**

  SET FORMAT TO

- **Comments**

  If you create your format file in the dBASE word processor, it is best to assign the file name an .FMT extension in the MODIFY COMMAND statement, so that you don't need to rename **291♦** the file or include the extension name in every SET FORMAT command.

  As an alternative to writing complex format programs in a word processor, you might want to consider using a program that automates the creation of format files—SED **316★** or dFORMAT, for example.

SET FUNCTION

■ **Structure**

SET FUNCTION number TO character_expression

■ **Description**

The SET FUNCTION command reprograms one of the keyboard's 10 function keys **167★** to a specified expression. Thereafter, when the user presses that key, the entire expression will be issued automatically from the keyboard.

■ **Usage**

When you load dBASE, the function keys are assigned default settings that issue selected commands at a single keystroke. If these settings are not particularly useful to you, you can use the SET FUNCTION command to change them to commands that better suit your own dBASE work patterns.

The semicolon character in a SET FUNCTION expression has the same effect as pressing the Return key. For example, the following setting actually executes the SET DEFAULT **343★** command whenever you press F9:

```
. SET FUNCTION 9 TO "SET DEFAULT TO B;"
```

If you omit the semicolon, the characters will be displayed at the dot prompt, but the command itself will not be issued until you press Return. This syntax is used for those commands that will require keyboard input before they are performed. For example, if you reprogram function key 10 as follows:

```
. SET FUNCTION 10 TO "MODIFY COMMAND "
```

every time you press F10, the words MODIFY COMMAND will appear at the dot prompt. You must then finish the command by entering a file name and then pressing Return.

More than one command may be issued from a single function key by ending each command in the character expression with a semicolon.

```
. SET FUNCTION 7 TO "SELECT 2; USE Accounts;"
```

A maximum of 30 characters may be assigned to one function-key expression.

■ **Caution**

The semicolon is used for two confusingly different purposes in dBASE: In the SET FUNCTION command, a semicolon represents the carriage-return character; however, when placed at the end of a command line, an undelimited **98◆** semicolon character is a non-executable continuation symbol indicating that the current command is continued on the following line (see Command Structure **62★**).

■ **dBASE II equivalent**

SET Fn TO character_expression
where *n* is the number of the function key.

■ **Comment**

Most often, you will want to use the same function-key settings for every dBASE session. To avoid having to reprogram the keys at each session, you can include these control parameters **73★** in your *CONFIG.DB* file **66★**, so that they are set automatically when you load dBASE. The syntax for this form of the SET FUNCTION command is:

```
Fn = character_expression
```

where *n* is the function-key number.

SET HEADING

■ **Structure**

SET HEADING ON
SET HEADING OFF

■ **Description**

The SET HEADING command controls the display of field names **154◆** or other expressions as column headings in commands that display elements from a database. By default, HEADING is set ON: A LIST **200★** or DISPLAY **116★** command presents a line of field names above the first actual record that is displayed. The column width for each field is determined by the width of the field itself or the width of the field heading, whichever is larger.

When SET HEADING is OFF, no headings are displayed and the width of each display column is determined by the defined width of the field.

■ **Usage**

An illustration of the use of SET HEADING can be found in the *Schedule* procedure discussed in the SET INDEX **372★** entry. This procedure (part of the real-estate program) has the task of displaying a table of homes that are for sale, along with the number of contractual days remaining for the real-estate agent to close each sale.

Schedule uses DISPLAY ALL to present two columns of information: a simple field value and a calculated value. Because of the calculated value, the heading for this table would be complex and not very readable:

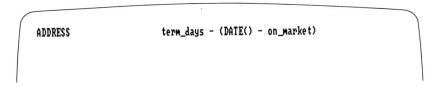

```
ADDRESS                 term_days - (DATE() - on_market)
```

For this reason, the procedure sets the default headings OFF and creates its own headings:

```
SET HEADING OFF
CLEAR

? "*** Unsold properties, in order of remaining days to sell: ***"
?
? "     Address:                          Days Remaining:"
? "     --------                          ---- ----------"
```

The result is a clearer, more readable table of values. When the table is complete, the procedure sets HEADING back to the ON condition. (In general, it is good practice for a procedure to return a control parameter **73★** to its default setting before relinquishing control, since other procedures in the program might require the parameter to be in its default state.)

■ **Caution**

There are occasions when it may be important to know how a certain value was obtained. In these cases—usually when you are working at the dot-prompt **62♦** level—you may prefer to leave SET HEADING ON.

■ **dBASE II equivalent**

None

SET HEADING TO can be used to incorporate an additional title string into a dBASE II report form.

■ **Comment**

The SUM **426★** and AVERAGE **31★** commands also display headings and are therefore affected by the SET HEADING command.

SET HELP

- **Structure**

  SET HELP ON

  SET HELP OFF

- **Description**

  Normally, dBASE offers immediate help when you issue a command that contains a syntax error:

```
. USE Address
. LIST FOR city = San
Variable not found
                   ?
LIST FOR city = San
Do you want some help? (Y/N)
```

As you become more expert in dBASE, you may wish to disable this feature. To do so, use the SET HELP OFF command. To reactivate the feature, just SET HELP ON again.

- **Usage**

  When SET HELP is ON, an affirmative answer to the help question will bring up an appropriate screen from dBASE's on-line help facility **170♦**.

- **dBASE II equivalent**

  None

  However, the HELP command is available in dBASE II.

- **Comment**

  dBASE also offers the HELP **170★** and ASSIST **28★** commands for on-the-spot assistance. These features can be accessed quickly by pressing the F1 or F2 key, respectively.

SET INDEX

■ **Structure**

SET INDEX TO index_file_list

■ **Description**

The SET INDEX command opens one or more index files **156♦** located on disk. Up to seven indexes may be open at once: The first index in the list will control the order in which the database is displayed; the others are opened only for updating. When changes occur in the contents of the database, all open index files are automatically maintained in working order.

By default, dBASE assumes that index files will have an .NDX extension name **155♦**. If you have assigned some other extension to an index file, you must include the extension name in the SET INDEX command. If no disk drive is specified, dBASE will look for the index files on the default disk.

Upon opening a controlling index file (that is, the first file in the list), dBASE positions the record pointer **258★** at the first record in the *ordered* database.

■ **Usage**

You may want to create several indexes for a given database, so that you can use the database in different orders for different purposes. When you subsequently make changes in the database by adding or deleting records, or by revising the contents of current records, you will want to make sure that all indexes are kept current: SET INDEX provides a convenient means of accomplishing this.

■ **Database example**

The following short example uses a database called *Assets*, which stores data about a small company's depreciable assets, including the name of each item, its original value, the date it was purchased, and its age:

```
. USE Assets
. LIST
Record#  ITEM                    VALUE PURCHASED  AGE
      1  typewriter            1240.00 05/30/79   6.3
      2  personal computer     2495.00 03/15/83   2.5
      3  printer, daisy-wheel  1250.00 03/15/83   2.5
      4  printer, dot-matrix    650.00 05/15/84   1.4
      5  copier                1835.00 12/20/84   0.8
      6  office desk            850.00 02/27/80   5.6
.
```

Three indexes have been created for use with this database: *ITEM.NDX*, *VALUE.NDX*, and *AGE.NDX*. The following SET INDEX statement opens all three indexes, putting Item in control of the order of the database:

```
. SET INDEX TO Item, Value, Age
. LIST
Record#  ITEM                      VALUE PURCHASED AGE
      5  copier                  1835.00 12/20/84  0.8
      6  office desk              850.00 02/27/80  5.6
      2  personal computer       2495.00 03/15/83  2.5
      3  printer, daisy-wheel    1250.00 03/15/83  2.5
      4  printer, dot-matrix      650.00 05/15/84  1.4
      1  typewriter              1240.00 05/30/79  6.3

.
```

Let's examine dBASE's behavior when one record is subsequently deleted from *Assets*:

```
. DELETE RECORD 3
      1  record deleted
. PACK
      5 records copied
Rebuilding index - C:Item.ndx
      5 records indexed
Rebuilding index - C:Value.ndx
      5 records indexed
Rebuilding index - C:Age.ndx
      5 records indexed

.
```

As you can see, all three of the indexes are "rebuilt," reflecting the change in the content of the database itself.

■ **Program example**

The real-estate program is designed to update and maintain a real-estate database called *Property*, which contains listings of houses that are for sale. (See the SET PROCEDURE 383★ entry for an overview of this program.) Depending upon the needs of the owner/client, the agency may sign a contract that allows them 45, 90, or 180 days to list and sell a given house: The *Schedule* procedure used in the program has the task of calculating the number of days that remain before each of the agency's listing contracts expires. *Property* contains two fields of information relevant to this contractual detail: *on_market*, the date on which the house first went onto the market; and *term_days*, the total number of contractual days the agency has in which to sell the house. The contract days remaining on any given date must be calculated from these two fields.

Two indexes are associated with *Property* ♦: *ADDRESS.NDX*, which orders the records alphanumerically by street address, and *SCHEDULE.NDX*, which orders them by the number of days remaining in the sales contract. Both of these indexes already exist before the real-estate program begins its work.

The following command was used to create the *Schedule* index:

```
. INDEX ON term_days - (DATE() - on_market) TO Schedule
```

In this case, the index key is a calculated numeric value: the number of days remaining in the contract. The expression *DATE() – on_market* gives the number of days a house has been on the market; subtracting this value from *term_days* yields the number of contract days remaining for a sale.

The *Schedule* procedure uses the *Schedule* index to display the records of all unsold houses in order of contract days remaining, from fewest to most:

```
*** Unsold properties, in order of remaining days to sell: ***

     Address:                       Days Remaining:
     --------                       ---- ----------
  4452 Sixth Avenue                       10
  15 Peach Lane                           24
  3555 Alta Street                        24
  50 17th Street                          70
  18 Jackson Avenue                       98
  55 Sayer Lane                          179

Press any key to continue...
```

Here is the procedure:

```
PROCEDURE Schedule
*----- Displays records from the Property database
*         in order of days remaining in the term
*         of the contract.
*

SET HEADING OFF
CLEAR
```

(continued)

```
? "*** Unsold properties, in order of remaining days to sell: ***"
?
? "    Address:                            Days Remaining:"
? "    --------                            ---- ----------"

SET INDEX TO Schedule
REINDEX

daystosell = "term_days - (DATE() - on_market)"
DISPLAY ALL address, &daystosell FOR .NOT. sold OFF
?
WAIT

SET·INDEX TO Address
SET HEADING ON
RETURN
```

Records can be added to the database through another procedure in the real-estate program, so the two indexes—*Schedule* and *Address*—may need to be updated at various points in program performance. With this in mind, your first inclination might be to keep both indexes open at all times, so that the indexes will be updated appropriately whenever a record is added.

However, the *Schedule* index also relies on an external factor to maintain records in the proper order: the current value of the system-date function, DATE() 103★. This value changes every day, of course, so merely updating the index whenever a record is added may not be sufficient: To ensure complete reliability, the index must be updated before every use. Therefore, as soon as the *Schedule* procedure opens the *Schedule* index, it immediately updates it with the REINDEX 284★ command. Then, when the procedure's work is complete, it reinstates *Address* as the controlling index. (In this case, there is no point in keeping *Schedule* open as a secondary index, because it must be updated before every use in any event.)

■ **Caution**

In planning an application that requires the use of several indexes, keep in mind that dBASE imposes an upper limit of 15 files (of all types 156★) open at one time.

■ **dBASE II equivalent**

SET INDEX

■ **Comment**

As shown in the preceding example, the REINDEX command offers an alternative way to update an existing index file when it is not possible or effective to keep all indexes open for updating.

SET INTENSITY

■ **Structure**

SET INTENSITY ON
SET INTENSITY OFF

■ **Description**

SET INTENSITY controls the reverse-video display format of full-screen input templates. SET INTENSITY—and therefore reverse video—is normally ON. When you issue the SET INTENSITY OFF command, field and variable templates will no longer appear on the screen in reverse-video mode.

■ **Caution**

If you SET INTENSITY OFF without supplying field delimiters **345 ◆**, you will have no visible field-width template:

```
. SET INTENSITY OFF
. USE Property
. APPEND
```

```
Record No.      14
OWNER_L
OWNER_F
ADDRESS
CITY
NEIGHBORHD
HOME_AGE
BEDROOMS
BATHROOMS
GARAGE      ?
SQ_FOOTAGE
ASKING_PR
CUR_BID               :
SOLD        ?
SALE_DATE   / /
SALE_PRICE
ON_MARKET   / /
TERM_DAYS
DESCRIPTN   memo
```

However, you can use the SET DELIMITERS **345★** commands to supply characters to mark the width of the input fields:

```
. SET DELIMITERS ON
. APPEND
```

```
Record No.      14
OWNER_L       :          :
OWNER_F       :          :
ADDRESS       :          :    :
CITY          :          :
NEIGHBORHD    :          :
HOME_AGE      :    :
BEDROOMS      :  :
BATHROOMS     :. :
GARAGE        :?:
SQ_FOOTAGE    :    :
ASKING_PR     :      :  :
CUR_BID       :      :  :
SOLD          :?:
SALE_DATE     : / / :
SALE_PRICE    :      :
ON_MARKET     : / / :
TERM_DAYS     :   :
DESCRIPTN     :memo:
```

■ **dBASE II equivalent**
 SET INTENSITY

■ **Comment**
 The SET COLOR **331★** command selects the colors used in normal and full-screen modes. Through this command, the default reverse-video display of black on white can be changed to any other available color combination.

SET MARGIN

■ **Structure**
SET MARGIN TO column_number

■ **Description**
SET MARGIN sets the left margin of the printer for subsequent printed output from dBASE. By default, the left margin is set at column 0.

■ **Usage**
The *Prntinfo* procedure listed and described in the SET DEVICE **347**★ entry contains an example of the SET MARGIN command. This procedure prepares a report from a selected record of the database called *Property*. (You can see a sample of the report in the SET DEVICE entry.) To accomplish an approximate horizontal centering of the report on the printed page, the program sets the left printer margin at column 12:

```
SET PRINT ON
SET MARGIN TO 12
```

Upon completing the report, *Prntinfo* resets the margin to its default value of 0, so that other parts of the real-estate program will not be affected by the setting:

```
SET MARGIN TO 0
```

■ **dBASE II equivalent**
SET MARGIN

■ **Comment**
The SET MARGIN command has no effect on screen display.

SET MENU

■ **Structure**
SET MENU ON
SET MENU OFF

■ **Description**
SET MENU controls the display of dBASE's built-in help menus for full-screen modes. Each menu describes the use of the keyboard—in particular, cursor keys and control-key combinations—for a specific full-screen mode.

SET MENU is OFF by default. If you wish to see full-screen help menus, issue the SET MENU ON command before entering full-screen mode.

■ **Usage**

The keyboard-control menus are helpful reminders of how to manage the cursor during full-screen dBASE operations. Here is an example of the menu display as it appears in the APPEND **19**★ mode:

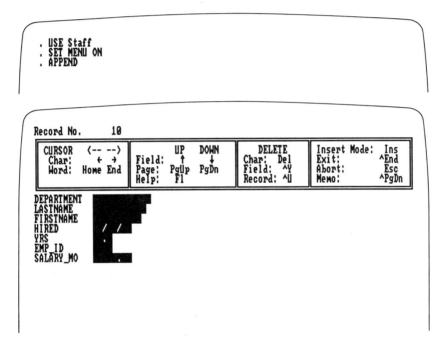

■ **dBASE II equivalent**

None

■ **Comments**

The F1 function key toggles menus on and off from within the full-screen modes, regardless of the initial SET MENU status.

If you use the keyboard menus frequently, the MENU setting may be included in your *CONFIG.DB* **66**★ file. However, most experienced dBASE users prefer to leave this control parameter **73**★ at its default OFF status, toggling the menus ON with the F1 key when they are needed.

SET PATH

■ **Structure**
SET PATH TO path_list

■ **Description**
The SET PATH command sets up a list of alternate subdirectory **250★** paths for dBASE to search, in their specified order, whenever a given file cannot be found in the default directory.

■ **Usage**
You must use *complete* path names in the SET PATH command, separating subdirectory names by a backslash (\). For example, the following command establishes two alternate paths, both on drive B:

```
. SET PATH TO B:\Accounts\New\Calif, ;
  B:\Accounts\New\Oregon
```

Subsequently, if the default directory does not contain a requested file, dBASE will automatically search for the file in the *Calif* directory and then, if necessary, in the *Oregon* directory.

■ **dBASE II equivalent**
None

■ **Comment**
Subdirectories are created and maintained in DOS **133★**, versions 2.0 and later. The MKDIR (or MD) command creates a subdirectory, and the CHDIR (or CD) command changes the current default subdirectory. RMDIR (or RD) removes a subdirectory, TREE displays all the directories on a disk in hierarchical format, and PATH establishes a list of alternate subdirectories for file searches (this DOS command is the same as the dBASE SET PATH command).

SET PRINT

■ **Structure**

SET PRINT ON
SET PRINT OFF

■ **Description**

SET PRINT controls dBASE output to the printer. When SET PRINT is ON, output that normally appears only on the screen is also sent to the printer. This includes:

☐ Any messsages that dBASE itself displays on the screen.

☐ Commands entered directly from the dBASE dot prompt **62◆**.

☐ The results of display commands such as ? **5★** and TEXT...ENDTEXT **431★**.

However, it does not include full-screen operations or the output of @...SAY **9★** commands.

■ **Usage**

In direct-command mode, SET PRINT ON enables you to record on paper a series of commands that you issue to dBASE from the keyboard, along with their results. In program mode, SET PRINT ON allows you to create "custom" printed output.

■ **Database and program example**

The *Prntinfo* procedure listed and discussed under the SET DEVICE **347★** entry is a program that prepares printed reports from individual records in a database called *Property*. The bulk of the procedure consists of ? commands that display various items of information from a single selected record of the database. Before any information is displayed, *Printinfo* issues a SET PRINT ON command. Then, when the report from a given record is complete, it resets the parameter to OFF. In this way, the program controls exactly what information will be sent to the printer, and when. Note in particular that with SET PRINT ON, even the contents of an entire memo field **217★** (*descriptn*, in this case) may be sent to the printer via the command:

```
? descriptn
```

■ **Caution**

The use of the SET PRINT ON command requires considerable care because of an annoying quirk in dBASE: If you issue the SET PRINT ON command when your printer is either not on or not available for operation, you will experience the following mysterious dialogue:

```
. SET PRINT ON
No paper error writing device PRN
Abort, Retry, Ignore?
```

At this point the correct procedure is to turn your printer on and press R (for Retry). If you press A (for Abort) instead, you will be dropped out of dBASE into your computer's operating system 133♦:

```
Abort, Retry, Ignore? a
A>
```

This is *not* a graceful exit from dBASE. The consequences can range from mildly annoying to completely disastrous. When you leave dBASE normally, via the QUIT 271★ command, any open files that have been updated are automatically saved on disk before the exit is completed. However, this process does *not* occur when you drop out of dBASE because of a printer error, and valuable data may be lost. For this reason, it is important to include a prompt message *before* a SET PRINT ON command in a program, reminding the user to turn on the printer.

■ **dBASE II equivalent**
SET PRINT ON
The same caution applies to dBASE II.

■ **Comments**
The IBM personal-computer keyboard offers a toggle that has the same effect as SET PRINT ON and SET PRINT OFF. To use the toggle, press Ctrl-P: The first time toggles the printer on, the second toggles it off again. The Ctrl-PrtSc keyboard command dumps only the current contents of the screen to the printer.

See EJECT **145★**, SET CONSOLE **335★**, SET DEVICE **347★**, and SET MARGIN **378★** for further information about printer operations.

SET PROCEDURE

- **Structure**

  SET PROCEDURE TO file_name

- **Description**

  The SET PROCEDURE command opens a special type of program file called a procedure file, making all of the subroutines (procedures) contained in the file available for performance. By default, SET PROCEDURE searches on the current disk drive for a file with a .PRG extension name **155◆**. For example, the command:

  ```
  SET PROCEDURE TO Info
  ```

  searches for a file called *INFO.PRG* on the default disk drive. If the procedure file has some other extension, or is located on a drive other than the current default, you must include this information in the SET PROCEDURE command:

  ```
  SET PROCEDURE TO C:INFO.REP
  ```

  This command searches for the procedure file named *INFO.REP* on drive C.

- **Usage**

  Whether SET PROCEDURE is performed as a direct command from the dBASE dot-prompt **62◆** level or from within a program, only one procedure file may be open at a time. If a program needs to perform various procedures that are located in more than one file, it *must* close the currently open procedure file (using the CLOSE PROCEDURE **57★** command) in order to open a new one.

  A procedure file ◆ may contain up to 32 procedures, each beginning with a PROCEDURE **263★** statement and each normally containing a RETURN **301★** statement to send control back to the calling program. Like any other program file, the procedure file may be developed in the dBASE word processor **466★**. To open the word processor, just use the MODIFY COMMAND **219★** statement with the name of your procedure file:

  ```
  . MODIFY COMMAND Info
  ```

Remember, though, that if you wish to create a procedure file larger than 4,096 bytes, you will have to use an external word processor to create an ASCII text file containing your procedures. dBASE can *use* these longer procedure files without difficulty—it just can't create or modify them in the built-in word processor.

Procedure files offer several clear advantages over the alternative of storing each subroutine in a program file of its own:

□ They reduce the number of open files during program performance.

□ They reduce the number of disk accesses required.

□ They make it easy to store and locate *all* the components of a given program.

■ Database and program example

The *Property* database ♦, and the real-estate program that works with it, are presented here to illustrate the use of a procedure file. (A complete listing of this rather large program appears in the Appendix.)

The *Property* database itself stores information about homes that are for sale and listed with an imaginary real-estate agency. The database contains 18 fields, representing all five of the field types **98♦** available in dBASE III. The first five fields identify the owner and location of a home. The next five contain the vital statistics of the home: age, number of bedrooms and bathrooms, square footage, and whether or not there is a garage. The next seven fields describe financial and contractual matters: the asking price and current bid (if any) on the home, the sale price and date of sale for a house that has already sold, the date the home came onto the market, and the number of contractual days allowed the realtor to sell the house. The final field—*descriptn*—is reserved for a promotional blurb describing the features of the house.

Two of the fields in the *Property* database are logical fields (*garage*, indicating whether or not the property includes one, and *sold*, specifying whether or not the property has been sold) and two are date-type fields (*sale_date*, recording the date of sale, and *on_market*, indicating the date the property went up for sale). The remaining fields are either character or numeric, except for *descriptn*, which is a memo field **217★**.

Here is the structure of the database:

```
. USE Property
. LIST STRUCTURE
Structure for database : B:Property.dbf
Number of data records :        8
Date of last update    : 08/30/85
Field  Field name  Type       Width    Dec
    1  OWNER_L     Character      20
    2  OWNER_F     Character      20
    3  ADDRESS     Character      28
    4  CITY        Character      20
    5  NEIGHBORHD  Character      20
    6  HOME_AGE    Numeric         3
    7  BEDROOMS    Numeric         1
    8  BATHROOMS   Numeric         3      1
    9  GARAGE      Logical         1
   10  SQ_FOOTAGE  Numeric         4
   11  ASKING_PR   Numeric         9      2
   12  CUR_BID     Numeric         9      2
   13  SOLD        Logical         1
   14  SALE_DATE   Date            8
   15  SALE_PRICE  Numeric         9      2
   16  ON_MARKET   Date            8
   17  TERM_DAYS   Numeric         3
   18  DESCRIPTN   Memo           10
** Total **                     178

.
```

The real-estate program is a menu-driven dBASE III program designed to offer the realtor all the functions needed for managing and using the *Property* database. It consists of a top-level 266♦ controlling section stored in a file named *MENU.PRG* and a set of procedures stored in the *PROPERTY.PRG* procedure file. The program allows the real-estate agent to perform any of six different operations involving the *Property* database:

☐ Add new home listings to the database.

☐ Change the status of a listing (record a new asking price, a new bid, or a sale).

☐ Search for all the listings that match the requirements of a given potential buyer.

☐ Examine a schedule of contract days remaining for unsold properties.

☐ Calculate a mortgage.

☐ Generate a "spec sheet" (a promotional information sheet about a given home).

Here is a listing of the real-estate program's controlling section, *Menu*:

```
*------------------------------------------------------ MENU.PRG
* Controls the activities of the real-estate program.
*   Uses the Property database and the Schedule and
*   Address indexes.
*

SET TALK OFF
SET BELL OFF
SET CONFIRM ON
SET ESCAPE OFF

USE Property INDEX Address
CLOSE PROCEDURE
SET PROCEDURE TO Property

DO WHILE .T.
    choice = 7
    CLEAR
    @ 8, 30 SAY "Real Estate Menu"
    @ 9, 30 SAY "---- ------ ----"
    @ 10, 25 SAY "1. Add a new home listing."
    @ 11, 25 SAY "2. Record a bid or sale."
    @ 12, 25 SAY "3. Search for listing(s)."
    @ 13, 25 SAY "4. Examine listing schedule."
    @ 14, 25 SAY "5. Compute a mortgage."
    @ 15, 25 SAY "6. Print an information sheet."
    @ 16, 25 SAY "7. Quit"
    @ 18, 25 SAY "Choice? <1,2,3,4,5,6,7> " GET choice PICTURE "9" ;
      RANGE 1, 7
    READ

    DO CASE
        CASE choice = 1
            DO Add
        CASE choice = 2
            DO Sale
        CASE choice = 3
            DO Reqmnts
        CASE choice = 4
            DO Schedule
        CASE choice = 5
            DO Mortgage
        CASE choice = 6
            DO Prntinfo
        CASE choice = 7
            CLEAR
            CLOSE PROCEDURE
            SET TALK ON
            SET BELL ON
            SET CONFIRM OFF
            SET ESCAPE ON
            RETURN
    ENDCASE

ENDDO
```

To run the program, the user simply enters the following command at the dBASE dot prompt:

```
. DO Menu
```

The bulk of the main program section is devoted to three tasks:

☐ Displaying a recurring menu on the screen.
☐ Accepting a menu choice from the keyboard.
☐ Calling the appropriate procedure to perform a selected activity.

Here is the menu the program displays on the screen:

```
    Real Estate Menu
    ---- ------ ----
1. Add a new home listing.
2. Record a bid or sale.
3. Search for listing(s).
4. Examine listing schedule.
5. Compute a mortgage.
6. Print an information sheet.
7. Quit

Choice? (1,2,3,4,5,6,7)  ▯
```

To accomplish each of the menu activities, the main program uses one of six procedures located in the procedure file *PROPERTY.PRG*. For this reason, the procedure file is opened at an early stage in the program:

```
SET PROCEDURE TO Property
```

With the procedure file open, the main program section can "call" ♦ any of the procedures the file contains, via a DO **122**★ command like this one:

```
DO Mortgage
```

The various procedures in the *PROPERTY.PRG* file are listed as illustrations in several different entries in this book. The following outline of the file gives the name of each procedure, a comment describing its purpose, and the entry and page where you will find the entire procedure listed (see also the Appendix 470★):

```
PROCEDURE Add
*----- Appends a new record to the Property database.
*
        [See SET FORMAT 365★]

PROCEDURE Sale
*----- Records a bid or sale of a house.
*
        [See IF 171★]

PROCEDURE Reqmnts
*----- Filters the Property database, searching for homes that
*        match the requirements of a given client.
*
        [See SET FILTER 357★]

PROCEDURE Schedule
*----- Displays records from the Property database
*        in order of the days remaining in the term
*        of the contract.
*
        [See SET INDEX 372★]

PROCEDURE  Mortgage
*----- Calculates a monthly mortgage payment.
*
        [See PICTURE 252★]

PROCEDURE Prntinfo
*----- Prints a specification sheet for distribution
*        to potential buyers of a given home.
*
        [See SET DEVICE 347★]

PROCEDURE Get_rec
*----- Finds a record number, given an address.
*    .
        [See SEEK 317★]

PROCEDURE Yesno
*----- Handles prompt and input for a yes-or-no question.
*        Returns answer in the logical variable yn.
*
        [See PARAMETERS 245★]

PROCEDURE Minmax
*----- Accepts min and max requirements for the REQMNTS procedure.
*
        [See PUBLIC 269★]
```

As you can see, there are nine procedures in all. The first six are responsible for the main activities of the program; the remaining three perform subsidiary functions and are called from several points in the program. The following structure diagram illustrates the hierarchical organization of the entire real-estate program:

Structure Diagram of the Real-Estate Program

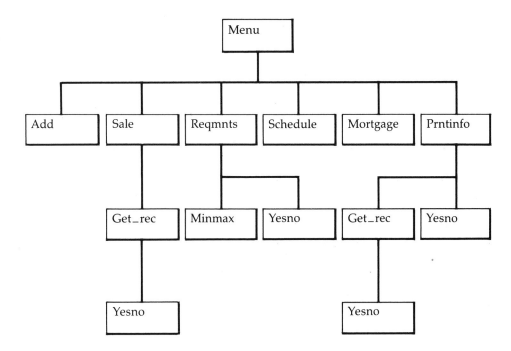

- **Caution**

Before a program attempts to open a procedure file, it is important to make sure that no other procedure file is already open. Notice that, to be safe, the real-estate program therefore issues a CLOSE PROCEDURE command in advance of the SET PROCEDURE command:

```
CLOSE PROCEDURE
SET PROCEDURE TO Property
```

- **dBASE II equivalent**

None

In dBASE II, every program, no matter how small, is stored in a file of its own.

■ **Comments**

Procedure files need not be application-specific. One of their most valuable uses is to store general-purpose utility functions that can be used by many different programs to perform routine tasks.

Several other important dBASE III commands are available to improve the performance and structure of programs you write. For example, the PARAMETERS **245**★ statement and the DO...WITH command allow one procedure to "pass" information to another, and the PUBLIC **269**★ and PRIVATE **259**★ statements can control access to variable values by creating "global" and "local" variables..

See the Programming **264**★ entry for further discussion of programming concepts and dBASE programming tools.

SET RELATION

■ **Structure**

SET RELATION TO field_name INTO database
SET RELATION TO RECNO() INTO database

■ **Description**

The SET RELATION command establishes a relationship between the record pointers **258**★ of two open databases.

Normally, the record pointers in all open databases move independently of one another. However, SET RELATION establishes a dependency between the currently selected **322**◆ database and a related database that is open in another work area **454**◆, so that when the pointer of the current database is moved, the pointer in the related database also moves to the corresponding record.

The controlling database is the one that is currently selected when the SET RELA-TION command is issued; the related, or *linked*, database is the one that is named in the SET RELATION command. The related database can be identified by its actual file name **155**★ or by an alias **14**★.

The relation between the databases can be based on a field that is common to both or on record numbers. If a field key **194**★ is used, the related database *must* be indexed **176**◆ on that field. If the relation is to be based on record numbers, however, the RECNO() **279**★ function must be specified as the key in the SET RELATION command, and the related database must remain in record-number order—that is, *not* indexed. Each time the record pointer is repositioned in the controlling database, dBASE searches for a corresponding key-field value in the related database. If the value is found, the pointer is moved to that record. If the value is not found, the EOF() **147**★ function becomes true for the related database.

■ Usage

The SET RELATION command is essential for working with a system of database files thar are all related to the same application: When two or more files are open at once, SET RELATION facilitates locating related data items in different work areas.

■ Database example

A short example of a system of related databases is described in the JOIN **189★** entry. Briefly, the system involves two databases: *Bksales* and *Authors*. The *Bksales* database contains a list of best-selling titles from a national bookstore chain. Since the list may include several titles by the same author and we don't want to duplicate lengthy entries, author profiles are stored separately, in the *Authors* database. The two databases have one field in common: *author_num*, which contains an individual code number for each author. Besides *author_num*, the *Bksales* database contains no information about authors or publishers and the *Authors* database contains no information about book titles or sales.

The database called *Salesort* is a copy of *Bksales*, sorted **402◆** in descending order by *unit_sales* (the field that contains each book's sales to date). In the following sequence, *Salesort* is opened in work area 1 and *Authors* is opened in work area 2:

```
. SELECT 1
. USE Salesort INDEX Booknum ALIAS Books
. SELECT 2
. USE Authors INDEX Author
. SELECT Books
```

Because the related database, *Authors*, is indexed on the *author_num* field, the following SET RELATION command is used to establish a relationship between the two open databases:

```
. SET RELATION TO author_num INTO Authors
```

Now, whenever the pointer moves in *Salesort*, dBASE will search for the corresponding author number in *Authors*. This means that from work area 1, the currently selected area, we can access information from work area 2 simply by referring to the name (or alias) of the database in that area (see SELECT **322★**). The following sequence of commands illustrates this relation between the two databases:

```
. GOTO 4
. ? title
Mystery of the East

. ? Authors -> last_name
Bloomfield

. ? Authors -> first_name
Janice

. ? Authors -> publisher
Linton

.
```

As you can see, the book title is contained in the *Salesort* database, whereas the corresponding author and publisher names are stored in the *Authors* database, yet both can be accessed without reselecting the work area.

- **Program example**

The following program, called *Bookinfo*, opens these same two databases, establishes the same relation between them, and then displays a title profile based on information stored in both databases:

```
*------------------------------------------------------BOOKINFO.PRG
* Prints information sheets about the books
*    described in two files:
*
*    SALESORT.DBF contains information about book sales.
*    AUTHORS.DBF contains an author profile.
*

PARAMETER bkno

SET TALK OFF
SELECT 1
USE Salesort INDEX booknum ALIAS books
SELECT 2
USE Authors INDEX author
SELECT books
SET relation TO author_num INTO authors
```
(continued)

```
CLEAR

bkno = UPPER(bkno)
SEEK bkno

IF EOF()
    ?
    ? "Book #" + bkno + " is not in the file."
ELSE
    CLEAR
    ? title
    ?
    *----- Draw a line the same length as the book title.
    width = LEN(TRIM(title))
    DO WHILE width > 0
        ?? "-"
        width = width - 1
    ENDDO

    IF "F" $ bkno
        ? "Fiction by "
    ELSE
        ? "Nonfiction by "
    ENDIF

    ?? TRIM(Authors -> first_name), Authors -> last_name
    ? "Published by:", Authors -> publisher
    ?
    ? "Unit sales to date:    " + STR(unit_sales, 6)
    ? "Average monthly sales: " + STR(month_avg, 6)
    ?
    ? "This book is #" + STR(RECNO(), 2) + " on our list."
    ?
    ? "Author profile:"
    ? "---------------"
    SELECT Authors
    ? profile
    ?
ENDIF

CLEAR ALL
RETURN
```

The program accepts a book number as a parameter **245◆** (the *Salesort* database is indexed on the *book_num* field in this application), searches for the book in *Salesort*, and then displays the title summary. Here is a sample run of *Bookinfo*:

```
. DO Bookinfo WITH "f298"
```

```
Mountain Romance
----------------
Fiction by Janice Bloomfield
Published by: Linton

Unit sales to date:     67646
Average monthly sales:   7866

This book is # 3 on our list.

Author profile:
---------------
Janice Bloomfield has written over one-hundred
romance novels during her twenty-year career as a
storyteller.

.
```

It is interesting to note that three different sorts are in effect in this application:

□ *Salesort* is itself a sorted version of *Bksales*, arranged in descending order of total unit sales. For this reason, the record numbers of *Salesort* can be used to rank each book in the list.

□ *Salesort* is also indexed by book number, so that the SEEK **317★** command will be able to locate books.

□ Finally, *Authors* is indexed by author number, so that the relation between the two databases will work properly.

■ **Caution**

If a database contains a memo field **217★**, information from that field can be accessed only from within the work area in which the database itself is located. This is true regardless of whether the database has been linked with another open database through a SET RELATION command. Consider the following example, again using the *Salesort* and *Authors* databases in work areas 1 and 2, respectively (the currently selected work area is 1):

```
. GOTO 4
. ? title
Mystery of the East

. ? Authors -> last_name
Bloomfield

. ? Authors -> profile
Unrecognized phrase/keyword in command
    ?
? Authors -> profile
Do you want some help? (Y/N) No

.
```

The *profile* field is a memo field in the *Authors* database, but dBASE issues an error message if you try to access that particular field from within another work area. To display the contents of *profile* for the current record, you must first select work area 2:

```
. SELECT Authors
. ? profile
Janice Bloomfield has written over one-hundred
romance novels during her twenty-year career as a
storyteller.

.
```

This is the technique the *Bookinfo* program uses for gaining access to and displaying the author profile.

■ **dBASE II equivalent**
None

■ **Comments**
You can establish up to 10 different database relations with the SET RELATION command—one in each of the 10 available work areas. This allows a fairly complex series of interrelationships within a system of database files.

To terminate an existing relation, use the SET RELATION TO command with no parameter. This will leave the databases open, but remove the link between them.

The JOIN command actually creates a new file from two different databases—an operation that is similar to, but more permanent than, SET RELATION. JOIN also has problems with memo fields.

SET SAFETY

- **Structure**

  SET SAFETY ON
  SET SAFETY OFF

- **Description**

  SET SAFETY determines whether or not dBASE will warn you before overwriting a file that already exists on disk. The default setting is ON: When you issue a command that would result in overwriting an existing file, dBASE asks you to confirm the operation before proceeding.

  When SET SAFETY is OFF, dBASE omits the warning and confirmation process: The disk operation is performed immediately, whether or not it results in destruction of an existing file.

- **Usage**

  Normally, SET SAFETY should be left ON. When you are issuing direct commands to dBASE, SET SAFETY helps prevent the loss of important data:

```
. CREATE Stock
Stock.dbf already exists, overwrite it? (Y/N)
```

  To abandon the write operation, press N (for No).

  Some programs intentionally create new versions of already-existing files. In this kind of controlled situation, SET SAFETY should be OFF, so that the process can occur without interruption. However, the program should reset SAFETY to its default ON mode before returning control to the dBASE dot prompt 62♦. (For an example of this usage, see the *General* program listed in the SAVE 309★ entry.)

- **dBASE II equivalent**

  None

- **Comment**

  The SAFETY warning message is not suppressed by a SET TALK OFF command.

SET SCOREBOARD

- **Structure**
  SET SCOREBOARD ON
  SET SCOREBOARD OFF

- **Description**
  The SET SCOREBOARD command controls dBASE's use of the upper right corner of the screen for special messages. The default setting is ON, which means that dBASE will display messages on the first screen line when appropriate (error messages for invalid data entry, for example—see RANGE 272★).

  When the setting is OFF, dBASE no longer displays these messages, and row 0 is guaranteed to be free for uninterrupted use by a program 264◆.

- **Usage**
  Normally, SET SCOREBOARD should be left ON. However, you may occasionally want to exert strict control over the entire display screen, including row 0. In such a situation, you can temporarily set the SCOREBOARD parameter to OFF, but be sure to reset it to its default ON status when the program or operation is finished.

- **dBASE II equivalent**
  None

- **Comment**
  SET SCOREBOARD was not documented in version 1.0 of dBASE III.

SET STEP

- **Structure**
  SET STEP ON
  SET STEP OFF

- **Description**
  SET STEP is a program debugging 267◆ tool that allows you to examine the action of a program one command at a time. After you issue the SET STEP ON command, a subsequent program performance will pause after each command and wait for you to respond to the following message on the screen:

```
Type any key to step - ESC to cancel
```

■ **dBASE II equivalent**
SET STEP

■ **Comment**
Other dBASE debugging tools include SET ECHO **351**★ and SET DEBUG **339**★.

SET TALK

■ **Structure**
SET TALK ON
SET TALK OFF

■ **Description**
SET TALK specifies whether or not dBASE will display messages on the screen after the performance of many commands. The default setting is ON, meaning that the messages are displayed. The OFF setting inhibits the messages.

■ **Usage**
Many dBASE commands result in a message showing what sort of action has taken place. For example, messages might indicate how many records have been affected, where the record pointer **258**★ is positioned, or what value has been assigned to a variable **459**★. During an interactive **62**◆ session with dBASE, these messages are often useful and important, and SET TALK should therefore remain ON.

Program performance, on the other hand, is likely to be compromised by the appearance of such messages on the monitor, particularly if the program itself exerts detailed control over the appearance of the screen. For this reason, most programs will contain a SET TALK OFF command somewhere near the beginning, and a SET TALK ON command near the end (see *Comment*).

■ **Caution**
Whenever you get no apparent result from a dot-prompt command, check the SET TALK status before seeking other explanations for the problem.

■ **dBASE II equivalent**
SET TALK

■ **Comment**
It is good programming practice to reset all control parameters **245**★ to default status before returning control to the calling program or procedure, so that subsequent dBASE activities will not be affected.

SET UNIQUE

■ **Structure**

SET UNIQUE ON
SET UNIQUE OFF

■ **Description**

The SET UNIQUE ON command controls the creation of a special kind of index file **156◆** from an INDEX **176★** command. By default, SET UNIQUE is OFF: Under this status, the normal behavior of the INDEX command is to create an index file that includes every record of the current database. However, when SET UNIQUE is ON, the INDEX command produces an index that excludes any records that duplicate key-field **194★** values already included in the index.

■ **Usage**

SET UNIQUE ON is useful whenever a database contains one or more entries of identical values *in a given field*: It enables you to isolate, count, and access all the unique entries. Each value will be represented only once in the new index.

■ **Database example**

The following example uses a database called *Reorder*, designed to store a list of spare parts and the names of their suppliers. Here is a partial listing:

```
. USE Reorder
. LIST item_no, supplier
Record#  item_no    supplier
      1  M728       Acme, Inc.
      2  X11        Smith & Co.
      3  N987       Acme, Inc.
      4  G222       Allbright Parts
      5  M991       Allbright Parts
      6  M891       Smith & Co.
.
```

The following sequence of commands generates a list of the company's parts suppliers, with no duplicates in the list:

```
. SET UNIQUE ON
. INDEX ON supplier TO Supplier
. LIST supplier
Record#  supplier
       1  Acme, Inc.
       4  Allbright Parts
       2  Smith & Co.

.
```

- **Cautions**

  An index created with SET UNIQUE ON is not a complete index, and is not to be relied upon when changes are made to the database itself.

  Be careful to turn the SET UNIQUE status back to OFF once you have generated an index: Normal indexing is performed in the default OFF mode.

- **dBASE II equivalent**

  None

- **Comments**

  SET UNIQUE does not filter duplicate values in fields other than the key field.

  Other dBASE commands such as SORT **402★** and DISPLAY **116★** are not affected by the SET UNIQUE status.

  Other index-related commands include SET INDEX **372★**, REINDEX **284★**, FIND **160★**, and SEEK **317★**.

SKIP

- **Structure**

  SKIP *numeric_expression*

- **Description**

  In the currently selected **322◆** database, SKIP moves the record pointer **258★** a specified number of records forward or backward from its current position.

- **Usage**

  Without a numeric parameter, SKIP moves the pointer forward one record. With a negative parameter, it moves the pointer backward. In an unindexed database, SKIP follows record-number order; in an indexed **176◆** database, it follows the indexed order.

■ **Database example**

The following sequence uses a database called *Stock*, which currently has 25 records. When the database is opened, the record pointer is automatically positioned at the first record in the file. A series of SKIP commands moves the pointer forward one record at a time:

```
. USE Stock
. ? RECNO()
        1
. SKIP
Record no.     2
'
. SKIP
Record no.     3
'
. SKIP
Record no.     4
'
```

Notice that the new record number is displayed on the screen after each SKIP. (This is true only if the SET TALK 398★ status is ON.)

These next SKIP commands result in jumps forward or backward ◆ by several records at a time:

```
. SKIP 5
Record no.     9
'
. SKIP -4
Record no.     5
'
. SKIP 10
Record no.    15
'
. SKIP -15
Record no.     1
'
```

When a SKIP command attempts to move backward from the first record, the BOF() 35★ function becomes true:

```
. ? BOF()
.T.
'
```

Likewise, an attempt to SKIP forward beyond the last record sets EOF() **147★** to true:

```
. SKIP 30
Record no.     26
.
. ? EOF()
.T.
.
```

■ **Caution**

Notice that the record number displayed in the preceding example is one beyond the last actual record in the database (see the EOF() entry for further discussion of this behavior). A subsequent SKIP command will result in an error message:

```
. SKIP
End of file encountered
            ?
SKIP
.
```

■ **dBASE II equivalent**

SKIP

■ **Comments**

The GOTO **169★** command moves the record pointer to a specific record in the database.

With linked databases (see SET RELATION **390★**), a SKIP command issued from the currently selected **322◆** work area also moves the pointer in the related database.

SORT

■ **Structure**

SORT   *scope_clause*   ON field_name/*indicator*   ,*field_name*/*indicator*   ,...
condition_clause   TO file_name

■ **Description**

The SORT command creates a sorted ◆ copy of the current database and stores the result on disk as a new database file. The ON clause specifies the key field **194★** or fields upon which the sort will be performed. Only character, numeric, and date fields **99♦** may serve as keys to the sort. The TO clause specifies the name of the new file that will be created on disk (dBASE supplies the default extension name **155♦** .DBF).

The scope **312★** and condition clauses, both optional, can be used to specify a subset of records to be included in the sorted version of the database. Without these clauses, the entire database is sorted.

Each field name in the ON clause may include an optional indicator to specify the sorting order:

Indicator:	Order:
/A	Ascending
/D	Descending
/C	Alphabetic case ignored
/AC	Ascending, case ignored
/DC	Descending, case ignored

By default, SORT arranges the records in ascending order, uppercase first.

■ **Usage**

Use SORT when you wish to create a new disk copy of all or part of a database in a sorted order: Unlike INDEX **176★**, the SORT command results in a complete new database file on disk, not just an index file **156♦**.

■ **Database example**

A client-billing database called *Lawfirm* is used in the following examples. The database stores billing records from three departments of a (fictitious) law firm. Each record contains the department name, the client's name, the amount billed, the billing date, and the payment date. Here is a selection from the database:

```
. USE Lawfirm
. LIST
Record#  DEPARTMENT  CLIENT          AMOUNT BILLING_DT PAYMENT_DT
      1  Litigation  XYZ Enterprises 2593.88 08/15/84   12/05/84
      2  Corporate   SuperTek Co.    1872.42 09/01/84   11/15/84
      3  Labor Law   MultiGlom, Inc.  521.55 09/01/84   09/15/84
      4  Corporate   BBB Corporation 2113.20 09/15/84   11/01/84
      5  Litigation  Acme Co.        4988.89 10/01/84   11/30/84
      6  Litigation  Expo Ltd.       3889.21 10/15/84   01/20/85
      7  Labor Law   Doe Properties   733.28 11/01/84   01/15/85
.
```

The first example sorts the database on the *amount* field, in descending numeric order:

```
. SORT ON amount/D to Amt
  100% Sorted          7 Records sorted
```

The resulting file, *AMT.DBF*, is stored on the current disk. The SORT command does not open the new database. To examine the sorted file, you must first USE **454★** it:

```
. USE Amt
. LIST
Record#  DEPARTMENT  CLIENT           AMOUNT BILLING_DT PAYMENT_DT
      1  Litigation  Acme Co.        4988.89 10/01/84   11/30/84
      2  Litigation  Expo Ltd.       3889.21 10/15/84   01/20/85
      3  Litigation  XYZ Enterprises 2593.88 08/15/84   12/05/84
      4  Corporate   BBB Corporation 2113.20 09/15/84   11/01/84
      5  Corporate   SuperTek Co.    1872.42 09/01/84   11/15/84
      6  Labor Law   Doe Properties   733.28 11/01/84   01/15/85
      7  Labor Law   MultiGlom, Inc.  521.55 09/01/84   09/15/84
.
```

The next example uses a condition clause to select only the records from the Litigation Department for the sorted version of the database:

```
. SORT ON client FOR department = "Litigation" TO Litigate
  100% Sorted          3 Records sorted
.
. USE Litigate
. LIST client, amount
Record#  client           amount
      1  Acme Co.        4988.89
      2  Expo Ltd.       3889.21
      3  XYZ Enterprises 2593.88
.
```

Finally, this last example demonstrates the use of primary and secondary keys—*department* and *amount*, respectively—for the sorting operation. First, the departments are sorted in alphabetical order; then, within each department, the billing amounts are sorted in descending numeric order—that is, largest to smallest:

```
. SORT ON department, amount/D TO Deptamt
  100% Sorted              7 Records sorted
.
. USE Deptamt
. LIST department, amount, client
Record#  department   amount client
      1  Corporate    2113.20 BBB Corporation
      2  Corporate    1872.42 SuperTek Co.
      3  Labor Law     733.28 Doe Properties
      4  Labor Law     521.55 MultiGlow, Inc.
      5  Litigation   4988.89 Acme Co.
      6  Litigation   3889.21 Expo Ltd.
      7  Litigation   2593.88 XYZ Enterprises
.
```

■ Cautions

Because sorted files are not linked to their original databases, they are *not* automatically updated when changes are made to the original database, even if both files are open in different work areas (see SET RELATION 390★). Nor is there a RESORT command comparable to the REINDEX 284★ command.

Only field names can be used as keys in a SORT command. The syntax will not accept any type of expression. (The INDEX command *does* allow expressions as keys.)

■ dBASE II equivalent

SORT

■ Comments

If you sort a database that has an associated memo file 156◆ (.DBT), dBASE will automatically make a properly sorted copy of the memo file to go with the sorted database. However, dBASE will not allow the use of a memo field 217★ as a key to the sort.

See the Sorting 406★ entry for a discussion of the differences between SORT and INDEX. See also INDEX, SET INDEX 372★, and REINDEX.

Sorting

Sorting a database means rearranging its records in a defined order. To specify a sorting operation, you must select one or more fields **154★** as the keys **194★** to the sort: The rearrangement will be made on the key or keys that you select. In dBASE III, sorts can be performed on character, numeric, or date fields, resulting in alphabetic, numeric, or chronological sorts, respectively. Memo or logical fields cannot be keys.

By selecting more than one key field for a sort operation, you can specify the order the sort should take in the event of a "tie" in the primary key. For example, consider a sort in which the primary key is *lastname* and the secondary key is *firstname*. If the *lastname* field contains identical values in more than one field—six Johnsons, say—dBASE will order the tied records according to the values in *firstname*.

Two different commands are available to sort a dBASE database: INDEX **176★** and SORT **402★**. Both result in the creation of a new file on the current disk, but they differ greatly in the *type* of file **156★** they create:

☐ The INDEX command creates an index file, with the extension name .NDX. dBASE uses this index file to determine the sequential order in which to *display* the database, but the actual physical order of the database does not change.

☐ In contrast, the SORT command creates an entirely new copy of the database, with a .DBF extension name. The new copy of the database is physically sorted in the order specified in the SORT command.

The INDEX command has some important advantages over the SORT command:

☐ An index file takes up less disk space than a new copy of the entire database.

☐ INDEX accepts expressions in the key. SORT accepts only field names.

☐ dBASE will automatically *update* an open index file when you make changes in the database it indexes. For example, if you add or delete records, or change values in the key fields, dBASE will adjust the index accordingly, so that the database will continue to be displayed in sorted order.

☐ You may create more than one index file for a given database. Only one of these indexes is in control at a given time, but up to six additional indexes may be open concurrently, and all open indexes are updated when changes occur in the database.

☐ The REINDEX **284★** command is available to re-sort any indexes not open during an update. SORT, on the other hand, requires creation of yet another new file in order to update after changes to the original database.

The SORT command, in turn, has a couple of advantages over INDEX:

□ SORT allows both ascending and descending sorts. (Ascending means A to Z, smallest number to largest number, earliest date to most recent date. Descending means just the opposite.) SORT even allows you to specify ascending or descending order for each separate key of a multiple-key sort. The INDEX command sorts only in ascending order.

□ The SORT command permits a sort operation to be performed on a selected group of records specified with a scope **312★** clause, a condition clause, or both. The INDEX command always sorts the entire database (see SET UNIQUE **399★**, however).

See the individual command entries, and also SET INDEX **372★**, FIND **160★**, and SEEK **317★**, for further details on usage.

SPACE()

■ **Structure**
SPACE(numeric_value)

■ **Description**
The SPACE() function provides a string **98♦** consisting of a specified number of space characters. The numeric argument of SPACE() expresses the desired length of the string.

■ **Usage**
The argument of SPACE() may be any valid numeric expression resulting in a number from 0 through 254—the maximum length of any string in dBASE III.

The SPACE() function may be used to separate two output strings by a specified number of spaces:

```
. ? "test1" + SPACE(20) + "test2"
test1                   test2
.
```

Perhaps more significantly, however, SPACE() may be used with the LEN() **197★** function to display a string right justified within a horizontal display field. Let's say, for example, that a certain database has a character field named *item* and you wish to display the values of *item* right justified in a 20-space field. To accomplish this, you could write a program containing a line like this:

```
? SPACE(20 - LEN(TRIM(item))) + TRIM(item)
```

In this expression, the formula *20 – LEN(TRIM(item))* determines the number of spaces that must be output ahead of each value of *item* to ensure that *item* will be right justified within the 20 spaces. For instance, if a given record contains an *item* value that is 5 characters long, the LEN() expression will result in a value of 5. Hence, the SPACE() function in this case will yield a string of 15 blank spaces, and the value of *item* itself will be displayed in the last five positions of the display field.

■ **Database and program example**

The following database, called *Children*, contains the names, addresses, and birth dates of a group of young children (such a database might be maintained by a baby-sitting or birthday-party service):

```
. USE Children
. LIST OFF
LASTNAME      FIRSTNAME  ADDRESS        CITY           STATE ZIP   BIRTHDATE
Harte         Susan      45 Rose St.    San Francisco  CA    94110 05/24/78
Young         Elizabeth  1824 First St. Oakland        CA    94725 12/18/79
Washington    Jacqueline 76 Charles Pl. Daly City      CA    94012 03/05/80
Morris        George     231 Wood Rd.   San Francisco  CA    94118 07/29/78
Colborne      Robert     89 Maple Dr.   Berkeley       CA    94710 02/15/77
McDonald      Karen      214 Sixth St.  Richmond       CA    94201 12/18/81
```

The users of this database would like to create a specially formatted list of these children and, ultimately, print the list onto a set of gummed labels. The left side of each label will identify the nature of the five lines of information the label will contain; the right side will display the actual information about a given child. This personal information is to be justified at the right margin of the label. The *Kidlist* program has been designed to produce this specially formatted list:

```
*------------------------------------------------ KIDLIST.PRG
* Produces a directory of the names, addresses, birthdays,
*    and ages of the children in the Children database.
*

SET TALK OFF
SET SAFETY ON

USE Children
INDEX ON lastname + firstname TO Nameind
GOTO TOP

DO WHILE .NOT. EOF()
    name = TRIM(firstname) + " " + TRIM(lastname)
    ? "Name:            "
    ?? SPACE(25 - LEN(name)) + name
    street = TRIM(address)
    ? "Address:         "
    ?? SPACE(25 - LEN(street)) + street
    csz = TRIM(city) + ", " + state + " " + zip
    ? "City, State, Zip:"
    ?? SPACE(25 - LEN(csz)) + csz
    dob = DTOC(birthdate)
    ? "Birthdate:       "
    ?? SPACE(25 - LEN(dob)) + dob
    da = (DATE() - birthdate)
    yr = INT(da / 365)
    mo = (da - yr * 365) / 30
    age = STR(yr, 2) + " years, " + STR(mo, 4, 1) + " months"
    ? "Age:             "
    ?? SPACE(25 - LEN(age)) + age
    ?
    ?
    SKIP
ENDDO

SET SAFETY ON
SET TALK ON
RETURN
```

409

Here is the output the program produces:

```
Name:                        Robert Colborne
Address:                        89 Maple Dr.
City, State, Zip:          Berkeley, CA 94710
Birthdate:                          02/15/77
Age:                    8 years,  2.6 months


Name:                          Susan Harte
Address:                        45 Rose St.
City, State, Zip:      San Francisco, CA 94110
Birthdate:                          05/24/78
Age:                    6 years, 11.5 months


Name:                        Karen McDonald
Address:                       214 Sixth St.
City, State, Zip:          Richmond, CA 94201
Birthdate:                          12/18/81
Age:                    3 years,  4.6 months


Name:                        George Morris
Address:                       231 Wood Rd.
City, State, Zip:      San Francisco, CA 94118
Birthdate:                          07/29/78
Age:                    6 years,  9.3 months


Name:                    Jacqueline Washington
Address:                      76 Charles Pl.
City, State, Zip:          Daly City, CA 94012
Birthdate:                          03/05/80
Age:                    5 years,  2.0 months


Name:                        Elizabeth Young
Address:                      1824 First St.
City, State, Zip:           Oakland, CA 94725
Birthdate:                          12/18/79
Age:                    5 years,  4.6 months
```

To accomplish the effect of right justification, *Kidlist* requires the use of the string functions LEN(), STR() **416★**, TRIM() **440★**, and SPACE(). Notice how the SPACE() function is used to display each item of information right justified within a display field of 25 spaces:

```
name = TRIM(firstname) + " " + TRIM(lastname)
? "Name:                    "
?? SPACE(25 - LEN(name)) + name
```

■ **Cautions**

Sending an argument greater than 254 to the SPACE() function results in a string of 254 spaces and the following error message:

```
*** Execution error on SPACE() : too large
```

An argument of 0 results in a null string—that is, a string with no characters in it—and an argument less than 0 results in a null string, plus the following error message:

```
** Execution error on SPACE() : negative
```

■ **dBASE II equivalent**

None

■ **Comments**

The SPACE() function can be used to initialize a variable as a string of blank spaces:

```
. STORE SPACE(10) TO newvar
. DISPLAY MEMORY
NEWVAR      pub   C  "             "
    1 variables defined,      12 bytes used
  255 variables available,  5988 bytes available
.
```

The TRIM() function removes spaces from the end of a string value.

SQRT()

- **Structure**

SQRT(numeric_expression)

- **Description**

The SQRT() function returns the square root of its argument, which must be a positive number.

- **Usage**

The following program, *Sqrttable*, produces a table of square roots, given arguments from 1 through 20. The table is stored in a database called *Sqrroots*, which contains only two fields: *x* for the numeric argument, and *sqrt_x* for the resulting square root:

```
*-------------------------------------------------- SQRTTABL.PRG
* Creates a square-root table in the database called Sqrroots.
*

SET TALK OFF
SET SAFETY OFF

USE Sqrroots
ZAP

recs = 20
DO WHILE recs > 0
    APPEND BLANK
    recs = recs - 1
ENDDO

REPLACE ALL x WITH RECNO()
REPLACE ALL sqrt_x WITH SQRT(x)
DISPLAY ALL

SET TALK ON
SET SAFETY ON
RETURN
```

Notice the use of ZAP **469★** to clear any existing records from the database. Without this command, the new values would simply be added to the end of the existing file. Here is the output from the program:

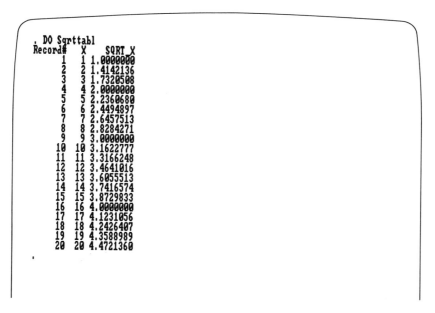

```
. DO Sqrttabl
Record#    X     SQRT_X
     1     1  1.0000000
     2     2  1.4142136
     3     3  1.7320508
     4     4  2.0000000
     5     5  2.2360680
     6     6  2.4494897
     7     7  2.6457513
     8     8  2.8284271
     9     9  3.0000000
    10    10  3.1622777
    11    11  3.3166248
    12    12  3.4641016
    13    13  3.6055513
    14    14  3.7416574
    15    15  3.8729833
    16    16  4.0000000
    17    17  4.1231056
    18    18  4.2426407
    19    19  4.3588989
    20    20  4.4721360
```

By revising the first of the two REPLACE **291★** commands in the program, you can produce a table of any square roots that you wish to examine. For example, the following REPLACE commands fill the argument field (x) with values from 101 through 120 and from 100 through 2000, respectively:

```
REPLACE ALL x WITH RECNO() + 100

REPLACE ALL x WITH RECNO() * 100
```

(You will need to make sure that the field widths in your *Sqrroots* database are large enough to store the resulting numeric values, or the program will display an error message and terminate performance.)

■ **Caution**

An attempt to send a negative number to the square-root function will result in the following error message:

```
**Execution error on SQR() : negative
```

■ **dBASE II equivalent**

None

■ **Comments**

In general, the number of decimal places in the result of SQRT() will be same as the number of decimal places in the argument. However, there will always be at least two digits after the decimal point in the result, even if there are fewer in the argument, unless you specify otherwise via the SET DECIMALS **340★** command. All of these factors are irrelevant if the result of SQRT() is to be stored in a database, as in the preceding example: In that case, the number of decimal places is determined by the field definition.

The other mathematical functions provided by dBASE are EXP() **152★**, LOG() **205★**, and ROUND() **302★**. The statistical commands AVERAGE **31★**, SUM **426★**, and TOTAL **436★** are also available for use with databases.

STORE

■ **Structure**

STORE expression TO variable_list
variable_name = expression

■ **Description**

The STORE command assigns a value to one or more variables **459★**. The expression in STORE is evaluated, and the *result* is stored in the variable or variables listed.

The alternate and perhaps more commonly used form of the dBASE assignment statement ♦ stores a value in a single variable. The variable name is always to the left of the equal sign in this format; the expression to be evaluated and stored in the variable is to the right.

The dBASE assignment statement, in either form, may be used to initialize a new variable or to assign a new value to an existing variable. If you assign a new value to an existing variable, the previous value is lost.

■ **Usage**

In this book, the alternate form of the assignment statement is almost always used, both because it is quicker and because it is closer to the syntax of assignment statements in other programming languages:

```
princ = 0
rate = 0
term = 0
```

The one advantage of STORE is that you can assign the same value to more than one variable. For example, the following statement initializes these same three variables to zero with just one command:

```
STORE 0 TO princ, rate, term
```

The value to be stored in the variable can be a simple literal (constant) numeric value, as in the preceding examples, or a complex expression, as in the following two assignments:

```
fact = (r1 + 1) ^ (-t1)
mort = (princ * r1) / (1 - fact)
```

If the assignment statement is storing a new value in an existing variable, the variable may itself be part of the expression to be stored. Consider the following examples, involving numeric, string **98♦**, and logical **99♦** variables, respectively:

```
x = x + 1
street = TRIM(street)
ok = .NOT. ok
```

The first of these statements increments the value of the variable *x* by 1. The second eliminates trailing blanks from the string variable *street*. The third reverses the logical value stored in *ok*: If *ok* previously contained a value of .F., it now contains a .T., and vice versa. In each of these cases, the previous value of the variable is lost.

■ **Cautions**

In dBASE III, it is legal, though ill-advised, for a variable to have the same name as a field **154★** in the current database—*address*, for example. If you then use the name *address* in a command, dBASE will assume that you are referring to the database field by that name. If you wish to access the value in the variable named *address*, you will have to use this notation:

```
M -> address
```

A better idea is to avoid the ambiguity in the first place by using a different name for the variable.

Up to 256 variables may be in use at once in dBASE III, but the variables and the values they contain may, together, take up a maximum of 6,000 bytes.

■ **dBASE II equivalent**
STORE
The alternate assignment-statement format is not available in dBASE II.

■ **Comments**

The DISPLAY MEMORY **118★** command allows you to examine all of the currently defined variables, along with their values and types.

All or a selected portion of the current variables may be erased from memory with the RELEASE **288★** command.

The variables currently in memory may be stored together in a disk file, via the SAVE **309★** command. The RESTORE **298★** command reads the saved variables back into memory from disk.

In addition to the assignment statement, there are three input commands that also create new variables: INPUT **182★**, ACCEPT **12★**, and WAIT **461★**. These are used in dBASE programs to obtain input from the keyboard and store it for use in program processing.

Finally, dBASE III is willing to change the data-type of a current variable, if you assign a new value that is different from the current type. Again, this practice is legal but not advisable—it is better to create a new variable for the new type of value.

STR()

■ **Structure**
STR(numeric_value, length ,*decimals*)

■ **Description**
Given a numeric value, the STR() function returns a string **98◆** of characters representing the number. The second and third arguments of the STR() function,

length and *decimals*, indicate the length of the string to be returned and the number of decimal places that will be included in the character representation, respectively. The *decimals* argument is optional.

■ **Usage**

The STR() function is useful for incorporating numeric values into concatenated **65★** strings of characters. The following example, taken from the *Kidlist* program discussed in the SPACE() **407★** entry, uses STR() to incorporate two numeric values—*yr* and *mo*—into a concatenation that is ultimately assigned to the variable *age*:

```
age = STR(yr, 2) + " years, " + STR(mo, 4, 1) + " months"
```

The string value resulting from the first of these STR() functions is two characters long and includes no decimal places. The string generated by the second STR() function is four characters long, with one place after the decimal point (notice that the specified length of the resulting string must allow for the decimal point itself). Here is an example of the result:

```
6 years, 11.5 months
```

Where necessary, STR() rounds the result in the string equivalent of its numeric argument:

```
. ? STR(123.562, 3)
124

. ? STR(123.562, 5, 1)
123.6

.
```

In the first of these two examples, the *decimals* argument is omitted, so the result of the function is a string representing a rounded integer. In the second example, the numeric value is rounded to one decimal place in the resulting string.

■ **Cautions**

If the second argument of STR() specifies a length that is not great enough to hold the resulting string of characters, including the decimal point, dBASE will display a string of asterisks. If the second argument is omitted altogether, the resulting string will represent a rounded integer, right justified in a 10-character display field:

```
. ? STR(123.562, 2)
**

. ? STR(123.562, 5, 2)
*****
.
```

```
. ? STR(123.562)
       124
.
```

■ **dBASE II equivalent**

STR()

■ **Comments**

STR() is often used in conjunction with other dBASE functions and commands to create multiple-key indexes 176♦, compound condition expressions 287♦, special programming effects, and the like.

The VAL() 456★ function produces a numeric value from a string of digits.

String functions

Eleven of the dBASE functions might be called string functions, because they work with string values or supply some information about a string ♦. Ten of these can easily be categorized into functional pairs, the two members of each pair performing more-or-less opposite tasks.

One pair of functions is available specifically to give you access to your computer's ASCII 28★ code:

□   Given a string of characters as an argument, the ASC() 26★ function supplies the ASCII code number (from 0 through 255) of the first character in the string. (ASC() is often used in other programming languages as a tool for implementing character-by-character input validation, but in dBASE, the sophisticated powers of the @...SAY...GET 9★ commands are more likely to be used in this context.)

- ☐ Its converse, CHR() **50★**, supplies the ASCII character corresponding to a code number from 0 through 255. CHR() is more likely than ASC() to be of value in dBASE programs because it allows you to use and display the graphics characters generated by the upper end of the IBM personal computer's extended ASCII code.

Another pair of string functions deals with substrings:

- ☐ AT() **30★** takes two string arguments and returns a number indicating the character location of the first string inside the second. If the first string is not present in the second, AT() returns a value of 0.
- ☐ SUBSTR() **423★** takes three arguments: a string and two numbers. The numbers represent a location in the string and a length in characters, respectively. SUBSTR() extracts a substring of the specified length, starting from the designated location in the string argument.

Two functions deal with the alphabetic case of a string of characters:

- ☐ LOWER() **213★** supplies a lowercase version of its string argument.
- ☐ UPPER() **451★** supplies an uppercase version of its string argument.

Another very important pair of functions works with the space character in strings:

- ☐ SPACE() **407★** supplies a string consisting of a specified number of blank spaces. It can be used in conjunction with LEN() **197★**, TRIM() **440★**, or both, to center or right justify a string.
- ☐ TRIM() eliminates *trailing* spaces from a string. Its most important use is in working with string fields from databases: Because each string value from a database automatically takes on the full defined width of its field, such field values often have unwanted extra spaces tacked on to the end of the significant characters. TRIM() removes these spaces so that they will not interfere with other string operations, such as concatenation **65★**.

The STR() **416★** and VAL() **456★** functions deal with data-type conversions:

- ☐ STR() yields a string version of its numeric argument.
- ☐ VAL() returns a numeric version of its string argument, assuming that the string consists of digital characters.

The final string function is unpaired:

- ☐ LEN() returns the length, in characters, of its string argument. Significantly, when its argument is a string-field value from a database, LEN() returns the defined field width.

For more detailed information and examples, see each function under its own entry.
See also String Operators **420★**, Concatenation, and Data Types **98★**.

String operators

Three string **98♦** operators are available in dBASE III—two for concatenation **65★** and one for substring operations (checking whether one string is contained inside another):

Operator:	Function:
+	Concatenation—blanks in original positions
–	Concatenation—blanks to end of resulting string
$	Substring check

Concatenation simply means joining ♦: Concatenation operators join one string to another. Both dBASE concatenation operators produce a new string whose length is equal to the combined lengths of the original strings, but they differ in the way they handle trailing blanks. The + operator simply combines the two strings exactly as they are, maintaining the original positions of any trailing blanks. The – operator ♦ moves all trailing blanks to the end of the resulting string.

The following illustrations produce concatenations from the string variables *s1* and *s2*. Each of these variables contains trailing space characters. The + operator leaves these spaces in place, separating the two parts of the resulting string. The – operator pushes the spaces to the end of the concatenated string:

```
. s1 = "dBASE    "
dBASE

. s2 = " III    "
 III

. ? s1 + s2
dBASE    III

. ? s1 - s2
dBASE III

.
```

Note, however, that the resulting strings are still of equal *length*—the combined lengths of *s1* and *s2*:

```
. ? LEN(s1)
      10
. ? LEN(s2)
      10
. ? LEN(s1 + s2)
      20
. ? LEN(s1 - s2)
      20
.
```

While its output may look similar, the – operator does not have the same effect as the TRIM() 440★ function, which actually *removes* trailing blanks:

```
. ? TRIM(s1 - s2)
dBASE III
. ? LEN(TRIM(s1 - s2))
      9
.
```

The substring operator, $ ♦, tests for the presence of one string inside another and returns a logical value 99♦, .T. or .F., indicating whether or not the substring is present:

```
. ? "A" $ "dBASE"
.T.
. ? "a" $ "dBASE"
.F.
.
```

The following example of the $ operator uses the *Invntory* database discussed in the SUBSTR() **423**★ entry.

```
. USE Invntory
. LIST
Record#  ID      ITEM          QTY  COST   VALUE
     1   12B123  ruler         150  0.21    31.50
     2   76C987  notebook      225  0.45   101.25
     3   32A971  blotter        76  1.51   114.76
     4   76F971  calculator     35  3.75   131.25
     5   23D971  desk clock     25  7.88   197.00
     6   32H231  desk organizer 110  2.37   260.70
.
```

Imagine that the ID number of each of these inventory items contains specific coded information about the category and usage of the item. You would like to be able to locate inventory items that meet certain conditions coded by a specific character or sequence of characters in their ID numbers. The following examples show the use of the $ operator for substring searches inside the values stored in the *id* field:

```
. LIST FOR "F" $ id
Record#  ID      ITEM          QTY  COST   VALUE
     4   76F971  calculator     35  3.75   131.25

. LIST FOR "C" $ id
Record#  ID      ITEM          QTY  COST   VALUE
     2   76C987  notebook      225  0.45   101.25

. LIST FOR "9" $ id
Record#  ID      ITEM          QTY  COST   VALUE
     2   76C987  notebook      225  0.45   101.25
     3   32A971  blotter        76  1.51   114.76
     4   76F971  calculator     35  3.75   131.25
     5   23D971  desk clock     25  7.88   197.00
.
```

The $ operator can also be useful for input validation in dBASE programs. (To extract a substring from a string value, use the SUBSTR() function.)

The string operators are used extensively in database and program examples throughout this book.

SUBSTR()

■ **Structure**

SUBSTR(character_expression, start ,*number*)

■ **Description**

The purpose of the SUBSTR() function is to allow a command or program to identify and access a portion, or substring, of a given string **98♦** of characters. SUBSTR() takes three arguments:

☐ A character expression representing the original string from which the substring is to be accessed.

☐ A numeric expression representing the target substring's starting position in the original string.

☐ The number of characters to be accessed from the original string—that is, the ultimate length of the target substring.

The final argument, *number*, is optional; if it is not included, SUBSTR() returns the substring beginning at *start* and ending at the last character of the original string.

■ **Usage**

The first argument of SUBSTR() may be any valid character expression, including:

☐ A character-type field or variable.

☐ The result of a function that returns a string.

☐ A literal (constant) string value enclosed in quotes or square brackets.

☐ A concatenated **65★** expression combining two or more strings.

The numeric arguments may be any expressions that result in valid numeric values. Here are some examples:

```
. var1 = "Now is the time."
. ? SUBSTR(var1, 8, 8)
the time

. ? SUBSTR(TIME(), 4, 2)
20

. ? SUBSTR("A database-management program", 3, 8)
database

. ? SUBSTR("A database-management program", 3)
database-management program
.
```

The following REPLACE **291★** command, used in an example in the UPPER() **451★** entry, contains two illustrations of the SUBSTR() function:

```
. REPLACE ALL item WITH UPPER(SUBSTR(item, 1, 1)) + ;
  LOWER(SUBSTR(item, 2))
```

The first SUBSTR() returns the first character of the value stored in the *item* field, which is then used as the argument in UPPER(). The second SUBSTR() returns all the characters from the second to the last, for use as the argument in LOWER() **213★**. The effect of the entire REPLACE command is to give each value in the *item* field an initial capital letter, followed by lowercase letters.

The following assignment statement, used in an example in the TIME() **433★** entry, contains yet another illustration of SUBSTR():

```
s1 = VAL(SUBSTR(TIME(), 7, 2))
```

In this expression, the SUBSTR() function returns the last two characters of the system-time string, representing the seconds. The VAL() **456★** function converts this value to a number, which is then assigned to the variable *s1*. (Notice that the presence of the final argument of the SUBSTR() function in this example is not strictly necessary, since TIME() always returns a string that is exactly 8 characters long.)

■ **Database example**

The following database, called *Invntory*, contains information about a group of inventory items (for more work with this database, see UPPER(), LOWER(), and String Operators **420★**):

```
. USE Invntory
. LIST
Record#  ID      ITEM            QTY   COST   VALUE
      1  12B123  Ruler           150   0.21    31.50
      2  76C987  Notebook        225   0.45   101.25
      3  32A971  Blotter          76   1.51   114.76
      4  76F971  Calculator       35   3.75   131.25
      5  23D971  Desk clock       25   7.88   197.00
      6  32H231  Desk organizer  110   2.37   260.70
.
```

The first field of information, *id*, is a character field that contains coded ID numbers for each item in the inventory list. Examining these ID numbers, you can see that the third character is always a letter of the alphabet and all the other characters are digits. Let's imagine that this third ID character has some special significance to the user of the database—identifying the category of each inventory item, for example. Given this significance, the user might want some way of sorting the database by the ID letters, even though these letters are embedded within the values of the *id* field. The following INDEX 176★ command performs this task:

```
. INDEX ON SUBSTR(id, 3, 1) TO Id_ind
      6 records indexed
. LIST
Record#  ID     ITEM            QTY   COST  VALUE
      3  32A971 Blotter          76   1.51  114.76
      1  12B123 Ruler           150   0.21   31.50
      2  76C987 Notebook        225   0.45  101.25
      5  23D971 Desk clock       25   7.88  197.00
      4  76F971 Calculator       35   3.75  131.25
      6  32H231 Desk organizer  110   2.37  260.70
.
```

As you can see, the records of the database have been placed in order by ID letter—that is, by the third character of the *id* field. The SUBSTR() function in the INDEX command supplies access to this single embedded character.

To test the validity of this particular indexing process, use the FIND 160★ command on the indexed database:

```
. FIND C
. DISPLAY
Record#  ID     ITEM       QTY   COST  VALUE
      2  76C987 NOTEBOOK   225   0.45  101.25
.
```

FIND successfully locates the record whose embedded ID letter is C, and the DISPLAY 116★ command then prints the record on the screen or report.

■ **Caution**

If the second argument of SUBSTR() (*start*) is greater than the length of the character value in the first argument (and SET TALK **398★** is ON), dBASE will display an error message and SUBSTR() will return a null string—that is, a string containing no characters:

```
. ? SUBSTR("test", 5, 1)

***Execution error on SUBSTR() : start point out of range

.
```

■ **dBASE II equivalent**

$()

Note that $ is a string *operator* **420★** in dBASE III.

■ **Comment**

The $ operator yields a logical value—true or false—indicating whether or not one string is embedded in another. The AT() **30★** function supplies a numeric value representing the character location of one string inside another.

SUM

■ **Structure**

SUM   *scope_clause   expression_list   TO variable_list   condition_clause*

■ **Description**

The SUM command computes and displays totals from the numeric fields of a database. You can use the expression-list clause to designate specific fields or arithmetic field expressions you wish to total. The TO clause, which is also optional, allows you to store the results of SUM in variables you name in the variable list: The values in the expression list are assigned consecutively to the variables listed.

The scope **312★** option may include any one of the three scope clauses available in dBASE III: ALL **7★**, NEXT **239★**, or RECORD **282★**. The default scope is ALL: That is, if the scope clause is missing, SUM works on the entire database. The condition option allows you to use a FOR **164★** or WHILE **463★** clause to select specific records for the summation process.

■ **Usage**

The results of the SUM command are normally displayed on the screen immediately after you issue the command itself. To save these results, you must include a TO clause in the command, to specify the names of the variables in which you want to save the summed values.

■ **Database example**

The database called *Staff* contains information about the employees of a small company. *Staff* has three numeric fields: *yrs*, for the number of years each employee has worked for the firm; *emp_id*, for the employee's ID number; and *salary_mo*, for the employee's monthly salary:

```
. USE Staff
. LIST
Record#  DEPARTMENT   LASTNAME    FIRSTNAME  HIRED     YRS  EMP_ID SALARY_MO
      1  Production   Morris      John       11/03/82  2.5    4521   1850.00
      2  Marketing    Southby     Anne       08/22/81  3.7    3134   2315.00
      3  Clerical     Peters      Larry      06/10/83  1.9    3412   1350.00
      4  Clerical     Broussard   Marie      05/05/81  4.0    8712   1275.00
      5  Production   James       Fred       02/22/77  8.2    6563   1675.00
      6  Marketing    Smith       June       03/29/80  5.1    6823   2475.00
      7  Clerical     Liles       Carter     09/29/77  7.6    8799   1400.00
      8  Production   Washington  Liz        11/05/74 10.5    7321   1700.00
      9  Clerical     Ludlum      Donald     03/30/77  8.1    7412   1250.00
.
```

The first of the following SUM commands finds the total monthly salary expense that the company incurs. The second finds two sums: the total years of service accumulated by all the company's current employees, and the total monthly salary expense. The third uses SUM with an arithmetic expression to find the total yearly salary expense incurred by the company. And finally, the fourth SUM command uses a FOR clause to sum the salaries of only the employees in the Clerical Department:

```
. SUM salary_mo
       9 records summed
   salary_mo
    15290.00
.
. SUM yrs, salary_mo
       9 records summed
   yrs      salary_mo
   51.6     15290.00
.
```

```
. SUM salary_mo * 12
       9 records summed
   salary_mo * 12
        183480.00
.
. SUM salary_mo FOR department = "Clerical"
       4 records summed
   salary_mo
    5275.00
.
```

■ **Program example**

The following program, called *Summary*, creates departmental summary reports from the *Staff* database. The program illustrates the use of the TO clause to store the results of the SUM command in variables:

```
*------------------------------------------------ SUMMARY.PRG
* Presents summary statistics about any one of
*   the departments in the Staff database.
* Requires department name as a string parameter.
*

PARAMETER deptname

*----- Make sure deptname has correct case format.
*
deptname = UPPER(SUBSTR(deptname, 1, 1)) + LOWER(SUBSTR(deptname, 2))

SET TALK OFF
USE Staff

*----- Determine statistical values.
*
COUNT FOR department = deptname TO emps
AVERAGE yrs, salary_mo FOR department = deptname TO avgyrs, avgsal
SUM salary_mo, salary_mo * 12 FOR department = deptname TO totmo, totyr

*----- Convert values to strings of characters.
*
emps_c = STR(emps, 2)
avgyrs_c = STR(avgyrs, 4, 1)
avgsal_c = STR(avgsal, 9, 2)
totmo_c = STR(totmo, 9, 2)
totyr_c = STR(totyr, 9, 2)

*----- Build underlining string.
*
width = 0
line = ""
DO WHILE width < LEN(deptname)
    line = line + "-"
    width = width + 1
ENDDO

*----- Display summary report.
*
CLEAR
? deptname, "Department"
? line  +  " ----------"
? "  Number of employees:      "
?? SPACE(12 - LEN(emps_c)) + emps_c
? "  Average years with firm: "
?? SPACE(12 - LEN(avgyrs_c)) + avgyrs_c
```

(continued)

```
? "   Average monthly salary:    "
?? SPACE(12 - LEN(avgsal_c)) + avgsal_c
? "   Total monthly salaries:    "
?? SPACE(12 - LEN(totmo_c)) + totmo_c
? "   Total yearly salaries:     "
?? SPACE(12 - LEN(totyr_c)) + totyr_c

SET TALK ON
RETURN
```

The program uses SUM to find the total monthly and yearly salary expenses for a given department and store these values in the variables *totmo* and *totyr*, respectively:

```
SUM salary_mo, salary_mo * 12 FOR department = deptname TO totmo, totyr
```

A call to *Summary* requires one string parameter 245♦: the name of the department for which a report is to be created. Inside the program, this string is stored in the variable *deptname*. (Alphabetic case is not important in issuing this string parameter because the program takes care of adjusting the string properly for use in the FOR clause.) Here are examples of output from *Summary*:

```
. DO Summary WITH "clerical"
```

```
Clerical Department
-------- ----------
   Number of employees:             4
   Average years with firm:        5.4
   Average monthly salary:     1318.75
   Total monthly salaries:     5275.00
   Total yearly salaries:     63300.00
.
```

```
. DO Summary WITH "PRODUCTION"
```

```
Production Department
---------- ----------
   Number of employees:            3
   Average years with firm:      7.1
   Average monthly salary:   1741.67
   Total monthly salaries:   5225.00
   Total yearly salaries:   62700.00
   .
```

(Both the *Summary* program and the *Staff* database are discussed further in the AVER-AGE **31★** and COUNT **85★** entries.)

■ **Caution**

Without any parameters at all, the SUM command totals all numeric fields in the database—even those for which the summation process serves no useful purpose:

```
. SUM
       9 records summed
   YRS    EMP_ID    SALARY_MO
  51.6     56697     15290.00
   .
```

A summation of employee numbers is obviously meaningless, but the SUM command supplies it anyway.

■ **dBASE II equivalent**

SUM

■ **Comment**

Other dBASE III statistical commands include TOTAL **436★**, AVERAGE, and COUNT.

TEXT...ENDTEXT

- **Structure**

  TEXT

  ...lines of text to be sent to the screen and/or the printer...

  ENDTEXT

- **Description**

  The TEXT...ENDTEXT block provides a convenient tool for outputting several sequential lines of text from a program to the screen or printer. It takes the place of a series of ? (print line) commands. The ENDTEXT statement is required to close the structure.

- **Usage**

  The TEXT...ENDTEXT structure may be used in any dBASE program that outputs long passages of literal text. It does not require quotation marks, and all spacing within the block is duplicated exactly.

- **Program example**

  The following short program shows how TEXT ... ENDTEXT might be used to print a form business letter:

```
*-------------------------------------------------- PRNTLET.PRG
* Print a letter acknowledging receipt of an
*    unsolicited job resume.
*

PARAMETER name
SET PRINT ON

TEXT

                    BigCo, Inc.
                    1234 Main Street
                    Smalltown, CA. 91234

ENDTEXT

? "                    ", DATE()
?
?
?
? "Dear", name
?
```

(continued)

```
TEXT

    Thank you for sending us your resume and your application for
    employment at BigCo. Your qualifications are excellent, and we
    feel certain that your prospects for employment in the field
    are good.

    Unfortunately, we do not have any openings at present. We will
    keep your resume on file, and contact you if an appropriate
    position becomes available.


                                        Yours sincerely,


                                        P. Smith,
                                        Personnel Manager


ENDTEXT

SET PRINT OFF
RETURN
```

Notice that the name of the job applicant is passed to the program as a parameter **245♦** (*name*) in the WITH clause of the DO **122★** statement that initiates program performance; for example:

```
. DO Prntlet WITH "Arthur Johnson:"
```

■ **Cautions**

Do not attempt to use macros **215★**, variables **459★**, or even comments **4♦** within a TEXT...ENDTEXT block. Everything inside the block is displayed or printed *literally*.

If you inadvertently omit the ENDTEXT statement, everything to the end of the program will be printed or displayed as text.

■ **dBASE II equivalent**

TEXT...ENDTEXT

TIME()

■ **Structure**

TIME()

■ **Description**

The TIME() function reads the computer's system time and supplies a string **98♦** of characters representing it. The string returned by the TIME() function is eight characters long and is presented in the hr:mn:sc format. The system time is based on a 24-hour clock:

Time:	Meaning:
00:00:00	Midnight
06:00:00	6:00 a.m.
12:00:00	Noon
18:00:00	6:00 p.m.
23:59:59	One second before midnight

■ **Usage**

The result of TIME() represents the setting of the system clock at the moment the function is performed. For instance, to display the current time, you might issue a ? command:

```
. ? "The time is " + TIME() + "."
The time is 12:16:31.
```

Notice that, because TIME() returns a character string, its value can be concatenated **65★** with another string.

■ **Program example**

The following program, called *Clock*, produces a time display that changes every second (the program also displays the system date):

```
*----------------------------------------------------- CLOCK.PRG
* Displays the date and the time, given a specified
*   date-format style. Uses BOX.PRG.
* Program ends when user presses the Escape key.
*

PARAMETER style

SET DATE &style
CLEAR

DO Box WITH 10, 29, 15, 49
@ 21, 26 SAY "Press <Esc> to end program."

@ 12, 35 SAY DATE()
DO WHILE .T.
    @ 13, 35 SAY TIME() + " "
ENDDO

RETURN
```

To perform this program, you must supply, as a parameter 245◆, a string of characters representing the style in which you want the date to be displayed (see SET DATE 337★):

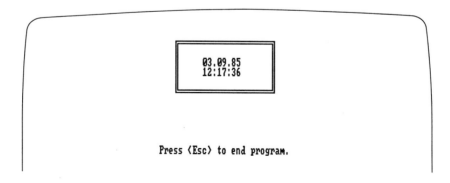

```
. DO Clock WITH "french"
```

The result of this particular command will be a display of the date and time in the following format:

```
03.09.85
12:17:36
```

```
Press <Esc> to end program.
```

Notice that *Clock* makes use of a program called *Box* (listed in the CHR() **50★** entry) to draw a border around the date and time display.

Clock displays the time from within an "endless" loop:

```
DO WHILE .T.
    @ 13, 35 SAY TIME() + " "
ENDDO
```

This loop continues to display new values of TIME(), producing the effect of an ever-changing digital clock, until you press the Escape key to end the process.

- **Caution**

  Do not confuse the distinct natures of the TIME() and DATE() **103★** functions. DATE() returns a date-type **99◆** value upon which you can perform date arithmetic **100★**, and dBASE also provides a special set of functions that allow you to create and manipulate dates. The TIME() function simply returns a string of characters representing the system time; dBASE offers no specific facilities for "time arithmetic," although you can use certain string functions **418★** to isolate and evaluate the components of the time string (see *Comments*).

- **dBASE II equivalent**

  None

- **Comments**

  The following short program, called *Minute*, demonstrates a technique in which the TIME() function is used to measure the passage of time. The program simply allows one minute to elapse, and then rings the system bell:

```
*------------------------------------------------------MINUTE.PRG
* Lets a minute go by and then rings the bell.
*

SET TALK OFF
CLEAR

s1 = VAL(SUBSTR(TIME(), 7, 2))

IF s1 = 0
    s1 = 60
ENDIF

s2 = s1
@  8, 15 SAY s1 PICTURE "System seconds started at ##."
@ 10, 15 SAY "System seconds now at   ."
DO WHILE s2 <> s1 - 1
    s2 = VAL(SUBSTR(TIME(), 7, 2))
    @ 10, 37 SAY s2 PICTURE "##"
ENDDO

? CHR(7)

SET TALK ON
RETURN
```

435

The key to the *Minute* program is the use of the SUBSTR **423★** function to isolate the number of seconds in the current time setting (the seconds are represented by the last two digits of the time string). The VAL() **456★** function then converts this value to a number:

```
VAL(SUBSTR(TIME(), 7, 2))
```

This expression is used twice: first to assign the starting time to the variable *s1*, and subsequently to assign the readings of the passing seconds to the variable *s2*. The program ends, and the bell is rung, when *s2* has a value 1 less than *s1*. (Notice the use of the CHR() **50★** function with the ASCII **28★** value 7 to ring the system bell.)

You might want to use, or expand upon, the technique illustrated in this program in two types of situations:

☐ When you want to measure the amount of time taken by a certain activity.

☐ When you want to control the duration of a certain programmed activity, such as the display of a message on the screen.

TOTAL

■ **Structure**

TOTAL   ON field_name   TO file_name   *scope_clause   FIELDS field_list   condition_clause*

■ **Description**

Given an open database that contains at least one numeric field, the TOTAL command produces a "totals" database file on disk. The purpose of the newly created database is to store numeric totals, by categories of records, from the original database. To specify the totals categories, you must begin by sorting **402◆** or indexing **176◆** the original database on a desired key field **194★**. You then supply the name of this field in the ON clause of the TOTAL command and TOTAL uses the field as a reference for determining categories: Each time the value in this field changes, moving sequentially from one record to the next, TOTAL begins a new totals category.

The TO clause specifies a name for the new database. (You may also specify a drive destination other than the default drive.)

The FIELD clause allows you the option of specifying which numeric fields you wish to have totaled. If you omit FIELDS, *all* numeric fields in the original database will be totaled, whether appropriate or not.

The scope **312★** specification, which is optional, consists of an ALL **17★** or NEXT **239★** clause. If a scope is not specified, ALL is assumed: In other words, TOTAL works on the entire original database. The condition option permits you to use a FOR **164★** or WHILE **463★** clause to select specific categories for totaling.

■ **Usage**

TOTAL produces one totals record for each *category* in the original database.

■ **Database example**

The *Staff* database contains information about the employees of a small company. Included in the database are fields for each employee's department, first name, last name, date hired, years with the firm, employee number, and monthly salary:

```
. USE Staff
. LIST
Record#  DEPARTMENT  LASTNAME    FIRSTNAME  HIRED      YRS   EMP_ID  SALARY_MO
      1  Production  Morris      John       03.11.82   2.5     4521    1850.00
      2  Marketing   Southby     Anne       22.08.81   3.7     3134    2315.00
      3  Clerical    Peters      Larry      10.06.83   1.9     3412    1350.00
      4  Clerical    Broussard   Marie      05.05.81   4.0     8712    1275.00
      5  Production  James       Fred       22.02.77   8.2     6563    1675.00
      6  Marketing   Smith       June       29.03.80   5.1     6823    2475.00
      7  Clerical    Liles       Carter     29.09.77   7.6     8799    1400.00
      8  Production  Washington  Liz        05.11.74  10.5     7321    1700.00
      9  Clerical    Ludlum      Donald     30.03.77   8.1     7412    1250.00
.
```

The company would like to find two totals for each of the three departments represented in this database: the total monthly salary expense for each department, and the total years of employment that have been accumulated by all the current employees in each department. The first step in accomplishing this task is to index the database on the *department* field:

```
. INDEX ON department TO Deptind
. LIST
Record#  DEPARTMENT  LASTNAME    FIRSTNAME  HIRED      YRS   EMP_ID  SALARY_MO
      3  Clerical    Peters      Larry      10.06.83   1.9     3412    1350.00
      4  Clerical    Broussard   Marie      05.05.81   4.0     8712    1275.00
      7  Clerical    Liles       Carter     29.09.77   7.6     8799    1400.00
      9  Clerical    Ludlum      Donald     30.03.77   8.1     7412    1250.00
      2  Marketing   Southby     Anne       22.08.81   3.7     3134    2315.00
      6  Marketing   Smith       June       29.03.80   5.1     6823    2475.00
      1  Production  Morris      John       03.11.82   2.5     4521    1850.00
      5  Production  James       Fred       22.02.77   8.2     6563    1675.00
      8  Production  Washington  Liz        05.11.74  10.5     7321    1700.00
.
```

With the database thus indexed, the following TOTAL command will produce a new database called *Stafftot*, in which the *yrs* and *salary_mo* fields will be totaled by department:

```
. TOTAL ON department TO Stafftot FIELDS yrs, salary_mo
.
```

To examine the totals, we must first open the new database and then list the relevant fields:

```
. USE Stafftot
. LIST department, yrs, salary_mo
Record#  department    yrs salary_mo
      1  Clerical     21.6   5275.00
      2  Marketing     8.8   4790.00
      3  Production   21.2   5225.00
.
```

As you can see, *Stafftot* consists of three records—one for each of the three department categories.

■ **Cautions**

The new database created by the TOTAL command will be identical in structure **100♦** to the original database, except that memo fields **217★** will not be included. As a result, the totals database is likely to contain irrelevant information in most of the untotaled fields. For example, here is a listing of the entire *Stafftot* database:

```
. LIST
Record#  DEPARTMENT  LASTNAME  FIRSTNAME  HIRED      YRS EMP_ID SALARY_MO
      1  Clerical    Peters    Larry      06/10/83 21.6   3412   5275.00
      2  Marketing   Southby   Anne       08/22/81  8.8   3134   4790.00
      3  Production  Morris    John       11/03/82 21.2   4521   5225.00
.
```

Notice that the fields *lastname*, *firstname*, *hired*, and *emp_id* contain the values from the first record in each department category in the original *Staff* database. All of these fields are extraneous in *Stafftot*.

Before you use the TOTAL command, make sure that the numeric fields to be totaled are wide enough for the resulting values. If they are not, TOTAL will fill in the fields with asterisks in the totals database. The following experiment with a meaningless database called *Test* illustrates this behavior (and also shows that the TOTAL command does not transfer memo fields from the original database to the totals database):

```
. USE Test
. LIST
Record#  KEY  NUM  NOTES
     1    A    234  Memo
     2    A     34  Memo
     3    A    979  Memo
     4    B    797  Memo
     5    B    431  Memo
     6    B    123  Memo
     7    C    111  Memo
     8    C     21  Memo
     9    C    321  Memo

. TOTAL ON key TO Tottest FIELD num
     9 Record(s) totalled
     3 Records generated
Numeric overflow (data was lost)

. USE Tottest
. LIST
Record#  KEY  NUM
     1    A    ***
     2    B    ***
     3    C    453
.
```

As you can see, the totals for categories A and B were too large to fit in the *num* field in *Tottest*, and the memo field *notes* is missing from the new database.

■ **dBASE II equivalent**

TOTAL

■ **Comment**

TOTAL is a rather clumsy command, best used sparingly. For most situations in which you want to compute statistics from a database, the other dBASE statistical commands—AVERAGE 31★, COUNT 85★, and SUM 426★—will prove much more useful.

TRIM()

■ **Structure**

TRIM(character_expression)

■ **Description**

Given a string **98♦** of characters, the TRIM() function supplies a new version of the string without any space characters at the end **♦**. The string value resulting from TRIM() will thus be shorter than the original string by the number of trailing spaces contained in the original.

■ **Usage**

The argument of the TRIM() function may be any valid character expression. However, TRIM() is most typically used to eliminate ending spaces from character-field values, which always conform to the width of the field as defined in the structure of the database. For example, if the character field named *states* has a width of 15, and you enter the value "OHIO" in that field, the value will actually be stored as:

```
"OHIO           "
```

In other words, the entire unused width of the field is automatically filled with space characters. This can be a problem if you want to display the field value in a concatenated **65★** expression:

```
. ? states + " is my home state."
OHIO           is my home state.
.
```

In this instance, the space characters displayed after the word "OHIO" are clearly undesirable. Fortunately, the TRIM() function will eliminate them:

```
. ? TRIM(states) + " is my home state."
OHIO is my home state.
.
```

■ **Database example**

The database called *Children* contains the names, addresses, and birth dates of a group of children. All of the fields are character, except for *birthdate*, which is a date-type **99◆** field:

```
. USE Children
. LIST OFF
LASTNAME    FIRSTNAME  ADDRESS        CITY           STATE ZIP    BIRTHDATE
Harte       Susan      45 Rose St.    San Francisco  CA    94110  05/24/78
Young       Elizabeth  1824 First St. Oakland        CA    94725  12/18/79
Washington  Jacqueline 76 Charles Pl. Daly City      CA    94012  03/05/80
Morris      George     231 Wood Rd.   San Francisco  CA    94118  07/29/78
Colborne    Robert     89 Maple Dr.   Berkeley       CA    94710  02/15/77
McDonald    Karen      214 Sixth St.  Richmond       CA    94201  12/18/81
.
```

The following examples show how the TRIM() function can be used with this database to display certain combinations of data in usable formats:

```
. LIST TRIM(firstname) + " " + lastname
Record# TRIM(firstname) + " " + lastname
      1 Susan Harte
      2 Elizabeth Young
      3 Jacqueline Washington
      4 George Morris
      5 Robert Colborne
      6 Karen McDonald
.
```

```
. LIST TRIM(city) + ", " + state + " " + zip
Record# TRIM(city) + ", " + state + " " + zip
      1 San Francisco, CA 94110
      2 Oakland, CA 94725
      3 Daly City, CA 94012
      4 San Francisco, CA 94118
      5 Berkeley, CA 94710
      6 Richmond, CA 94201
.
```

Here is how the city, state, and zip-code display would appear without the TRIM() function:

```
. LIST city + state + zip
Record#  city + state + zip
      1  San FranciscoCA94110
      2  Oakland      CA94725
      3  Daly City    CA94012
      4  San FranciscoCA94118
      5  Berkeley     CA94710
      6  Richmond     CA94201

.
```

■ **Program example**

The *Children* database is also discussed in the SPACE() **407★** entry, where the *Kidlist* program is used to produce a specially formatted set of mailing labels for the children listed in the database. The most interesting feature of this program is its ability to right justify the elements of the data, and the TRIM() function is instrumental in this process. For example, consider the following passage from the program:

```
csz = TRIM(city) + ", " + state + " " + zip
? "City, State, Zip:"
?? SPACE(25 - LEN(csz)) + csz
```

In the first line of this sequence, TRIM() eliminates the extraneous spaces from the end of the value in the *city* field. Here is an example of the resulting string, which is stored in the variable *csz*:

```
Oakland, CA 94725
```

Without the TRIM() function, the string would have been left with several unwanted spaces after the *city* value.

■ **Cautions**

Using the TRIM() function on an empty field—or any other character value that contains only spaces—will result in a null string (a string value containing no characters):

```
. test1 = "            "
. test2 = TRIM(test2)
.
. LIST MEMORY
TEST1        pub  C  "           "
TEST2        pub  C  ""
      2 variables defined,       14 bytes used
    254 variables available,   5986 bytes available
.
```

TRIM() has no effect on *leading* blanks, and therefore cannot be used to eliminate blanks resulting from number-to-string conversions by the STR() **416★** function. (Because such values are stored right justified in their field width, blank spaces are located *before* the value.) However, the SUBSTR() **423★** function can be useful in extracting the relevant characters from such STR() output:

```
. numvar = 1234
. ? TYPE("numvar")
N
.
. newvar = STR(numvar)
. ? TYPE("newvar")
C
.
. ? TRIM(newvar)
      1234
.
. ? SUBSTR(newvar, 7)
1234
.
```

■ **dBASE II equivalent**

TRIM()

In dBASE II, performing the TRIM() function on an empty field or a string value that contains only spaces results in a string that contains exactly one space.

■ **Comment**

The SPACE() function is, in a sense, the converse of TRIM(): SPACE() *supplies* a string of characters consisting of a specified number of blank spaces.

TYPE

■ **Structure**

TYPE file_name   *TO PRINT*

■ **Description**

The TYPE command searches the current or specified disk for the named text file **157♦**, and displays the file's contents on the screen. The TO PRINT option sends the contents to the printer as well.

■ **Usage**

TYPE can be used to list the contents of program files (.PRG), format files (.FMT), alternate files (.TXT), or any other ASCII text file. Here are two examples:

```
. TYPE A:CONFIG.DB
BELL = OFF
COMMAND = ? DATE(), TIME()
CONFIRM = ON
DEFAULT = B
F10 = DO Menu
HELP = OFF
MARGIN = 10
MAXMEM = 320
MENUS = ON
MVARSIZE = 12
PATH = A:\
```

```
. TYPE BLANKS.PRG
PARAMETER NUM

SET TALK OFF
COUNT TO cur

DO WHILE num > 0
    APPEND BLANK
    num = num - 1
ENDDO

GOTO cur + 1

SET TALK ON
BROWSE
RETURN
```

Notice that the file name's extension **155♦** is *required* in the TYPE command.

■ **Caution**
Other types of dBASE files—including .DBF, .NDX, and .DBT—are not stored in ASCII text format, and therefore cannot be displayed using the TYPE command.

■ **dBASE II equivalent**
None

■ **Comment**
TYPE is the dBASE equivalent of the DOS **133**★ TYPE command ◆.

TYPE()

■ **Structure**
TYPE("variable_name")
TYPE("field_name")

■ **Description**
Given a variable **459**★ name or field **154**★ name, the TYPE() function returns a single letter that indicates its data type **98**★. The result of TYPE() is always one of the following characters:

Character:	Data type:
C	Character
N	Numeric
D	Date
L	Logical
M	Memo
U	Undefined

The variable- or field-name argument must be delimited **98**◆ as a string value—that is, surrounded by quotes or square brackets.

■ **Usage**
One important use of the TYPE() function is to determine the data type of a value entered from the keyboard in response to an INPUT **182**★ statement. (INPUT will accept character, numeric, date, or logical data.)

The following passage from the *Typetest* program discussed in the INPUT entry shows how the TYPE() function can be used to test the value of an INPUT variable:

```
INPUT "Enter any type of expression: " TO var
?
?? "==> "
t = TYPE("var")

DO CASE
    CASE t = "C"
        ?? "character value: "
    CASE t = "N"
        ?? "numeric value: "
    CASE t = "D"
        ?? "date value: "
    CASE t = "L"
        ?? "logical value: "
ENDCASE
?? var
```

Since this passage appears inside a DO WHILE loop, sample output from the program might look like this:

```
Enter any type of expression: 1234
==> numeric value:        1234

Enter any type of expression: "test"
==> character value: test

Enter any type of expression: .T.
==> logical value: .T.

Enter any type of expression: CTOD("12/25/55")
==> date value: 12/25/55

Enter any type of expression:
```

■ **Caution**

An undelimited string variable name can be used as the argument of TYPE() if the value stored in the variable is itself the name of a currently defined field or variable. For example, imagine you are working with a billing database containing a date-type field called *date_due*. You have created a string variable, *fld*, which always contains the name of the field you are currently working with. In this situation, TYPE() can be used as illustrated in the following passage:

```
. fld = "date_due"
date_due
.
. ? TYPE(fld)
D
.
```

However, the use of a macro will not be successful:

```
. ? TYPE(&fld)
Variable not found
        ?
? TYPE(date_due)
.
```

■ **dBASE II equivalent**

TYPE()

■ **Comment**

TYPE() returns a U if its argument is an illegal expression or contains an undefined variable or field. Therefore, TYPE() can be used to test for the existence of a variable.

UPDATE

■ **Structure**

UPDATE ON field_name FROM file_name REPLACE field_name WITH expression
,field_name WITH expression ,... RANDOM

■ **Description**

Given a "target" and a "source" database, both open in different work areas **454◆**, the UPDATE command replaces the data in selected fields of the target database with data from the source database. UPDATE requires a key field **194★** common to both databases in order to match target records with source records.

The database that is currently selected **322◆** at the time UPDATE is performed becomes the target; the source database is specified in the FROM clause of the UPDATE command.

The ON clause identifies the key field, which is typically a numeric or character field. The two databases must be arranged in one of two ways relative to this key:

☐ Both databases must be indexed **176◆** or sorted **402◆** by the key field.

☐ If the RANDOM option is used, the target database must be *indexed* by the key field, but the source database may be arranged in any order.

The REPLACE clause identifies the field or fields that will receive new values in the target database. Each field name is followed by a WITH clause containing the expression that will be evaluated to supply the new value.

The WITH expression may contain references to fields in the target database, the source database, or both. Target-database fields may be specified by their names alone, but references to fields in the source database must include the name or alias **14★** of the database itself, in the form:

```
database -> field_name
```

The REPLACE clause may include numeric, character, logical or date-type **99◆** fields. The WITH expression must, of course, evaluate to the same type as the field that is to receive the value.

■ **Usage**

As its name implies, UPDATE is often used as a tool for updating ◆ a master file from individual chronological files: Daily, weekly, or monthly transaction information is stored in temporary files and then transferred periodically to the master file, which contains the accumulated data from all of the individual chronological files.

■ Database example

The following example of the UPDATE command uses a database called *Bksales*. This database, which you can read more about in the entries for JOIN **189★** and SET RELATION **390★**, contains records of book sales from a national bookstore chain: specifically, the total number of copies sold for 10 of the chain's best-sellers. Each month, *Bksales* is updated with the sales from the previous month. The database that contains the previous month's sales is given the name of the month represented. Here are listings of both *Bksales* and *Sept*:

```
. SELECT 1
. USE Bksales INDEX num ALIAS Books
. LIST book_num, title, unit_sales
Record#  book_num title                  unit_sales
      1  F162     The Orchid                  59643
      5  F182     The Mission                 65880
      2  F298     Mountain Romance            67646
      9  F509     Mystery of the East         66834
      3  N123     Nights of London            39806
      7  N340     The Perfect Cook            76835
     10  N556     Images of Japan             81252
      6  N774     Politics Among Us           34131
      4  N866     Paris: Art at Home          51193
      8  N881     Traveler in Europe          40749
.
```

```
. SELECT 2
. USE Sept
. LIST
Record#  BOOK_NUM MONTH_SALE
      1  F162           1831
      2  F298            534
      3  N123            983
      4  N866           3412
      5  F182            664
      6  N774           4319
      7  N340            426
      8  N881           1988
      9  F509            321
     10  N556           3118
.
```

As you can see, *Bksales* and *Sept* have one field in common: *book_num*. This character field contains coded identification numbers assigned to each book in the database. *Bksales* has been indexed by *book_num* (*INDEX num*), but *Sept* is unindexed. In *Bksales*, the total number of copies sold is stored in the *unit_sales* field; in *Sept*, the corresponding field is *month_sale*.

In order to update *Bksales* from *Sept*, the UPDATE command must be issued from work area 1, where *Bksales* is located:

```
. SELECT Books
. UPDATE ON book_num FROM Sept REPLACE unit_sales ;
  WITH unit_sales + Sept -> month_sale RANDOM
     10 records updated

.
```

Notice that each value of *unit_sales* in the *Bksales* database is to be replaced by the value *unit_sales* + *Sept* -> *month_sale*. (Since the *month_sale* field is in the source database, any reference to it must include the database name or alias.) Notice also that the RANDOM clause is included in this command because *Bksales* is indexed but *Sept* is not.

The new version of *Bksales* shows the results of the UPDATE command:

```
. LIST book_num, title, unit_sales
Record#  book_num title            unit_sales
      1  F162     The Orchid           61474
      5  F182     The Mission          66544
      2  F298     Mountain Romance     68180
      9  F509     Mystery of the East  67155
      3  N123     Nights of London     40789
      7  N340     The Perfect Cook     77261
     10  N556     Images of Japan      84370
      6  N774     Politics Among Us    38450
      4  N866     Paris: Art at Home   54605
      8  N881     Traveler in Europe   42737

.
```

■ **Caution**

Unfortunately, the UPDATE command does not allow the use of RECNO() 279* (the record-number function) as the key to the updating operation. The key must be a structure field that is contained in both the source and the target database. (See the SET RELATION entry for an example of a command that does allow RECNO() as a key.)

■ **dBASE II equivalent**

UPDATE

However, the syntax of the command is less versatile in dBASE II.

■ **Comments**

UPDATE is probably most commonly used for updating numeric fields in the target database. However, the command's syntax allows work with character, logical, and date-type fields as well. This means that you can perform concatentations **65★**, logical tests **207◆**, and date arithmetic **100★**, using data from the source database. In the case of concatenations, keep in mind the following two points:

☐ The width of a database field is fixed. If a concatenation results in a string that is too large to fit in the field, the string will be cut down (truncated) to the width available.

☐ A character value that is smaller than the field in which it is located will contain trailing blanks to fill out the width of the field. For this reason, you should use the TRIM() **440★** function or the – operator **420◆** to concatenate field values in an UP-DATE operation.

UPPER()

■ **Structure**

UPPER(character_expression)

■ **Description**

Given a string **98◆** of characters, the UPPER() function returns a new version of the same string, in which all letters of the alphabet are converted to uppercase.

■ **Usage**

The argument of UPPER() may be any valid character expression:

☐ A character-type field or variable.

☐ The result of a function that returns a string.

☐ A literal (constant) string value enclosed in quotation marks or square brackets.

☐ A concatenated **65★** expression combining two or more strings.

Here are several examples:

```
. stock_no = "12a4500D"

. ? UPPER(stock_no)
12A4500D

. ? UPPER("dBase III")
DBASE III

. ? UPPER("Today is " + CDOW(DATE()) + ".")
TODAY IS TUESDAY.

.
```

■ **Database example**

The following database, called *Invntory*, contains five fields of information about items of stock. The character field *item* stores a brief description of each object:

```
. USE Invntory
. LIST
Record#  ID      ITEM              QTY  COST   VALUE
      1  12B123  ruler             150  0.21    31.50
      2  76C987  NOTEBOOK          225  0.45   101.25
      3  32A971  Blotter            76  1.51   114.76
      4  76F971  CALCULATOR         35  3.75   131.25
      5  23D971  Desk Clock         25  7.88   197.00
      6  32H231  desk ORGANIZER    110  2.37   260.70
.
```

Notice that the *item* values are stored in inconsistent and random case formats: Some are all uppercase, others are all lowercase, and still others are mixed. This situation often occurs when records are entered into a database by several different people, or over a long period of time.

The following REPLACE **291**★ command uses the UPPER() function to put all of the *item* values in the *Invntory* database into a consistent format:

```
. REPLACE ALL item WITH UPPER(item)
      6 records replaced
. LIST
Record#  ID      ITEM              QTY  COST   VALUE
      1  12B123  RULER             150  0.21    31.50
      2  76C987  NOTEBOOK          225  0.45   101.25
      3  32A971  BLOTTER            76  1.51   114.76
      4  76F971  CALCULATOR         35  3.75   131.25
      5  23D971  DESK CLOCK         25  7.88   197.00
      6  32H231  DESK ORGANIZER    110  2.37   260.70
.
```

Alternatively, the following rather complex REPLACE command gives each item description an initial capital letter, followed by all lowercase letters. This handy feat is performed using a combination of the UPPER(), LOWER() 213★, and SUBSTR() 423★ functions:

```
. REPLACE ALL item WITH UPPER(SUBSTR(item, 1, 1)) + ;
  LOWER(SUBSTR(item, 2))
      6 records replaced
. LIST
Record#  ID      ITEM           QTY  COST  VALUE
      1  12B123  Ruler          150  0.21   31.50
      2  76C987  Notebook       225  0.45  101.25
      3  32A971  Blotter         76  1.51  114.76
      4  76F971  Calculator      35  3.75  131.25
      5  23D971  Desk clock      25  7.88  197.00
      6  32H231  Desk organizer 110  2.37  260.70

.
```

The SUBSTR() function is used twice here, to isolate the specific parts of the *item* string to be converted by UPPER() and LOWER(), respectively.

■ **Caution**

If the values stored in a character field follow an intentional pattern of mixed upper- and lowercase formats, that pattern can be very difficult to restore after a REPLACE ALL command that converts everything to uppercase.

■ **dBASE II equivalent**

!()

■ **Comment**

The LOWER() function converts the letters of a string to lowercase.

USE

■ **Structure**

USE *file_name* *INDEX index_list* *ALIAS alias_name*

■ **Description**

The USE command opens ◆ a database file **156**◆ into the currently selected **322**◆ work area. Optionally, USE can also open as many as seven index files **156**◆ associated with the database, and assign the database an alias **14**★ name.

■ **Usage**

The simplest form of the USE statement searches on the current disk for a database file (with a .DBF extension **155**◆):

```
. USE Property
```

If the database has one or more memo fields **217**★, USE automatically opens the associated memo file, which has the same file name but a .DBT extension.

Potentially, up to 10 database files can be open concurrently in dBASE III—one in each of the 10 work areas ◆. When you open multiple files in this manner, it is sometimes convenient to assign a short, meaningful alias to each database, for use in subsequent SELECT **322**★ statements:

```
. SELECT 1
. USE Bksales ALIAS Books
. SELECT 2
. USE Authors
. SELECT Books
```

The final SELECT command in this example uses the database's alias, *Books*, to move back to work area 1. (See SELECT and Aliases for more information on this subject.)

Normally, USE opens the database with the record pointer **258**★ positioned at record #1:

```
. USE Lawfirm
. ? RECNO()
        1
.
```

However, when an index file is opened along with the database file, USE places the record pointer at the first record in the *indexed* order:

```
. USE Lawfirm INDEX Client
. ? RECNO()
        4
.
```

If you open more than one index file, the first index in the list becomes the controlling index: the others are opened only for potential updating, in the event that you revise the database itself:

```
. USE Lawfirm INDEX Client, Amt, Paid
```

In this example, the database will be displayed and operated on in alphabetical order by client name, because *CLIENT.NDX* is the controlling index; *AMT.NDX* and *PAID.NDX* are available only for updating.

■ **Caution**
A given database (and index file) may be open in only one work area at a time. Any attempt to open a file that is already open in another work area results in an error message:

```
. SELECT 1
. USE Bksales
. SELECT 2
. USE Authors
. SELECT 3
. USE Bksales
ALIAS name already in use
        ?
USE Bksales
.
```

■ **dBASE II equivalent**
USE

■ **Comment**
USE alone, issued without parameters, closes the database and associated indexes in the currently selected work area. Files open in other work areas are not affected.

VAL()

■ **Structure**

VAL(character_expression)

■ **Description**

Given a string **98◆** of characters consisting of digits and a decimal point (optional), the VAL() function supplies the numeric equivalent of the string. If the first character of the string argument is not a digit, VAL() returns a value of zero.

■ **Usage**

In programming situations, it is occasionally necessary to perform mathematical operations on a number that is stored as a string of digit characters. The VAL() function converts such a string to a numeric value, which can then be used arithmetically. Here is a simple example:

```
. ? 2 * VAL("443")
886.00
.
```

■ **Program example**

The program called *Minute*, listed and discussed in the TIME() **433★** entry, uses VAL() and SUBSTR() **423★** to convert the seconds portion of the system time to a numeric value (TIME() always returns a string value):

```
VAL(SUBSTR(TIME(), 7, 2))
```

This expression can be expanded into a formula that converts any TIME() string into a numeric value measuring the number of seconds that have elapsed since midnight. The following command was issued when the system time was 12:07:01:

```
. ? VAL(SUBSTR(TIME(), 1, 2)) * 3600 + VAL(SUBSTR(TIME(), 4, 2)) * 60 ;
+ VAL(SUBSTR(TIME(), 7, 2))
43621.00
.
```

The formula in the preceding example is one possible approach to performing "time arithmetic" in dBASE III. To find the amount of time that has elapsed between two TIME() settings, *t1* and *t2*, convert both settings to seconds elapsed since midnight, and then subtract one from the other:

```
diff = t2 - t1
```

Given this difference in seconds (*diff*), the following formulas will find the number of hours, minutes, and seconds that have elapsed:

```
hour = INT(diff / 3600)
min = INT((diff - (hour * 3600)) / 60)
sec = diff - (hour * 3600) - (min * 60)
```

Here is one way you might use the results of these calculations:

```
. diff = 10432

. hour = INT(diff / 3600)
. min = INT((diff - (hour * 3600)) / 60)
. sec = diff - (hour * 3600) - (min * 60)

. ? "Time elapsed: " + SUBSTR(STR(hour), 9, 2) + " hours, " + ;
  SUBSTR(STR(min), 9, 2) + " minutes, " + SUBSTR(STR(sec), 9, 2) + " seconds "
Time elapsed:  2 hours, 53 minutes, 52 seconds
.
```

(This approach works only if both *t1* and *t2* are time settings within the same 24-hour day. If they are not, the "time-arithmetic" algorithm will also need to include one or more of the dBASE date functions 102★.)

■ **Cautions**

For display purposes only, VAL() rounds its result to two decimal places:

```
. ? VAL("443.126")
  443.13
.
```

However, when you perform arithmetic on the numeric result of VAL(), you can expect the results to represent the full decimal value of the original string:

```
. ? VAL("443.125")
    443.12
: ? 2 * VAL("443.125")
      886.25
.
```

(VAL() rounds according to the usual arithmetic conventions.)

In some early releases of dBASE III, VAL() rounds to the nearest *integer* for display purposes.

Given a string that does not begin with a digit, the result of VAL() will always be zero. Given a string that begins with one or more digits but is followed by nondigital characters, VAL() simply converts the digits and ignores the remainder of the string:

```
. ? VAL("test")
    0.00
: ? VAL("443test")
      443.00
.
```

■ **dBASE II equivalent**

VAL()

■ **Comment**

The STR() **416**★ function performs the opposite operation, converting a numeric value to a string.

Variables

A variable is a symbolic means of storing and accessing a data value. A dBASE variable has a name, a data type **98★**, and a current value. When you create a variable, dBASE stores its name and current value together in memory. Thereafter, whenever you refer to the variable by name, dBASE fetches the value that is stored in it.

Like field names **154◆**, variable names may be up to 10 characters long and may include letters, digits, and the underscore character (the first character must be a letter). Four variable types **98◆** are available in dBASE: character, numeric, date, and logical. (The TYPE() **444★** function can be used to determine the data-type of a variable, or whether the variable even exists.)

Up to 256 variables may be defined during a given session, and dBASE allocates 6,000 bytes of memory to store them. An MVARSIZ command can be included in the *CONFIG.DB* **66★** file to increase the amount of memory space allocated for variables, but the maximum *number* of variables is fixed. You can use the RELEASE **288★** command to clear memory space of variables that are no longer needed.

There are several ways to create a variable and assign it a value. Perhaps the most common is to use one of the two forms of *assignment statement*:

□ The STORE **414★** command, which assigns a value to one or more variables.

□ The *variable = value* syntax, which handles only one variable at a time.

New variables can also be created through three program statements that read values from the keyboard: INPUT **182★**, ACCEPT **12★**, and WAIT **461★**. Finally, dBASE's AVERAGE **31★**, COUNT **85★**, and SUM **426★** commands can optionally assign calculated statistical values to variables.

Any of these commands can also change the value of an existing variable. (The @...GET command cannot create a new variable, but does allow you to edit the value of a current variable from within a program—see @...SAY...GET **9★** and READ **275★**.) Be aware, however, that when you assign a new value to a variable, the old value is lost, since a variable can store only one value at a time.

The DISPLAY MEMORY **118★** command displays all currently defined variables, their types, and their values. It also tells you the total number of variables defined, and how much memory space they are taking up. The current value of a *specific* variable can be displayed on the screen, sent to the printer, or both, through the ? **5★** command or the @...SAY command.

One or more variables and their current values can be stored, via the SAVE **309★** command, in a special disk file called a memory file **157◆**. (Memory files have the default extension name **155◆** .MEM.) The variables stored in a memory file can be read back into active memory at a later time through the RESTORE **298★** command.

The availability of a variable depends upon where it was created. Variables created during the performance of a program are said to be *local* ◆ by default: That is, when the program or procedure **383◆** that created the variable relinquishes control, the variable is released from memory. Variables created from the dot-prompt **62◆** are *global* ◆: They are available at any level of dBASE. A global variable used in a program remains in memory even when the program terminates.

Within a program, variables may be declared global via a PUBLIC **269★** statement located near the beginning of the program *before* the variables are initialized. In contrast, a PRIVATE **259★** statement may be issued at a specific procedure level to hide global variables, so that identical variable names can be reused. (See SET PROCEDURE **383★**, PUBLIC, and PRIVATE for further details about management of local and global variables.)

A variable value, or parameter, can be passed to a program or procedure by the WITH clause of the DO **122★** statement that initiates performance of the program. Inside the procedure itself, a PARAMETERS **245★** statement sets up a variable to receive the passed value.

Finally, dBASE allows a very special use of character variables through the ampersand symbol (& **1★**): If you precede a variable name with this symbol, the variable becomes a *macro* **215★**. When a macro appears in a dBASE command, the value of the macro variable is substituted *literally* into the syntax of the command itself. For example, if the variable named *var* equals " TO PRINT", then the command *LIST &var* will be read as *LIST TO PRINT*. (See the & and Macros entries for details.)

WAIT

■ **Structure**

WAIT *message   TO variable_name*

■ **Description**

A dBASE program can use the WAIT command to create a pause in its own performance. The pause continues until the user presses any key on the keyboard.

By default, WAIT displays the following message on the screen while the pause is in progress:

```
Press any key to continue...
```

If you prefer, you can supply your own message to appear in place of the default message.

The TO clause, which is also optional, allows you to supply the name of a variable in which the user's keystroke will be stored as a string input value.

■ **Usage**

A typical use of WAIT in a program is to allow the user to examine a screenful of information before the program continues on to some other activity.

A good example appears in the *Mortgage* procedure listed and discussed in the PICTURE **252★** entry. (This procedure is part of the real-estate program used to illustrate many of the entries in this book.) *Mortgage* calculates a mortgage balance and monthly payment, and displays the results on the screen, where the user may examine the display as long as necessary. When the user presses a key on the keyboard, the display disappears and the real-estate program continues.

The following passage produces the display and the ensuing pause:

```
CLEAR

@8, 25 SAY princ PICTURE "Principal:      $###,###"
@9, 25 SAY rate PICTURE "Interest:        ##.##"
@10, 25 SAY term PICTURE "Years:            ##"
@11, 25 SAY "------------------------"
@12, 25 SAY mort PICTURE "Payment:       $#,###.##"
?
?
WAIT "                      Press any key to continue."

RETURN
```

The WAIT command in this passage includes a message clause almost identical to the default message. However, the prompt supplied here is centered beneath the other information displayed on the screen. Here is a sample of the output from the passage:

```
              Principal:    $120,000
              Interest:       13.25
              Years:            30
              -------------------------
              Payment:      $1,350.93

              Press any key to continue.
```

(See the PICTURE entry for further discussion of this procedure.)

- **Caution**

A validation loop must be included after the WAIT command if you wish to restrict the range of acceptable responses. However, a preferable approach to this kind of situation is to use an @...GET **9◆** statement with PICTURE and RANGE options to obtain the desired response.

- **dBASE II equivalent**

WAIT

However, the optional message clause is not part of the syntax in dBASE II.

- **Comments**

As a keyboard-input command, WAIT differs from dBASE's other two input commands, ACCEPT **12★** and INPUT **182★**, in some significant ways:

- ☐ WAIT results in the storage of a single keystroke value in a variable.

- ☐ WAIT does not wait for the user to press Return to complete the keyboard input.

- ☐ WAIT always stores the keyboard input as a string value in a character variable.

WHILE

- **Structure**

  … WHILE condition_expression …

- **Description**

  WHILE is one of two optional condition clauses (the other is FOR **164★**) available for use with some database commands. A condition clause selects specific records **284★** within the default or specified scope **312★** of a dBASE command: Only those records are acted upon by the command that contains the condition clause. To be selected, a record must meet the condition expressed in the clause: That is, the expression must evaluate as true for the record in question. The WHILE clause causes the command to begin executing at the current record and continue sequentially forward through the database until a record is encountered that does not match the expressed condition.

- **Usage**

  The position of the record pointer **258★** is an important consideration when you write commands with WHILE clauses. Such a command begins at the *current position* of the record pointer and stops at the *first* record that does not meet the WHILE condition. (For this reason, you will usually want to use a sorted **406♦** database when you expect to use commands with WHILE clauses—see *Cautions*.) When the action of the command is complete, the pointer will be positioned at *the record following* the last record that was actually acted upon.

- **Database example**

  The examples in this section use the database called *Staff,* which contains information about a group of employees. The *Yrsind* index arranges the database in order of number of years of employment, *yrs*:

```
. USE Staff INDEX Yrsind
. LIST
Record#  DEPARTMENT   LASTNAME   FIRSTNAME  HIRED     YRS  EMP_ID  SALARY_MO
      3  Clerical     Peters     Larry      06/10/83  1.9  3412    1350.00
      1  Production   Morris     John       11/03/82  2.5  4521    1850.00
      2  Marketing    Southby    Anne       08/22/81  3.7  3134    2315.00
      4  Clerical     Broussard  Marie      05/05/81  4.0  8712    1275.00
      6  Marketing    Smith      June       03/29/80  5.1  6823    2475.00
      7  Clerical     Liles      Carter     09/29/77  7.6  8799    1400.00
      9  Clerical     Ludlum     Donald     03/30/77  8.1  7412    1250.00
      5  Production   James      Fred       02/22/77  8.2  6563    1675.00
      8  Production   Washington Liz        11/05/74 10.5  7321    1700.00
.
```

The following DISPLAY **116★** commands illustrate the effect of the WHILE clause. At the beginning of the sequence, the GOTO TOP **169◆** command positions the record pointer at the first record in the indexed database. The first DISPLAY command moves the record pointer to the fourth record—that is, the record *following* the final record that is displayed. The second DISPLAY command begins its action at the fourth record and processes through to the end of the database. Since the WHILE clause made an attempt to evaluate a record past the last record (*yrs < 12*), the EOF() **147★** function now returns a value of true:

```
. GOTO TOP
. DISPLAY WHILE yrs < 4
Record#  DEPARTMENT   LASTNAME    FIRSTNAME   HIRED     YRS  EMP_ID  SALARY_MO
      3  Clerical     Peters      Larry       06/10/83  1.9   3412   1350.00
      1  Production   Morris      John        11/03/82  2.5   4521   1850.00
      2  Marketing    Southby     Anne        08/22/81  3.7   3134   2315.00

. ? RECNO()
      4

. DISPLAY WHILE yrs < 12
Record#  DEPARTMENT   LASTNAME    FIRSTNAME   HIRED     YRS  EMP_ID  SALARY_MO
      4  Clerical     Broussard   Marie       05/05/81  4.0   8712   1275.00
      6  Marketing    Smith       June        03/29/80  5.1   6823   2475.00
      7  Clerical     Liles       Carter      09/29/77  7.6   8799   1400.00
      9  Clerical     Ludlum      Donald      03/30/77  8.1   7412   1250.00
      5  Production   James       Fred        02/22/77  8.2   6563   1675.00
      8  Production   Washington  Liz         11/05/74 10.5   7321   1700.00

. ? EOF()
.T.
.
```

■ **Cautions**

Despite contradictory documentation on the subject, the WHILE clause does *not* set the default scope to ALL **17★**. Even when used with commands that *have* default scopes of ALL, the WHILE clause behaves the same: It begins processing at the current record. (To test this, repeat the preceding sequence of commands using LIST **200★** instead of DISPLAY: The same behavior will result.) If you want a command with a WHILE clause to act over the entire database, starting from the first record, you must issue a GOTO TOP command first, or else explicitly specify a scope of ALL:

```
. USE Staff INDEX Yrsind
. LIST WHILE yrs <= 4
Record# DEPARTMENT   LASTNAME   FIRSTNAME  HIRED     YRS EMP_ID SALARY_MO
      3 Clerical     Peters     Larry      06/10/83  1.9   3412 1350.00
      1 Production   Morris     John       11/03/82  2.5   4521 1850.00
      2 Marketing    Southby    Anne       08/22/81  3.7   3134 2315.00
      4 Clerical     Broussard  Marie      05/05/81  4.0   8712 1275.00

. LIST WHILE yrs <= 2
Record# DEPARTMENT   LASTNAME   FIRSTNAME  HIRED     YRS EMP_ID SALARY_MO

.
```

```
. LIST ALL WHILE yrs < 2
Record# DEPARTMENT   LASTNAME   FIRSTNAME  HIRED     YRS EMP_ID SALARY_MO
      3 Clerical     Peters     Larry      06/10/83  1.9   3412 1350.00

.
```

If you attempt to use a command with a WHILE clause on an unsorted database, the command may miss records that meet the WHILE condition, because performance terminates at the first record that evaluates as false.

- **dBASE II equivalent**
  WHILE

- **Comments**
  The FOR condition clause *does* automatically set the default scope to ALL.

  The following database commands take an optional condition clause (WHILE or FOR): AVERAGE 31★, CHANGE 48★, COPY TO 82★, COUNT 85★, DELETE 106★, DISPLAY, JOIN 189★, LABEL FORM 195★, LIST, LOCATE 202★, RECALL 278★, REPLACE 291★, REPORT FORM 295★, SORT 402★, SUM 426★, and TOTAL 436★.

Word processors

The dBASE III program has a built-in word processor (or text editor ◆) that can be used for writing programs **264◆** or for entering text into memo fields **217★**. There are two ways into the word processor, depending upon the kind of document you wish to produce:

☐ To write a dBASE program, use MODIFY COMMAND **219★** to invoke the word processor. You must supply a file name **155★**; dBASE will supply a default extension of .PRG. MODIFY COMMAND stores printable ASCII text files **157◆**.

☐ To write or edit memo fields, use any one of the full-screen operations APPEND **19★**, CHANGE **48★**, or EDIT **141★**. When the input template appears, position the highlight over the memo field and press Ctrl-PgDn to invoke the word processor. The resulting file will have the same file name as the database file itself, with an extension name of .DBT. Memo files are not ASCII text files.

■ Keyboard controls

dBASE's word-processing operations are controlled via a special set of keyboard commands. Some of these commands use the cursor-movement functions available on the number pad at the right side of the IBM personal-computer keyboard. Others use special "control characters" identical, in many cases, to the keyboard functions in the WordStar word-processing program.

Cursor movement: To move the cursor one line up or down, or one space to the right or left, use the Up-, Down-, Right-, and Left-arrow keys located on the number pad at the right side of the keyboard. (Make sure the NumLock key is toggled for cursor-movement rather than for numeric data entry: If numbers appear on the screen, press NumLock once.) Alternatives to the arrow keys are Ctrl-E, Ctrl-X, Ctrl-D, and Ctrl-S, respectively.

The PgUp and PgDn keys can be used to jump several lines up or down in a document. The End and Home keys (or Ctrl-F and Ctrl-A) move the cursor one *word* to the right or left, respectively. Ctrl-Left-arrow or Ctrl-Right-arrow (or Ctrl-Z or Ctrl-B) jump the cursor to the beginning or end of the current line.

Deletions and insertions: The Ins key (or Ctrl-V) toggles between *insert mode* and *typeover mode*: The message INSERT ON will appear at the upper right corner of the screen when you are in insert mode. In typeover mode, Ctrl-N will insert a blank line between two lines of text; in insert mode, pressing the Return key will insert a line. Ctrl-Y deletes a line. Ctrl-T deletes the word to the right of the cursor. The Del key (or Ctrl-G) deletes the character at the current cursor position. The backspace key is "destructive": That is, it doesn't simply move the cursor back—it actually moves the cursor one space left and deletes that character.

After you have made deletions or insertions in a paragraph, you can use Ctrl-KB to "reformat" the paragraph.

Reading from and writing to external files: Ctrl-KR reads the contents of an ASCII text disk file into the current document. This is a convenient way to incorporate part of some other program or document into the program you are currently writing. Ctrl-KW writes the current document to a disk file. Both Ctrl-KR and Ctrl-KW result in a screen prompt asking you for the name of the file you wish to read from or write to.

Exiting the word processor: To exit and save your current work, press Ctrl-End, Ctrl-W, or Ctrl-PgUp. To exit without saving, press Esc or Ctrl-Q.

If you use MODIFY COMMAND to edit an existing text file, dBASE will automatically save a backup copy of the previous version of your file, giving it a .BAK extension.

■ **External word processors**

The largest document you can produce in the dBASE word processor is 4K bytes (4,096 characters). If you wish to write a program file larger than that—or if you simply want to write your dBASE programs in another word-processing environment—you may use any word-processing or text-editing program that produces a file consisting only of printable ASCII characters (the unformatted mode of Microsoft Word, for example).

If your computer has sufficient memory beyond the 256K required for dBASE itself, you can access an external word processor from within dBASE via the RUN 306★ command, or even install a different word-processing program for program files, memo fields, or both (see the *CONFIG.DB* **66★** entry for details).

YEAR()

- **Structure**

  YEAR(date-type value)

- **Description**

  Given a dBASE date-type **99◆** value, the YEAR() function supplies a four-digit number representing the year in which the date falls.

- **Usage**

  The argument of YEAR() may be a date-type field or variable value, or it may be the result of the DATE() **103★** or CTOD() **92★** function:

```
. USE Bills
. ? YEAR(date_due)
 1985

. ? YEAR(DATE() + 1000)
 1988

. STORE CTOD("07/04/1776") TO indepndnce
. ? YEAR(indepndnce)
 1776
.
```

Notice that YEAR() supplies the correct century of a date that falls before the year 1900.

- **Program example**

  The *Booklist* program included in the MONTH() **236★** entry produces a series of publication announcements from a database called *Books*. The program uses YEAR() to produce part of the final line of each announcement, which designates the season and year in which the book will appear. This is the command that produces the year display:

```
?? YEAR(pub_date)
```

- **Caution**

  YEAR() works only on a date-type argument. An attempt to send a string of characters to YEAR() will result in an error message:

```
. ? YEAR("2/27/51")
Invalid function argument
                       ?
? YEAR("2/27/51")
.
```

■ **dBASE II equivalent**
None

■ **Comment**
Because dBASE always displays date-type values in six-digit format (mo/da/yr, for example), YEAR() is the only means available in dBASE for identifying date values earlier than January 1, 1900. (See the CTOD() and DTOC() **139★** entries for a detailed discussion on creating and manipulating non-twentieth-century dates.)

ZAP

■ **Structure**
ZAP

■ **Description**
The ZAP command deletes all records **284★** from the current database, but leaves the file open and its structure intact.

■ **Usage**
Here is an example of the use of ZAP on a database called *Stock*:

```
. USE Stock
. COUNT
        25 records

. SET SAFETY ON

. ZAP
Zap B:Stock.dbf? (Y/N) Yes

. COUNT
      No records

.
```

Before the ZAP, *Stock* has 25 records. After, it has none.

The confirmation question ("Zap B:Stock.dbf?") is displayed only if the SET SAFETY **396★** status is ON. If you are performing a ZAP from within a program, and if you have absolute confidence in your convictions, you should SET SAFETY OFF to suppress this question. (If you do so, remember to include a SET SAFETY ON before the end of the program, to reset the default.)

■ **Caution**
ZAP is terminal. Its work cannot be undone unless you have created a backup copy of your database beforehand (see COPY TO **82★**).

■ **dBASE II equivalent**
None

■ **Comment**
Use the DELETE **106★** and PACK **243★** commands for selective deletion of records.

APPENDIX

This appendix contains the structure of the *Property* database and the complete listing of the real-estate program that manages it.

```
. USE Property
. DISPLAY STRUCTURE
Structure for database : B:Property.dbf
Number of data records :        8
Date of last update    : 08/30/85
Field  Field name  Type        Width    Dec
    1  OWNER_L     Character      20
    2  OWNER_F     Character      20
    3  ADDRESS     Character      28
    4  CITY        Character      20
    5  NEIGHBORHD  Character      20
    6  HOME_AGE    Numeric         3
    7  BEDROOMS    Numeric         1
    8  BATHROOMS   Numeric         3      1
    9  GARAGE      Logical         1
   10  SQ_FOOTAGE  Numeric         4
   11  ASKING_PR   Numeric         9      2
   12  CUR_BID     Numeric         9      2
   13  SOLD        Logical         1
   14  SALE_DATE   Date            8
   15  SALE_PRICE  Numeric         9      2
   16  ON_MARKET   Date            8
   17  TERM_DAYS   Numeric         3
   18  DESCRIPTN   Memo           10
** Total **                      178

.
```

The real-estate program consists of two files: *MENU.PRG*, the top-level controlling program, and *PROPERTY.PRG*, the procedure file. In order to use the program, you will also need to have available the following data and format files:

PROPERTY.DBF 384♦
PROPERTY.DBT 384♦
ADDRESS.NDX 374♦
SCHEDULE.NDX 374♦
PROPIN.FMT 366♦

The program is completely menu driven. To begin, type *DO Menu*. Then, just follow the screen prompts to perform the desired task.

```
*------------------------------------------------------------ MENU.PRG
* Controls the activities of the real-estate program.
*    Uses the Property database and the Schedule and
*    Address indexes.
*

SET TALK OFF
SET BELL OFF
SET CONFIRM ON
SET ESCAPE OFF

USE Property INDEX Address
CLOSE PROCEDURE
SET PROCEDURE TO Property

DO WHILE .T.
    choice = 7
    CLEAR
    @ 8, 30 SAY "Real Estate Menu"
    @ 9, 30 SAY "---- ------ ----"
    @ 10, 25 SAY "1. Add a new home listing."
    @ 11, 25 SAY "2. Record a bid or sale."
    @ 12, 25 SAY "3. Search for listing(s)."
    @ 13, 25 SAY "4. Examine listing schedule."
    @ 14, 25 SAY "5. Compute a mortgage."
    @ 15, 25 SAY "6. Print an information sheet."
    @ 16, 25 SAY "7. Quit"
    @ 18, 25 SAY "Choice? <1,2,3,4,5,6,7> " GET choice PICTURE "9" ;
      RANGE 1, 7
    READ

    DO CASE
        CASE choice = 1
            DO Add
        CASE choice = 2
            DO Sale
        CASE choice = 3
            DO Reqmnts
        CASE choice = 4
            DO Schedule
        CASE choice = 5
            DO Mortgage
        CASE choice = 6
            DO Prntinfo
        CASE choice = 7
            CLEAR
            CLOSE PROCEDURE
            SET TALK ON
            SET BELL ON
            SET CONFIRM OFF
            SET ESCAPE ON
            RETURN
    ENDCASE

ENDDO
```

```
*-------------------------------------------------PROPERTY.PRG

PROCEDURE Add
*----- Appends a new record to the Property database.
*

SET FORMAT TO Propin
APPEND

CLOSE FORMAT
RETURN



PROCEDURE Sale
*----- Records a bid or sale of a house.
*
CLEAR
? "             *** Record a bid or sale on a home. ***"
?
?
DO Get_rec
IF EOF()
     RETURN
ENDIF

CLEAR
@ 2, 10 SAY "Address:   " + address
@ 3, 10 SAY "Owner:      " + TRIM(owner_f) + " " + owner_l
@ 4, 10 SAY asking_pr PICTURE "Asking:    $###,###.##"
@ 5, 10 SAY "Bid:"

IF cur_bid = 0
     @ 5, 20 SAY "None"
ELSE
     @ 5, 20 SAY cur_bid PICTURE "$###,###.##"
ENDIF

IF .NOT. sold
     @ 6, 10 SAY "Still available"
ELSE
     @ 6, 10 SAY sale_price PICTURE "Sold at:  $###,###.##"
     @ 7, 10 SAY "On:           " + DTOC(sale_date)
ENDIF

@ 8, 10 SAY "=========================================="
?
IF sold
     WAIT "              Press any key to continue. "
     RETURN
ENDIF

DO Yesno with 10, 10, "Change the asking price? "
IF yn
     @ 11, 15 GET asking_pr
     READ
ENDIF
```

(continued)

```
DO Yesno WITH 13, 10, "Change the current bid?   "
IF yn
    @ 14, 15 GET cur_bid
    READ
ENDIF

DO Yesno WITH 16, 10, "Has the house sold?        "
IF yn
    REPLACE sold WITH .T.
    @ 17, 15 SAY "Price? " GET sale_price
    READ

    DO Yesno WITH 18, 15, "Today? "
    IF yn
        REPLACE sale_date WITH date()
    ELSE
        @ 19, 15 SAY "When?   " GET sale_date
        READ
    ENDIF
ENDIF

RETURN


PROCEDURE Reqmnts
*----- Filters the Property database, searching for homes that
*        match the requirements of a given client.
*

CLEAR
?
? "  ** Search for homes that match these requirements: **"
?
? "        1. price range...............>"
? "        2. square footage range......>"
? "        3. age range.................>"
?
? "        4. number of bedrooms........>"
? "        5. number of bathrooms.......>"
? "        6. garage required...........>"
done = .F.
reqs = ""
validate = ""
choice = 1
DO WHILE .NOT. done
    @ 12, 12 CLEAR
    @ 12, 12 SAY "Which requirement? <1,2,3,4,5,6> ";
      GET choice PICTURE "9" RANGE 1, 6
    READ
    stchoice = str(choice)

    IF stchoice $ validate
        ? CHR(7)
        @ 14, 14 SAY "You have already specified"
        @ 15, 14 SAY "a value for this requirement."
    ELSE
        IF LEN(validate) <> 0
            reqs = reqs + " .AND. "
        ENDIF
```

(continued)

```
        DO CASE
            CASE choice = 1
                @ 14, 14 SAY "price range:"
                DO Minmax WITH 4
                reqs = reqs + " (asking_pr >= " + min;
                    + " .AND. asking_pr <= " + max + ")"
            CASE choice = 2
                @ 14, 14 SAY "footage range:"
                DO Minmax WITH 5
                reqs = reqs + " (sq_footage >= " + min;
                    + " .AND. sq_footage <= " + max + ")"
            CASE choice = 3
                @ 14, 14 SAY "age range:"
                DO Minmax WITH 6
                reqs = reqs + "(home_age >= " + min;
                    + " .AND. home_age <= " + max + ")"
            CASE choice = 4
                bdrms = "  "
                DO WHILE LEN(TRIM(bdrms)) = 0
                    @ 14, 14 SAY "number of bedrooms: " GET bdrms ;
                        PICTURE "99"
                    READ
                ENDDO
                @ 8, 40 SAY bdrms PICTURE "99"
                reqs = reqs + "bedrooms = " + bdrms
            CASE choice = 5
                bthrms = "   "
                DO WHILE LEN(TRIM(bthrms)) = 0
                    @ 14, 14 SAY "number of bathrooms: " GET bthrms ;
                        PICTURE "9.9"
                    READ
                ENDDO
                @ 9, 40 SAY bthrms PICTURE "9.9"
                reqs = reqs + "bathrooms = " + bthrms
            CASE choice = 6
                @ 10, 40 SAY "Yes"
                reqs = reqs + "garage"
        ENDCASE

    validate = validate + stchoice
ENDIF

    IF LEN(validate) < 60
        DO Yesno WITH 19, 16, "Another requirement? "
        done = .NOT. yn
    ELSE
        done = .T.
    ENDIF

ENDDO
```

(continued)

475

```
reqs = reqs + " .AND. .NOT. sold"
SET FILTER TO &reqs
COUNT TO n
CLEAR

IF n = 0
    ?
    ? "** No homes available matching those requirements. **"
ELSE
    SET HEADING ON
    DISPLAY ALL address, asking_pr, sq_footage, home_age, ;
        bedrooms, bathrooms OFF
ENDIF
?
WAIT

SET FILTER TO
RETURN



PROCEDURE Schedule
*----- Displays records from the Property database
*          in order of days remaining in the term
*          of the contract.
*

SET HEADING OFF
CLEAR

? "*** Unsold properties, in order of remaining days to sell: ***"
?
? "    Address:                        Days Remaining:"
? "    --------                        ---- ----------"
SET INDEX TO Schedule
REINDEX
daystosell = "term_days - (DATE() - on_market)"
DISPLAY ALL address, &daystosell FOR .NOT. sold OFF
?
WAIT

SET INDEX TO Address
SET HEADING ON
RETURN
```

(continued)

476

```
PROCEDURE Mortgage
*----- Calculates a monthly mortgage payment.
*

SET CONFIRM ON
SET BELL OFF
SET TALK OFF
CLEAR

@ 6, 25 SAY "Monthly Mortgage Calculation"
@ 7, 25 SAY "------- -------- -----------"

princ = 0
rate = 0.00
term = 0
@ 9, 25 SAY "Principal amount? " GET princ PICTURE "######" ;
  RANGE 10000, 999999
@ 11, 25 SAY "Percent interest? " GET rate PICTURE "##.##" ;
  RANGE 5, 25
@ 13, 25 SAY "Term in years?    " GET term PICTURE "##" ;
  RANGE 10, 50
READ

rl = rate / 1200
tl = term * 12
fact = (rl + 1) ^ (-tl)
mort = (princ * rl) / (1 - fact)

CLEAR
@ 8, 25 SAY princ PICTURE "Principal:     $###,###"
@ 9, 25 SAY rate  PICTURE "Interest:        ##.##"
@ 10, 25 SAY term  PICTURE "Years:             ##"
@ 11, 25 SAY "------------------------"
@ 12, 25 SAY mort  PICTURE "Payment:      $#,###.##"
?
?
WAIT "                    Press any key to continue."

RETURN
```

(continued)

```
PROCEDURE Prntinfo
*----- Prints out a specification sheet for distribution
*          to potential buyers of a given home.
*

CLEAR
? "          *** Print a specification sheet for a home. ***"
?
?
DO Get_rec
IF EOF()
    RETURN
ENDIF

ok = .F.
DO WHILE .NOT. ok
    DO Yesno WITH 10, 10, "Is the printer ready? "
    ok = yn
ENDDO

SET CONSOLE OFF
SET PRINT ON
SET MARGIN TO 12
EJECT
SET DEVICE TO PRINT

? "     XYZ Realty"
? "     --- ------"
?
? "     Home Listing"
?
?
? "               " + address
? "               " + city
?
? "               (" + TRIM(neighborhd) + " District.)"
?
@ PROW() + 1, 15 SAY asking_pr PICTURE "$###,###.##"
?
?
? "               Features of home:"
? "               --------- -- -----"
? "                    > ", sq_footage, "sq. feet"
? "                    > ", bedrooms, "bedrooms"
? "                    > ", bathrooms, "bathrooms"
IF garage
    ? "                    >  garage"
ENDIF
?
?
? "======================================================="
?

? descriptn
?
```

(continued)

478

```
SET CONSOLE ON
SET DEVICE TO SCREEN
SET MARGIN TO 0
SET PRINT OFF
RETURN


PROCEDURE Get_rec
*----- Finds a record number, given an address.
*

SET TALK OFF
SET BELL OFF
SET CONFIRM ON
SET EXACT OFF

SET INDEX TO Address

done = .F.
r = row()
DO WHILE .NOT. done
    street = SPACE(28)
    @ r + 1, 10 SAY "What is the street address?" GET street
    READ

    street = TRIM(street)
    SEEK street

    IF EOF()
        @ r + 3, 15 SAY "*** Record not found. ***"
        DO Yesno WITH r + 4, 19, "Try again? "

        IF yn
            @ r + 1, 10
            @ r + 3, 15
            @ r + 4, 15
        ELSE
            done = .T.
        ENDIF

    ELSE
        done = .T.
    ENDIF

ENDDO
RETURN
```

(continued)

```
PROCEDURE Yesno
*----- Handles prompt and input for a yes-or-no question.
*          Returns answer in the logical variable yn.
*

PARAMETERS currow, curcol, question
PUBLIC yn

SET BELL OFF

valid = .F.
answer = " "

DO WHILE .NOT. valid
    @ currow, curcol SAY question GET answer PICTURE "!"
    READ
    valid = answer $ "YN"

    IF valid
        answer = "." + answer + "."
        yn = &answer
    ELSE
        ? CHR(7)
    ENDIF
ENDDO
RETURN



PROCEDURE Minmax
*----- Accepts min and max requirements for the REQMNTS procedure.
*

PARAMETERS loc
PUBLIC min, max

min = "      "
max = "      "

DO WHILE LEN(TRIM(min)) = 0 .OR. LEN(TRIM(max)) = 0
    @ 16, 16 SAY "from: " GET min PICTURE "999999"
    @ 17, 16 SAY "to:   " GET max PICTURE "999999"
    READ
ENDDO
@ loc, 40 SAY min + " to " + max

RETURN
```

Douglas Hergert

A native Californian, Douglas Hergert received a Bachelor of Arts degree in English and French from Washington University, St. Louis, Missouri, in 1974. After graduation, he spent five years in the Peace Corps, teaching English in Afghanistan and Senegal. Doug is the author of several books, including *Mastering Framework*, *BASIC for Business*, and *Doing Business with Pascal*.

The manuscript for this book was prepared and submitted to Microsoft Press in electronic form. Text files were processed and formatted using Microsoft Word.

Cover design by Steve Renick.
Cover airbrushed by Stephen Peringer.
Interior text design by Craig A. Bergquist & Associates.
The high-resolution screen displays were created on the IBM PC AT and printed on the Hewlett-Packard LaserJet.

Text Composition by Dwan Typography, Sebastopol, CA, in Palatino with Times Roman Italic and Helvetica Bold, using the Omni composition system and the Mergenthaler Linotron 202 digital phototypesetter.

OTHER TITLES FROM MICROSOFT PRESS

Running MS-DOS 2nd edition. The Microsoft guide
to getting the most out of its standard operating system
Van Wolverton $21.95

The Peter Norton Programmer's Guide to the IBM PC
The ultimate reference guide to the *entire* family
of IBM personal computers *Peter Norton* $19.95

Command Performance: Lotus 1-2-3 The Microsoft desktop
dictionary and cross-reference guide *Eddie Adamis* $24.95

Variations in C Programming techniques for developing
efficient professional applications *Steve Schustack* $19.95

Word Processing Power with Microsoft Word
Professional writing on your IBM PC *Peter Rinearson* $16.95

Presentation Graphics on the IBM PC How to use Microsoft
Chart to create dazzling graphics for corporate and
professional applications *Steve Lambert* $19.95

Getting Started with Microsoft Word A Step-by-step guide
to word processing *Janet Rampa* $16.95

Managing Your Business with Multiplan How to use
Microsoft's award-winning electronic spreadsheet
on your IBM PC *Ruth K. Witkin* $17.95

Online A guide to America's leading information services
Steve Lambert $19.95

Silicon Valley Guide to Financial Success in Software
Daniel Remer, Paul Remer, and Robert Dunaway $19.95

Out of the Inner Circle A hacker's guide to computer security,
"The Cracker" (Bill Landreth) $ 9.95

A Much, Much Better World *Eldon Dedini* $ 6.95